VIDAL AND HIS FAMILY

From Salonica to Paris

VIDAL AND HIS FAMILY

From Salonica to Paris

The Story of a Sephardic Family
in the Twentieth Century

EDGAR MORIN

Translated by Deborah Cowell
Foreword by Alfonso Montuori

sussex
ACADEMIC
PRESS
Brighton • Chicago • Toronto

2 4 6 8 10 9 7 5 3

First published in 2009 by
SUSSEX ACADEMIC PRESS
PO Box 139
Eastbourne BN24 9BP

Distributed in North America by
SUSSEX ACADEMIC PRESS
Independent Publishers Group
814 N Franklin St, Chicago, IL 60610, USA

British Library Cataloguing in Publication Data
A CIP catalogue record for this book is available from the British Library.

Library of Congress Cataloging-in-Publication Data
Morin, Edgar.
  [Vidal et les siens. English]
  Vidal and his family : from Salonica to Paris, the story of a Sephardic
    family in the twentieth century / Edgar Morin ; translated by
    Deborah Cowell.
    p. cm.
  ISBN 978-1-84519-274-7 (pb : alk. paper)
  1. Nahoum, Vidal, 1894–1984. 2. Jews—France—Biography.
  3. Jewish merchants—France—Biography. 4. Nahoum, Vidal,
  1894–1984—Family. 5. Nahum family. I. Title.
DS135.F9N34613 2008
305.892′4044092—dc22
[B]

2007047678

Typeset and designed by SAP, Brighton & Eastbourne.
Printed and bound by CPI Group (UK) Ltd, Croydon, CR0 4YY
This book is printed on acid-free paper.

Contents

Contents

Contents

Foreword by Alfonso Montuori

At the beginning of the 21st century many—indeed arguably all— of the issues facing humanity have become planetary. From the economy to the environment, from the nature of "identity" (individual, cultural, national...) to immigration, we are increasingly aware of how tremendously interconnected humanity has become. The compression of time and space – through the internet and commercial air travel, for instance – has meant that everything is happening faster, and the events in distant cities and nations can have an immediate impact on us.

Our established ways of thinking about the world are unable to help us make sense of this new reality. Edgar Morin has been at the forefront of the efforts to help us grapple with the complexity, uncertainty, and ambiguity of the new world. *La Methode*, his six-volume magnum opus, is a masterwork of contemporary thought. It overturns the focus on determinism, reductionism, certainty, and simplicity that marked Modernity, and invites us to engage in complex thought, a kind of thinking that does not reject but actually feeds on uncertainty, interconnection, and complexity. One of the things that makes Morin's scholarship so uniquely important is that it is not divorced from even the most intimate aspects of his life. While it is common to say that all scholarship is on some level autobiographical, with Morin there is no question that we find the motivation and passion for his scholarship not in the abstraction of disciplinary questions, of passing intellectual trends, but in the complexities of his own life and times (Montuori, 2004).

In this undoubtedly transitional time, when the term post-modern has shown itself unable to capture the complexity and radical rupture of our age, Morin looks to the past – his own past, the past of his father, and his family – and to the future. By articulating his own roots in a novel way, one that reflects the principles of the complex thought Morin has painstakingly developed (Morin, 2008), he shows us a way of thinking about humanity that can also project us into a more interconnected, planetary future (Morin & Kern, 1999). Morin often cites Pascal's dictum that one cannot understand the part without understanding the whole, and cannot understand the whole without understanding the part. This "holographic" principle is evident throughout *Vidal*. We are brought into the details of individual lives, share their fears, joys, their passions, their letters, songs, and hear about their meals. At the same time, we are also aware of the larger context, swept along in the events that forced Vidal and his people across Europe. Along the way we witness cosmopolitan moments of creativity, diversity, and coexistence, when different cultures and languages and practices mingled, and moments of cruelty, war, hatred, "purification" and hyper-nationalism, culminating in the horrors of World War II.

Edgar Morin applies the principles of complex thought to the story of his own father's life, and weaves a remarkable tale that is also, holographically, a history of Sephardic Jews, of Europe, of humanity's interactions, connections, and hybridizations, of the emotions, memories, views, sounds and smells of distant times and places, and of Edgar Morin himself. It is at times told with the wistfulness of a man reminiscing about his family and at other times with the eye of a historian capturing the complexity of history's triumphs and tragedies. In a few charming and poignant passages, Morin traces the journey of one of his favorite dishes, the Salonician *pastellico*, from his family's tables, as it journeys through Europe, and across the world, as the Ottoman *borek*, the Greek *tiropita*, and the Spanish *empanada* which is now found in the New World. In every culture the dish picks up some changes and is modified to fit the local aesthetic sensibilities and/or constraints. And this is also the fate of the individuals whose lives Morin follows.

In an age where Huntington's *The Clash of Civilization* (Huntington, 1998) has dominated discourse and even policy, and the study of globalization seems polarized between pro- and anti- factions, Morin weaves a different story and provides us with a different, more complex perspective. He shows us the ravages of cultural, religious, and national conflicts, to be sure, and their effects in the everyday lives of his family. But he also shows the creativity that emerges out of cultural interactions, the way human curiosity and adventurousness combine in an excitement to *create together* that is so apparent in the arts, and sadly so often lacking in politics, not to mention the rhetoric of nationalism and essentialist approaches to identity. What is so refreshing about Morin's account is the way he documents the everyday creativity that emerges out of the encounter of different cultures. This cultural creativity is an integral part of cultural encounters, ironically often at the same time that there are clashes and antagonisms. This reflects Morin's complex concept of the dialogic: not an either/or logic of either cultural clashes or cultural creativity; not a dialectic whereby two cultures are somehow subsumed in a higher synthesis; but a *dialogic*, where cultures and interactions can be complementary, concurrent, and antagonistic all at the same time.

For Morin every culture and every individual – every "system" in somewhat more abstract technical terminology – is a *unitas multiplex*, a unity in diversity. It cannot be reduced to one label, one "identity," one "essence." In the last pages of this book, Morin asks, who was Vidal, what was his place, where did he belong geographically? And the answer is complex. To say Vidal was a French Jew would be to represent only a part of his life, to deny

Salonica and Livorno and Spain and life on the cusp of Europe and Asia. Vidal was all this and more.

As Morin writes:

> Vidal experienced an Oriental-Occidental poly-identity from which he derived great satisfaction: although he was first and foremost a Salonician, a child of Salonica, his small but true homeland turned paradise lost, essentially irreducible to any other place in the Sephardic world, he was also specifically Judeo-Spanish, more broadly a son of the Jewish people, and more broadly still Mediterranean, and he became a Frenchman both by chance and by predilection. He was Salonician, Sephardic, Mediterranean and French in a concentric and interwoven fashion. He was never from a single "place." He was neither nomadic nor sedentary, but sedentarized and nomadizable. (p. 294)

I personally feel a great kinship here with Vidal. My father was Italian and my mother Dutch. They were diplomats who lived in Beirut, Athens, and London, and whisked me away from Holland, where I was born, when I was six months old. My passport says I'm Italian but I've never lived there. I do identify with Italy, but not just Italy. I was brought up speaking five different languages. For the sake of convenience, living in the US I initially used to answer the question "where are you from" by saying I was Italian. I knew people's eyes would glaze over if I explained the real story to them. Increasingly I am not alone: there is even a name for people like me – "Third Culture Children." The unitas multiplex is sometimes hard to articulate and explain. Morin writes that likewise

> (Vidal) would introduce himself as Mr. Vidal to strangers or new acquaintances, partly through Oriental prudence, in order to conceal his true identity for a time, and partly because he wanted to be integrated into the French world. (p. 293)

But *Vidal* is not just for and about individuals who have grown up living in different cultures. Morin's book shows not only the importance of recognizing and articulating the complexity of our origins, but he also reminds us that this complexity lies within all of us. As Gianluca Bocchi and Mauro Ceruti have shown, there is no such thing as ethnic "purity" in Europe. Any claims to land or ethnic identity are all based on an arbitrary point in history at which a decision has been made to stop following the thread to greater cultural and genetic complexity (Bocchi & Ceruti, 1997). If we take a good look, if we keep following the thread of history, of our cultural and genetic roots, our complexity is far greater than we may imagine. And the word "mutt" President Obama self-deprecatingly used to refer to the fact that his father is black and his mother white, is in fact applicable to all human beings.

It is both the *awareness* and the *articulation* of complexity that is problematic in an age when we are still drawn to simplistic essentialisms (My country right or wrong! You're either for us or against us!), when disjunctive thought runs rampant creating oppositions between "us" and "them," when the social imaginary is filled with images of nations and cultures and tribes at war, and there is little or no recognition of the rich creative interchanges that have arguably been at the root of every advance in human civilization.

Morin challenges us to think differently, to see different, largely hidden dimensions of the world, both at the macro- and micro-levels, and envision different possibilities based on this new perspective. He invites us to see the richness of the human journey through cultures, individuals, stories, historical events. Through the vigorous and unforgettable figure of Vidal Nahoum and "his people" and their travels and travails, Morin reminds us of the power of human creativity to shape our lives, our culture, and our destiny.

ALFONSO MONTUORI
San Francisco

Sources

Bocchi, G., & Ceruti, M. (1997). *Solidarity or Barbarism: A Europe of Diversity against Ethnic Cleansing*. New York: Peter Lang.

Huntington, S. (1998). *The clash of civilizations and the remaking of the world order*. New York: Simon & Schuster.

Montuori, A. (2004). Edgar Morin: A partial introduction. *World Futures: The Journal of General Evolution*, 60(5), 349–355.

Morin, E. (2008). *On complexity*. Cresskill, NJ: Hampton Press.

Morin, E., & Kern, B. (1999). *Homeland Earth: A manifesto for the new millennium*. Cresskill, NJ: Hampton Press.

Preface to the French Edition

Vidal was born in 1894 in the Ottoman Empire's great Macedonian port. His great-grandfather came from Tuscany and spoke Italian. His mother tongue was fifteenth-century Spanish. He learned French and German as a child. When he was an adolescent, he dreamed of living in France; he was deported there as a prisoner, and then liberated by the French Prime Minister. He lived through the Balkan wars, the collapse of the Ottoman Empire, and two World Wars. His life spanned most of the 20th century, until his death in 1984.

Like every individual point in a hologram, which contains all the information about the whole of which it is a part, Vidal's unique experience also contains the maturity, decline and death of a culture – that of the Sephardim, or Spanish Jews; it includes the transition from imperial city to nation-state, the complex of modern relations between Jews and gentiles, the complex of relations between East and West, and, ultimately, the history of the 20th century itself.

Vidal cannot be isolated from his family. And so this book also tells the stories of the men and women in his immediate family and in his wife's family, but it does so schematically and discontinuously. Vidal is the center of the book, and I wanted it that way because Vidal is my father.

He is both the object and subject of this book, which is an attempt to restore some life to his life. It is because he is the true subject of this book that I did not want to create interference by using the "I" of the narrator-witness. So when, as his son, I inevitably come into his story, I refer to myself in the third person, to objectify myself, and I have retained his use of the first person in all the passages included here from his spoken autobiography. It is because he is the object of this book that I want to describe him as objectively as possible, and therefore I refer to him in the third person; at the same time, because I want to minimize the distance between myself and him, I call him by his first name, Vidal.

And so this book *about* and *for* my father is not "my father's book."[1] The reverence that inspired me did not call for a work of edification; it implied that I should attempt to write a truthful book. For this reason, the book is not in the least respectful, or at least not in the usual sense of the word. Vidal felt that loving someone meant being able to tease him. The author of these lines, who has inherited something of this trait, does not think it disrespectful to tease or make fun of the people he loves.

I began to feel the need to write a book about my father on the day after his death, in August 1984. At that time, I envisaged a joint project with Véronique Grappe-Nahoum and Haïm Vidal Sephiha, who both agreed to help me.

Véronique, who is my daughter and Vidal's granddaughter, is a historian at the EHESS (l'École des hautes études en sciences sociales); in 1978 she had asked Vidal to let her record his spoken autobiography on audio cassette. Almost the whole of that unpolished narrative, which is sometimes disorganized and distorted, is reproduced here in italic script, and in fact constitutes a book within this book.

Haïm Vidal, guardian and defender of the language and culture of the Spanish Jews, and holder of the first university chair devoted to their language (which survived outside of Spain for five centuries), directs the research conducted by the *Vidas Largas* association into Sephardic culture, and has published its key work, *L'Agonie des judéo-espagnols.*[2]

So before this book was written, both of them made essential contributions, and afterwards, while I was writing it, they helped me with their comments, criticism and information. But I became possessed by my subject, and took over all the writing myself; in the end, I became the author.

The sources for this *historical account*, apart from the oral autobiography, are the following:

- Vidal's personal archives: beginning in his childhood in Salonica he had amassed a great number of postcards (which he collected), and later he hoarded the many letters that he received or sent (he kept typed copies); he also kept his prison diary,[3] the draft of his marriage proposal, and many other personal, familial or professional documents;
- The monumental *Histoire des Israélites de Salonique*, in seven volumes, by the erudite Salonician scholar Joseph Nehama,[4] without which I could not have written this book. It also helped me trace the origins of the Nahum and Frances families on one side, and the Beressi and Mosseri families on the other, which were united in the marriage between my father and my mother;
- Certain works or articles, which I cite in the course of the book, concerning the Spanish Jews, in Spain, during their emigration to Tuscany or under the Ottoman Empire.

After I had formed the project, personal difficulties initially prevented me from writing. The first person I would like to thank is Jacques-Antoine Malarewicz, who persuaded me that writing it would be the best way of overcoming them.

I thank my cousins, who contributed their information and corrections, and in particular Fredy Pelosoff, who recorded his mother's memoirs on audio cassette; Chary Ledoux, whose memory enlightened me on numerous occasions about the Nahum family's past; and Henri Pelosoff and Edgard Nahum. Finally, I thank my daughter Irène for her contribution, her mother Violette Narville for her criticism, and Edwige, for having both read me and chosen me. I thank Monique Cahen for her encouragement, her patience and her attentive criticism of the manuscript.

Lastly, I thank my colleagues at the Centre d'Études Transdisciplinaires for their kind and unstinting assistance: Marie-France Laval, Marie-Madeleine Paccaud and Nicole Phelouzat-Perriquet, each of whom lent me their particular skill.

VIDAL AND HIS FAMILY

From Salonica to Paris

The Story of a Sephardic Family
in the Twentieth Century

Prologue

Nosotros fuemos echados de la Spagna, y en malo modo.[5]
RAFFAELE NAHUM TO HIS CHILDREN

THE SEPHARDIM

The year 1453. The Byzantine Empire is in ruins. The Ottoman Empire takes its place, choosing Constantinople as its capital, and re-naming it Istanbul. Four centuries of *pax ottomanica* in Eastern Europe and the Eastern Mediterranean follow. The defeated Christian population is tolerated there, as it was in Muslim Spain.

The year 1492. After the fall of Granada, Islam is driven out of Western Europe. Spain forces Jews and Muslims to choose between exile and conversion. August 2, 1492 is the deadline by which Jews wishing to remain faithful to Mosaic Law must leave. On August 3, Christopher Columbus, a fervent Catholic whose ancestors may have been converted Jews, heads West for what will later be known as the New World. Most of the tens of thousands of Jews who refuse to convert head East.

Estimates of the Jewish population in Spain have varied greatly. In the past, they were thought to have represented a third of the total population, but nowadays it is believed that there were 400,000 of them at their height, and probably 250,000 in Spain in the 14th century.[6] These descendants of Israelites had been established in the Iberian peninsula for 1,500 years. They had begun to settle in Roman Spain before the complete expulsion of the Jews from Palestine. Scattered colonies of Jews prospered in Medieval Spain, divided between the Christian and Muslim kingdoms.

The Muslims tolerated their Christian and Jewish minorities (with the exception of two waves of persecution under the Almoravid and Almohad dynasties, in 1086 and 1172); the Christian princes also tolerated their Jewish and Muslim minorities. In comparison with other Jewish communities in the rest of Christian Europe in the Middle Ages, the Jews in Christian Spain enjoyed an exceptional situation: they were not imprisoned in ghettoes, nor were they subjected to restrictions and harassment. Instead, they lived in something like independent rabbinical republics, with their own ordinances and their own law enforcement. The Jews were not segregated in any particular professions, and although many of them were merchants and scholars, some were also craftsmen, and even vine-growers and farmers.

Nevertheless, outbursts of anti-Jewish feeling flared up from time to time during the 14th century. Although the Jews were protected by princes, the common people accused them of deicide, of making ritual sacrifices of Christian children, and exploiting the poor through their monopolies on commodities or usury. The year 1391 saw massacres of Jews that resulted in mass conversions to Catholicism. As well as conversions by fear, there were some genuine religious conversions. For instance, a man called Salomon ha Levi became Pablo de Santa Maria and bishop of Burgos. Some of the converts would become fervent Christians. But many *conversos* were still secret "Judaizers." Publically, they went to Mass, obeyed the rites of the Church, and ate fish on Fridays; but in secret, at home, they recited Jewish prayers and blessings, abstained from eating unclean food, or at least made every effort to celebrate the Passover festival with their families. They kept in touch with relatives or friends who had not converted, and thus they retained their umbilical tie to Judaism. Although the Church tolerated the Jews, "Judaizing" *conversos* were condemned as heretics. The Spanish Inquisition was created in 1480, with the specific intention of unmasking Judaizers camouflaged as Christians. Between 1481 and 1488, there were 700 convictions in Seville.[7] Also in 1480, Jewish neighborhoods or *juderías* were turned into ghettoes. In 1491, some Jews were sentenced to death in Avila for the ritual murder of a Christian child. The arrival of Christian Europe's anti-Semitism in Spain coincided with the triumph of Christianity in the Iberian peninsula: Granada fell in 1492, and in the same city the Catholic Kings, Isabella and Ferdinand, signed the decree requiring the Jews to convert or leave.

The majority converted, and among these Marranos Judaism would either die out gradually, or survive in secret, undergoing a variety of modifications over the years. Those who refused baptism left in a hurry, taking their house keys with them. They did not know that they would not be allowed to return for centuries to come. 10,000 Jews left Aragon, and approximately 50,000 left Castile in 1492.[8]

Some went to Portugal and Navarre, but they were driven out in 1498. The diaspora of the Sephardim, or Spanish Jews, expanded as small groups settled in Holland and Provence, larger groups in North Africa,[9] and the largest of all in the East, in the Ottoman Empire, where they were given sanctuary by Bayazid II. They made their homes in the port cities of Istanbul, Izmir and especially Salonica, which received 20,000 of them.

Prologue

SALONICA

Salonica is a port on the Aegean Sea, a chunk bitten out of the Thermaic Gulf, on the Northern side of the Chalcidic peninsula. According to Strabon, the city was founded by Cassandra, Alexander the Great's general and brother-in-law, who named it after his wife Thessalonika. Under the Roman Empire, it was linked to Italy and Byzantium by the Via Egnazia; at Salonica, where the Vardar Valley opens out, this road meets the road that serves all of the Balkan territories as far as the Danube plain.

Depending on the prevailing historical circumstances, Salonica has either been a remote village, nestling at the wrong end of the sea and the farthest-flung point of the land, or, on the contrary, the port that serves as principal outlet and trading post for a hinterland rich in agricultural, pastoral and mining resources, and a cosmopolitan city receiving the maritime traffic that passes between the Eastern and Western Mediterranean. Under the *pax romana*, Paul of Tarsus, the son of a Pharisee who had received a revelation from Christ on the road to Damascus, came to preach to the Hellenized Jews of Salonica. He was yet to make the radical division that isolated the Christian offshoot from its Jewish source. He told his fellow believers that Jesus' second coming, "which will deliver us from the wrath to come," was imminent. He was driven out of the city, and wrote his two Epistles to the Thessalonians from Corinth. Thus, in the first century after Christ, Salonica, or Thessalonika as it was then known, was the point of convergence for the Greek, Jewish and new Christian stock; the dialogic[10] between them would determine the emergence and development of European culture.

After the Empire was divided up, Salonica, by that time a great Byzantine city, was besieged by the Goths, Huns, Avars and Bulgarians, attacked by Arab pirates, captured for a few days by the Normans from Sicily (in 1184), sacked by the crusaders, surrendered to the Venetians, and finally conquered in 1430 and ruled for several centuries by the Turks. The city was depopulated, with just a handful of Greeks remaining in it; a few Turks settled there later, but it was the admission of around 20,000 Sephardim that repopulated and reanimated the city, and it expanded rapidly in the first decades of the 16th century.[11]

Salonica had become a new Sepharad in miniature. As in the old Sepharad, pre-1492, steeples, minarets and synagogues coexisted peacefully. For two centuries, Salonica was a true microcosm of Spain, in which Catalans, Aragonese, Castilians, Andalucians and Majorcans lived side by side, each group collecting around its own synagogue, without merging; later, Provençals (*Provinsya*), Calabrians (*Kalabria*), Pouillais (*Poulia*), North Africans (*Mograbis*), Poles and Russians (*Ashkenaze*) came. In time, Castilian swallowed up the other Iberian languages, as it had in Spain. Castilian also prevailed over Greek, the language of the Romaniot Jews, and Yiddish, that

3

of the Ashkenazim who had emigrated to Salonica, and for centuries to come every Jewish immigrant was integrated into Spanish Jewish culture. Thus Salonica repeated the pattern of late fifteenth-century Spain: it Castilianized the Spanish and Hispanicized the immigrants from other countries. The paradoxical result was that a pure form of Castilian became the specifically Jewish language of Salonica: not modern Castilian, but the Castilian of the fifteenth century, which does not use the *jota*, and includes words that have been forgotten in Spain today. It is both a living language and a museum language, and delights modern Spaniards when they hear it. In the 19th century, however, this language was not really seen or thought of as Spanish by the Sephardim; to their minds, as to those of the Turks, Greeks or Macedonians, it was *djidio*, the Jewish language. Hence the astonishment of certain 19th-century Salonicians on overhearing some priests from Castile, who had come to observe these rejects of Spanish origin *in situ*: "How strange, Jewish priests!"

As the centuries passed, Spain began to seem very far away. And yet it had been hard to uproot. The Sephardi immigrants never became numb to the pain of exile, and for many years some families held on to the keys to their houses in Spain. What they felt was more than the age-old Jewish sense of exile: it was the grief of having been expatriated far from the cherished Sepharad, as many songs that have been preserved to this day attest; this feeling, although attenuated, would remain alive in Vidal who, in 1970, when he was over 70 years old, wanted to see the "land of his ancestors" again.

Salonica not only became a microcosm of Spain within the Ottoman Empire; it also became a "macédoine"[12] within Macedonia. In the province of Macedonia, ethnic Greeks, Slavs and Turks, with their different religions, lived side by side and overlapped. In Salonica, there was a concentrated macédoine surrounding the predominantly Sephardic element. The Turks formed a minor ingredient in this mix (for a long time they would not exceed 10 percent of the population). The Turkish world enveloping Sephardic Salonica did not penetrate it, except by capillary action: *djidio* absorbed a few Turkish words, music underwent Turkish influence, and a gastronomic osmosis occured between the parent Mediterranean cuisines of Spain and the East.

From the middle of the 16th century up to 1912, the Sephardim were the majority in Salonica. During this period, they accounted for more than half of the population, the rest being 20 percent Turkish, 20 percent Greek and 5 percent Bulgarian. Although the Jews had been homogenized by Spanish-Jewish culture, they were themselves a genetic mish-mash. In addition to the Spanish Jews, whose ancestors were Israelites, but whose gene pool must have been added to over the centuries as a result of rapes, illegitimate love affairs and conversions, and whose physical types were extremely diverse, there were the "Romaniots," or Greek Jews, and later there were immigrants from Germany, Poland and Russia, not to mention the descendants of converted Christian slaves (every wealthy family in the 16th century had one or several domestic slaves, who naturally adopted the religion of Moses). The entire city was attuned to its Sephardic majority, which imposed Saturday as an official holiday for all religious groups and for all the city's activities, including the mail.

As Vidal recalls in his recorded autobiography: *First of all, Saturday was a public holiday in Salonica, and the Muslims, Orthodox and Bulgarians would all close their shops, because Saturdays were sacred . . . Friday would have been the Muslim day . . . The Muslims went to the mosque, but they went back to work again afterwards, whereas on Saturday, the customs, the post office, everything was closed.*

Moreover, in contrast to cities with a Turkish majority (Istanbul, Izmir) or cities of the Ottoman Empire such as Alexandria or Damascus, where the lower orders were Egyptians or Arabs, while Turks occupied the higher echelons of society, Salonica had Jews ranged from the top to the bottom of the social ladder: they were financiers, big businessmen, doctors, scholars, laborers, dockers, porters and servants, as well as craftsmen, shopkeepers and carters. There were even Jewish landowners and farmers. The Sephardic city represented a complete society. It was not composed of rich Jews and poor non-Jews, or dominant non-Jews and oppressed Jews; Jews belonged to all social classes and practiced every profession.

As in Spain before 1480, the Jewish neighborhoods were not ghettoes. On the contrary, the Jews' wooden houses occupied the open center of the city, from one side of the port to the other, as far as the hills, where the square Turkish houses built of stone began, while the Greek neighborhood lay at the periphery, on the south-eastern side. Salonica's walls protected the city from invaders, rather than protecting the gentiles from the Jews. The Sephardic city was autonomous. In 1523, it obtained a charter of liberation from the Sublime Port, making it a little republic endowed with almost complete internal sovereignty. Until the 19th century, the council of rabbis collected taxes for the Empire and fixed the sum owed by each person; the council had the right to conduct trials within the community, and could inflict fines, beatings, or imprisonment, as well as excluding the miscreant or heretic by anathema (*herem*). At first, every synagogue had its own school (Talmud Tora), where boys learned to read and write in Spanish; it also had its own tribunal (Beit Din), its charitable interest-free lending societies, its aid to the poor, and so on. Moreover, as early as 1515, the community owned a printing press (the first Ottoman printing press would not appear until 1728).

The Sephardic people were privileged in comparison with the other subject peoples of the Ottoman Empire. They were welcomed in, and not subjugated. Their habitat was given to them, not conquered. They could build their own temples, whereas even the most beautiful Christian churches were converted into mosques and had minarets attached to them. The

Empire's other ethnic groups dreamed of liberation, but the Sephardim enjoyed a liberty that could not be found elsewhere. Subesequently, beginning in the 19th century, this difference would be exacerbated: the subjugated groups would want their own nation-state, while the Sephardim would do everything they could to avoid being swallowed up by a nation-state.

"THE GOLDEN AGE"

The 16th century saw Turkish power at its peak, during the great era of Soliman the Magnificent. Exchange between the West and the East intensified. Venice was the new Athens, extending its commercial empire over the whole of the Mediterranean; the city became Salonica's principal trading partner. Later, Venice would be rivaled by Ancona, Genoa and Livorno, where the grand duke of Tuscany allowed Jewish immigrants to settle in 1593.

The Sephardic diaspora made possible the gradual creation of a network consisting of dispersed members of the same family, or people who came from the same place. This network not only covered the ports of the Ottoman Empire and Italy, but also those of Spain (where intense communication with the Marrano population continued until the end of the 17th century), North Africa, Holland, and, further afield, the ports of the Hanseatic League. This inter-Mediterranean and inter-European network of trust made it possible to offer credit, make deals where a person's word was his bond, and transfer capital.

At the same time, Salonica became a center of industry, devoted principally to the production of drapery, and secondarily to that of silk and carpets. Macedonian wool was processed and sold within the Empire (in particular to the army of Janissaries); it was also exported. Finally, in the 16th century, Salonica became the center of an ephemeral Renaissance. Marrano men of letters, educated at the Universities of Coimbra, Lisbon, Alcala and Salamanca, came in great numbers to settle in Salonica. They knew Latin, were expert in the discourse of both Greek and Arab profane philosophy, and brought the culture of the Spanish Golden Age with them to Salonica. One such man was Moses Almosnino, a polymath of unbounded curiosity, who knew Hebrew, Turkish, Latin and Castilian, and wrote and published his book, *Extremos y Grandezas de Constantinopla* in Spanish (it would be printed after his death in Madrid, in 1638).

The commerical power of Salonica even turned political for a moment. Following an *auto-da-fé* ordered by the Pope, who sent Jews and Marranos from Ancona to be burned at the stake in 1565, Salonica succeeded for a time in persuading the other Sephardic communities of the Turkish Empire to boycott the port of Ancona, the majority of whose trade was with the

East. The city found itself deserted for a few months in 1566, but then private interests regained the upper hand, and the anti-Ancona league disintegrated. Nevertheless, under Salonica's initiative, a Jewish community had, for a while at least, dared to retaliate to persecution; it was the only time this ever happened in the history of Europe.

The first great Turkish defeat, at Lepanto (in 1571), where Ali Pacha's fleet of three hundred galleys was destroyed, actually promoted the rise of Salonica. The reason was that Venice, the true victor at Lepanto, continued to reign supreme over Mediterranean trade, and retained Salonica as the hub of its business with the Ottoman Empire. In fact, the economic fading of Salonica would follow the decline of Venice, which began to become apparent after the capture of Candie by the Turks (1669). Although Salonica's cultural deterioration began at the same date, economic deterioration would not be the principal cause of it. Instead, it came as the result of a Messianic disaster.

MARRANISM AND SHABBATAISM

It is said that in Spain today there are still some strict Catholic families in which the father confides the secret of the family's Jewish origin to his eldest son on his deathbed. There are still families in Spain who refuse to eat pork. Given this background, it is not surprising that in the 16th and 17th centuries, and even at the beginning of the 18th century, descendants of *conversos*, who were ostensibly Christians, left Spain for Sephardic communities in Italy or the East, and revealed their Jewish faith there. In Salonica, they have left their names on tombstones, where their names are inscribed in Latin script, and their dates of birth and death follow the Gregorian calendar.

Often, the Inquisition was the cause of their flight. It remained insatiable (and would not be suppressed until 1834). It uncovered clandestine Jews, conducted the investigations for their trials, and set up *autos-da-fé*. In 1680, in Madrid, 70 Marranos were brought to *auto-da-fé* and 18 of them were burned to death. In 1682, in Lisbon, an *auto-da-fé* condemned 90 clandestine Jews, four of whom were burned to death. In 1715, the Inquisition discovered a secret association of 20 families with a clandestine rabbi and temple. Each *auto-da-fé* provoked departures of Marranos, whether because they were Judaizers or because they feared that they would be denounced as such. There were other Marranos whose motive for leaving was not fear, but the pressure of an inner truth which had become invincible. One of them was Dr. Fernando Cardoso, a court doctor, favorite of the powerful, friend of Lope de Vega, prize-winning poet and successful author. One day, when he was a mature man who had never been the object of suspicion or denunciation, he unexpectedly left the Spanish court and sought asylum in the Venice ghetto (which had a Sephardic majority at the time). There, he changed his name to Isaac, and offered medical care to the poor; he wrote *De la excellencia de los leos hebreos* in Castilian to demonstrate the superiority of the Mosaic Law over that of all other religions.[13] His younger brother Miguel went to Livorno, changed his name to Abraham and became an apostle and theologian of the Messiah Shabbatai Zevi. Also in the mid-17th century, Urile de la Costa, a young man raised as a strict Catholic who was treasurer of a church in Oporto, emigrated to Amsterdam, where he declared himself a Jew.

Marranos flocked to Salonica during the 16th and 17th centuries; by this time, they had ceased any strict observation of Mosaic Law. They had become accustomed to eating non-Kosher food, and had neglected the rites of the synagogue. They were not circumcised. In their eyes, Judaism was not dependent upon the strict obedience of rules; instead, it was essentially an intimate faith in the Lord and his promise. The rabbis' conservatism meant that they would not be allowed to call themselves Jews, and would have some difficulty returning to the bosom of the synagogue. However, their presence undoubtedly had an indirect influence on other Jews who had never ceased to abide by Mosaic prescriptions. This period saw a regression of the Law in favor of faith. The message of the Kabbala,[14] a vision at once mystical, philosophical and cosmic, spread to the detriment of that of the Talmud, the code of ritual prescriptions. The Kabbala reinterpreted Genesis: it was not divine intervention but divine exile that was responsible for the creation of the world. Creation was degeneration, where disorder proliferated, Good and Evil split asunder, and Man was estranged from himself; Israel was the center of both the cosmic tragedy and the attempt to rectify this original degeneration; the Messiah, who would ensure the redemption of the world and that of Israel, had to embrace evil in order to suppress it. Kaballist speculation and the mysticism of Safed, in Palestine (most of the visionaries were Salonicians of Aragonese descent), began to ferment in Salonica. By 1568, doubtless as a result of this potent injection of Marranism and Kabbalism, Salonica was readying itself for the imminent coming of the Messiah. This state of feverish expectation lasted a few years, but ten years later it had all been forgotten.

Preparations began again in the middle of the 17th century. News of the horrific pogroms committed by Polish peasants reached the Sephardic community. The affliction suffered by the Jews in Spain, where the Inquisition continued to send Judaizers to the flames, and the afflictions in Poland heralded the imminent coming of the Redeemer. And at last the Messiah appeared. In a moment of inspiration, a young mystic from Smyrna, Shabbatai Zevi, pronounced the unpronounceable name of YHVH, thus revealing that he was the Messiah. He performed miracles, and announced the Salvation. A shock wave swept through all the Sephardic communities, not only arousing popular fervor, but convincing the majority of the rabbis. The news spread to all the Jewish communities in Europe, and merchants from Hamburg and Amsterdam were even known to set out for Jerusalem.

Salonica, where Shabbatai Zevi came to prophesy in 1655, was turned upside down. Many merchants destroyed their accounts and prepared themselves for the blessed time to come. At first, the Sultan believed Shabbatai Zevi to be an inspired prophet, and respected him. However, the intense agitation among the Sephardic people, and Shabbatai's claim that he would take over the kingdoms of the earth, persuaded the Sultan to take a preliminary precaution: he had Shabbatai Zevi imprisoned in a fortress. Tens of thousands of the faithful gathered around it, waiting in jubilation for the Message to be fulfilled. The Sultan then ordered Shabbatai to choose between being put to death or converting to Islam. Shabbatai converted (in 1666).[15]

Whereas, fifteen hundred years beforehand, the Pharisees had victoriously prevented the Jews of Palestine from recognizing Jesus as their Messiah, with the result that, through Paul's intermediary, he became the Savior of the gentiles, between 1650 and 1666 the rabbis, along with the faithful, supported the Messiah *en masse*. Nevertheless, Shabbataism, whose theologians and scholars were men like Nathan of Gaza and Abraham Cardoso, brought a new gospel, based on the Kaballist cosmogony of the divine Exile and the redemption of the whole Universe, which was expressed in a richer and more mystical and complex vision of the relationship between Good and Evil (with a sense of the complementarity between asceticism and debauchery, akin to that of the Cathars, and the same fascinated compassion for sin and degradation that one finds in Dostoevsky's novels). A new religion was trying to emerge among the Sephardim, in the wake of the Marrano experience and the recurrence of anti-Jewish persecution: a post-Judaism that might perhaps have embraced the gentiles of its own accord. What destroyed the new faith was Shabbatai's sudden and incomprehensible conversion to Islam.

So the religion that was trying to be born was crushed, and Shabbataism became a mere sect. After Shabbatai's abjuration, his most fervent partisans found a rationalizing explanation to preserve the truth of his message. Some believed that Shabbatai had risen up to heaven and had left only a simulacrum of his body on earth. Others thought that he was accomplishing the next phase of his mission. He had to descend even further into the realm of error and falsehood. "The Messiah had to become a Marrano like me," wrote his apostle Abraham Cardoso, adding: "The essence of the mystery is that according to the Tora, we must all become Marranos before we can come out of exile."

Shabbatai began to preach in the mosques, which he was soon forbidden to do. He was exiled to Albania, and died in poverty there in 1676.

Shabbataism split into two secret branches, one within Judaism, the other within Islam. The Jewish branch underwent an uneven process of dissolution, like that of Judaism among the Marranos who had remained in Spain. However, certain families, such as the Cardosos, made prayers for a long time to come which expressed their expectation of Shabbatai's return.

Missionaries set forth from Salonica to preach the Shabbatean gospel to the Jews of Europe; as Scholem points out, the Hasidism of the Polish ghettoes, and the "Frankism" of the Austro-Hungarian Empire, with its two faces, Christian and Jewish, can be seen as offshoots of Shabbataism.

The Islamic branch, for which Salonica became the main center, divided into three sects. Like the secret Judaism of the Marranos, but this time chiefly within the Muslim world, Shabbataism became an occult religion, camouflaged by the practice of official worship at the mosque, and even pilgrimages to Mecca. Two hundred Sephardi families became Muslims after the Messiah's abjuration, and 300 families, including some of the richest and most influential, converted in 1686. The converts who remained Shabbateans were known as *Dönmes* (a Turkish word meaning apostate), and they would be viewed with distrust for a long time to come both by traditional Muslims and by de-Shabbataized Jews. There were 8,000 *Dönmes* in Salonica at the beginning of the 19th century, and, probably as a result of the same demographic growth experienced by the Sephardim, between 15,000 and 20,000 of them in 1912 (at that time, the *Dönmes* made up more than half of the town's Muslim minority, that is, 11 percent of the total population).

At the end of the 18th century, marriages were still taking place between *Dönmes* and Jews, and related families maintained contact with each other. However, by the beginning of the 19th century, Shabbataism had become isolated within the Islamic world, and family ties or shared beliefs did not prevent an almost complete breakdown of communication between the *Dönmes* and their Jewish neighbors. The *Dönmes* settled in their own neighborhood. In the 18th and at the beginning of the 19th century, they were the city's wealthiest and most active group. Although genuine Muslims were suspicious of them, the *Dönmes* were gradually integrated into Turkish society, and at the end of the 19th century they would play a very active role in the Young Turk reform movement. They would be the first group from the properly Turkish world to embrace secular, liberal and national ideas from the West, and propagate them. Thus, in this last incarnation of Marranism, the seclusion that was an aspect of the double *Dönme* identity would undergo a metamorphosis from which it would re-emerge as openness to secular ideas from the West. Once they had readapted in this way, the *Dönmes* would take their place at the forefront of the movement to Europeanize Turkey.

Dominique Aubier has made the exaggerated claim that Spain's unconscious secret is Judaism.[16] Would it be an exaggeration to say that Salonica's unconscious secret is Marranism? Without the Marranos, who were Jewish in their souls, but had abandoned the rites and had been more or less Christianized by the time they came to Salonica to join the first wave of Sephardic immigrants, neither the mystical, Kabbalistic atmosphere nor the excited expectation of the Messiah would have come about. The experience

10

of a double (Christian/Jewish) Marrano identity found an echo in the new (Muslim/Jewish) experience of the *Dönmes*. Salonica's secret would not only remain hidden, it would become dormant during the 18th century. This can partly be explained by the fact that the Spanish Marranos stopped arriving in such large numbers, and partly because the *Dönmes* cut themselves off from the Jewish community. The Jewish community found itself back under the control of the traditional rabbis, and became even more isolated from outside influence as trade with the West lessened and the city entered a long period of economic decline.

THE DARK CENTURY

When the century of the Enlightenment was dawning in Europe, Salonica had fallen into intellectual obscurity and economic lethargy. Profane studies were banned, as were all ideas suspected of heresy. While the European textile industry was flourishing thanks to new techniques, Salonica's drapery industry, incapable of withstanding the competition, collapsed and died.

The decline of the textile industry and that of Venitian trade weakened Salonica's economy. Moreover, the Turkish wars caused the Sublime Porte to devalue its currency and increase taxation, which exacerbated Salonica's economic decline.

Salonica did not directly suffer the effects of the Turkish defeats, the Hapsburg *reconquista* in Europe or the Russian conquests in Asia. However, the city did suffer the by now chronic insubordination of the Janissaries, who frequently revolted and wrought havoc, as well as attacks by Maltese pirates in the Thermaic Gulf, and a resurgence of bandits in the Macedonian countryside, not to mention epidemics of plague and cholera, earthquakes and fires.

The Sephardic city shrank into itself, and concentrated on small-scale business and crafts. Nevertheless, Salonica's renaissance would soon begin, first outside the Sephardic world, and then on its margins.

Greek trade was the first to revive. With the treaty of Kutchuk-Kaïnardji (1770), the victorious Russians obliged the Turks to give Russian ships freedom of navigation, and this allowed the Greek arms dealers, who were protected by the Orthodox Empire, to make their entry into big maritime business under the Russian flag. Then the Franks, first the French, followed by other Westerners, came to settle in Salonica, and with them came trading posts and bridgeheads with the great commercial and industrial expansion in the West.

The treaty signed in 1535 by François I and Soliman the Magnificent was the prototype for the "capitulations" that gave France a near-monopoly over Ottoman trade with the Western powers. This treaty, which was renewed eleven times and lasted until 1740, was declared irrevocable and perpetual, but the right acquired by France ceased to be a monopoly. At the end of the 17th century, Great Britain set up a consulate in Salonica, and Austria followed suit. The Western consuls were merchants, and they protected the other French, English or Austrian merchants or brokers, who settled in the Frankish quarter. The consuls employed Greeks and Sephardim as *drogomans* (consular interpreters who took messages between the consulate and the Turkish authorities, and carried out customs formalities for arms dealers and importers who were nationals of the consulate), or as "servants" (performing all kinds of services for the consulate and its merchants).

Consular protection initially gave Western merchants the monopoly over trade with Europe. However, as business expanded, this protection would be extended to Greeks and especially to Jews of Livornese origin. The Franks gradually left the broking side of their activities in the hands of these protégés, who, in the 19th century, become representatives for the Western firms and companies. Ultimately, this consular protection, which also extended to the individual's family, would afford a minority of Greeks and Jews from the Turkish ports, and Salonica in particular, exemption from the laws and taxes of the Sublime Porte, enjoyment of the privileges accorded to nationals of Western powers (inviolability of their homes, immunity from local police and Turkish tribunals), and also escape from the constraints to which members of the Jewish community were subjected, notably the collective tax or *haradj*. Accordingly, within the Sephardic community these protégés (or *beratlis*) enjoyed superior status, privilege and what amounted to a monopoly.

THE LIVORNESE

In 1593, the grand duke of Tuscany authorized foreigners, including Jews, to settle in Livorno, which was then a fishing village. In the 16th and 17th centuries, Livorno took in Catholics from England, Moors from Spain, Jews driven out of Oran by the Spanish in 1667, and Marranos from Spain and Portugal. In the 17th century, the city became a great port, competing with Venice and Salonica, with which city Livorno also had trade relations. Moreover, during the 18th century, Livornese Jews, who were often of Sephardic or Marrano descent, but were strongly Italianized, settled in Salonica, undoubtedly attracted by the *beratli*'s privileges, for which they were also eligible. They benefited from the protection of the Austrian consul there (Austria represented Tuscany's interests from 1737 on), and could also take advantage of English, and especially French protection (since France directly controlled Tuscany between 1800 and 1815). These Livornese would form the bulk of the Frankish colony that was beginning to take control of international trade and brokerage in Salonica. "They soon established a preponderant position in the local market and played the principal role in transactions with the West."[17] Among these Livornese were the Nahums, the Franceses and the Beressis, who settled in the city towards the end of the 18th century, and the Mosseris, who arrived in the middle of the 19th century.

While the established Sephardim of Salonica had become Easternized, the Livornese were thoroughly Westernized. They had been raised on the profane culture of the West, and had already absorbed the secular poetry and the new ideas for which Tuscany was a breeding-ground in the second half of the 18th century. It was in Livorno in 1764 that Beccaria published his *Dei delitti e delle pene*, repudiating the notion of punishment and any other form of repression. Pietro-Leopoldo of Habsburg-Lorraine, grand duke of Tuscany between 1765 and 1790, was a perfect example of an "enlightened despot." In 1786, he promulgated a penal code inspired by Beccaria's ideas and, for the first time in Europe, he abolished the death penalty, torture and the crime of lese-majesty; in 1787 he abolished the Inquisition, and he also favored the ideas of the physiocrats. It was this environment that had molded the Livornese Jews who would, at the end of the century, come to settle in Salonica.

The Livornese, who initially came as consular protégés, and then became naturalized Italians after the unification of the peninsula, were bound neither by the Turkish state nor by the Jewish administration; they were also exempt from the tax which the former obliged the latter to collect. From the beginning, they were responsible for forging the link with the modern West. Later, benefiting both from their immunity from rabbinical power and from an economic privilege enjoyed neither by the Turks nor by the other Jews, they would bring the modern, secular, technical and economic West to Sephardic Salonica.

The Livornese were, in a sense, neo-Marranos, who were secularized rather than Christianized. They wore European clothes, shaved off their beards, and spoke Italian at home; the wealthier ones sent their sons to be educated in Tuscany, often at university. Throughout the 19th century, the Livornese of Salonica, who lived together in the Frankish quarter, practiced endogamy, marrying within their micro-community. There were probably 2,000 descendants of Livornese or Tuscans there in the middle of the 19th century; when Italy became a nation in 1861, it recognized 3,000 Italians in the city.

Exempt from taxation, enjoying privileged status, and speaking Italian and French, the Livornese acted as a linchpin bringing together Sephardim, Greeks, Tuscans, Austrians, French, and, more broadly, Ottomans and Westerners. They served as bridgeheads in the Ottoman Empire for Western firms and companies. It was also families of Livornese origin who, during the 19th century, would become the city's economic and cultural leaders. After having established and developed big business, they became importers of western techniques, founders of modern banks (Modiano), and creators of new industries (Moses Allatini). The richest and most progressive of the big Livornese families were the Allatinis, followed by the Mopurgos, the Fernandez, the Modianos and the Pereras. They were all related to one another, and together they constituted a new power. Moses Allatini's brother-in-law, Salomon Fernandez, was consul to the grand duchy of Tuscany, and David Mopurgo was consul to Spain. They were exempt from all the constraints of the Turkish and rabbinical authorities.

They would take advantage of their power and their influence to bring the Enlightenment to Sephardic Salonica. Moses Allatini was their principal leader.

Lazarus Allatini, who was born in Livorno in 1776, founded the Allatini and Modiano trading business in Salonica in 1796; the firm opened branches in every European country. He married Anne Mopurgo, and sent their son Moses, born in Salonica in 1809, to study medicine in Italy (possibly at Bologna). Moses Allatini set up in practise as a doctor in Florence. This, then, was a man who reached maturity in Italy at a time when 18th-century Enlightenment had been absorbed by the cultured bourgeoisie, when the ideas responsible for the French Revolution were fermenting among the students, when the Ancien Régime had been supplanted by the Napoleonic Empire, and when Tuscan, the language of classical Italian culture, had also become the language of modern ideas. The peiod of Moses Allatini's intellectual development coincided with the romantic generation of the Resurgimiento. As a descendant of Jews expelled from Spain by the Inquisition and the absolute monarchy, he inevitably shared the liberals' hatred of absolutism and clericalism. His father's death in 1834 brought him to Salonica to run the family business, but this would not prevent him from continuing to tend to the sick. After developing a business exporting Macedonian grain to the West, and particularly to Italy, a great consumer of hard wheat, Moses Allatini brought the industrial revolution to Salonica when he set up the Allatini mills, and later a brickworks, a brewery and a tobacco factory.

At the same time, he opened the doors to the cultural revolution. He took risks, founding and encouraging secular schools and newspapers, but he was also careful: he never directly attacked the rabbinate, and gave subsidies to religious works. Although most of his efforts were directed towards the Sephardic community, he acted ecumenically, working with Greek colleagues and giving subsidies for the building of Greek schools. By the time Moses Allatini died in 1882, he had accomplished a great and bloodless revolution: he had simultaneously brought the West's 18th and 19th centuries to Salonica.

Prologue

THE TRIUMPH OF THE ENLIGHTENMENT

The Enlightenment came to Salonica through three separate channels, into the three juxtaposed worlds of the Sephardim, the Greeks and the Turks. In all three cases, an intelligentsia educated in the West or in the Western manner was formed and expanded; its members were doctors, lawyers, attorneys, educators, and journalists; non-religious schools were founded, along with a press and other associations through which ideas and new customs were propagated. There was only one difference, but it was an essential one from the point of view of ideas. Among the Greeks and the Turks, modernism and secularism were closely linked to the affirmation and development of nationalism, whereas the Sephardim were not only indifferent to any form of nationalism, but would do all they could to avoid being integrated into the nation-state.

We will concentrate here on the Sephardim. The propagation of the Enlightenment was effected in the Italian, Spanish and French languages, an extraordinary example of linguistic cooperation that produced a bastard child, which Haïm Sephiha has christened "Fragnol," and of which numerous examples can be found in the writings of Vidal and his family.

The Spanish spoken in Salonica in the 19th century underwent a certain Italianization, doubtless under Livornese influence, by comparison with that spoken in Istanbul. (Had it been influenced by the Italian *f* – producing *fifo* instead of *hijo* as in Spain or Istanbul – or did it retain the ancient Latin *f*, lost in modern Spanish?) Naturally, the Sephardim continued to write in Spanish and in Hebrew script in their private correspondence, and this custom would be preserved until the end of the century. Increasingly, however, as the new schools expanded, the Sephardim began to adopt the original Latin script, and the bulk of the newspapers and books that flooded Salonica after 1870 or 1880 would be in Spanish, written in Latin script. Because of these books and newspapers, *djidio* Spanish would cease to be a dialect and would become a fully-fledged language in its own right. It was revitalized by being re-Latinized, and would only begin to die out in the 20th century, when the inhabitants of Salonica emigrated to the West and the city became Greek after 1912, and especially after 1922. French, which was gaining ground in Salonica, did not compete with Spanish. Reciprocally, Spanish did not stand in the way of French; although French ceased to be the sovereign language of diplomacy and trade in the 19th century, it remained one of the languages of trade, and in particular it remained the language of culture. It continued to be the principal Western language in the Ottoman Empire, where France, historically the protector of the Catholics and former ally of Soliman the Magnificent, ran religious schools, and later non-religious ones. In Salonica, French was taught in all of the modern schools founded after 1850, those of the *Dönmes* and the Greeks, but espe-

15

cially those of the Sephardim. And although the "Livornese" continued to speak Italian to each other, used Italian in their transactions and founded an Italian school, they would be responsible for propagating the French language. Indeed, the Italian culture of the 19th century was itself highly Francophile, and a large proportion of Italians spoke French. Italian brought French along in its wake, and then gradually died out, although certain families continued to speak it at home. French spread to nearly all categories of the population. In this instance, the prestige of French was connected to the fact that France was seen as the homeland of liberty, and to the myth of Paris. There was an unbridled taste, which Haïm Vidal Sephiha called galloping Gallomania, for anything French: songs, clothes, perfume, anything *made in France* or *made in Paris*. The spread of secular ideas encouraged Gallomania, which in return increased the spread of secular ideas.

Sephardic Salonica therefore became polyglot and bicultural. In a sense, it became "Neo-Marrano" – although, in contrast to the classic Marrano situation, where Jews are forced to adopt the religion of the gentile, in this case it was the Jews who appropriated gentile secularism. As we will see, this secularism, which put Jews and gentiles on the same level, would be resisted by the rabbis.

Moses Allatini accomplished the first step towards cultural *perestroika* by creating a French school in 1858. He brought in a progressive rabbi from Strasbourg to run it, thus attempting a historic compromise with the religious community. In the three years that it remained open, the school shaped a remarkable generation of young Salonicians, who spoke Turkish and French; but then it was forced to close, doubtless because of an ultimatum from the rabbis. Shortly beforehand, in 1856, Salomon Fernandez had founded a modern-style Italian school. In 1866, the Salem school opened, followed by a few others that taught French. In 1873, the Universal Israelite Alliance, flying the banner of progress, with headquarters in Paris, founded a boys' school in Salonica, open to all denominations, followed by a girls' school, and then a professional training school and a school for workers' children.

The teaching there followed the French model, and included the study of languages, sciences and literature; business studies were added to the curriculum. This type of teaching spread throughout Turkey, and by 1912 the Alliance had 52 schools in the European part of Turkey and 63 in the Asian part. After 1885, non-religious, Western-style schools proliferated, including Mr. Gattegno's Franco-German school, which Vidal would attend. At the beginning of the 20th century, the French secular Mission would produce *bacheliers* who had no difficulty going to France and pursuing their higher education there.

The market in profane books took off. While a progressive printer, Saadi Halevy, was publishing profane writings in Jewish Spanish, French books were also flooding into Salonica. In 1878, again at Moses Allatini's instigation, the first newspaper in Spanish, *La Epoca*, appeared. It was followed by numerous other dailies, of which five or six in Spanish survive, and two or three in French. There was the *Journal de Salonique*, and a quantity of progressive and optimistic titles including *El Liberal, El Imparcial, La Nueva Epoca, El Nuevo Avenir, La Accion, El Tiempo, El Messagero*. The Socialist press also appeared on the scene, with *El Avenir, L'Avanti* and *La Solidaridad Ovradera*, and, at the beginning of the 20th century, a Zionist newspaper, *La Renacencia*, was launched. One hundred and five Spanish-Jewish newspapers were founded in Salonica between 1860 and 1930, as compared to 33 in Istanbul and 23 in Izmir, which indicates the extent to which Salonica was leading the Enlightenment movement. At the same time, newspapers from Paris and Vienna were sold in Salonica. The local and international press supplied the Sephardic people with news from Europe and around the world, and the Dreyfus Affair would impassion public opinion.

Associations and clubs were created, and they proliferated. Barouh Cohen, a free thinker, founded a Masonic lodge that recruited from all ethnic groups. The Club des Intimes, founded in 1875, was an exclusively Sephardic reform club that brought together the Italian and French educated elite. It succeeded in partially secularizing the community's board of governors (in the past governors had simply been nominated by the grand rabbi) and in imposing elections by restricted suffrage to this board.

The irruption of the Enlightenment was resisted by the conservative rabbinate and by strictly practicing Jews. The rabbinate had formidable weapons at its disposal, including anathema, which exiled reprobates; it could also have anyone who offended against rabbinical authority arrested by the Turkish police. But the consulates protected progressive thinkers. Accordingly, in 1873, a man called Matalon bought a lamb from a Greek butcher, had his meat roasted in a Greek tavern and ate it openly while also drinking wine which was not Kosher. The rabbinate had the Turkish police arrest him, but the French consul had him released as a French national.

The rabbinate cast the anathema against the Israelite Alliance for teaching French, the language of the infidel. The conservatives raged at the schools and newspapers, which they considered to be breeding-grounds of impiety. In 1874, they created the Etz Haïm society to fight against modern ideas, but nothing could stem the irresistible propagation of the Enlightenment, and, in 1880, the highly orthodox Talmud Tora was obliged to reform by introducing Italian and French into its teaching program.

Political ideas came in to the Sephardic city, but there was very little actual political activity. The progressive haute bourgeoisie took the lead in reforming the community, almost in total isolation. Liberal ideas spread, but there was no real protest, because the Sephardim had no desire to free themselves from the Ottoman Empire and form a nation, or to merge completely with the Turks. Nevertheless, politics filtered down from the top, with the entry of a few Sephardic intellectuals into the Young Turk movement (where they came into contact with *Dönmes*), and up from the bottom, with the introduction of socialist ideas among Jewish dockers and workers. It was not until 1911, after the reforms brought about as a consequence of the Young Turk revolution, but just before the city's annexation by Greece, that Salonica would elect a Sephardic representative, Emmanuel Carasso.

The propagation of the Enlightenment, which began between 1856 and 1858, gained speed after 1875, and finally triumphed before the beginning of the 20th century. The inner transformation it accomplished in each person would also be revealed by the outer signs of clothing and hairstyle. Until the mid-19th century, the Sephardim had continued to wear their traditional Spanish dress, the *antari* (a kind of toga), *capitana* (doublet), and *djoubé* (coat with sleeves), or, for the wealthy, the *beniche* (silk cape), *mestas* (slippers) and *bonete*. Naturally, the small Livornese minority were already wearing western-style dress, which was an infraction of the Tora, and marked them as miscreants ("Thou shalt not wear a cloth woven of diverse threads, of linen and woolen mixture"). They also shaved off their beards, another infraction of the Law. Gradually, and especially after 1876, the wearing of European suits and the shaving of beards spread at the same time as modernism and the Enlightenment; moustaches were worn in the western style, and had even disappeared entirely among the younger generations by the beginning of the 20th century. At the same time, religion was in retreat: modernizers still respected the Sabbath as a day of rest, but they no longer respected its interdictions; rigorous alimentary restrictions were also forgotten and people limited themselves to not eating pork. The progress made by secularism was erratic and, within the same family, some brothers remained religious while others became free thinkers.

The abandonment of the stringent prescriptions of Mosaic Law meant that the Sephardim could frequent non-Kosher restaurants; in Turkey or abroad, it allowed them to eat at the same table with people of other religions, and thus led to the formation of friendships between Jews and gentiles. Although purists would not tolerate a gentile entering their homes, others invited and were invited by them. This was the case for the Nahums, who were taken in by their Turkish neighbors after an earthquake. Jews and gentiles began to go out together to drink raki and eat meze, barbounias, shish-kebabs and dolmes in the restaurants and cafés that lined the seafront. The pleasures and leisure activities of the West were also adopted by progressives from the wealthy classes, including entertainment, theatre, cafés where singers (on tour from France) performed for clients, reading, excursions and tourism. Western first names, already frequent among the Livornese, became common: for girls, Flor, Elena, Clara, Luna, Corinne, Fortunée and Daisy began to compete with Rachel and Sarah. For boys, Isaac was supplanted by Isidore, and Haïm became Henri.

Thus, the progressives had ceased to see Western gentiles, particularly those from France, as heathens, unclean, or persecutors, and instead saw them as models of civilization. However, there was a limit to the modernization of manners. For instance, there was no mixed marriage in Salonica. The custom of very early marriages disappeared, so that boys married after the age of 20 and could "sow their wild oats" at leisure. But marriages were still arranged by families, even modern ones; they had to be made within the same social class, and if possible within the same clan. Although girls in progressive families were educated at school (as was the case with the Franceses, who sent their daughter Elena to the Italian school of Dante Alighieri), women remained subordinate and dependent. Men and women lived in separate worlds. Women talked to each other from their windows, and set up their stools in the street to do their mending, alterations, or knitting, or put the finishing touches to *fideos* while discussing women's business; men met away from home, and discussed men's business in front of their stores, on café terraces, or in the clubs; they had their own separate outings. There was a nursery rhyme, set to a Turkish tune, which taught little boys to mock women's arguments, and which Vidal would sometimes sing nostalgically to himself in Paris:

Ya basta bula Djamila
De pelear con las vezinas
Por un cantaro, la negra
Que vos se rumpio.[18]

Salonica's cultural revolution was inseparable from its technical and economic transformation. In 1852 the first steam boat arrived in the harbor, and the blast of its horn terrified the Salonicians. Between 1877 and 1888, a railway line was built connecting Salonica to Usküb (Skoplje), and thereafter to the Serbian network and the West. The Simplon Orient Express would link London, Paris, Vienna, Belgrade, Salonica and Istanbul. In 1890, the installation of gas began in the city; in 1893, that of tram lines; in 1896, the system distributing drinking water was installed. Hygiene made progress. Salonica's demography grew prodigiously, not as the result of an influx of immigrants, but because of reduced infant mortality. Most families still had from four to eight children. *Coitus interruptus* and condoms only made their appearance with the generation that came of age in the 20th century.

Accordingly, Salonica expanded from 50,000 inhabitants in 1865 to 90,000 in 1880, 120,000 in 1895 and 170,000 in 1912. The proportions remained the same: 56 percent were Sephardim (5 percent of whom were consular protégés, with 12 schools and 32 synagogues), 20 percent were Turks, half of whom were *Dönmes*, 20 percent were Greeks, 4 percent Bulgarians and various other nationalities.

19

IN THE TURKS' COUNTRY

Salonica was extremely prosperous at the end of the 19th century, just before the Ottoman Empire began to crack apart. The 18th century had seen its gradual erosion by the neighboring Christian empires of Russia and Austria. Russia seized the northern provinces in Asia, while Austria took Belgrade, Albania, Dalmatia and Herzegovina. Russia and Austria continued to apply pressure from the outside in the 19th century, while internally the emergence of Balkan nationalism dismembered the Empire: Serbia acquired autonomy in 1817, Greece won its independence in 1830, Romania became an independent principality in 1858, and Bulgaria achieved emancipation in 1877. The Congress of Berlin ratified the accession of the Danubean and Balkan states to national sovereignty. The situation became increasingly explosive: in addition to the rivalry between Austria–Hungary and Russia, who were busy dividing up the Turkish Empire between them, there was the *Drang nach Osten* of Wilhelm's Reich, along with offensives from the English and the French, who had formerly protected Turkey from Russia (during the Crimean War), but now seized Egypt (1882) and Tunisia (1881) respectively, and then attempted to hold the two central empires in check. All these conflicting designs on the Ottoman Empire were combined with the exacerbation of nationalism among groups who were not only against the Empire that oppressed or threatened them, but also against each other, because they laid claim to the same territories in which rival populations were tangled up together. Accordingly, in 1912, Greece, Serbia, and Bulgaria joined forces against Turkey; then, after their victory, they fought each other: Greece, with the support of Serbia, would go to war with Bulgaria for control of Macedonia and Salonica. But even when Salonica entered the eye of the cyclone (between 1908 and 1912), the city seemed destined to enjoy peace, and indeed prospered from the conflict by supplying the campaigning armies.

The Ottoman Empire had split apart internally in the 18th century, as we have seen. The Janissaries had reached a point of chronic insubordination and overthrown the Sultans. The Empire was in need of reforms. These began in 1826 with the bloody suppression of the Janissaries, which came as a relief to Salonica, for they had continually threatened the city with pillage and devastation; however, it also killed off the garment industry, which had supplied the Janissaries' uniforms. An era of reform (or Tanzimat) was proclaimed in 1831. Mahmud II put an end to all discrimination against non-Muslims and officially proclaimed freedom of religion. A Constitution was promulgated in 1876. Civil equality was accorded to all of the *rayas* (minorities), who were now in principle eligible to accede to public office, and, in 1890, the tax department stopped collecting taxes by community, and began to do so on an individual basis instead. But the Tanzimat, like all belated, badly applied and sabotaged reform programs, contributed to the decline rather than putting a stop to it. The 1876 Constitution was suspended in 1878. By mid-century, the expansion of nationalism had created an irreversible centrifugal force, which the Young Turk revolution[19] would end up intensifying, in spite of the euphoria and harmony of its early days, by provoking the affirmation of a new Turkish nationalism amid the ruins of the multi-ethnic empire.

The new Turkish nationalism had developed in Salonica, and the Young Turk revolution broke out there in 1908, following the uprising of Salonica's garrison. Significantly, the descendants of the *Dönmes* were the mainsprings in this process. Like the Livornese among the Sephardim, the *Dönmes*, who were also of Sephardic origin, had nurtured the Enlightenment and introduced it among the Turks. There were 10,000 of them in Salonica at the end of the 19th century, working as craftsmen, merchants and bankers, and they had created an intelligentsia of doctors, lawyers and attorneys educated in Lausanne or Paris. They had founded two Franco-Turkish schools, were Turkified and secularized, and many of them rejected both Islam and Shabbataism to become free thinkers. It was this Dönme environment that shaped the officers and intellectuals of the Young Turk party. In Salonica, in 1908, they started the insurrection that would depose the Sultan, Mustafa Kemal, whose pink house in Salonica still stands today, and who lived among the *Dönmes* and attended their schools. The *Dönmes* would be absorbed by the Turkish society whose maturation they had codetermined, accelerated and amplified. Many would leave Salonica after Greece's annexation of Macedonia, and the last of the *Dönmes* were expelled in 1922, when the Greek and Turkish populations changed places. In Turkey, their descendants became secular republicans. In the 20th century, there was a further diaspora of *Dönmes* throughout the world, some of whom may have taken the Messiah's secret message with them. In a sense, these people carry within them the secret of Salonica.

THE SALONICIAN HYBRID

The Jewish communities in the West, and those in the Slav East, were closed to influence from the outside world until the end of the 18th century and the 20th century respectively. In contrast, as we have seen, the Sephardic communities of the Ottoman Empire, and particularly the largest of them, those of Salonica, which for centuries had given the city its identity, remained open to the gentile world. Salonica communicated with the West via Venice and then Livorno, with the Ottoman East and the Egyptian South.

This openness was amplified by the cosmopolitan nature of the Mediterranean port, which was a result of Sephardic influence, and which in return redoubled Sephardic openness. The plurisecular tolerance of the Turks had made it possible, by taking in the Sephardim without subjugating them. In Salonica, the Turks generally worked as soldiers and civil servants, and they left civil society to the Jews. Moreover, while the Turks had been fighting on their borders without respite ever since the 16th century, peace had reigned without interruption in Salonica. With one exception (the siege of Morosini in 1687), the city was never under threat while it was part of the Turkish Empire. During these centuries, Salonica was always an extraverted, exhibitionistic, active, cheerful and talkative city. The Sephardim who settled in Salonica had brought with them a two-fold, Jewish and Spanish identity. The Marranos who continued to emigrate there for the next two centuries added their own complex two-fold identity to the mix. For although the Marranos were Jews in their souls, it was a long time since they had respected the Jewish rituals, and unconsciously they carried within them Paul's message that faith is superior to the Law, the pre-secular message that obedience to the detailed prescriptions of the Tora is superfluous or superstitious. Hence the expansion and the momentary triumph, which was greater in Salonica than elsewhere, of Shabbatean Messianism, the embryo of a new, properly post-Marrano religion, which was destroyed only by its Messiah's conversion to Islam. However, what was left of Shabbataism recreated, this time in a closed fashion, the open, double identity of Marranism. (And in the end, it was their double, contradictory consciousness that made the *Dönmes* the first in the Turkish world to be receptive to the Enlightenment, and become its propagators.)

Accordingly, we can understand why it was so extraordinarily easy, in the 19th century, to introduce and disseminate the Enlightenment to the Sephardic city, with its unconscious Marrano cultural inheritance, based on the Livornese ferment with its two-fold identity, Western and Eastern, Jewish and secular.

Furthermore, it is because the cultural revolution came from above, as a result of the economic strength and the political immunity of the Livornese, that resistance from conservatives and traditionalists was so weak, in spite of the fact that spiritual power, temporal enforcement and the thunderbolt of anathema were in their hands.

The Sephardim had, in the 16th century, brought to the East the cultural riches of the first West (which had itself been fertilized by the Arab culture of the East), that of Christian-Islamic-Jewish Iberia. In the 19th century, they absorbed the second West of secularism, the Enlightenment, and modern civilization. On several occasions, Salonica's Sephardic culture was a privileged element in the historic Mediterranean whirlwind where East and West re-generate one another. Except in the darkest moment of the 18th century, Salonica was always a "mixer" of East and West, and continued to produce a very rich cultural hybrid.

However, the Enlightenment, the reforms, the Young Turk revolution, and the eventual disintegration of the Ottoman Empire and the Hellenization of the city, would shatter the Salonician city-homeland. Whereas the Greeks, Bulgarians and Turks would find their homeland in a nation-state, the Salonician Sephardim only wanted to escape absorption by a nation-state. As it turned out, the arrival of the nation-state would indeed break up their little homeland, and the Sephardim of Salonica were destined to be dispersed in the West or diluted in Greece. The Sephardic spirit remained very much alive for a time, carrying within it the vague consciousness of a common secular destiny, and Salonician emigrés would remain profoundly faithful to the memory of their little lost homeland. But integration in one place or another would finally be achieved. The children of Salonicians, immersed in their new homelands, would not know that it was the very originality of Sephardic culture and identity that had allowed for its own dilution in the countries of the West.[20]

I

The Nahum Family

A LIVORNESE FAMILY

Vidal was born in Salonica, in the Ottoman Empire, on the "Frankish" date of March 14th, 1894, to David Nahum and Dona Helena Frances.

Nahum is a Hebrew word, which, like its variant Nehama, means "consolation." The word is also a forename, which became a family name among the Sephardim. The Bible mentions the predictions and maledictions of a minor prophet called Nahum, who announced the fall of Niniveh. Vidal liked to imagine that he was descended from this man, who although minor was a prophet all the same, and with mock seriousness, which was one of his favorite forms of humor, he claimed that he still possessed the ancestral gift.

The family must originally have come from Aragon, as Joseph Nehama tells us, since a Nahum family was affiliated to the Aragonese synagogue in Salonica. But Vidal's family did not come directly from Aragon to Salonica. Did his ancestors leave Spain at the time when Jews were obliged to choose between conversion and exile? Were they among those Marranos who only emigrated during the centuries that followed? When did they settle in Livorno? They were probably still there at the middle of the 18th century, and indeed a branch of the family seems to have stayed in Tuscany, since the historiography of the Risorgimento indicates that one Isaac Nahum was active in the army there. Salomon Nahum may have lived in Sicily for a short time, as Vidal remarks: *My father used to tell us that our Livornese ancestors left for Sicily first, and from Sicily they went to Salonica.* In fact, the Nahum family attended a synagogue known as New Sicily (Sisilya Hadach), whose other patrons were a group of families including the Amars, the Ezrattis, and the Sephihas.[21] The Nahums' attendance of this synagogue confirms their recent settlement in Salonica, where there was a synagogue of Old Sicily (Sisilya Yachan), but it does not prove that they had ever settled even briefly in Sicily, since no particular synagogue existed for the Livornese.

Vidal's great-grandfather, Salomon Nahum, was probably born in Livorno. His grandfather, David S. Nahum, had four brothers, the eldest of whom had a son who was a physician; the youngest had two sons to whom he gave forenames which were then considered unusual, Adolphe and Edgar (perhaps because he admired Adolphe Thiers, the republican and liberal thinker under the monarchy, and Edgar Quinet, the great republican and intellectual leader of the young in 1840s France, who was exiled in 1851). This must have been how the exotic forename of Edgar entered the family, before its reincarnation in the 20th century, once in Belgium (by Léon D. Nahum's son), and again in France (by Vidal's son).

At the beginning of the 19th century, Salonica had 65,000 inhabitants, more than half of whom were Sephardim. David S. Nahum was contemporary with the reforms of Mahmud II. During his lifetime, Salonica experienced great difficulties. There was a series of epidemics, including the cholera epidemic, which, between April and September 1832, literally decimated the population, followed by the catastrophes of 1838, 1847 and 1855. The city's economy remained depressed, and a number of Salonicians emigrated, particularly to Egypt.

However, when the Livornese clan settled in Salonica, a new period of development, both economic and cultural, began. The Age of Enlightenment was soon to emerge. Dr. Moses Allatini returned from Florence in 1834 to take over the running of the Allatini firm, and would later expand it, as we have seen (Prologue). David S. Nahum may have been quite close to Moses Allatini; Vidal says of his grandfather: *It was a very good family, they had a very good situation . . . his position in the Allatini mills was more like that of a partner.*

In 1830, David S. Nahum had married a Miss Botton, or rather, as Vidal used to insist, with conviction, "de Botton" (I am not sure whether he was convinced or had convinced himself that it was true, or whether it merely amused him to think that his grandmother might have had aristocratic origins). In any case, he notes in his oral autobiography that his grandmother in particular came from a very good family; and as it turns out the de Bottons were indeed one of the "great" Livornese families. The couple had eight children: Gracia or Riquetta (1833), Salomon (1836), who married twice and fathered eleven daughters, Joseph (date unknown), Jouda (1839), Avram (1842), Youri (1845), Sara (1848) and finally David.

David S. Nahum died in 1851, aged 48, while his wife was pregnant with his sixth son. The new-born, apparently counter to tradition, would take his father's name, David, but he would do so in order to honor the memory of a father who died before his birth. It was this last-born and second David, David D. Nahum, who would be Vidal's father. Vidal knew his grandmother, who died in 1908, fifty-seven years after her husband: *I never knew my grandfather, but I did know my grandmother, who was absolutely devoted to her grandchildren and her sons . . . I was 14 when I lost my grandmother, but I have never forgotten the tenderness in her eyes when she looked at me.*

After the death of David S. Nahum, his eldest son Salomon took his place in the Allatini firm. David D. (1851–1920) was still a child when his older brother married; this marriage and a second one would produce eleven daughters with French and Italian forenames (Alegra, Sol, Lucia, Elise, Marie, etc.).

How was David D. Nahum's character marked by the fact that he never knew his father? Whatever its effect may have been, he benefited from the love of an extremely tender mother, who must have focused especially on this, her last-born orphan. He probably went to the French school founded by Allatini (since the Universal Israelite Alliance's school was only set up in 1875), where he learned Italian, Turkish and Greek. His first job, like his brother's, was at the Allatini mills; later, he established himself as an independent trader in Macedonian hard wheat. He began to work with the French consul to Salonica, who exported grain and tobacco to France, and he facilitated his dealings with the Turkish dignitaries. Accordingly, for four or five years, from around 1875 to 1880, he was *drogoman* to the French consul, and acted as an interpreter and intermediary between him and the Turkish authorities. It was at this time that progressive families, especially the men, began to dress in the *franka* manner. David D. Nahum was one of the first to favor the new customs, as well as the new style of dress, and he was enthusiastic about France, its ideas and its manners. *Djidio* was still spoken within the family and to close friends, but French increasingly supplanted it in conversations about ideas, debates, etc. David D. Nahum was, in an inseparable fashion, resolutely modern and passionately Francophile. Since he was linked to the French consul, Dumonteil La Grèze, who was himself a merchant, and exported tobacco and grain to France, it may have been business that took him to the World's Fair of 1878. He returned from this trip filled with wonder at what he had seen, and he was still telling his children about Paris and the Fair in the 1900s: *Yes, he used to tell us all about it . . . He used to sing "Allons au Tro, tro, tro, trocadéro. A l'omnibus, bus, bus de Chaillot."*

In 1878 war broke out between Russia and Turkey. David was indifferent to this war, until the Russian victory conferred "a great advantage" on all the non-Turks living in the Empire: *The Russians made the Turkish government give up its authority over all the inhabitants of European Turkey who weren't Muslims. So those who were French, English, Italian, German or American fell under the jurisdiction of their consulates . . . so for us it was a dream, there were no more taxes, there was no military service.*

Indeed, David Nahum, who must already have been a *beratli* protected by the French consulate, took advantage of the Russo–Turkish treaty to acquire in full the advantages of Italian nationality. He managed to use his Livornese ancestry to persuade the consulate, and all of his children were accorded Italian nationality. Although the decision to take Italian nationality was not an arbitrary one, since the family had still been in Tuscany in the 18th century, they did not experience it in a patriotic fashion. David D. Nahum had already become a *selanikli*, and had adopted Spanish as his own language; for his children's generation, Italian was no more than a memory handed down by their parents.

Many families of Italian origin requested and obtained Italian nationality.

Other families sought Spanish nationality, several centuries on; some acquired other nationalities or bought them by baksheesh, and all these changes of nationality protected them from taxes, from military service and from the Turkish police.

Italian nationality gave David Nahum rights, dignity and privilege. People with Livornese ancestry who, like him, were able to acquire Italian nationality, and those who could acquire a western identity from a consulate, either through their business contacts, or by some other means, were truly privileged. Although they remained within the Ottoman Empire, they were no longer its subjects, in the political sense of the word, meaning "objects." They enjoyed an effective *habeas corpus* that was denied even to the Ottomans. David's son Vidal remembers the advantages conferred by this *habeas corpus: It really was an advantage because suppose my brother was at the café-concert – I was very young, I might have been fifteen years old, and he was already twenty – well, if he felt like taking up two seats instead of one, and a policeman said to him: "You're taking up two seats, sir," he would reply, "It's none of your business, I'm Italian."*

In 1879, after his return from Paris, where he had "sown his wild oats," David married. He was 28 (that is, the age when people marry today), and his young bride, who was also from a "very good family" of Livornese origin, Dona Helena Frances, was 17. She was born in 1862, to Jacob Frances (born in 1816), a wholesale textile merchant, and Sara Bitti (born in 1846). (Jacob Frances had two other daughters, Flore and Régine, and two sons, Vidal and Azriel.) Did the Franceses leave France for Spain before the reign of Isabella the Catholic, or Spain for France after having to choose between conversion and exile? Could they be related to Manoel Boccara Frances, a Marrano living in Lisbon in 1590, who became a Jew in Amsterdam, before settling in Livorno in around 1658 and meeting his death on the road to Florence? In any event, the Franceses also came from Livorno. Dona Helena attended the Dante Alighieri Italian school, which not only testifies to her very definite Livornese ancestry, but also to the modernism of the Frances family: at the time it was unusual for daughters to be educated at school. Vidal: *My mother, when she married, was, how can I put it, imbued with a certain, how can I put it, knowledge, not only of foreign languages and history and geography, but she was absolutely up-to-date, which meant she suited my father very well, because he was also very modern.*

David was fond of teasing his wife: *My father used to tease my mother. He used to say that he had seen with his own eyes that whenever a pretty woman came in to my maternal grandfather's store, my grandfather would tell her: "Madam, I do not sell to the public, but I'm prepared make an exception for you, only first I will have to take your measurements . . . So, to allow me to take your measurements, please step into my office." Then my mother would say: "Stop it, for goodness' sake."* David D. Nahum enjoyed shocking his wife with a joke, making her protest; what he liked was to succeed in "getting a rise out of" his wife, although she was quite aware that it was a joke and a game. Vidal inherited his father's taste for teasing of this kind.

Dona Helena gave birth to six children between 1881 and 1897: Henriette, Léon, Jakob known as Jacques, Haïm known as Henri, Vidal, and Mathilde. In 1882, at the age of 30, David D. Nahum added metallurgy to his import–export activities. He represented big Belgian companies and became official *drogoman* to the Belgian consul. He even took over the running of the consulate's office in 1901, when the usual holder of the post was absent. His position as *drogoman* was the source of immense pride to David and his family: *He was very proud, because every time there was a special occasion, or a festival, whether it was a Muslim holiday or some other kind, the Belgian consul would go and visit the prefects, mayors and other consuls, and my father, wearing his top hat and tails, would accompany the consul in his big two-horse carriage, which was always guarded by a* kawas, *a uniformed bodyguard.* On December 14, 1902, the consul presented David with a civic medal, first class. In Vidal's imagination, this medal was magnified to become the "Order of Léopold," which was how he would always refer to it afterwards.

The family would never cease to reminisce about this episode. An envoy from the consul asked David D. Nahum to come to the consulate at once, without giving any explanation. The family's reaction was one of alarm, anxiety and expectation. *I get back from school, my mother says to me . . . I can see she's very worried, my brother too, all of them, they tell me: "They came to get Papa and Léon, my eldest brother, the consul sent them, I wonder why . . . Let's hope there's no problem, you never know what might happen."* (A clear demonstration of the Oriental fear that any attention from the heights of officialdom potentially signals danger. The danger in this case was not of penal sanction, since the Belgian consul had no authority to use harsh measures, but of a sudden fall from favor.) Time dragged on, and still they waited: *Luckily, one hour later the consul's car appears, all prettied up for the occasion, with the* kawas *at the front, and my father with a medal, which the consul had wanted to give him in my brother's presence, at a ceremony that was attended by the handful of Belgians who were in Paris . . . who were in Salonica.* David descended from the carriage, bearing the medal proudly on his chest. A decoration was something fabulous to a community who, for centuries, had experienced persecution, ignorance, disdain, tolerance, prosperity and esteem but never the glory conferred by a medal. It seemed an immense distinction, to be measured by the distance away rather than the area of Belgium. A far-away king had deigned to take notice of the Balkans, and to honor the merit of David Nahum. On his father's death, Vidal received the medal and the title, had them framed under glass and ever afterwards displayed them in a conspicuous position in his successive apartments. In France, he was convinced that the Legion of Honor itself was no match for the Order of Leopold.

David Nahum's business prospered. In around 1880, he was made responsible for the Russian oil depot at Bakou, which was exported by the

Mantachoff firm, and at the beginning of the century he would transfer responsibility for the metallurgical sector to his eldest son, Léon. As a sign of his prosperity, he built an imposing two-story house made of wood, after the fashion of the time, in a street known as "la Dzinganeria," a name that attests to the former presence of gypsies there. It was situated in the Frankish quarter, so called not in memory of the Normans or of Simon de Montferrat, who had come to Salonica centuries earlier, before the fall of Byzantium, but because of the French and other Westerners who settled there in the 17th and 18th centuries. It was not an exclusively Jewish quarter, and was inhabited by wealthy families, while in the Campagnes quarter the Sephardic upper-middle class built western-style villas, like the villa Allatini.

THE DAWN OF THE 20TH CENTURY

The dawn of the 20th century was a blur to me, says Vidal. The birth of the century came like a sunrise to Salonica. Sephardic Salonica was flourishing. It had benefited from the expansion of trade with the Ottoman hinterland, with the Balkan countries, with Mitteleuropa, Austria-Hungary and Germany, with Russia, and with the West, particularly France and Belgium.[22] The luxuries, manners and ideas of the West all arrived together. Enlightening ideas spread along with electric lighting and streetcars. Salonica's Sephardic dockers launched the first union movement in the Ottoman Empire. In 1911, *La Solidaridad ovradera*, a newspaper in the Spanish Jewish language, announced the first socialist conference. The newspapers from Paris, London, Berlin and Vienna were read and discussed in the clubs that sprang up everywhere. French *café-concert* artists came to Salonica on tour, and everything that sang of Paris, the mythical city, was received with great enthusiasm.

But the 20th century also began with an earthquake and a bombing. *I remember there was an earthquake in about 1902, I was still very young . . . The inhabitants were advised to leave their apartments . . . As a result, because the Turkish houses, the Muslims' houses, were single-story, they took us into their homes . . . We had Muslim neighbors next door with whom we were on very good, fraternal terms, we used talk to each other, chat, we visited one another, and we were invited to one another's houses.* (This indicates that the zone in the Frankish quarter the Nahum family moved into was also inhabited by Turks, which indicates that territorial segregation had lessened.)

In 1903, the Bulgarian *comitadjis* attacked the Ottoman Bank. *I remember it very clearly, because I was 9 years old: one evening, at about 8 or 9 o'clock, we lived about 300 meters from the place, we heard a massive explosion, and because there had been a lot of disturbances lately, we wondered what it could be; luckily the whole family was together, my father, my mother, my brothers and sisters, and so my father went to the window to find out . . . No one knew anything, everybody was*

*running down the street, they were all running away, and gunshots were coming from
all directions. A few seconds later, we learn that it's the Bulgarians, they've blown up
the Ottoman Bank and immediately the Turkish police force sends its officers into the
street and we see the first Bulgarian prisoners being dragged out; they were picking
them up here there and everywhere, whether they had anything to do with it or not,
they were killing them, they were shooting them, they were putting them onto carts,
it was a horrible sight . . . Finally, shortly afterwards, when everything was a bit
[calmer], the firemen came, all the ones who had put out the fire at the bank . . . an
hour or two later we were all ready and waiting at the windows . . . the neighbors
opposite found out that it had started in a grocery that was opposite the bank. The
police realized what an incredible job they'd done: because it was a grocery, there was
an endless stream of customers, which meant that all day, from morning to night, the
customers came in one after another and stood in line to take away their shopping,
and in fact all they were taking away was soil that had been dug out to make the
tunnel, but neither the police nor the neighbors guessed anything was up, the customers
kept coming out with their parcels, with their bags . . . that's my first memory.*

Vidal began to attend the Franco–German school at the age of six. His
father could have sent him to the German school, particularly since he
intended to have him specialize in the Austrian and German markets, but
there was no question of his not learning French: *The Germans had started an
exclusively German school in Salonica, they were trying to take pupils away from the
Franco-German school which was private . . . so my father didn't want that, and as
it turned out he was absolutely right.* On completing his studies, Vidal acquired
a diploma that seems to have been equivalent to the *baccalauréat*, since it
allowed Vidal's schoolmates to pursue their further education in France.
Vidal would have liked to study medicine himself, as his friend Matarasso
did. Was it because he wanted to follow his friend, who left for France, or
was he genuinely attracted by the career? In any event, when he left school
in 1910, his father insisted that he began to earn his living immediately in
Salonica. For a long time, possibly for the rest of his life, Vidal would regret
not having become a doctor, but he would never hold it against his father;
he neither showed nor felt the least resentment. David D. Nahum was an
approachable, jovial man, a *bon vivant* who enjoyed a joke, but he inspired
respect and veneration in his sons, and particularly in Vidal.

This was because the family represented a very powerful community. At
this time, families had several children and extended, through uncles, aunts
and cousins, into kinds of tribes linked by a network of relationships that was
always a network of mutual assistance and solidarity. It was often a
cosmopolitan network, including brothers, uncles and cousins in Livorno,
Alexandria, Usküp (Skoplje) or other places. At the end of the 19th century,
it expanded to take in the great cities of the West, particularly Vienna and
Paris, when the emigration to the West began, with young people who
wished to study and practice medicine, pharmacy and dentistry there.

Within the nucleus of the family, the father's authority was undisputed, as was respect for the mother. If the father died young, the eldest son became head of the family and protector of his mother and his siblings, even if he was barely an adolescent. There was never any lapse in authority. On the father's death, the brothers formed a community in which the eldest brother held the deciding vote. All loving warmth seems to have been concentrated in the affection between brothers and sisters, and was nurtured by the ever-present memory of their deceased parents. The affectionate diminutives dating from early childhood (*pacheco*, little pacha, *patico*, little duck, *queridico*, little darling), were often used for an entire lifetime (thus for the rest of his life Vidal remained Vidalico to his brothers, and even, to some extent, to his son). The Nahum family community not only survived exile and dispersion; it became, as we will see (Epilogue), increasingly vigorous as a result.

Marriages were unions between families on the same social level, and were arranged and dictated by the parents. Marriage brokers (*kazamenteros*), who might be amateur (that is to say, people who enjoyed matchmaking), or quasi-professional, made suggestions to parents or were asked by them for their assistance. In David D. Nahum's generation, and even later, marriages took place within the Livornese caste; there were numerous marriages between cousins, and certain families were, literally, inextricably interrelated. It was considered proper, especially for girls, to marry in order of age. Indeed, the parents of a girl who was not very pretty would refuse the well-born lover of a younger sister until the elder girl found a husband. Things were arranged so that young people would meet as if by accident, in order to see how they liked one another. If inclination was slow in coming, parents would put pressure on their son and especially on their daughter. One of Vidal's elder brothers had a mistress, but was forced to bow to his parents' insistence that he marry a young woman who, as it happened, was very beautiful, had a good dowry and came from a good family. As in 19th-century novels, he wept before going to the wedding ceremony. However, even in those days, Jacques Nahum, David's second son, and his sister Mathilde married for love. Marriage based on inclination or love was not really acceptable until the following generation, the one that was born in France. Therefore, the modernism and up-to-date ideas of advanced families like the Nahums only slowly wore down the influence of traditional rules related to matrimony.

Marriage, until the end of the 19th century, was still confined to families who came from the same city. The Sephardim of Salonica and Istanbul held one another in contempt,[23] barely trusted one another and would not have dreamed of allying with one other through a blood tie. These prejudices, specific to an urban civilization, had lessened by the turn of the century (Jacques married a girl from Belgrade in Usküb). They disappeared after the emigration to France, where passionate love and strangers to the city made a simultaneous irruption into *selanikli* marriage, and broke down the ancient rules.

Despite the divisions, and even hostility, between one city and the next, the Sephardim were united in their aversion for the Ashkenazim, whom they called "pollaks:" this aversion (which was in fact reciprocal) would take concrete form when they met physically in France. They did not frequent the same synagogues (belonging to different rites), and they would have only very superficial relationships with each other; when German Jews fleeing the Nazis emigrated to France, Vidal did not see them from the perspective of a co-religionist, but from that of a Sephardi faced with an Ashkenazi. And finally, when the plump, soft, delicate women of Salonica, who could not stand the cold, and were accustomed to comfort and idleness, arrived *en masse* at Auschwitz, they would be the object of irony and mocking laughter from the thin, tough, uncompromising Polish Jewesses. The Ashkenazim jeered as they were led to the gas chamber.

BROTHERS AND SISTERS

The Nahum brothers, like their mother and their father, were mostly tall, over 5 feet 10; they had black hair, pale skin, and almost all of them had blue eyes. If they were not dressed *franka*-style, they would look like Circassians (Tcherkesses) from Caucasia, whose women were highly prized in the harems of the Sultans, or like Chleuhs from Southern Morroco, both of whom are tall, straight-backed, with fair skin and blue eyes. In the West, when conventionally dressed, they did not look as if they came from the East. It was their manner of speaking (all of the Nahums had an accent, albeit a very slight, indefinably Balkan one), and especially some of their gestures and expressions, that made their Eastern background apparent. Dona Helena Frances was a tall woman like her husband, with blue eyes and regular features, which increased the frequency of blue eyes and tall stature among her children. David D. Nahum was a dignified man and a *bon vivant*. He had an air of authority and leadership, but he also knew how to make himself approachable, and liked to make jokes when at home with the family. He was modern and "up-to-date," meaning that he was well informed about all the latest changes and developments. Dona Helena Frances was a cultured, reserved, modest woman. They made a harmonious couple.

As we have seen, David and Hélène were non-practicing: *My father wasn't very . . . orthodox; for instance, on Saturdays, you weren't supposed to light the fire, but he lit it anyway.* Furthermore, they did not respect the prescriptions and culinary interdictions of Mosaic law. They only retained a repugnance for pork (which Vidal would maintain for his entire life; not for the meat itself, but only for its name, since Vidal was very fond of ham, which he in no way identified with pigs). Notably, even within the tribe made up of descendants of the Livornese, secularism made very uneven progress. (For instance, Raffaele Nahum, son of Salomon Nahum, and nephew of David S. Nahum, remembers that at the beginning of the 20th century his father continued to respect the prescriptions concerning food and the interdictions regarding the Sabbath. He had a Turk come to light his fire on Friday evenings, and anyone who came into his home had to touch the *mesouza*, kiss it, and say amen.)

The main Jewish festivals were respected and celebrated: *So my father would try and take us to the temple, not all four brothers, but at least one or two of us, because we were a bit reticent, we wanted to take advantage of the festivals to go walking in the woods.*

Clearly, respect for the rituals diminished further with the generation of David D. Nahum's sons, since they tried to play hooky from the synagogue during the big festivals. However, the whole family celebrated Passover, ate unleavened bread for eight days, and spent two or three days celebrating the festival of Purim.[24] David also had children make little houses decorated with flowers to put in the courtyard of his home, for the festival of Sukkot. Were they scrupulous about fasting at Kippur? Vidal, for one, never went without food. He liked to joke that when he was ill, as a very young boy, his father asked the rabbi to give him a dispensation exempting him from fasting, and that this dispensation was still valid. One wonders whether David D. Nahum, with his healthy appetite, would have been able to keep up his fast completely. David D. Nahum's children would stop respecting Kippur once they came to the West, with the exception of the eldest daughter, Henriette, whose husband was religious. The festivals that the Nahums celebrated were the joyous ones, which symbolized their cultural and ethnic belonging to the Jewish community, but did not imply a relationship of penitence to God. In fact, David seems to have been a deist, believing in a tutelary "Good Lord," but not in the Revelation. His sons would be something like deists themselves. As we will see later, when they were at the height of their tribulations, during their detention in prison, Henri and Vidal would softly sing prayers asking God's forgiveness for their sins.

David's eldest son, Léon, who was born in 1883, resembled him physically, and especially resembled him in his bearing and dignity. He was a "very handsome man." His manners, his respectability, his imposing presence and his elegance were admired by his brothers. He had the reputation of being a great lover of women and a Don Juan. In 1910, he married a very beautiful woman, Julie Menahem, who came from a big, progressive family of Livornese origin (her father was a member of the Intimes reform club and lived in the Campagnes quarter). Léon ran the metallurgical side of his father's business. He and his wife Julie made numerous trips abroad to Western Europe, both on business and as tourists, as we know from the cards they sent to his parents in 1906 from London, in 1909 from Budapest and Vienna, and in 1910 from Venice, Paris and Vienna. Léon moved first to Brussels, where the big Belgian companies he worked for as a correspondent had their headquarters, in about 1911; then he went to live in Istanbul with his wife and his daughter Chary (born in 1911 in Salonica), to oversee the construction of the Anatolian railroad, which had been undertaken by the Belgian companies for which he acted as proxy. Léon had authority over his brothers, and his moral pre-eminence would become clear after their father's death, in 1920.

Jacques, born in 1885, was discreet, very private, thoughtful, perhaps shy. He spoke very correct and formal French, and had a taste for literature. He would probably have preferred to be an intellectual, but like the rest of his brothers he was obliged to make his career in business. His first job was at the Modiano Bank in Salonica, and he was later appointed branch manager at Usküp (Skoplje). In 1914, the Cohens, a family of Serbian nationality from Belgrade, came to live in the city, and Jacques met Sophie Cohen, a young Sephardi woman raised as a Serb, at a hotel. He obtained consent for their marriage, which was a love match. Jacques would retain the Italian nationality acquired by his father until the end of his life. After the First World War, he would settle in Brussels, work in Léon's firm, and always retain his love of literature.

Henri was a carefree, womanizing joker. Vidal was very admiring of his brother, who was four years older than him. They would be arrested together by the French military police in Salonica in 1915, and would go through deportation in a warship, prison and concentration camp together, which would further strengthen the bond between them.

Henriette, the eldest girl, born *de facto* in 1881 but *de jure* in 1885 (after her arrival in France), married Élie Hassid in 1904. It was a marriage of convenience. He worked at the Modiano bank in Salonica, and was manager of a small branch office. Although he did not strictly respect Mosaic Law, he was religious and much more of a traditionalist than the Nahums.

Henriette was very active, energetic, devoted to the family, and somewhat domineering. She seemed to want to enjoy the prerogatives and the authority of the head of the family, especially as far as domestic problems, arguments or misunderstandings were concerned. Even in his earliest memories of her, the author always saw her as something of a matron, who dominated her husband. She was concerned about questions of class, rites, rank and proprieties.[25] She brought her Salonician consciousness of social class with her when she moved to France, where she continued to disdain *gentes bachas* (the lower classes). Her two daughters, Liliane and Aimée, would take piano lessons. In Paris, she would move to a bourgeois neighborhood, the 17th arrondissement.

Mathilde, the youngest, born *de facto* in 1897, then *de jure* in 1903 was cherished and admired by everyone. She was very beautiful, with dark hair, blue eyes and a slender and perfect figure. When she was an adolescent in Salonica, her beauty transfixed a fifteen-year-old boy, David Matarasso, who was two years her junior. Wanting to express his love to her, but finding himself lost for words, he consulted a public letter-writer, who gave him the following sentence to copy out: "Oh my love, I love you so much that no word is capable of expressing my love." He timidly handed the note to Mathilde and ran away. Shortly afterwards, as she had not responded to his message, he dared to speak to her directly; the beauty replied with scorn: "You're too short for me, and anyway, you made a spelling mistake." In the seventies, the author of this book met David Matarasso in São Paulo, where he had emigrated; sixty years on, he remembered the episode with tears in his eyes. The lovely Mathilde did accept the proposal of a distinguished soldier in 1917. After spending three days on leave in Marseilles, where he had come to see his sister Sophie, Jacques Nahum's wife, Bouchi Cohen, a cavalry captain in the Serbian army, would fall in love with Mathilde, find favor with her, and ask for her hand.

II
Adolescence

YOUNG VIDAL

Vidal, the last of the four brothers, born on March 14, 1894, was loved tenderly by his parents, and never ceased to be their Vidalico. The name Vidal is a Hispanized version of Haïm, which means "life." By the end of the 19th century, however, the Sephardim had begun to use the two forenames independently of one another, and Haïm became equivalent to Henry, probably because of the H. Naturally, in a French-speaking environment, Vidal's elder brother Haïm would be known as Henri.

Vidal is 5 feet 10 inches tall; his hair is black, and he has blue eyes flecked with gray and green. He is slim and straight-backed. He is not as elegant and dignified as Léon, nor as discreet and calm as Jacques, and he is not a womanizer like Henri. However, he has a very quick and curious mind, and is highly sensitive to feminine charms. He is a *joueur,*[26] in every sense of the word. He likes to inject a spirit of playfulness into his relationships with his close family or friends, and he likes games of chance: not card games or roulette, but lotteries. In France, he will never miss a single draw on the national Lottery, from the day of its inception onwards, but he will never have any luck. He also buys Crédit National bonds because there is a chance of winning the draw. He dabbles on the Stock Exchange – in secret, because both his first and second wives, as well as his eldest brother Léon, scold him about this dangerous penchant. Still, he is always very prudent, never risking big amounts; Vidal simply likes to cast his line and try his luck.

Vidal and his brother Henri love to sing. All their lives, they sing in the mornings, while walking down the street; they whistle or hum *mezzo voce* as soon as they have finished eating, and if it has been a good, convivial meal, they break into song and urge their table companions to sing in turn. Vidal's son remembers his father singing like a bird in the early morning, while he is still dozing heavily himself. He sings Mayol songs from the 1900s, songs by other French singers, Spanish tunes, popular melodies, occasionally an old Turkish chant. Throughout his life, Vidal sings songs from every period of his life.

Vidal is very cheerful, and laughs at anything; Henri likes "kidding," whereas Vidal has an immoderate appetite for jokes. He laughs with pleasure and to give others pleasure. Laughter is his natural mode of communication.

Vidal is very fearful. Having been raised in a family and in an environment where there were no pets, he is afraid of dogs and has never liked their company; on his way home at night from the *café-chantant*, he whistles and sings as he walks to reassure himself, for which his brothers mock him. He is afraid of arguments and fights, but when he thinks a member of his family is in danger, he is capable of becoming a wolf. One day, when his son, aged 15, is accosted near the store by a gentleman who speaks and smiles at him engagingly, Vidal comes out, scowling ferociously at the stranger, who flees under his terrifying glare.

Vidal is also very anxious. Once, when he was very young, he took the train with his parents to the outskirts of Salonica on an excursion to the countryside (a sign that the recent western custom of rural recreation had been taken up by the Nahum family). All the way through the walk, he worried that his parents would miss the train home, and would not leave them in peace: "*Papa, el treno se va fuyir.*" Vidal is not profoundly anxious, however, nor is he tormented, or racked by guilt; his anxiety, although very keen, is also very superficial. He will never lose his anxiety over timetables. He always gets to the station at least an hour before his train is due to leave. If his wife knows the train time, she will tell him not to be in such a hurry to take the métro or a taxi, and so he will find a way of lying to her about the real departure time, so that he can satisfy his irresistible psychological need to get there early. Then, having found out by experience that he lies to her and adds on an extra hour, his wife tries again to make him leave later, which means that next time he has to add on an extra hour and a half. In the end, no one will ever know the real departure time of his trains, but he will always find a way of arriving at least an hour early. Despite his great love of family, Vidal, like his brother Henri, his immediate elder, is very sociable. He strikes up friendships easily, anywhere, on the train, in the street, on the bus.

At the same time, Vidal is curious about everything. In fact, he is curious about the whole world. At thirteen, he uses the advertising sections of *Mon dimanche* and *Annonces philatéliques* to exchange stamps and postcards. He accumulates stamps, without classifying them, and will continue to accumulate them until the end of his life. He receives "views" of Brussels, Dinant, Malines, Anvers, Strasbourg, Troyes, Grenoble, Sassari and Kutira Hora (Bohemia). He writes, with an offer to exchange postcards, to Miss Cornélie Monday of Montreal. She sends him a card showing the Pacific Railway bridge over the Saint Laurence, near Montreal, on March 4, 1907: the card is addressed to Mr. Vidal D. Nahum, of Salonica, Turkey, Europe, and states: "Accept exchange with pleasure." Their correspondence continues until 1910. At the age of 66, on April 22, 1960, Vidal writes to Miss Cornélie Monday:

Dear Madam,

1907 . . . 1908 . . . 1909 . . . 1910 . . .

At that time, I was living in Salonica, and I exchanged postcards with you from there. Since 1912–27, I have been living in Paris. When the President of our Republic visited Montreal, I remembered your address.

I am writing to you in case you are still at this address, and hope to hear from you.

I remain, Madam, or Miss, your obedient servant.

The letter is returned. The address, whether wrongly read or wrongly copied out by Vidal so many years later, was incorrect. Vidal had written to 1159, Bordeaux Delorimier, whereas it should probably have been Boulevard Delorier; in any case, the letter was stamped "address unknown."

Around 1908 or 1910, between the ages of 14 and 16, Vidal begins to go out. For a long time, he has been wanting to go to cafés and the theatre like his elder brothers. He supports his school football club:

Every Sunday, especially since it was our day of rest, we went straight after lunch, in the afternoon, to the football pitch, either to watch our team train, or for a match against another club. When the match was over, those of us who were in the final year were allowed to use the alumni's club, and we all went to the club.

At the club, there was a kind of head waiter who served beer, hardboiled eggs, fried eggs, light snacks, and also a member of the mandolin club — because in Salonica the mandolin was the specialty — and he would start playing the mandolin and people would get up to dance, which meant that the girls and the young men . . . Once the sessions at the club were over, in little groups of three, four, five, six, or seven, we each had our particular friends, we went to a very well-known restaurant, which served very good food, and where they made us extremely welcome . . .

Véronique: But how come you had money to go to a restaurant?

Because in the final year of high school my father already used to give us our "little week" [literal translation of semanadica*] . . . , and I was swapping postcards, and stamps, I always had a little bit of money coming in.*

And in 1910,[27] when I finished my studies, and started working, we organized things better. For example, we would go to football matches in a horse-drawn carriage, we would treat ourselves to the best restaurants, and so on.

There were also evenings out to see the touring theater companies that used to come to Salonica and put on two or three shows, there were classical French plays as well as Italian operas, performed by Italian companies . . .

At sixteen, Vidal is initiated into adult entertainments. At 6 o'clock, shops and offices close, and clerks and businessmen, bachelors and married men alike, go to meet their friends and acquaintances in cafés, where they chat while drinking beer, or *raki* with *mezes*, buying boiled eggs or salted pistachios from street vendors. They talk over the events in Europe. Vidal remembers the Steinhel affair:

He's a painter or a sculptor whose wife was the mistress of the President of the Republic, it was quite a scandal! Vidal is very partial to any news about

38

Presidents of the French Republic. His brothers discuss the *Drang nach Osten*, Germany's entry into Turkey and the Balkans (*Some thought it was a good thing, others didn't*), and, of course, talk over the day's news.

Then everyone goes home for dinner. They dine late, as in Italy or Spain, and, afterwards, *with the family, we would chat, we would talk, because there was no radio or TV*. This is how Vidal comes to hear his father's memories, and family anecdotes like the one about his ancestor Tchilibon, who came home drunk one night with a pair of oars he had bought from a fisherman.

David Nahum does not follow the custom of Salonica's elite and take summer holidays in the spa or leisure towns of Europe: Vichy, Baden-Baden or Montecatini. Instead, for several years, and for three or four weeks at a time, he rents a little apartment in a seaside resort about forty miles from Salonica, where his wife, accompanied by Mathilde and Vidal, receives treatment for her rheumatism. He sees that they are settled in, then returns to Salonica, and comes back to collect them when the cure is over. In summertime, he organizes family excursions. The Eastern railroads provide a service of pleasure trains, which leave early in the morning for a little village, where a buffet is prepared for the travelers.

In the years between 1908 and 1912, Vidal is preparing to learn his trade. He is fourteen years old at the time of the Young Turk revolution, and eighteen when Salonica is annexed by Greece (in 1912). He leaves school at sixteen or seventeen, and is employed in a bank's branch office managed by Élie Hassad, his elder sister Henriette's husband. Vidal "does everything" there: accounting, receipts, payments, errands, secretarial work, security.

The years between 1908 and 1912 are also convulsive and decisive years for Salonica and the Balkans. The Young Turk revolution of 1908, which begins in Salonica, is greeted with a few days' euphoria by all Salonicians, Moslems, Christians and Jews alike: *I was fourteen years old, the schools were closed, and we went to the Place de la Liberté every day*, remembers Vidal. The speakers hold forth in Turkish, Spanish, French, Bulgarian and Romanian: "They encourage people to forget their hatred, to strive for harmony, to love one another, everyone sings the *Marseillaise*, people embrace in the street, the Comitadjis and Anthartes [guerillas whom the Sephardim consider to be bandits] come out of their hiding places and embrace each other in the squares and in the cafés . . . rabbis, Orthodox priests, pappas and imams walk down the streets arm in arm . . . some proclaim the resurrection of the dead, or predict the union of all Balkan States."[28] A Constitution is announced, along with a parliament representing all of the Empire's inhabitants, who are henceforth citizens. However, this attempt to create an Ottoman supernationality has come too late. The Macedonians, Bulgarians and Greeks of the Empire have been magnetized by the nation-states of Greece, Serbia, and Bulgaria, which now lay claim to them. The Young Turk revolution will end up creating one more Nation State, Turkey, instead of turning the Ottoman Empire into a confederation of peoples. From now on, the guerillas are not only fighting against the Turks, but also against each other. The other Empires add fuel to the fire in the Balkan cauldron. The period that begins in 1908 with the Young Turk revolution, and whose first act finishes in 1912, the year of the Balkan war fought by the Greeks, Serbs and Bulgarians, first against the Turks, then against each other (and which notably results in Greece's annexation of Salonica), sees a general explosion of nationalism, including Turkish nationalism, all over the Balkans; this is the twilight of the Empire and its cosmopolitan cities. Until 1912, however, the city of Salonica remains in the calm eye of the hurricane. Its economic prosperity continues to grow. Exports increase from 25 million Turkish pounds, in 1900, to 40 million in 1911, and imports from 57 million in 1900, to 120 million in 1911.[29]

In 1911, an apparently minor event in the Ottoman Empire's process of disintegration turns the life of David D. Nahum's family upside down: the Italo-Turkish war. Italy lays claim to Tripolitania (now Libya), sends an ultimatum and launches its attack. Salonica's once-privileged Italian nationals suddenly become enemies and are subject to arrest. David D. Nahum does his best to find a way out. The Italian consul has left Salonica in haste, but he has left *a kind of stand-in behind, a chargé d'affaires if you like*, and David Nahum obtains the Turkish authorities' agreement to let him have two or three weeks to prepare for his departure, *because all the same there were quite a few of us, there was my father, my mother, the four boys and my younger sister.* The elder sister, Henriette, had ceased to be Italian when she married Élie Hassid. Léon, the eldest brother, who, as we have seen, is responsible for the metallurgical sector of his father's business, is in Brussels, where he has set up a bridgehead office. The family flees Salonica. David Nahum leaves for Vienna accompanied by his wife, Vidal and Mathilde. He sends Jacques and Henri to join Léon in Brussels. David Nahum asks the Italian embassy in Vienna to help him to find a clerical post for his son Vidal, who can speak German and knows about bookkeeping.

A day or two later, an Austrian insurance company gives me an appointment to see them. I turn up, first they test me, then they tell me: "OK, you're accepted, you will work here as a clerk." It was quite an imposing building. On the first floor, there were three offices; on the second floor, three offices, including my office, where the boss was Mr. Wagner; there was a lady, two other gentlemen and myself. Well, it all went very well, the boss was very pleased with me, my colleagues were not so pleased, because I worked too fast, they told me you mustn't work so fast. When it came to handing in my documents, what I'd written, all that, I came into contact with a young lady who worked on the floor below, a Miss Schwartz, Wilhelmine Schwartz, she was very sweet, very nice. I was pretty taken with her and everything, so I asked if I could accompany her when we left the office; unfortunately we had to go in different directions, and when I tried to walk with her for a while anyway, she didn't want me to, and she said: "No, no, if my father or if my mother or if my sister saw us together." Well, to cut a long story short, she was very harsh with me . . . And then when I put a bit more pressure on her, when I made myself a little clearer, she said: "Listen, be reasonable, you're only 18, and I'm 20, so it's impossible; anyway, I don't want to get married, I'm not going to marry an 18-year-old boy, it's ridiculous!"

Vidal continues to work at the same office as Wilhelmine for six months, and then, after Italy's very rapid conquest of Tripolitania, the war comes to a sudden end. David leaves by boat from Trieste with his wife, Vidal and Mathilde; his other sons, Léon, Jacques and Henri come and join him on the same boat bound for Salonica: *It was like a big party, my father was overjoyed, and we weren't the only ones either, there were at least three or four Salonician families in the same situation, Italians like us, the Modianos and all of them with their children, so, on board ship, we really lived it up, and the journey lasted a week.*

Vidal remembers a patriotic Italian song from this war, which he will sing for the rest of his life, although he is entirely indifferent to the conquest of Tripoli:

Tripoli sara italiana!
Sara italiana al rumbo de canone.
Vogua vogua corrazate![30]

He will especially remember Wilhelmine, his first love.

As soon as they return, in 1912, the Greco-Turkish war breaks out: *Unfortunately, on the first day we got back, we saw some little skirmishes between Greek, Turkish and Bulgarian soldiers.* Salonica falls into the hands of the Greeks. The Balkan territories are now divided up into isolated nation-states. Little Greece swallows up what had once been the great port of the Ottoman Empire. David D. Nahum's business is immediately affected.

Then comes the Balkan war of 1912 to 1913. Everything comes crashing down. Turkey has collapsed. The Russians don't want to send oil to Salonica any more, because Salonica is no longer Turkish . . . There are different laws, different customs regulations, etc. Well, it was all ruined. The metallurgy business is ruined too, because European Turkey is cut up into pieces. The whole of European Turkey, which used to come to Salonica for its supplies, is divided into four parts, one part for the Bulgarians, one for the Serbs, and so on. Well, to cut a long story short, then what happens? My eldest brother leaves for Constantinople, where he continues to represent Belgian metallurgical factories, and my father carries on with the oil business in Salonica, but on a very, very modest scale . . .

The situation causes a new wave of migration. Migration towards the West had already begun at the end of the 19th century, with the young people who felt irresistibly attracted to Paris or Vienna, either to practice medicine, dentistry or pharmacy, or to try their luck there. The next waves of young people will be motivated by their reluctance to do military service for a nation-state, first Turkey, and then Greece. Departures of young Sephardic Jews for Egypt, Paris, London, Lausanne, Barcelona, New York and Buenos Aires are unleashed by the law following the Young Turk revolution of 1908 that obliges all Ottomans to enter active service. The Hellenization of Salonica (in 1912 and 1922) will increase emigration.

These migrations, where each wave creates a bridgehead for the next,[31] scatter throughout the West but especially focus on Vienna,[32] the great cosmopolitan capital open to the East and to the West, and especially to France.

Vidal is not old enough for military service in the years between 1908 and 1912. Ever since leaving school, however, his desire has been to go to France. But he does not want merely to visit the country, he wants to live there. In his eyes, France is poetry incarnate. The texts he learned by heart at the Franco-German school have left their mark on him. Throughout his life, he recites, with emphasis, as he had been taught to do, "Tell me one thing, Count. Do you know Don Diego?" then, changing places, he takes the role of Don Gormas, and replies, with equally emphatic disdain: "Who made you so vain," and: "Presumptuous young man." He also loves: "Be seated, Cinna," and then, with implacable imperial authority: "Sit;" also, "Oh Time, suspend your flight," "My father, the hero with the gentle smile"; "It was snowing. The bitter winter melted into an avalanche." To him, these lines were never mere memories of his school days, but remained a living and ardent presence, and he was stirred with emotion every time he recited them.

Vidal also loves Parisian songs. He is delighted when the downstairs neighbor, a dental surgeon who has studied in Paris, comes to visit and sings the songs he learned there with the Nahum brothers. He especially loves the songs that sing of the City, and there is one in particular that he finds enchanting:

Paris! Paris! Ô ville infâme et merveilleuse!

In January 1913, he writes, in an exercise book: "Poincaré! Poincaré! When will I be one of your inhabitants!" The term is, interestingly, incorrect: Poincaré, then President elect of the Republic, is seen by Vidal as some kind of lay sultan, who may not rule over "subjects" like an Oriental despot, but, in Vidal's Oriental view, does not preside over citizens either. Hence the term "inhabitant," which implies neither subjection nor citizenship.

As soon as he left school, Vidal asked his father to let him try his luck in Paris. His father refused. He wanted his youngest son to stay close to him, in Salonica. But, when they return from Vienna, after Greece's annexation of Salonica, Vidal, who has gone back to his boring job as factotum for Élie Hassid, succeeds in persuading his father. David Nahum knows that the new situation will be unfavorable to his business, and he foresees that he will have to leave Salonica sooner or later; so he gives his son permission to leave, but warns him that he is unlikely to find a position to suit him in Paris. Vidal hopes that his male and female cousins (the dental surgeon Paul Nahum, a pharmacist, a chief accountant, a clerk in a boiler-making company, and another in a shop selling articles for the home), who are already established in Paris, will be able to help him: *They all made me very welcome, and they all helped me in my search . . . Well, I would show up somewhere, for example, at an insurance company, but there would be no job for me there; at a bank it was the same story, or else they were offering miserable conditions, they were paying 50 francs a month, and just then, 50 francs a month! I'd already rented a furnished room, which I was paying 30 francs a month for, so it was impossible . . . I held out for five, six weeks . . . Then, as my parents had predicted, I went home.*

On his return, Vidal does not go back to his job with Élie Hassid, but starts in his father's office with his brother Henri, who is in charge of the metallurgical sector for Greece, now that Salonica is a Greek city. By this time, Léon has settled in Constantinople in order to continue working in the Turkish market and overseeing the construction of the Istanbul to Ankara railroad. Their father continues in the oil business, which has slackened off considerably.

Sephardic Salonica becomes part of the Greek world, and is absorbed into the framework of a modern nation–state. After forced exchanges of population, Greeks arrive *en masse* in Turkey, while the Turks are driven out of Salonica. Having become Ottoman citizens *in extremis*, the Sephardim are now obliged to become Greek. Those who, after a fashion, remain outside the nation–state are people like David Nahum and his family, who have acquired a foreign nationality. They are integrated into the Greek state system, with its laws and its taxes, but are not subjected to military service.

Once it has become part of Greece, Salonica loses its important economic role as the great port for the Balkan hinterland. Worse: Salonica is now trapped, without yet knowing it, in the historic tornado that is forming at the beginning of the century in the Balkans.

The weakening of Ottoman power exacerbates Bulgarian, Greek and Romanian nationalism, and these states lay claim to the populations that speak their language and practice their religion. However, because a number of regions are populated by Bulgarians, Greeks, Macedonians, etc. who are all mixed up together, Balkan nationalisms exacerbate one another, and the victors fight over the spoils that their coalitions have seized from the Turks. Austria-Hungary has ceased to be the protector of the Christians against the Turks: now it is the Empire that has subjugated the Slav nationalities of the South, and this exacerbates its conflict with Russia, protector of the Slavs and Orthodox Christians. Thus, the disintegration of Ottoman power creates an area of low pressure, out of which the devastating cyclone of the Great War will emerge.

The summer of 1914 arrives. In 1978, aged 84, Vidal will remember in detail (the newspapers from Paris, London, Vienna and Berlin are read in Salonica) the visit of the Austrian heir to the throne, Arch-Duke Franz-Ferdinand, to Sarajevo: *Great preparations, celebrating, triumphal arches, Austrian flags everywhere, and here comes our prince, arriving in Sarajevo with a full military escort . . . Well, at that time, Austria-Hungary was asking the Serbs to apologize and make reparations. Then the Russians – or the Tsar – says to Emperor Franz-Josef: "Well excuse me, wait a moment, the Serbs are my people, part of my family, we're all Orthodox Christians, you can't touch the Serbs."*

Emperor Wilhelm supports Emperor Franz-Josef, saying: "You must make reparations." And that's how the First World War began . . .

Vidal's life would be marked for ever by all the unforeseen events which, in just two years, wiped out the formidable Empire that had been created in the 15th century, and transformed the multisecular nature of Salonica. As causes of this catastrophe, Vidal identifies the terrorism of the Comitadjis and the Young Turk revolution, which he had witnessed himself at 9 and 14 years of age, and without which *they wouldn't have deposed the Sultan, Abdul Hamid, whom all the historians recognize as the greatest diplomat of the century*, and *there would have been no annexation of Bosnia-Herzegovina, there would have been no First World War*. Deeply affected by this period, which would ring the death-knell of his little city homeland, Vidal would continue to believe, seventy years on, that the cataclysm was a mere accident and that Salonica could have remained what Sephardism had made of it.

III
The First World War

The war breaks out in 1914, but does not affect Salonica immediately. King Constantine declares Greece neutral, although Prime Minister Venizelos wants to pledge his country's support to the Allies. Turkey has aligned itself with the central Empires. Salonica seems destined to remain an island of neutrality in the war that is setting Europe ablaze. But in October 1915, after the repeated failures of the Anglo–French landings in the Dardanelles between March and August of that year, and Bulgaria's entry into the war on the side of the central Empires, the French command, violating Greek neutrality, transports all of the French forces in the Dardanelles, and a portion of the British forces, to Salonica, in order to form the Eastern army there. The King's troops are disarmed. After they have been suppressed by the Bulgarians, Serbian troops come to Salonica to reform. Venizelos rebels against the King and forms a provisional government in the enclave of Salonica, but Greece will remain neutral until the King is deposed, in July 1917. When the French arrive in Salonica, they think they are landing in some god-forsaken Balkan backwater. To their surprise, they are greeted by people who speak French, and they discover that there are local daily newspapers in French. People discuss French singers and politicians with them. The Sephardic merchants suddenly find themselves presented with a new market: supplying the Eastern army: *So me and my brother Henri, and my father, we decided to go into supplying the army. We began with equipment in our sector, metal goods: shovels, for example, or pickaxes, barbed wire, girders, sheet metals . . . Well I must say, we had a very good relationship with them, very friendly . . . the engineer who was in charge of buying supplies was very pleased to work with people who could already speak French so well.*

In the same year, in May 1915, Italy enters the war on the side of the Allies and, once again, the privilege of being Italian turns into a catastrophe for the Nahums. Léon, henceforth an enemy alien, has to flee Istanbul in secrecy before he is arrested. Léon leaves with his wife and four-year-old daughter, Chary, all carrying picnic baskets, for a hotel beside the sea; early the next morning, they sail away on a caique that takes them to a neutral boat anchored outside territorial waters. They then sail back to Salonica. In Salonica, however, young Sephardim of Italian nationality who are of an age to do military service have been identified and are being called up by the

Italian consulate: *In Salonica, there were about thirty or forty Italians of an age to bear arms; and we said to ourselves, well really, it's got nothing to do with us, we don't know Italy well enough to go and do military service, we live in Salonica, which used to be Turkish but is now Greek, we don't want to go . . . we're not willing to go . . .* On around January 15 or 16, 1916, the Italian consul, having received no response to its draft of eligible nationals, has them arrested by the French military police, who take them away on a warship.

These young people, who have forgotten their Livornese origins, have never been to Italy and are often unable to speak Italian, arrive at a training camp where they are turned into soldiers. Then they are sent to the front. One of them, Albert Mosseri, Vidal's future relative by marriage, has told the story of his adventure. A captain, saber drawn, orders his company to advance: "*Uno, due, uno, due.*" The young Sephardi has been placed in the front line, and is terrified to be marching into battle. Since he is on the flank of his column, on every second "*uno, due*" he manages to take a step backwards, and thus patiently retreats to the tail end of the company. The last of the soldiers pass him, eyes staunchly fixed to the fore, and he falls face down on the ground and lies there without moving. The sound of "*uno, due*" gets fainter, then disappears; he jumps to his feet, throws off his uniform jacket, and flees in his shirtsleeves, deserting before he has fought a single battle.

Vidal and his brother Henri are also arrested by the French military police and taken away on a warship. But there is some mistake, and they disembark in Marseilles, where they are put in prison; from this prison, they are sent, not exactly to a concentration camp, but to the Abbey of Frigolet, which has been turned into a detention center. Why was such a mistake made? Why were they treated differently from the other true or false Italians of their age? Vidal had no idea. At least, that is the answer he always gave his son. He was, moreover, ashamed of his time in prison, which he referred to as "the pen," and he did not mention this episode from his life in front of anyone outside the family. However, what he had never wanted to tell, even to his son, he divulged in 1983, the year before his death, in an absolutely unexpected moment of confession, after lunch in a restaurant in Beaulieu-sur-Mer, and to people (his daughter-in-law's parents) who were practically strangers: for the truth was that he knew perfectly well why he had been transported to France and imprisoned there.

He had been imprisoned by mistake, but he understood the cause and the nature of that mistake.

First the cause: after the 1912 war, a Turkish depot of arms and damaged warships had been abandoned in the port of Salonica. David Nahum had somehow become responsible for selling this downgraded war equipment, and he had entrusted the business to his sons Henri and Vidal. A German importer from Hamburg had shown interest in it. Negotiations had begun by correspondence, and then the German merchant came to Salonica by train. He arrived on a Friday evening, and being an Ashkenazi, and religious, he refused to discuss business until the sabbath was over — behavior that astonished the Nahums. Then he disappeared. On Sunday morning, he negotiated to buy the equipment from the young Nahum brothers. We do not know how they envisaged transporting it. The German left for Hamburg again. We do not know whether the equipment was ever delivered. In any event, the French military police (who from time to time arrested spies they caught helping German submarines with signals or delivering military information to the enemy) must have found out about the deal the two brothers had made, while drawing up the dossiers on the young draft evaders indicated to them by the Italian consulate; this is what turned them into suspects and resulted in their being sent to Marseilles.

When his son heard about this episode, which Vidal had kept secret from him for his whole life, he thought Vidal meant that the merchant from Hamburg had come to Salonica during the war, or after the French Eastern army had established itself there, and he was amazed that it had been possible, during the First World War, to cross through enemy countries so easily by train. But when his cousin Edgard read this account, he assured him that it was unlikely that a civilian traveler could have crossed one or several fronts. Edgar, Vidal's son, nevertheless believed that it was not unimaginable for someone to have traveled to the enclave of Salonica which, although occupied by French troops, was part of a country that was still neutral. It was far more credible, however, to suppose that the journey took place before October 1915, either right at the beginning of the war (Romania and Bulgaria, which at that time were neutral, still offered a way through, allowing one to circumvent little Serbia and enter neutral Greece), or, more probably (although what is probable is not necessarily most certain), just before the hostilities were triggered off, in the weeks or even days leading up to August 1914.

In any case, the fact that Vidal and his brother were sent to prison in Marseilles, unlike the other young Italians, who were sent to a military camp on the Peninsula, can only be explained by the fact that the French military police were in possession of some information or denunciation concerning the two brothers' German business.

Vidal would remember the date of June 8 very clearly. He has a meeting to go to at his club, the friendly society of alumni of the Franco-German school, of which he was treasurer, to prepare for a big party. Vidal is completely absorbed in these joyful preparations. A week or two later, *one afternoon at the office, my Dad, my brother Henri and I are there, when two gentlemen in civilian dress come in and introduce themselves:*

"French police!"
"Oh! What do you want, French police?"
"Well, I'll tell you. Mr. Henri Nahum, Mr. Vidal, please come with us, you're needed at staff headquarters."

"Headquarters? Where's that?"
"Well, at such and such a school" [which they had requisitioned].
So my father says:
"We'll go tomorrow."
"Oh no, sir, they must go there at once."
"Very well, I'll come with them."
And off we went, all five of us. When we arrived in front of the school, with a sentinel standing guard at the door, of course, they wouldn't let my Dad in. So he says:
"But why not?"
"Oh no, no, sir."
So my father, poor man, he didn't know what to do. We didn't know what had happened, my brother Henri and I; they show us into an office, a room; we see a gentleman we know who is already there, Mr. Seyas, who was a pharmacist, and another, Mr. Venezia, who was in cereals, and a couple of others, there were four or five of them.
So they say:
"You'll be coming with us."
"And what for?"
"What for? The Italian consul wants us to go back to Italy, so here we are, waiting."
The night passes, and of course we're sitting on chairs or on the floor. And then the others, three or four Italians, are called, and we don't see them again. Why? [This indeed indicates that the two brothers' dossier contains something peculiar, which sets them apart from the other Italians]. *The day goes by, and the second night, the same thing, we ask, I ask everyone I can find, they tell me:* "Oh, no, sir, we don't know anything, you'll have to wait, you know, you just have to wait."
In the meantime, my father and my eldest brother are trying to get something done at the Italian consulate, with the French police, and since my brother [Léon] *was already supplying the army, he goes to see a commandant, he sees a colonel, they tell him:*
"No, no, you have no reason to worry . . . "
David Nahum, taken by surprise by his two sons' arrest, is powerless to stop what is happening.
The next morning, about 10 or 11 o'clock:
"Up you get, on your feet!"
At that time there was a group of us there: in the meantime two Albanians had arrived, two Greeks, two Muslim priests, a group of about fifteen people, along with another of my compatriots, another Salonician [as we can see, even sixty years later, Vidal really thinks of Salonica as his homeland], *also of the Jewish faith, whom we knew. So there were fifteen of us, and suddenly the door opens. Two police officers come in:*
"Come along with us, and bring your belongings."

"But we have no belongings, we haven't got anything."
"Never mind, you'll take nothing since you have nothing."
"And where are we going?"
"To the port, you're going to leave on a boat."
So we go out into the street with a policeman on either side of us, and, fifty or a hundred yards away, we see my father and my mother, who had already been informed about our departure, why and how we didn't know, along with a first cousin of ours, a guy who knew a thing or two, a very, very smart guy. And then we see him . . . He tries to get closer:
"No, no, no, don't try to come any closer!"
So to cut it short the convoy left, but in fact there were no handcuffs, nothing at all . . .

The tearful family follows the convoy of prisoners, with Henri and Vidal among them, down to the port. David asks their cousin to reach his sons and slip them a few gold coins.

From the school to the port, it was let's say five hundred, six hundred or seven hundred yards . . . although it was the end of January, the weather was pleasant and mild. As we approached the port, the cousin I mentioned tries to work out a way to reach us, because my brother was on the right, I was on the left, and the police were on either side. He tries to come closer to me. The policeman pushes him away and says to him: "No, no, no, you can't do that, keep your distance." So he contrives, I don't know how he manages it, he turns around or he goes around the whole convoy and comes up from the other side, where my brother is, and another policeman, and he's in such a hurry that he stumbles a bit, but he gets close to my brother, and shoves something into his hand. The policeman pushes him back, but in the meantime my brother has taken whatever it is, and put it in his pocket, and we carry on down the path, and finally we arrive at the port. The boat is waiting on the quay, and they make us climb aboard. My father and my mother are standing down below, and we wave to them.

They embark on the *Sainte-Anne*, a troop transporter, which leaves Salonica on 27 January 1916, at two-thirty.

They take us to the cabins, and then the first selection takes place. The captain calls out in Greek:
"What's-your-name, up you get!"
Two soldiers, two conscripts, take away those whose names are called.

Five people are separated from the others: two Muslim priests, an Albanian, and the two Nahum brothers. The captain sends this group to the infirmary.

To the infirmary, well, we don't know what it meant. We go down the corridors in the boat, which has been requisitioned for troop transport, and which was once a transatlantic liner. We arrive at the infirmary, it's a big room with beds laid out for forty or fifty patients. We managed to communicate more or less with the Turks, I knew a few words, my brother knew a few words, they didn't speak Spanish or French, or Albanian.

Two hours later, the captain comes back and says:

"Henri Nahum, why are you here?"

"Well, er, we've been asking ourselves the same question."

"Well, he says, the boat's already raised anchor, we're on our way to Marseilles. You'll be fed, but you can't leave the infirmary, or open the portholes, because there are German submarines in these waters, we mustn't let any trace of light escape during the night. There's a little thingumajig there for you to wash in."

One day, two days, three days, all the time we can hear that the boat is making its way onwards. On the fourth or fifth day, we stop, and so, very cautiously, I open the porthole, and I see land,[33] and the portholes must have been watched from up above or down below, because a soldier comes, or a sailor comes, shouting "Hey! Hey!"

As soon as the journey begins, Vidal starts keeping a journal which he writes in pencil in a little pocket notebook.

27th January 1916, 6 p.m. Soup, haricot beans, tea, bread, water. NB: ration insufficient for man, adequate for invalid. The lack of water is a real problem, and when we ask, nothing, nothing at all.

28th January, 7 a.m. ½ a pint of coffee, biscuits dating from 1880??

28th January, noon. Lentils with boiled meat, bread, water.

28th January, 5 p.m. Good soup, red beans, tea, bread, all in large quantities.

On the same day, Vidal writes the following letter to his family. It is written on two pages torn out of the notebook in which he is keeping his log; he never manages to send it.

On board the Sainte-Anne,

28 January 1916, en route to Marseilles.

My dear family,

I am bored here on the ship, with nothing to do except eat, drink and sleep, so I am writing you a few lines to let you know that Henri and I are absolutely fine. We eat and sleep in a huge room with twenty-four beds in it; Henri, a Serb and I are the only occupants, which works out at eight beds each. The meals they serve to us are all very well prepared and copious. I am very anxious to know what is happening on your side, and what Mama and Papa have done; if there is still time, they must definitely go to Switzerland, and not anywhere else; in any case, send us your news by telegram to Bellon, 34 Boulevard de la Paix, in Marseilles, and especially let us know about dear Sophie, we would be very glad to have good news of her. If Papa and Mama are still in Salonica, they must not worry at all on our account, we are very, very well and hope to be able to see you shortly after our arrival in Marseilles; so if they want to they should leave for Switzerland, because that is where we are thinking of going – to Lausanne.

This letter seems to indicate that Vidal is worried the affair of the sale of military equipment will have repercussions on his father, and he encourages his parents in insistent terms to leave for the neutral country of Switzerland, in order to avoid any trouble. He also expresses his own hope of going to Switzerland, which means escaping from the war that has now begun to persecute him: all of the countries in which he might otherwise seek refuge are involved in the fighting, and would oblige him to be either a soldier or a prisoner.

On a double sheet, also torn from the notebook, Vidal writes to his friends from the alumni's club of the Franco-German school, whose treasurer he is. Evidently, he has not been able to hand over the accounts before his departure.

My dear friends,
Being en route for Marseilles, and very bored, I have decided to write you these few lines. I am sure you must have been very surprised to hear of my sudden disappearance. The war is to blame; any further explanations are pointless. When we are fortunate enough to see each other again, I will be able to tell you how quickly it all happened, not even leaving me the time to embrace my parents or shake hands with you. In any case, I am sure you won't forget me so quickly, and that you will still be kind enough to write me long letters, telling me what is going on where you are, the rumors surrounding my departure, etc. Tell me if you are enjoying yourselves: in fact, do so, enjoy yourselves as much as you can. Live life, because I have begun to believe that the future does not depend on us, and that sometimes it is just a long list of unanswerable questions, some of which are bitter.

Let's forget all that: I want to tell Raphaël that the total of . . . francs on the cash balance sheet breaks down as follows: Liaou owes 4.65 francs on an old account, there are around 86 francs for expenses incurred at the January 6 ball, which have not been paid yet (Liaou already knows about that); in addition, I gave Liaou 75 drachmas out of the cashbox, to pay the electricity bill.

That leaves me with 3.50 drachmas in the kitty. I received 68.70 drachmas from the gas company, less 13 drachmas that we owed . . . You'll easily be able to manage with that, Raphaël. As for me, I have other things to worry about.

The journal continues:
Saturday, 27th January, 7 a.m. Coffee with biscuits dating from the 1900 Fair; however, when they have been dipped in coffee for an hour, they could pass for 5 or 6 years old.

29th January, midday. Vegetable, noodles or grains [incomprehensible word accompanied by its Spanish translation: *harvaiesso, vetches* or *lentils*] *with meat, soup, water, bread, all in large quantities (why no fish on Saturday?[34]).*

29th January, 5 p.m. Good soup, haricot beans, tea.

30th January, 8 a.m. Coffee with biscuits dating from the Crusades.

30th January, 11.30 a.m. Soup with macaroni as fat as one-inch tubes, lentils with mutton, bread (still fresh), water.

30th January, 6 p.m. Rice, bread, water.

31st January, 8 a.m. Coffee, the usual biscuits. Thanks to some haviar given to us by a Serbian officer who's been keeping us company since midnight, we've used up all the bread we had. At 8 a.m. (Salonica time), it is still dark.

31st January, 12 o'clock midday. Soup, same macaroni as yesterday, red beans with pig, wine, bread [Vidal seems to have eaten the pig without any difficulty].

1st February, Tuesday. Coffee, bread [underlined]. *11.30 to noon, soup, haricot beans with a tiny little bit of meat, bread, water. 6.30 p.m., bread soup, haricot beans that were rather* bayat [stale or rancid], *tea, bread. Tomorrow noon, Marseilles.*

2nd February, morning, in Marseilles harbor, 7 a.m. Coffee, bread.

2nd February. Disembarked at Frioul at 10.30 a.m.

Frioul, 2nd February. A Serb shaves our hair very short, we file into a hall where we take a bath, and wait, with a flannel to cover us, for our clothes and underclothes to be returned to us after having been disinfected.

Departure from Frioul on board a tug for Marseilles, then four-horse car; we arrive, accompanied by an Inspector from the Sûreté, at the departmental pen, 10, Rue d'Athènes, Marseilles. All our companions in misfortune are given a warm welcome by the other prisoners, as they know each other from the Salonica joint [so the convoy is transporting people who had already been imprisoned for a time in Salonica, and meet up with other detainees who had left earlier: common law criminals, suspects, political prisoners, military offenders and deserters, enemy agents?].

As soon as we get down into the yard, a woman rushes up to my brother: "Henri, Henri, what are you doing here?" Then she turns to me for a minute: "And you?" Because she knew my brother better than me. She was a respectable woman from Salonica . . . A Frenchwoman from Normandy . . . She had been taken there because her husband, or rather her lover, was supplying the German submarines, and they'd caught him red-handed, and arrested him, and the poor thing, she was crying. Once all the upset was over, we were glad to have found a bit of warmth . . .

Vidal continues his journal in the prison of Marseilles police station.

2nd February, 5 o'clock. Soup, boiled apple, a small glass of wine, bread; we eat in a well-ventilated room.

3rd February. Slept well in a real bed, after having spent seven nights on straw mattresses with no covering of any kind.

3rd February, 8 o'clock. Coffee, bread.

3rd February, 10 o'clock. Soup, rice, with a little meat, wine, bread.

3rd February. From 12 until 2 o'clock, out in the pen garden. Breathe a little fresh air and see the sky.

3rd February, 5 o'clock. Soup, garbanzos with garlic, wine, bread.

4, 5, 6, 7, 8, 9, 10th February. Apart from the fact that we're rather bored for a few hours of the day, everything is fine most of the time; we're well-fed, have good accommodation, with good beds, apart from the lack of covering, which leaves me rather cold at night. We get on well with the inspectors who guard us during the day: they're fine men, as are the ones on duty at night, the "agents of the peace." Several faces to remember, especially André and Vassil. No news of anyone, and impossible to send any ourselves. Patience. We read the Marseilles newspapers in the morning and evening. "They" won't let us read the Paris newspapers. On the day we were imprisoned here, there were 37 men and 3 women including us; today, there are 20 men, and 1 woman (10th February, 6 p.m.).

12th February. The days go by very, very slowly, I am terribly bored, and (although I don't know why) I don't join in the games with the others, but they wouldn't amuse me anyway. All the time, the fact that I'm not sending any news to my parents puts me in a not particularly pleasant mood. I would also really like to know what's been going on at home since I left. I hope they are all absolutely fine. As I can do nothing at all to resolve the present situation, I wait patiently for someone to help me. Dear Papa, dear Mama, where are you at this moment? I am sure you are looking for us; I am also longing to see you already, and longing to see my dear mother looking at me tenderly at last. Life is only made for suffering, you just have to get used to it; I'm holding on, courageously I hope, because soon the day of freedom will come for me. Don't give up hope . . . (Marseilles, 12th February 1916, 2.30 p.m. Departmental pen.)

15th February, 6 p.m. After having eaten the regulation soup, a plate of lentils that we checked carefully (and found enough insects in it), I have some salami, a tangerine, some jam, what's left of a tin of chestnuts. As usual, we're bored between 11 in the morning and 5 in the evening, and from 6 to 8 or 9 o'clock when we go to bed, depending on the row being made by the men playing games, or the people joining in with the songs Vasili sings, which they seem to think compatible with a flute. All day we wait for an inspector or the police captain to turn up and tell us when they will set us free or send us to the next border. Still, we are patient [Vidal wrote impatient first, then corrected himself], *and if it weren't for the worry that my family still has no news from me, I wouldn't give a damn, but dammit, if I have to stay a few more weeks here with the "interns" of the pen for company, and I don't mean the little ones, oh no, f . . . that.* [Vidal is probably alluding to insects or mice, and the f . . . stands for "fuck." He has apparently picked up some Marseillais oaths, *nom de Dious, putaing*; his brother Henri starts speaking with a Marseillais accent, and keeps it for the rest of his life.] *Now I'm waiting for the "radical" evening paper, then good night and let's hope it's the last one in the pen. (15th February, 1916, 6 in the evening.)*

19th February. I've been rereading the last lines, written on the evening of the 15th, but my hopes of leaving the pen have still come to nothing. Carry on hoping, and a day will come when the great and beautiful sun of freedom will enjoy [he means it will shine, which he will enjoy] *for you too, as it does for other poor mortals. Shouldn't I ask myself why I'm so pessimistic about being in prison? In the thousands of days that Man has to live on Earth, should he be so bitter about spending a few of them, even a few hundred of them, in conditions different from those of his ordinary life? Well, philosophy aside, let's just note the day's impressions. The boredom that comes from being idle is greatest between 2 and 5 in the afternoon; during the rest of the day, at least we have something to do; we eat a few times a day, we read the newspapers – just the Marseilles ones, since we are not allowed the Paris ones.*

What else can I describe? Nothing, or almost nothing. The days go by and my poor mother doesn't know where or how we are. If only she could at least know that we are safe here, when she, whether in Salonica, or suffering on board some ship, is racked with worry about us. Here's hoping the person I asked to give her the first card I wrote has managed to get it to her in Salonica in time, and by now my wonderful mother will already have received news of me.

Whether it's for one thing or another, my dearest mother, why should you be condemned to suffer for your sons all your life?? Let Him on whom all things depend keep us safe [the first, indirect, appeal to God in this journal], *forget the time of suffering, and let that of pure joy begin! (19th February 1916, 3 p.m.)*

19th February. Saturday. Same time. Our day of rest, when we have fun with our friends in Salonica. Patience! Patience!

26th February, 5.30 in the evening. Saturday. Someone is ringing the bell! And every time I hear this bell, which is the bell on the door that the inspectors will come through with news for us, my heart beats a little faster, because since the morning, from 7.30 or even 7 a.m., until 9 or 9.30 in the evening, I've been waiting for the inspector to come, and call my name, though it has no importance to him, and take me God knows where! But the police captain says: "Be patient, in the next few days a decision will be made about all of you." We've heard that story more than once, including on the evening we arrived, on the 2nd of February, and now it's the 26th. I'm amazed to see that I haven't written anything for a week, although I have been very bored, and my legs can attest to that, often stamping their feet with irritation!

I still have no news of my wonderful parents, please let everyone be in good health, Amen. What are you doing this Saturday evening, dear parents? Mama, are you in Salonica or at some Italian or Swiss hotel? In either case, I am sure you must be shedding tears for us. I admit I often go to the barred window that looks out onto the Rue des Muguets to cry, but I can't. Rightly or wrongly, I hope you are in Salonica, dear Mama, amid all the dangers of war, it's true, but also surrounded by your sons and daughters, who will be able to tell you to be patient and comfort you for us. Whereas if you are in a foreign country, you will feel so isolated! How it hurts me to think this? And how is business? Beer? Palacci? Genié? What's happening? Oh, I will be well and truly ready for it when I finally get news of those who stayed behind in Salonica.

On March 2, 1916, Vidal notes, on the back of a report indicating his weight (68 kilos): *At a quarter to 5 this afternoon, extraction of my lower molar (second) along with the crown that covered it, after having spent the whole day in pain.*

The journal begins again:

Monday March 6, 1916. At the concentration camp in the Abbey of Saint-Martin-de-Frigolet, Graveson, near Tarascon. During the past week, we've had some good news: Papa is coming to Marseilles on board the Ernest-Simon.

Some information is missing here, which Vidal left out of his journal for safety's sake. Since their arrival in Marseilles – that is, on February 2 – Vidal and Henri have written to their cousins in Paris. We refer to Vidal's oral autobiography:

I had two cousins in Paris whom I knew were both drafted into the army: one was a lieutenant and the other was a captain, because one was a pharmacist and the other a dental surgeon. So I write to each of them – the superintendent had said: "You have permission to write, bring me the letters and I will have them sent off." Two days, three days go by, no answer. I write another letter, and again I take it to the superintendent.

"Ah, he says to me, very good, give it to me." A week goes by, and I say to my brother Henri:

"Listen, in the dormitory, there's a window looking onto the street, I'm going to try and call to a passerby through the bars on this window, and throw him a letter and a coin at the same time, so that he'll mail it." So my brother kept watch at the door, and I went to the window.

From this window on the Rue des Muguets, Vidal asks a sympathetic-looking passerby to mail a letter for him. When he refuses, Vidal asks other people, to no avail. Then it occurs to him to strike up a conversation with a girl, not mentioning the letter at first, but asking her for some information. On bidding her goodbye, he says, as if as an afterthought: "Oh, pardon me for asking, miss, but would you be kind enough to mail an urgent letter for me?" And so the message is sent.

Two days later, the superintendent summoned us to see him.

"A letter has arrived for you from Paris.

"Oh has it, good."

"But how did this happen? Your letters were never sent, I have your letters, here are your letters, so how did you get a reply?"

"Well, of course, since we gave you the letters . . . "

"Look, I'll say it again, don't you understand, your letters were never sent!"

"Well, one of them must have been."

"No, your letters weren't mailed."

Well, to cut a long story short, the reply was there, so I said to him:

"Please, since there is a reply, be kind enough to read it to us."

"Well, all right," he says, "OK, I'm willing to do that."

He reads. The letter is from one of our cousins [Paul Nahum, the dental surgeon], *who is the first to answer:* As luck would have it I'm on leave in Paris, but I can't understand what you're doing in Marseilles and why you have given me the address of a penitentiary. What on earth are you doing in a penitentiary? Whatever the reason, I have done as you asked me. I immediately sent a telegram to my uncle in Salonica, to let him know that you are in good health, and that you are at the address of the penitentiary; but for God's sake, write soon and explain to me why you have come and what you are doing in a penitentiary.

But the superintendent says: "Oh no you don't! No more letters!"

As soon as the news reaches him in Salonica, David Nahum makes his decision; he will leave for Marseilles on the first boat with his wife and his daughter Mathilde, entrusting his son Léon with entire reponsibility for his office in Salonica. Jacques has gone to Athens, to escape Italian conscription (Greece is still neutral). As soon as they land, David, Hélène and Mathilde go to the police station, where they are told that they have no information to give them: they should address themselves to the special section of the police, which is part of the Marseilles prefecture. There, they are informed that Vidal and Henri are at Saint-Michel-de-Frigolet, but that they need authorization from Paris to be allowed to visit them. David telephones his nephew Paul Nahum, who says: "Uncle, don't waste another minute, come as quickly as you can, I've already brought the matter to the attention of a Representative who is going to look into it."

David Nahum leaves Hélène and Mathilde in Marseilles, and takes the train to Paris at once. His nephew, Paul Nahum, who was born in 1870, and is the son of his elder brother Joseph, had emigrated to Paris before the beginning of the century; he had studied at the faculty of medicine and at the school of dentistry there, and had set himself up as a dental surgeon. He had taken French nationality, and become a freemason and a socialist; he was drafted as a health officer in 1914, and in 1916 was working in a Parisian hospital. (Paul Nahum was later to write a novel, which would have no success, except within his own family, called *Les surprises du divorce*.) As soon as his uncle had told him what was going on, Paul Nahum obtained a meeting with his friend Jean Longuet, socialist leader, grandson of Karl Marx, and Parisian Representative, who tells them that such an affair can only be resolved quickly and satisfactorily if the Prime Minister, Aristide Briand, intervenes personally; he asks him for an interview. In the meantime, David Nahum, who is staying with another nephew in the Rue d'Artois, goes every day to the Chamber of Deputies[35] until the interview is granted. The Prime Minister receives Jean Longuet and Paul and David Nahum in his office. David Nahum is wearing his elegant frock-coat, with the "Order of Leopold" pinned to his chest, and he presents his business card, which states that he is *drogoman* to the Belgian consul in Salonica. Briand asks for some explanations about the Nahum family's nationality:

"I don't understand . . . You were born what?"

"Well, in Salonica, Turkey."

"So you're Turkish."

He addresses Mr. Longuet:

"They're Turkish, then. Well, what next?"

"Then, after Turkey surrendered we opted to become Italian nationals."

"Oh yes, I know about that, my goodness it's complicated though. Fine, and now?"

"Now Salonica's Greek . . . "

"So that means you're Greeks?"

"Oh no."

"And you're not Turks?"

"No."

"And you're not Italian?"

"Well, no, we're not."

"Oh, what a muddle!"

He turns to the Representative:

"Mr. Longuet, I'm very sorry, I don't understand, it's all such a muddle, this Macedonian mish-mash. Still, we have nothing against them, have we? . . . Well then, since we've nothing against them, I'll give Marseilles the order to set them free, and let them do as they please."

And so, right in the middle of the First World War, while the battle of Verdun was raging, and hundreds of thousands of young men from many different countries were dying, Aristide looked down and took pity on two young Salonicians who were detained on a hill in Provence in the world's most delightful concentration camp, the Abbey of Frigolet, previously occupied by gentle monks who devoted their lives to prayer and to the production of an exquisite liqueur. On May 10, about a month after the interview with Briand, the two prisoners were set free.

We will return to Vidal's journal, which we interrupted before his departure for Frigolet, at the beginning of March – about the same time that David Nahum arrived in Marseilles to save his sons.

On Friday evening (3rd of March), around 6 o'clock, the steward announces that we must all be ready and waiting at 5 a.m. Spent a restless night because of the announcement that we are to leave: by 3.30 in the morning, everyone is ready, we have coffee, then off to Saint-Charles station, accompanied by two inspectors, all twenty-one of us who were in the pen take our seats in a third-class carriage in the train to Graveson; the journey takes twelve minutes and we arrive at Graveson, a tiny station in a cleft between great banks of rock; carrying our bags, and escorted by three soldiers, a corporal and a superintendent, we set off to Frigolet, that beautiful place. The women who lived in the only two houses in Graveson came out to watch us go by from their doorsteps. Finally, after a tough climb up a steep path for about a mile and a half or two miles, we arrive, panting, at Frigolet. On the way in, we see a few people who look like "Boches."[36]

There are indeed a number of German nationals imprisoned in the camp (Vidal is evidently imitating the others when he calls the Germans "Boches"), as well as some Italian socialists who oppose the war.

Saturday 11th of March 1916. Frigolet. In two hours' time, it will be exactly a week since I came here, and time goes by quickly, but at night, when all kinds of insects keep you awake, it's torture. You feel like getting a knife and cutting off the bits of you that the insects are eating alive. I had an awful time of it yesterday evening, I wish repulsive insects would leave their prey in peace! We've more or less settled into a routine: get up at a quarter past or half past 7, don't bother queuing up in the morning when the bugle sounds to get coffee. At 8.30, we go down into the yard, time goes by quite quickly until a quarter to twelve, when we lodgers eat at the canteen; mail is given out at noon, then soup in the evening at 4.30, bed between 8 and 1 o'clock, depending on our conversations with our comrades in misfortune. The Boches are well-represented here, all the typical Boche faces in all their glory. How they hate the French, who, they say, have made them suffer too much.

A little Kodak would do wonders here, to take a photo showing the endless line of prisoners coming in one door, in single file, and going out of the other, with their jerrycans and spoons in their hands. The toilets are "pearls" of convenience, you have to wait until it's getting dark just to be able to go and relieve yourself. To get up on to the latrines during the day, you'd have to be an acrobat not to fall in. I'm waiting every minute now for the good news that Papa, Mama and Mathilde are here under the clement sky of this wonderful French Provence. They won't take much longer. Be patient (10 a.m. 11th of March 1916).

April 1st 1916. Sometimes we suffer, sometimes we don't, sometimes we feel fine and sometimes we'd rather be in Guyana, never-ending nights during which we get no sleep, despite all our efforts, in the company of enormous rats, which are up to three feet tall, and all the different insects which eat you alive, and nights when even the most pitiful little sleep is a relief; in spite of myself, I get up three or four times to go to the toilet, a comfortable spot where the wind blows freely. But we're alive, and we're looking after ourselves as best we can. Dear Henriette and Léon in Salonica, Jacques in Athens, Mama and Mathilde in Marseilles, Papa in Paris, when will we all be together again? The Good Lord will unite us again soon. Patience.

Before leaving Marseilles for Paris, David Nahum pays a visit to Salomon Beressi, a friend from Salonica, who had moved to Marseilles in July 1914. He asks him to accompany his wife and his daughter to Frigolet when permission to visit eventually arrives. The permit arrives. After eight days' detention in Frigolet, Vidal and Henri are called in to see the superintendent. *And who do we find there, but my Mama, Mathilde and Mr. Beressi . . . We made a great fuss of each other, we were all in tears, I was a bit calmer, but my poor brother Henri could do nothing but cry, my mother was crying even harder, and so was Auntie Mathilde, but Mr. Beressi was crying hardest of all, and saying: "Just look at you!"* Salomon Beressi, who was a sensitive man, wept when he saw the two prisoners with their shaven heads and prison uniforms, so thin (relatively, anyway: Vidal weighed sixty-eight kilos on March 2, and would only return to his usual weight of seventy-three kilos on April 21). *They explain everything, they tell us what's been happening. The camp superintendent, a very, very nice man, says: "Listen, since you're all here together, I'll have some food sent up from the canteen, which you'll pay for, and you can go and have a meal together in my dining room." Well, it was really marvelous, and that man, the superintendent, he was a former French consul to Beirut or to Alexandria, now retired, but he had been drafted and put in charge of the concentration camp at Frigolet, and he had two big police dogs with him, and his wife and children (we'll have to go and see the Abbey one day, it's really beautiful).*

Two weeks later, having obtained another visitor's pass, Dona Helena and Mathilde, again accompanied by Salomon Beressi, return to Frigolet. Dona Helena informs her sons that their father has managed, with the help of his nephew Paul, to get an introduction to Jean Longuet, who has already contacted the Prime Minister.

May 10th, 1916. Wednesday. Continuation of this Journal which I have not written since April 1st. How have the last forty days been? Well, we've suffered a good deal, that's for certain, we have often prayed to God to set us free, reciting hymns we know from the Rosh Hashana and things from Kippur, which I sum up as follows: "I confess that I have sinned, but save us."

And God heard my voice, and justice has been done; this Wednesday morning, I got up early, feeling a little happier than usual. I don't know what is happening, but I do know that my father is working night and day on my behalf. Poor father, how good you are, and how will I be able to repay you for everything you have done for me? And you, darling Mama, day and night you think only of us, how will I be able to comfort you? My sister Mathilde, you deserve to live a happy life and you will surely be rewarded for all you are doing for us.

The secretary calls me in, an unforgettable conversation, the same with the superintendent. We're to leave right away. The others are all amazed and jealous. At last, Henri and I take up our heavy bags and walk with them under the hot sun for three quarters of an hour. Saved at last. <u>*Free.*</u> *Nothing went wrong on the journey. Arrived in Marseilles this Wednesday May 10 at 3 p.m., at Saint-Charles station, where Mama and Mathilde had been waiting an hour for us. Justice has been done. Long live France! Long live Poincaré! Long life and glory to the French army! Marseilles, Hotel Saint-Louis, Cours Saint-Louis.*

Friday:

A page has been torn out of the journal. But it was not the end of this journal that Vidal wanted to destroy, but a secret that concerned his love life, and which he would write the following year in the notebook, on September 29, 1917, on the back of the journal's last page.

First, we should make a few comments about this prison journal. During the journey by sea, it describes nothing but meals, which is understandable for three reasons: (1) They are the only events during these seven days of confinement; (2) Food is extremely important to Vidal; (3) Vidal is afraid of writing down his thoughts about the reasons for his arrest. Finally, probably because he was afraid that questions might be asked if his journal were discovered, he does not record any of the conversations and discussions that took place among the motley crew of detainees at Frigolet, who included enemy aliens from different countries, as well as internationalist revolutionaries.

The journal characteristically avoids the words "prison" and "prisoner." It is not only because he has picked up prison slang that Vidal speaks of the "pen" and its lodgers, but also because he is ashamed of the other words' scandalous connotations. Throughout his life, he will keep this episode secret, as if it were a stain on his respectability, and will only mention it to the closest members of his family, always referring to it as the pen or boarding house.

The uncertainty of this adventure, from the time of Vidal's arrest and departure up to his arrival at Frigolet, was met with a reaction of relatively nonchalant fatalism ("I don't give a damn," "f . . . that"), despite moments of anxiety. Whereas his brother Henri often felt demoralized, Vidal was mainly concerned about his parents. At Frigolet, once he has stopped worrying about what has happened to his parents, and is detained in better conditions with more space and company, he views this time as an interesting life experience. Boredom, which is continual during the sea voyage and frequent in the Marseilles prison, disappears completely. Vidal is sensitive to the "picturesque" aspect of camp life (the imaginary Kodak he would use to photograph the line of prisoners); he feels a sense of solidarity with his "companions in misfortune," and demonstrates his usual sociability, striking up friendships with all kinds of individuals, who have all kinds of personalities, nationalities and ideas, and notably include partisans of surrender and revolutionaries. Although he spends a good deal of time talking and taking part in discussions, he remains indifferent to politics and the war, despite the fact that they are the cause of his imprisonment. He is not receptive to the internationalist message of his Italian friends, from whom he learns revolutionary songs, which he will declaim with passion for the rest of his life. His only feeling is for his city, and his only attachment is to his tribe. Internationalism presupposes the nation, which it then rejects or overcomes. Vidal, however, is a-national; his only desire is to escape the nation from below, and by private means. It is because he is right at the bottom, on a micro-scale that bears no comparison to the macro-reality of nations, that he is unconcerned about the tragedy and the hecatombs of the Great War.

Vidal is happy as soon as he can buy himself some food. The two brothers must have changed the gold napoleons that their "smart" cousin had slipped them when they were leaving into French currency; they may have had some pocket money, and they probably received money from Salomon Beressi or from their mother; in any event, at Frigolet they were able to pay for haircuts, laundry, rope-soled shoes, scarves, bedcovers, a shoe-brush, a pipe, tobacco, perfume, bars of soap – even for their cell to be swept (1 franc) – newspapers, cheese, bananas, tangerines, eggs, sardines, apples, chocolate, jam and dried figs; they appear to have spent 500 francs in all. In two or three weeks at Frigolet, Vidal regains the fourteen pounds he had lost. The sorrow of having left behind the friends in Salonica with whom he "had fun" is forgotten during this period of living intensely. For the rest of their lives, Henri and Vidal will remember Frigolet with emotion, and even a kind of nostalgia. They will go back there on pilgrimages; first Henri, who writes the following to his brother in 1931, on the back of a postcard of Saint-Michel-de-Frigolet:

My dear Vidal,
I've just been to see Frigolet, and I am very happy and at the same time feel very

moved. I would have been very glad to have made this journey of remembrance with you, but we will do it together some time.

I'm enjoying a bit of Provençal sunshine, it's a real pleasure. Tomorrow, I'll be in Marseilles. Marseilles?

Very sincerely, Henri

Later, when Vidal came to stay in Avignon with his niece Chary, his brother Léon's daughter, he would take the opportunity to go back to Frigolet. When he was in his 70s and 80s, and even in the days leading up to his death, Vidal expressed his desire to make the pilgrimage to the concentration camp abbey one more time.

His time at Frigolet represented his richest and most powerful experience of the world. He was both a prisoner and a presumed spy there, living in a world of outcasts, suspects and rebels, and yet at the same time, unbeknown to him, he was protected by the Prime Minister of France at war. After Frigolet, he would not be exactly bourgeois, nor exactly plebeian, nor truly marginal either, but a little of all these things together, in juxtaposition. At Frigolet, his fatalism and his nonchalance got the upper hand over his anxiety. He drew on his capacity for living from day to day, his ability to weather the blows of fate, and his tendency to enjoy the highs and accept the lows. He demonstrated his ability to keep on starting his life over again, an ability further determined by the particularity of the Jewish condition: any form of settlement is precarious, and one's fate is fundamentally uncertain.

Their captivity does not end with their liberation from Frigolet. In Marseilles, Vidal and Henri are obliged to report to the police station, in order to obtain residence permits.

We got there, it was midday. First, we have lunch, and then, as luck would have it, at our hotel, in the dining room, there were some street singers because there had been a wedding:

Rien qu'à la pensée qu'elle est devant moi,
J'ai le cœur en émoi
(Just the thought that she's there before me,
Makes my heart miss a beat)

Well, it was a very happy song, and it lifted our mood, and straight away after lunch we went to the special police station.

They answer the questions from the inspector who fills out the form. They are asked for photographs, and their residence permits are issued to them.

So, we're very pleased to have these papers, and off we go downstairs. As we're walking out into the street, I notice that the papers say: "Nationality Italian."

Oh no, I say, that's no good, because if we're Italians we'll have to go back to Italy to do military service.

61

And so, after discussing the matter with their mother, Vidal and Henri send a telegram to their father asking him to intervene and rid them of their Italian nationality. The telegram is intercepted by the censor, and the two brothers are summoned by special police captain Borelli, who, after ranting and raving at them, agrees to let the telegram go, but demands that they state their nationality at once. They answer in chorus: "Salonicians." "What?" They had thought the matter through. To declare themselves Italians would mean being sent into the Italian army; to declare themselves Greek would mean being sent back to Salonica; to declare themselves Turkish would mean being arrested as enemy aliens; to declare themselves Belgian would mean being drafted into the Soldier-King's army. No other choice of nationality remained, and all were at war. Hence the logical necessity of declaring themselves nationals of what was indeed their little homeland, the city of Salonica.

But Salonica is not a nation-state, and the police captain is furious: "You're making fun of me, pals, I demand to know your nationality right away, otherwise I'm sending you back to jail." The two pals resist, and they are detained at the police station. But their telegram reaches their father, who once again alerts his nephew Paul, who in turn alerts Longuet, who alerts Briand, and David Nahum pleads his sons' cause one more time: "They're not Turkish, although they were born in the Ottoman Empire, they're not Greek, even though Salonica is Greek, they're not Italian, although they used to be Italian subjects, and so they can only be Salonicians." "It really is a Macedonian mish-mash," repeats the French Prime Minister, momentarily distracted by this peculiar conundrum from the torments of war. Then, convinced by the logic of David Nahum's argument, he immediately sends a telegram to Marseilles, ordering that the two brothers be set free, as Salonicians. They were probably imprisoned again on May 11, and they are released, this time for good, on the 16th.

The whole affair had turned out well thanks to the skill and intelligence of David Nahum, the crucial assistance of Paul Nahum, the generosity of kindly Salomon Beressi, the intervention of a great French socialist leader, and, finally, the miraculous ruling, worthy of Haroun al-Rachid, made by the highest authority of the French government. All of this powerfully confirmed Vidal's Oriental conception of power.

BOUCHES-DU RHONE REGION
RESIDENCE PERMIT

Family Name: Nahum.
First Name: Vidal.
Age: 22.
Nationality: Salonician.
Address: Rue d'Aubagne.

Mr. Nahum is authorized to reside in Marseilles with his family for the duration of the war. He is informed that he will not be allowed to travel during the hostilities unless in possession of a pass issued by the police captain, or, failing that, by the mayor of his place of residence.

He must strictly conform to all orders concerning inhabitants in general that are given in his town, either by the military or the civil authorities. He is warned that in the case of violation of the forementioned injunctions, he will be arrested immediately on presumption of espionage.

Marseilles, 18 May, 1916.

Special Inspector Borelli

The document in our possession is not the actual resident's permit, but an unofficial copy in Vidal's handwriting. On this copy, Vidal crossed out "Salonician" and wrote over it, at a later date, "Levantine Jew." In a postscript to this document, he wrote: "I say Levantine Jew, [signed] Borelli." In his own hand, he also copied out the incomplete copy of his identity card, no. 762003, issued to him in Marseilles on December 18, 1917 by Borelli himself, following the order of the prefect. The card is in the name of Nahoum (and not Nahum), and states the bearer's nationality as "Levantine Jew."

The "Levantine Jew" formula was only invented after the residence permit of 18 May, 1916 had been drawn up. Salonician nationality could only be a temporary lifeline. However, the status of minority immigrant offered all the advantages of French national protection without the military disadvantages that came with nationality. At this time, Sephardic Jews were arriving in great numbers in France, particularly in the aftermath of the great fire that swept through Salonica on August 5, 1917, and this prompted the invention of a special status for all these French-speakers who were neither Greek nor Turkish, and with whom Vidal could naturally align himself. For this reason, it is probable that in December 1917, when it was necessary to make out an identity card on the basis of the officially granted residence permit, police captain Borelli, perhaps troubled by this strange affair, himself retrospectively but illegally crossed out the word "Salonician" from the aforementioned permit, as if it were an error which had been corrected in 1916, at the time when it was originally written, and not in 1917, when Vidal's identity card was drawn up.

Although the residence permit still bears the spelling Nahum, the identity card is spelt Nahoum. Police captain Borelli, perhaps distracted by this strange affair, spelled the name in accordance with French phonetics, and thus differentiated Vidal and Henri's names from that of their family. Vidal did not consider rectifying the error at the time, because what mattered to him was not the spelling of his name, but the protection of a non-national identity. Henri would recover his original name Nahum at a later date, in Belgium, when he reverted to Italian nationality, which would leave Vidal as the only Nahoum among the Nahums – something that did not bother him in the least. In any event, thanks to his "Salonician" city nationality, and because of the vague infranationality implied by "Levantine Jew," Vidal would succeed in escaping the nation-state, which stood for the army, war and death. Thus, he was a Salonician for a period that may have lasted over a year, and would remain a Levantine Jew for a few years, until he temporarily used the Greek solution in 1925, before becoming a French citizen for good in 1931.

BE QUIET, MARSEILLES!

The Salonician identity, or that of Levantine Jew, had the advantage of being non-national, and, like Italian nationality in the Ottoman Empire between 1878 and 1912, it therefore exempted the Nahums from any form of servitude to a national state. In Marseilles, it allowed Henri and Vidal to avoid any form of military service. Other young Salonicians, who had become Greek after 1912, suffered the same fate in Marseilles as the young "Italians" from Salonica in 1915, when Greece entered the war on the side of the Allies (in July 1917). They were sent back to their pseudo-homeland, to be drafted into "their" army. This is what happened to Mony Covo, who would later become Vidal's nephew by marrying Liliane, Henriette's daughter:

Mony had problems, because being Greek he had to leave for Salonica to join the Greek army, and, as a result of that disaster [because the worst misfortune was to be drafted to fight in the service of a nation that one only belonged to in an abstract fashion], *he was put on a ship which was torpedoed . . . His boat from Marseilles to Salonica was a military transporter with about fifty Greeks on board, Greek Orthodox as well as Greek Jews, who were being sent to join the Greek army. And then the German submarine torpedoed them, but Mony had one especial piece of luck. His ship was very close to Malta. In Malta, the English were using corvettes or little reconnaissance boats to keep an eye on what was going on. They saw the ship sink. They came to the rescue at once. The survivors were on rafts, and the English torpedo boats in Malta came to fish them out, put them on boats, and transport them to Malta, to the hospital and doctors. Mony, poor thing, was on a raft, he was injured on the shoulder, well I don't know what it was exactly, but he was rescued, and then, a few days later, they up and send him to Salonica. And there, I think he got some time off, some pass, because since he was a survivor and had been injured by the torpedo, they couldn't put him in the army right away . . . and in the meantime there was the Armistice, and that was the end of it.*

Vidal and Henri's residence permits oblige them to remain in Marseilles for the duration of the fighting. However, the Nahums welcome this obligation. David Nahum, his wife, his sons Henri and Vidal and his daughter Mathilde, go to live at 70, Rue Paradis, in an apartment let to them by Mrs. Léonie Grandel, with whom they develop a very cordial relationship; she will give her reference for Vidal's identity card in 1917. Living in France could only be agreeable to David Nahum, who was still enraptured by the memory of his trip to Paris in 1878, and had probably already begun to consider settling there after Salonica became Greek.

The family feels quite at home in Marseilles. Marseilles is just like Salonica, only French instead of Sephardic. Like Salonica, it is a great port, and offers the same professional opportunities. It has a similar Mediterranean climate, with the same occasional gusts of cold wind: the Vardar in Salonica corresponds to the Mistral in Marseilles. The lifestyle is the same, with the same taste for idleness, leisure, pleasure, generally enjoyment of life, and "kidding around". The word "kidding" is adopted by the family soon after they settle in Marseilles.

In any case, the fire of August 1917 had wiped out Jewish Salonica; it not only destroyed houses, damaging 53,000 of them, but also 34 of the 37 synagogues, 10 of the 13 schools, all of the libraries, and all the public offices. It killed the soul as well as the body of the Sephardic city. It destroyed any thought of return in David Nahum, whose house was one of those that burned down. So the Nahums lost their home, but only after they had already found a new one, in Marseilles.

It was in Marseilles that the family was reunited. Jacques and Sophie arrived in 1916, probably during the summer. *So my brother Jacques, who was in Salonica, as soon as we were called up, he got out quick, he left Salonica . . . for Athens. He'd been able to get some papers in Salonica, saying he was* [indecipherable word, but in any case not "Italian"]. *And when he found out two or three months later that we were there, safe and sound and living in Marseilles, he managed to find a way too, got some different passports, and so he came to Marseilles as well, which meant that three of us brothers were there including myself, as well as my father, my mother and Mathilde.* It was in Marseilles that Jacques and Sophie's daughters were born, first Régine, then Hélène; both were declared French at birth.

David Nahum begins to work as a broker again. He obtains work permits for himself and his two sons from the prefecture and the chamber of commerce (Vidal states on his identity card that he is a "commercial clerk"). He establishes a permanent link with his son Léon, who has remained in Salonica at the head of his father's business, and has become a dignitary there, receiving General Sarrail at his table for dinner. Léon keeps his father informed about the needs of the French army in the East. "We're being asked for supplies, preserves, sardines in oil, butter cookies, chocolate bars, everything in the way of articles for soldiers, tinder wicks for lighters, postcards, pencils, ink." David gets in touch with his former business contacts in Marseilles, and obtains cases of soap for the army in the East from a manufacturer called Mr. Belon. Once again, David goes to work in several directions at once, tries a number of initiatives and provides jobs for his sons.

Staying behind in Salonica with Léon, the bridgehead of the family business, are Henriette, her husband Élie and her daughters Liliane and Aimée, who come to Marseilles in 1918 after the armistice. When she arrives in Marseilles, Henriette takes advantage of the move to make herself younger, bringing forward her date of birth and those of her daughters by four years; this rejuvenating operation conforms both to the traditional Eastern psychology of a mother who has every interest in reducing her unmarried daughters' age, and to the modern western psychology of rejuvenation.

Bouchi Cohen, a cavalry captain in the Serbian Army, comes on leave to Marseilles, where his sister Sophie is living, and meets beautiful Mathilde. Had he already seen her in Salonica? Is this their first meeting, and a case of "love at first sight?" In all events, cavalryman Bouchi requests Mathilde's hand three or five days later, and she accepts. The engagement is announced on September 7, 1917; a reception takes place on Sunday September 16, and, beforehand, on Friday 14, there is an engagement dinner for the family at Sophie and Jacques's house. The guests are, in order of seating, Dona Helena, with Bouchi on her right and Vidal (her favorite) on her left, followed by Mathilde between Bouchi and her father David, Mrs. Fauletier, Henri, Sophie, L. Medina, little Régine, Jacques and Sophie's daughter, and Jacques. After the engagement, Bouchi returns to the front. The family decides to postpone the wedding until the end of the war. Bouchi will return to Marseilles after the armistice, where, as Vidal says, he *starts living with his fiancée right away*. The wedding must wait until the Serbian family can move to Marseilles, and will finally be celebrated on March 12, 1919, at David's house, 70, Rue Paradis. The religious ceremony takes place at home, as is the custom in Salonica; this custom will still be in force when Liliane and Aimée get married, in the 1920s.

Vidal feels at home in Marseilles; he likes the city, and he likes the way of life there. Henri and he "have fun." Vidal rediscovers, with new friends, the amusements of his last years in Salonica.

Henri, who is a ladies' man, lives life to the full. These are happy years for the whole family.

Since my father is a bon vivant, and my mother is only too glad to go along with him, as are my brother and Mathilde, on Saturdays and Sundays, we'd maybe arrange to go to the outskirts of Marseilles, to some very nice places, where there were already some hotels. We'd have a meal, and stay the night, and then we'd go back to Marseilles either by the regional train, or by tram, there was one that traveled the whole twenty kilometers . . . We would finish our day's work at the office, and in the evenings we'd meet up in cafés in Canebière, my brother with his friends, and me with mine, we'd made some contacts, some very nice friends, very genuine, and among others there were two friends of mine who were doctors, one who had studied at Saint-Etienne and the other at Toulouse, and both of them had set up in Marseilles [Vidal is reunited in Marseilles with his two friends from the Franco–German school. One of them is Dr. Matarasso, with whom he had wanted to study medicine, and with whom he would remain in contact for the rest of his life, in a very affectionate friendship.] *Which meant that during the war things went very well, because I was working in a safe job, with no problems, we were protected from any kind of requisition.*

In Marseilles, Vidal had an important love affair, which he kept secret. While it amused him to tell his son and his granddaughters about pretty Wilhelmine, the young lady from Vienna with whom he fell in love in 1911, he never said a word about his love in Marseilles. He was even careful to tear the lines that referred to the woman he loved out of his notebook. He was afraid that his legitimate wives would discover this secret, and he did not want to reveal it to his descendants. We do not know whether the brother closest to him, Henri, was ever told about it. Here is what remains of his confiding in his black notebook:

29th September 1917, 70, Rue Paradis, Marseilles, 1.30 p.m.
It's not easy forgetting, for some time now everything has been going by before me, a few things are really making me think. Why do we meet like this, sometimes? Although I'm not really obsessed, I still think about her. And yet it's just a dream, it's impossible! Sometimes happiness is hidden in the most unexpected and incredible things. Well, fate says that I must see her again, let's see what time, the great regulator of all things, will do! In the meantime, I think that for seventeen months (?) I haven't written a single word here, time goes by so quickly, it's more than electricity, and it's true that I like this speed. Oh yes, I like it when the train . . . tram-driver . . . without . . .

The "unexpected and incredible" encounter in question is with a person with whom any union would be "impossible, a dream." It seems likely that these lines were written shortly after a separation, and that it had been more than a brief and intense encounter, because there has been "happiness," and the "seventeen months" which have passed since he gave up his journal may allow us to suppose that he met the unknown woman shortly after his liberation, around August 1917. It seems to have been necessary to keep this relationship a secret, since the first lines of the text are abstruse and mysterious, as if Vidal were taking pains to cover his words with a smokescreen, in case the journal were discovered and read. Moreover, if Vidal is writing after a separation, he expects to have to wait for a long time, and so time will feel slow to him, after it has been so quick, as indicated by the phrase *"time goes by quickly, it's more than electricity."* It seems, therefore, that it was during these seventeen months that time had speeded up, and that this love affair hurtling along at high speed intoxicated Vidal, who *"likes this speed,"* but may perhaps have feared derailment, since in the fragment that remains of the torn-out page, the word tram-driver survives. It also seems that the unknown woman is to leave Marseilles for a relatively distant destination. There are no clues to help us detect what makes it impossible for Vidal to envisage living with the unknown woman. Some taboo? Is she married? Does she have children? Or on the contrary, is she too young? Although it is not impossible that he will see her again, it could only be after quite a long time. Here, Vidal reveals what constitutes both his fatalism and his philosophy: "*Let's see what time, the great regulator of all things, will do.*" What did time do? Did he see the unknown woman again? Where? Under what circumstances? Did he lose her forever? Who was she? Was she a gentile, or one of "his people?" Would he love her for the rest of his life?

The armistice arrives, and Vidal, as we shall see, leaves Marseilles. For the Nahums, and especially for Vidal and Henri, who were eligible to be drafted into all four of the armies at war (Italian, Turkish, Greek and perhaps even French), Marseilles was an oasis of peace and incredible freedom, in the midst of a Europe put to the fire and the sword, and given over to the greatest and most collective butchery in history. The two brothers lived there with extraordinary unconcern.

Thus, in Marseilles, while Henri was pursuing his many amorous adventures, Vidal would have one, extraordinary, love affair. In the postcard that he sends from Frigolet thirteen years later, Henri can find no other way of expressing his emotion at the idea of returning to Marseilles, than writing twice over: "Marseilles. Marseilles?"

As for Vidal, he would still be overcome with nostalgia forty years later, on hearing Colette Renard's song:

> *Marseille, tais-toi Marseille!*
> *Tu cries trop fort!*
> [Marseilles, be quiet, Marseilles!
> You shout too loudly!]

His time in Marseilles and his Marseilles secret would resonate within him for the rest of his days.

IV

Move to Paris, Marriage
and Birth of a Son

The Nahums, who identify with the cause of the Allies, and see it as their opportunity for reunion, greet the armistice with joy. However, the event will prove disastrous for the family business, whose main source of income comes from supplying the Eastern Army.

It becomes urgent for Vidal to earn his living, and once again he feels an irresistible desire to go to Paris: *I managed to persuade my father and my brothers that I wanted to come to Paris to try and set up an office here, the same as we had in Marseilles, to start a new office in Paris. They agreed, and so I move to Paris, to number 28, Rue Saint-Georges, where I rent a little office. I rent a room with a family next door, and I set to work. In the meantime, Bouchi had been demobilized, he'd gone back to Belgrade, and had opened the store that he ran with his father, and he wanted merchandise; so he uses me as an agent in Paris for cloth, velvet, well, for whatever he wanted. And from there, he sends me other clients too; it worked out so well that my brother Henri came to Paris as well (to work with me).* Vidal and Henri set up shop under the sign "Nahum brothers, exports."

This passage from his memoirs reveals: (1) The strength of Vidal's desire to go to Paris, even though he is happy in Marseilles (is there a secret romantic motive?); (2) That he needs to obtain the consent of his father and his two elder brothers, although he is already 25 years old; (3) The vital role played by family relationships and the advantages of the familial diaspora in establishing a business network; and (4) Vidal's readiness to trade in absolutely anything, and his ease in moving from one kind of merchandise to another, from one place to another. The profession of broker or agent is ideally suited to polyvalence and polymorphism. For Vidal, as for his father, non-specialization is not so much a sign of economic archaism as evidence of his vitality and adaptability to changing and uncertain conditions. Even when he is obliged to start selling hosiery wholesale, Vidal will be careful to put a few of his eggs in two or three separate baskets.

In the meantime, Vidal buys cloth for Bouchi, and for other clients from central or Eastern Europe, as well as hosiery, thread and cotton.[37]

Then comes a stroke of luck: *So it's the beginning of 1919 . . . In the mean-time, during one of my return journeys to Marseilles, I'd met . . . I had gone to the*

69

fair in Lyons to make new business contacts which might be useful in the import–export trade, and, on my return from the fair in Lyons, luck would have it that I met a gentleman . . . so I tell him my story.

"Ah", he says, "I'm delighted to meet you."

He gives me his card:

"I'm Mr. de Rocasera, I'm the Representative for the Gironde. I'm a big businessman, and I need a young person, someone dynamic, listen, this evening" – the train was arriving in Paris – *"come and meet me tomorrow morning. But now you must come to my hotel."*

"But I already have a room."

"No, no, it's not worth it, you are my guest; you will take a room at my hotel, and tomorrow morning we'll have a long talk."

And indeed, there it was, the Hotel Cusset, in the Rue de Richelieu, it was a very grand hotel, elegant, not a third-rate hotel. The next morning, I see him after breakfast:

"To keep it brief, here is what it's about. I'm in the process, charged by the French government, of buying 5,000 pre-fabricated houses for the northern region, which is in ruins. I have been given the job of making this purchase, and I already have some proposals, I've already found an English factory to supply me with these houses over there. But I need an active, dynamic person to get things moving as quickly as possible . . . So I'm making you an offer . . . You'd have to go to London, and then . . . "

Well, I didn't want to tell him that my papers still said I was a Levantine Jew. And for the trip to London, the first thing he tells me:

"Well," he says, "you'll need a passport. To get your passport, you must get in touch with the Ministry of Foreign Affairs."

Luckily, at the Ministry of Foreign Affairs, here in Paris, on the Quai d'Orsay, there was an Armenian, a Mr. Balioudjian, in the section in charge of people from the East. I'll never forget him. He gave me a very kind reception, and so I told him my whole story, and he says to me:

"I understand, I understand . . . . And what do you want, now?"

"Well, I would like a passport so that I can go to London."

"Don't worry, you'll just have to go and register at the headquarters of the organization in charge of Levantine Jews in Paris, the president is Mr. So-and-so, here you are, I'll give you his address."

So I jump into a taxi, and off I go. I go and see this gentleman, his name was Rozales:

"Well, he says, there's no possible objection, I will give you all the certificates that you require."

I go back to the Ministry of Foreign Affairs to Mr. Baliodjian's office, he receives me very kindly, and I say to him:

"It worked out very well."

"Come tomorrow, your passport will be waiting for you."

The next day, I go to the British consulate, because you had to get a stamp on your passport to get into England, it all goes well, and I arrive in London with all the information from my Mr. de Rocasera. He's given me the address of a hotel in London to stay at (the Imperial Hotel, Russell Square), and the address of the manufacturer, whom he had already notified of my arrival, and the process gets under way. So I introduce myself, the contracts we need to sign are all ready, only I need a banker's guarantee, because it was a contract for I don't know how many million francs. So I send a telegram, and I don't remember how, but Mr. Rocasera tells me: "Fine, listen, in two days from now I will receive a payment from the Ministry for Reconstruction, and I will transfer the funds immediately."

And then, unfortunately, at that point, this is the beginning of 1920 (wrong, because the Identity Book Vidal obtained from the Metropolitan Police at Bow Station, probably in order to prolong his stay, was issued on March 5, 1919), *the pound sterling, which was worth 25 francs, the rate it had been for years, since before the war, goes up to 26 francs, then 27 . . . which means that the prefabricated houses which we had bought for, let's say, 300 pounds, which was 7,500 francs at the usual exchange rate, that made 8,075 francs when it went up to 28 francs; so we wait one day, two days for the rate to stabilize again; unfortunately, the rate, instead of going down, eats up more and more of the budget, so much so that he* [Rocasera] *tells me: "Listen, leave the deal standing for the time being, tell the manufacturer what's happening, and as soon as the currency has recovered we'll get moving again."* Vidal spends over a month in London. He returns to France on June 5 via Southampton, after having obtained a British identity card to prolong his stay – a card on which Sergeant Young, from the Aliens Department, feels the need to territorialize the individual, and writes under *nationality of birth: "Israelite from Turkey,"* and under *nationality of passport: "Israelite French passport."*

In just two days, his luck had changed. After the unexpected stroke of luck came an unexpected disaster. *To cut a long story short,* concludes Vidal, *the business didn't come off, and after that, the French franc kept on falling.*

This fall has a drastic effect on exports; although the Nahums continue to export to Yugoslavia, and Vidal finds new clients in Greece and Romania, it will not be enough.

THE FATHER'S DEATH

In the meantime, my father . . . luckily he was still working; apart from Yugoslavians, we had other clients, from Greece, Romania, and all that . . .

David begins to feel ill; he undergoes treatment for his heart, and he must realize that he is going to die, since on February 26 1919 – that is, before Vidal's trip to London – in an act of notary drawn up by Mr. Paul Maria of Marseilles, he transfers all powers to Vidal, who becomes his universal proxy. It is very likely that David Nahum's stay in Paris, during Vidal's absence in London, coincides with a consultation with a specialist. We know that he went into hospital for a time in Paris, before returning to Marseilles, where he remains until June 1920. In 1947, in response to a letter from Vidal, who has asked him for biographical information about his relatives, Paul Nahum writes that David "was suffering from a heart ailment caused by tobacco abuse." Vidal, when copying out word for word the information from his cousin Paul's letter, in order to send it to one of his nieces (Hélène), replaces "caused by tobacco abuse," with "brought about by long years of work, worry and trials."

David Nahum goes to Paris to attend Vidal's wedding, which takes place on June 22, 1920, and he never returns to Marseilles, probably on the advice of a doctor. He dies on August 9, at 109, Boulevard Voltaire. In a little pocket notebook, Dona Helena writes: "*La triste muerte de mi querido David, el 9 août, et 25 av.*" [The sad death of my darling David, on August 9, 25 av.] On the opposite page, she sticks an identity photo of her husband.

The Adenis firm, in the Place Voltaire, are directors of the funeral, which takes place on Wednesday 11 August 1920, at 12 o'clock: "Fifth-class convoy no. 1. Three berlines. Coffin in highly-polished oak, screws to bottom, padded and watertight upholstery, antiseptic salt, *grande taxe* engraved on pad. Purification, consistorial tax, authorization and procedures.[38] Letters of invitation in full mourning, carriage expenses, general gratuities. Plot in perpetuity at the Parisian cemetery of Bagneux, and fees: 3,405 francs received from M. Vidal Nahoum, 109, Boulevard Voltaire."

David D. Nahum was buried in plot no. 178, where his wife would join him in 1936. A rabbi said prayers over the tomb. Was it him who left the following inscription?

I have made my plaint and I lament David Nahum
Who was a loyal man.
Let his soul rest in peace.
Born Salonica, 1851, died 25 ab 5680.

David was an exceptionally intelligent man, energetic and astute, as his resourcefulness in his professional life shows; it made him *drogoman* to the French consul, principal *drogoman* to the Belgian consul, exporter of cereals, and then importer to Salonica of Belgian metallurgical products and of petroleum products from Bakou; he had no difficulty adapting to life in Marseilles, where he resumed his activities as a broker in completely different circumstances. He managed to find jobs for his sons Léon, Henri and Vidal in his business, and then released Léon, letting him work independently in the metallurgical sector. In Salonica, he had succeeded in protecting his family from the danger resulting from the Turkish munitions affair, and he had managed to free Vidal and Henri from the camp at Frigolet. He was a dignified man, and looked very respectable in the frockcoat that made such an impression on Vidal; but at the same time he was a *bon vivant*, appreciating the pleasures of the table, and probably those of the flesh too, and enjoying excursions: already in Salonica, he was in the habit of taking weekends off. He remained good-natured throughout a life of "work, worry and trials." What Vidal would not inherit, but Léon would, was his concern for correctness and dignity, and even sartorial elegance. However, Vidal resembled his father in other ways: he too would retain a cheerful nature and a capacity for happiness throughout a life of work, worry and trials; like his father, in spite of the work, worry and trials, which would never cease, he knew how to enjoy his leisure time and, more profoundly, how to enjoy life itself.

The end of the war and the father's death led to the restructuring of the family into separate units, which remained in constant communication. The Marseilles unit had almost reunited the whole family in 1918. All of David Nahum's sons were there (except Léon), as well as his two daughters; Henriette and her husband Élie Hassid had been the last to leave Salonica, and had come after the armistice to live in the family apartment in the Rue Paradis with their teenage daughters Liliane and Aimée. The Hassids would remain in Marseilles until at least November 1921.

The Marseilles unit disintegrates three years later, when Vidal leaves for Paris, followed by Henri. Mathilde leaves for Belgrade with her husband Bouchi; Jacques, whose business in Marseilles is failing, goes to Brussels to join Léon, who has set up Nahum Steel there; the firm deals mainly in Belgian metallurgical exports to the Balkans and the Middle East. Henriette remains in Marseilles, and her mother goes to live with her when she becomes a widow. Henriette, Élie, their two daughters and Dona Helena will be the last to leave for Paris, in November or December 1921, after it has been decided that Élie should become Vidal's associate in his brand new hosiery business.

Thus, two new family units are created: the Paris unit, with Vidal, Dona Helena, Henriette, Élie and their daughters Liliane and Aimée; and the Brussels unit, with Léon, his wife Julie and his daughter Chary, Jacques, his wife Sophie and their two daughters Régine and Hélène, and finally Henri, who goes to live with his brothers when the Paris office he runs with Vidal stops providing sufficient revenue.

The family continues to show solidarity. Léon remains its uncontested head, while Henriette, the eldest daughter, has her own area of authority in her role as chief advisor. Vidal unquestioningly obeys their petitions; for example, in 1921 he agrees to take on his brother-in-law Élie as his associate, and then, four years after the death of his wife, he gets married again, to one of Léon's sisters-in-law, on their advice. The tradition of mutual assistance and collective solidarity within the family will continue until all the protagonists from this generation have died. However, although the tradition continues, a vital break with the past has occurred: after Salonica, the birth rate among David's children drops sharply. Whereas generations before them had had five to ten children, Léon will have one daughter in Salonica, followed by a son in Brussels, Henriette will have two daughters in Salonica and no more, Jacques, two daughters, Vidal, an only son, while Mathilde will never have any children.

No real effort is required for the Nahums to adapt to life in France or Belgium. They speak and write French effortlessly, they have already been westernized by the Livornese tradition, and are even less religious than their parents' generation. But only two of them, Léon and Vidal, those who will have a son born in the new country, decide to take that country's nationality – a step which is made easier for them by this birth. Jacques and Henri will revert to being Italian, perhaps because it is more difficult for them than for Léon, whose son is born in Brussels, to obtain Belgian naturalization; perhaps they also feel more at home with this Mediterranean nationality, especially now that there is no longer a risk of their having to do military service. Henriette will retain the Greek nationality that her husband Élie Hassid acquired after 1912.

For Léon, and for Vidal, the process of assimilation to the host nation, however far it goes, begins with the birth of their sons.

MARRIAGE

In April or March 1920, in the period leading up to Passover, Vidal, who frequently goes to the Sentier neighborhood to buy fabric for his clients, runs into Salomon Beressi, an acquaintance from Salonica, who had been so dedicated in helping him when he was at the Frigolet camp.

Salomon Beressi, who was born in 1861 in Salonica, is 59 years old. He is the eldest of six brothers. The Beressis are very tall, even taller than the Nahums. They have black hair, full, well-defined lips, and brown eyes. The family seems to have originated in Bédéres or Bédarieux, in Provence. They lived in Tuscany for a long time, and Bederecit was changed to Bederessi there, before becoming Beressi. Salomon Beressi's grandfather probably settled in Salonica at the end of the eighteenth century.

Salomon Beressi's father, Joseph Beressi, born in 1830, had two children from his first marriage, Benjamin and Doudoun, and six children from his second marriage to Mathilde Mosseri: Salomon, Albert, Hananel, Jessua-Salvatore, Samy and Élie, who was born after his father's death. Joseph was killed in 1878 or 1879. Having left his home on horseback for a journey into the Macedonian mountains to visit clients or suppliers, he was captured by Bulgarian bandits. His horse came back to the stable on its own, lathered in sweat. Then an envoy from the bandits came to demand jewelry and money from Joseph's wife, giving her a finger that had been cut off from her husband's hand as identification. The woman gave everything she had, but her husband had already been killed. The family fell from great wealth to sudden destitution. For the first two years, the widow and her children lived on the reserves of garbanzos, lentils, dried beans and flour of which families kept several months' reserves in those days. The horses were sold. Afterwards, on every anniversary of Joseph Beressi's death, Salomon and his mother would donate money and gifts to an orphanage.

After his father's death, Salomon Beressi, then aged 17, promised his mother that he would become her protector and the head of this family of young children. He left school and found work. After climbing the ladder from one job to the next, he was quite soon able to start his own company selling iron goods, girders and hardware, in the neighborhood of Salonica known as "Los Ferreros." In particular, his company supplied the Nahum family, with whom he was on friendly terms.

Having become orphans at a very young age, the Beressi brothers could neither finish high school nor go to college; only Élie, the youngest child, born after his father's death, went to the Italian school. Shortly before 1900, Samy, the most enterprising brother, who in 1895 had worked on the construction of a railroad linking Salonica to the hinterland, was the first to leave for France, and it was he who convinced his brothers, including Salomon, to come and join him there. Salomon Beressi had married one of his cousins, Myriam Mosseri, who was born in 1877 in Salonica. Myriam Mosseri was the daughter of Salomon Mosseri and Myriam Mosseri, who were themselves cousins. Among the Mosseris, and to a lesser degree among the Beressis, there were a number of marriages between uncles and nieces and between first cousins. (Perhaps this was a hangover of a practice caused by the demographic constraints that prevailed in certain small Jewish communities in Tuscany, where it was difficult to find a husband or wife outside the family; another factor was the endogamy prevalent among Livornese families in Salonica).

The Mosseris are of average height, with black hair and brown eyes. They often have round faces, with expressions like those one sees in Tuscany or Emilia-Romagna. The name is probably an Italianization of Moche (Moses). They had uprooted themselves from Livorno to settle in Salonica more recently than the Nahums and the Beressis, as the fact that Myriam still speaks Italian with her sisters attests. As explained above, one of Myriam's nephews, Albert Mosseri, had been recruited by force into the Italian army in Salonica, at the same time that Vidal and his brother were taken to Marseilles.

Salomon Beressi and Myriam Mosseri had five children: Luna (1897), Pepo (1898), Corinne (1901), Benjamin (1909), and Emilie, known as Émy (1913). The family lived in a very large house, which Joseph Beressi had built, in Sainte-Sophie Street, near to the Greek church. The family's servant Tamar had her apartment on the first floor, with her husband and two daughters; the kitchen and the dining room, containing the Austrian dresser purchased by Joseph Beressi, were on the second floor; the bedrooms were on the third floor. Salomon Beressi had three toilets and a shower installed.

Twelve people lived in the house, including Tamar's family. Myriam Beressi, assisted by Tamar, cooked for them all. The men went to buy provisions. Street vendors came by selling vegetables. The family spoke Spanish at home, although Myriam and her sister Clara spoke Italian to one another. Myriam had attended an Italian school run by Catholic nuns, and she was strongly attached to her Livornese origins.

There was an Italian flag in the house, which they displayed in the window in times of trouble. The flag was put up in great haste when Hananel, Salomon's younger brother, took refuge there after he had stabbed a Turk during a fight.

Salomon Beressi wore western-style clothes with a Turkish fez, which he swapped in France for a hat.

Some cousins lived in the house next door, but Salomon Beressi had forbidden his children to make friends or play games with them. He would not even allow them to be called by the name Beressi; they were to be known as *los de por aqui* (the people next door). One of them had accompanied the Bulgarian who came to fetch the ransom for Joseph Beressi; Salomon and his mother believed that the man was implicated in the murder, or at least knew that Joseph Beressi was already dead when the ransom was paid. Furthermore, one of the *los de por aqui* had stabbed his own mother when she refused to give him a necklace he wanted for his fiancée. Salomon Beressi had disowned these people from his family. Luna, the eldest daughter, went to the Israelite Alliance school, where she learned French. Pepo often played truant. Corinne was never able to finish her studies, which were interrupted by the family's departure for France.

Following in Samy's footsteps, the five remaining Beressi brothers had all settled in France (or Spain in Élie Beressi's case) by the first decade of the century. Salomon's mother had come out to stay with them, as much out of a taste for French life as to visit her sons. Hananel Beressi had been in Marseilles since 1908. Salomon Beressi left Salonica for Marseilles with his son Pepo, in July 1914. War was declared one month later, and he remained separated from his family for the next year. Then, in September 1915, he managed to bring over his wife and his other children, as a pass issued by the Greek authorities indicates, in the name of Marie Beressi, 38, Luna, 17, Korina, 13, Benjamin, 8, and Emilie, 2.

The mother and her four children leave knowing that they will never return, taking six big trunks with them. The Freycinet company's ship, which is taking them to Marseilles, makes a stop at Naples, where Myriam is advised to get off, as there are fears that the boat will be torpedoed by a German submarine. During the crossing, Myriam, Luna and Corinne have their first taste of a very peculiar kind of cheese with holes in it. When they arrive in Marseilles, after a two-day train journey, Myriam feels utterly disorientated on finding that she cannot make coffee properly. After making several attempts in vain, she sends Corinne to ask the concierge, who teaches her how they do it in the West. Corinne is also very surprised to see that women rather than men go to market, and is horrified to see tripe and lungs hanging from butchers' hooks.

Salomon Beressi has a "commission and exports" office in Marseilles; he also supplies his brothers, who already have a store; he commutes between Paris and Marseilles, and, before the end of the war, sets up his Paris office in the Sentier, at 56, Rue Saint-Sauveur. He starts up an import–export business with Germany in 1919. He also opens a store selling novelties at number 10, Boulevard Barbès, not far from the Barbès-Rochechouart métro station, for his son Pepo. He lives at number 12, Rue Parmentier, in a neighborhood inhabited by many other Salonicians. The family lives with their servant from Salonica, Tamar, who will work for them for the rest of her life.

Salomon and his brothers have therefore "come home" to France, a few centuries later. The Beressi brothers make a success of their business, and become wealthy members of the bourgeoisie. One of them, Hananel, a very handsome, very elegant man, remains illiterate. He opens a business in the Sentier, but it is his employee and right-hand man, Joseph Pelosoff, who keeps the books and does the paperwork. No one could have guessed that Hananel does not know how to read. Every day, he goes and sits on the terrace of a big café, and spreads out his newspaper, which he examines attentively. As for Samy, he is the first member of his family to marry a gentile; he marries Gaby Lombard, with whom he has two sons, Roger (born in 1909) and Alex (born in 1911), and two daughters, Edith (1916), and Odette (1920), who will later become Ana Beressi. Fortune smiles on Samy: he develops a big wholesale business in the Sentier, becomes the owner of a department store in Paris, and moves into finance.

Most of the Mosseris have also settled in France; some of them are in Nice (like Albert Mosseri, who dies there), in Castres or in Montpellier, but most of them live in Paris, including Edouard Mosseri, Myriam's brother.

The Beressi and Mosseri families were already modern and secularized when they were in Salonica. Salomon, who is both a self-made and a self-taught man, has worked out his own systems of belief and morality. As an adolescent, it was obvious to him that no god would have allowed the cowardly murder of his father. Therefore he teaches his children that God does not exist and that humans have no need of this illusion; one must do good for its own sake, and not out of fear of God. Salomon Beressi continues to respect the important Jewish festivals, and especially Passover, because they are communal and familial celebrations. He is certainly one of the first men from his Salonician generation to practice birth control, and he decides to have no more children in France (Corinne, as an adolescent, will one day accidentally discover a peculiar little thing, transparent and rubbery, in a drawer of her father's bedside table).

Salomon Beressi is a man of extreme rectitude, whose sense of honor is far more acute than his sense of reputation. He is kind and sensitive, as Vidal testifies, remembering the tears Salomon shed on seeing him at the Frigolet camp, although his tragic adolescence and the hardships of his life have also made him tough. Luna and Corinne adore him. As Corinne will write, sixty-three years after her father's death (in 1921), when she is 83 years old, to her nephew Edgar: "Your grandfather Beressi was a genius and I admired him with all my heart . . . There are not many fathers like him. When he came home at night, I would rush to prepare him a warm footbath, in which I dissolved a handful of sea salt (I'd read that it relieves tiredness); then I would massage the soles of his feet – there was no public transport where we lived. I'd brush his hair and clean out his ears, and finish off by kissing his eyelids."

In 1920, Luna is 23 years old, Pepo 22, Corinne 19, Benjamin 11 and Émy 7. Luna's physical characteristics, in a passport issued in 1920, are listed as follows: height: five feet five inches; hair: black; forehead: average; eyebrows: black; eyes: brown; nose: straight; mouth: medium; chin: round; face: oval; complexion: flushed. Her face is of the Southern European type, and she could pass for Spanish or Italian. In some photos, she looks beautiful, but not in others. Corinne, her younger sister, is very pretty. Luna is reserved, while Corinne is more communicative. Pepo is, according to Corinne's description, sturdily built, impulsive, sweet, "crazy"; Benjamin is dreamy and naïve, Émy is open and direct. Salomon is very much in love with his wife, as we can see from this letter in *djidio*, which he writes to her from Frankfurt on March 6, 1920, shortly before running into Vidal in the Sentier:

Frankfurt, March 6, 1920

Dear Wife,

I received your treasured letter, and I am pleased to hear that you are all in good health; there is no need to worry about me, I am very well. I want to let you know, my darling, that this week I did some business, which initially looked promising, as I wrote to you last week, and was settled very satisfactorily on Thursday. Dear wife, I wanted to write to you on Thursday to wish you a happy Purim, but I was in Cologne, I motored there and back. Yesterday, I was tied up [enbrolyado] writing bills, and it's only today that I have had an hour to spare in which to write to you. I wish you all a happy Purim anyway. I am sure that you have ordered the masa [unleavened bread] for Passover.

Don't expect me home very soon, my dear Marika, you know that the 18th of this month is little Emilie's birthday, and last night in bed it occurred to me to ask what she wants me to buy her for her birthday present; even if she can't be bothered to write a word to her father, her father still thinks of . . . . [illegible word]. You write and tell me what she wants me to give her, I am putting 1,000 marks into the bank in her name. Write to me, I am so worried not to have received any letters from Benjamin; I asked him to write twice a week, and in every letter I write you I ask you to get him to write to me, but in the three weeks since I left Paris I have not received a single letter from this son of mine; I hope that you will oblige him to write, and let the master know so that he can correct his spelling. It was a pleasure to read the letter from Luna, which was well-written. As for Korina's letter, I couldn't read it . . . it was written with her foot and not her hand; she promised to write to me every day and give me the details of the takings [from the shop on the Boulevard Barbès where she was in charge of the checkout] each day, and instead she writes to me once a week with three receipts. In any event, I find this unwillingness to write incomprehensible.

As for Pepo's letter . . . it would be better if he asked one of his schoolmasters to teach him how to write and compose a letter; tell your son that it is a disgrace not to know how to write a letter and not to know how to spell a word, but all that is a result of the girls' negligence, because they do not pay attention and don't correct him when he writes. I hope that they will take good note of what I say . . . and you, my darling, write to me twice a week, drop everything else and write to your husband, and let me know everything that is happening. Say hello to dear Edouard . . . kiss all the children for me, and as for you my darling, your husband who loves you always sends you his warmest embrace.

Salomon

Vidal recounts his meeting with Salomon Beressi, in March or April 1920, in his oral autobiography:

"Well! What are you doing here?"

We embrace each other and all that. He says:

"You know it's our festival, Passover?"

"Yes, of course I know."

"And you're not going back to Marseilles, to be with your parents?"

"No, because I'm expecting two customers from Yugoslavia and Romania."

"But your brother is here with you?"

"My brother is going to go because he's more . . . how can I put it . . . more . . . what do you call that . . . not sincere . . . he's more . . . more keen on tradition, so he's quite determined to spend the holiday with Papa and Mama."

"What about you?"

"Me, I'm not leaving . . . "

"Fine, listen, since you aren't going away, come to my house, tomorrow night is the Passover celebration and it's the tradition to invite friends and people we know . . . So I'd be very pleased if you would accept my invitation, I don't want you to be alone in Paris on Passover evening."

Well, I accept, and we arrange a time. On the evening of the next day, he introduced me, so there were two girls, the mother and her sister, the uncle, etc., between ten to a dozen people, they seat me at the table, make me very welcome, there's a very friendly atmosphere, very warm; the father of my future wife – I didn't know she was my future wife yet – well, they give me a really wonderful welcome . . . make me lots of compliments . . . and they ask me to come back the next evening.

Sixty-four years later, Corinne, Luna's sister, gives her nephew Edgar,

Vidal's son, a fuller account of the meeting that was to result in Vidal's marriage.

"Your grandfather Beressi runs into your father, who was living in Marseilles. He asks him: 'How come you aren't celebrating Passover in Marseilles?' Your father answers: 'I'm expecting a customer from Yugoslavia who doesn't speak French, I have to accompany him to his hotel and go to the restaurant with him.' 'Come and celebrate with us at home on Passover evening, if you like.' He was not religious, on the contrary he was a strict atheist, but he followed tradition and often gave us lectures about how to behave. Your father accepts the invitation, and they arrange to meet at Pepo's – he had a store selling novelty goods. I used to go in the afternoons and work on the checkout for him, and in the evenings we'd go home in a hackney cab. Well, it's closing time. I'm at the back of the store, where there's a mirror [*in which she could see the stranger*], putting on my hat. My father can't come, and so he has asked a cousin of mine, Albert Hassid, to look after your father. I finish putting on my hat, and I have to go back out to the door of the store. We haven't been introduced yet, it's only when Edouard arrives that he introduces us. We arrive at our house. The table had been laid by Tamar [*the servant who worked for the family*], whom you may have known. Without doing it on purpose, she has seated your father next to your future and very dear mother, who I still miss terribly whenever I talk about her. She was my elder sister, she was six years older than me, and little by little, as we were growing up, the age difference wasn't very obvious [*according to her birth certificate, Corinne, born in 1901, is then 19 years old, and Luna, born in 1897, is 23, which only makes four years' difference*]. Around this big table, which had been laid for the celebration, there were quite a number of us. My parents, and my grandmother whom I loved and revered, I saw her every morning at 7 o'clock before doing the shopping for my Mama; she could speak Italian very well, but not French. Well, to get back to the Passover table, there was Edouard, Joseph Beressi and Uncle Jo, my future husband whom I was silently in love with, and he loved me passionately in return.

In the middle of the meal, your father starts whistling, and as Edouard had a big cage with canaries in it, and there was one that was ill and had stopped singing, I say: 'Listen, Edouard, your canary's recovered, he's singing.'

The whole table bursts out laughing. Always, after a good meal, or even before it has ended, as soon as he feels full and satisfied, Vidal begins to whistle a tune or a song, like a happy bird. On that day, neither the fact that this was his first invitation to dinner with the family, nor the ritual nature of the ceremonial meal inhibited him. Throughout his life, he would hum or sing whenever his stomach was satisfied.

"We ate dinner, sang and read the Haggadah. Your father fell in love with your much lamented mother at first sight."

We now return to Vidal's account: *The next day, again they made me very welcome, we read the prayer, and in the meantime, I say:*

"Listen, you've invited me twice now, I would like to invite you in return." So my father-in-law, or rather my future father-in-law (I didn't know it at the time) tells me: "Listen, you're very kind, but I don't go out in the evenings, because I am very tired, but invite my daughter and my son if you like, you can invite them."

Fine, so the next day, or the day after that, three days after I invite the daughter and the son to go to the opéra comique *to see* Carmen. *They accept, and I go and pick them up, etc. Well, I'm invited to their house again. One thing leads to the next, and I write to my parents to tell them I want to ask for her hand . . .*

Vidal has left something out of this account, although the episode in question is what gave him the idea of making the marriage proposal. In fact, Luna answers his note of invitation with a letter:

Paris, April 7, 1920
Dear Sir,
We were delighted to receive your invitation and we are very grateful to you. It is really very kind of you. Allow me to tell you that you are very considerate and have guessed exactly what we like: we adore the opéra comique . . . However . . . if by any chance you have not already booked the tickets, we would rather not go, because we have recently suffered a cruel loss. Death, that monster who knows neither law nor impediment, has spread his wings and snatched our very dear and deeply regretted aunt, "Mrs. Faraggi," away from us. I am sure you will understand the feelings that lead me to write to you in this way. And now I join Papa and Mama in asking you kindly to come and dine with us on Thursday evening, without fail "of course." I hope that we can count on you; until Thursday, then. Everyone at home asks me to give you their regards. Accept a friendly handshake from me.
   Luna.

It is on the back of this letter that Vidal begins the draft of his marriage proposal. He has previously asked permission from his parents: *I write to my parents asking for their consent. They say: "How do you expect us to give our consent? We know the gentleman very well, we don't know the daughter, but if you think the daughter suits you, if you like her . . . As far as the family is concerned, fine, since we know the parents very well, but make the request yourself, saying that we agree."*

It is then that Vidal writes the letter, in what Haïm Vidal Sephiha calls "Fragnol." His draft begins as follows:

Caro Salomon,
Kieriya qué Papa estouviera en Paris, qué el te fiziéra esta demanda. En su absence, i segura de la buena amistad del qué va recivir la prézente, mé decidi a escrivirte yo mezmo, por demandarte la mano de tu fija Mlle L . . . Tengo 27 anos [deleted]. No ajusto nada a mi demanda . . .

(Dear Salomon, I wish that Papa were in Paris, so that he could make this request on my behalf. In his absence, and being certain that you will receive this letter in a spirit of good friendship, I have decided to write to you myself to ask you for the hand of your daughter, Miss L . . . I am 27 years old [deleted] . . . I have nothing to add to my request . . . .)

So I show my letter to Mr. Beressi: "Ah, he says, that's very good, only I would have preferred them to be here too." "They can't . . . it's a long way from Marseilles to Paris, my father is rather elderly, and all that . . . "

What Vidal does not know is that Luna is not keen on the idea of getting married. The account that Corinne, Luna's sister, often gives to her nephew Edgar sheds a complementary light on what happened. [*After the marriage proposal*], "My father speaks to her, she doesn't want to know, she says: 'I don't know him, I don't want to.' My father tells me to talk to her when we are alone in our room, which I do as soon as the door is closed. I say: 'Hey, he's not bad, that boy, he's asked Papa for your hand, so are you going to accept?' Still the same answer: 'I don't know him and I don't want to get married.'"

Luna eventually accepts. The engagement takes place on April 13, 1920, followed by a reception on April 22.

> *Mr. and Mrs. Salomon Beressi*
> *have the honor of informing you of the engagement of*
> *Miss Louna Beressi, their daughter*
> *to Mr. Vidal Nahoum.*
> *We request the pleasure of your company at the reception which will take place on Thursday*
> *April 22, 1920, at 8.30 p.m.,*
> *at the Galeries des Champs-Elysées, number 55, Rue de Ponthiu.*

My father-in-law threw a first-class party at the Rue de Ponthieu, in a big room which afterwards became part of Claridge's Hotel; there were the six Beressi brothers, all of whom had excellent situations, all with their wives and children, and the Beressi cousins; plus my cousins, the dental surgeon, the pharmacist, the chief accountant, everyone from both families, well, it was a great success . . . And afterwards, we set a date for the wedding.

Apparently, Luna's grandmother made a disdainful face at the ring that Vidal gave his fiancée, an episode that would later be the object of semi-humorous arguments between Vidal and Corinne. These arguments would inevitably end with Vidal quoting the Turkish proverb: "He who gives little gives from his heart."

The wedding takes place on June 22, 1920, in the presence of David and Hélène Nahum, as well as Vidal's brothers and sisters, and of course the Beressi family. The contract stipulates a communal estate settlement. The couple leaves on honeymoon to the Alps, as a card written in Fragnol by

Vidal to his parents attests. It was sent from the Chamonix Palace on June 8, 1920, at 6 p.m., and the picture is of the frozen lake:

> Dear Papa and Mama,
> After a 4-hr car journey, we arrived today, the views were truly superb. You can't imagine what the ice and snow here are like. We are very, very well, and our only concern is that we haven't received any letters from you yet.
> I expect Corinne is to blame, she'll have taken the letters and left them in her "poche restante"[39] or purse. Anyway, we hope to receive some letters from you tomorrow, which I hope you have sent to us in Annecy. Until then, we send kisses to you all,
> Your Vidal.

Vidal is in love, as we can see from a card he sends from Mulhouse on October 14, 1920; the card shows a little girl who is looking intently at something:

> My darling little wife,
> Lunica Nahoum
> 10, Rue Mayran
> Paris
>
> Just like this little girl, I am looking hard for you, and I want to see you, my darling Lounica.
> Although I'm far away from you, all of my heart is with you, my Lounica. I can't wait to come and see you and kiss you.
> Your Vidalico who adores you.

Luna soon falls pregnant, but she miscarries, apparently due to natural causes, after three months. The truth is that Luna has had an abortion. Why? In 1917, she fell victim to the devastating Spanish 'flu epidemic, which killed nearly as many people as the First World War. Luna's case had been particularly alarming: Corinne writes, in the letter from which we have already quoted:

She was very seriously ill, and the family who lived in the neighborhood watched over her day and night. The doctor came every morning, afternoon and evening, and listened to her heart and lungs every time; he told my cousin Fortunée that as soon as there was any cause for alarm, she should get in a hackney cab and go to his house so that he could come at once.

Vidal (from his oral autobiography): *That damned Spanish 'flu attacked the heart. So her heart had been weakened* [she had a heart lesion], *and I didn't know anything about it; we get married; there was no medical examination in those days. Two or three months afterwards, she's pregnant, she consults her mother, her aunt, all that, and the result is that they decide not to keep the child.*

In fact, Luna does not realize how serious her lesion is until she is already pregnant, when the doctor advises her to terminate her pregnancy, since childbirth may well kill her. Luna then consults a *faiseuse d'anges,*[40] a woman specialized in abortion practices (which were illegal at the time), who gave her some plant-based treatment . . . *They made her take foot-baths, well, I don't know, to cut it short, there was an abortion. Everything goes well, the doctor comes, fine. Three months later, she's pregnant again.*

Once again, and again without telling her husband, Luna goes to consult the abortionist, but the second time around the treatment fails; the embryo, although thoroughly shaken and perturbed, endures. Now Luna must resign herself to the risk of giving birth.

Her father, Salomon Beressi, dies suddenly of a cardiac arrest on March 31, 1921, when he is only 60 years old. We can imagine how the grief over her father's death and her own reasons for anxiety, which she does not want to betray in front of her husband, must have been bound together in Luna. It is possible that Salomon Beressi had not been informed that childbirth might kill his daughter. Her mother, on the other hand, was told of the danger when Luna was pregnant for the first time, and this time she keeps the secret from Vidal. The midwife whom Luna decides to consult only lets Vidal know the situation when she is about five months pregnant.

So, the midwife examines her, all that, she comes to see me, and says: "Sir, everything is fine, only I'm going to ask you something, I need some information from you, here's my address, come tomorrow."

Fine, so I go the next day, and she says: "You know that your wife has a very agitated, very weak heart, and I admit I don't want to take responsibility for this birth! You will have to go and see a gynecologist, or an obstetrician who's better-qualified than I am, and here's an address."

So, being very careful not to upset her, I speak to her mother, her Dad had already died, and we decide to go and see a gynecologist, a Dr. Schwabe, who had a reputation . . . a kind of Dr. Schweitzer, you'd call him now.

After examining Luna, the doctor reassures her, but informs Vidal in confidence that mother and child are in danger; he tells him that whatever happens he thinks he can save the mother. He tells both of them that they must not have any more children. Luna goes to see him every two weeks and the pregnancy goes well.

BIRTH

The time comes for the baby to be born. At that time, babies were born at home, you had to have a nurse, and the doctor told her what needed to be prepared, bowls of hot water, and so on. The moment comes, in the middle of the night. The gynecologist turns up. He says: "Don't worry." Of course, I was terribly nervous, and all that. And so it went on, and the kid comes out, but he isn't breathing.

84

The child was born feet first, with the umbilical cord wrapped around his neck, and was apparently stillborn. *So I'm in the room next door, I hear a slapping noise, thwack, thwack, thwack. So, very timidly, I open the door a crack and I see him holding up a body like that, as if it were a little rabbit, and he carries on smacking it on its stomach, on its cheeks, on its heart. And finally, the child begins to cry. "Ah!" he says: "That's what I was waiting for," and he says to the nurse: "Go and look after the child, I'll look after the mother."*

Fifty-four years later:

8 July 1975, 6.30 a.m.
My dear Edgar, fifty-four years ago today! After a sleepless night, at dawn, around 4 o'clock, I hear Dr. Schwabe slapping something. I go to the door, and see that he is holding a little body by its feet.

Some minutes go by, which seem endless, and then you make your first cry, he puts you down on your Mama's bed, where she is lying all sore and tender, and he comes back to me: "It wasn't easy," he tells me, "I didn't want to stop hitting him, because he wasn't breathing. Get me an armchair so that I can rest for a while; I want to stay another two or three hours to make sure that Mama recovers and the child stays alive."

Then he asked me to make him some coffee. He went to see your Mama, and you, you were already waving your arms about and crying, and he told me that he was leaving, he wasn't worried about you, and that he would come back around around on this day, the 8th of July, it was very hot, just like today. Fifty-four years ago.

Happy birthday.
With love.
Your Dad.

The child is the first male to be born to the children of both David Nahum and Salomon Beressi. Thus, for the Nahums, it is imperative that he take the name of his grandfather David, who had died the year before. Similarly, for the Beressis, it is imperative that he take the name of his grandfather Salomon, who died a few months before his birth. Vidal and Luna are both charged by their respective families with this sacred mission. They think of reconciling the two sides by calling their son David–Salomon, but the child is immediately called little Davico by the Nahums, and little Salomonico by the Beressis. In order to avoid competition between the two forenames, and having seen the impossibility of inseparably uniting the two in one David–Salomon, Vidal and Luna decide to call him Edgar. The name had already been used in the family, in Salonica, and it is the forename that Léon has in mind for his son, who is born a few months after the son of his younger brother Vidal. This almost simultaneous birth and subsequent coexistence of two cousins with identical forenames (one with, the other without a d), is of no account to the two couples, for each has its own Edgarico: Léon's Edgard, nicknamed Dico,

85

and Vidal's Edgar, first called Bébéco by his family, and later Minou, for a very long time, by his father.

The child's Frenchification begins at once. He is declared a French national, whereas Vidal and his wife are still "Levantine Jews." The double forename David–Salomon, declared at birth, will be succeeded by the *de facto* forename Edgar, and later changed by deed poll.

The child, who will inevitably be an only child, is born. Against the doctor's advice, Luna wants to breast-feed him; she is so obstinate that the doctor gives in and allows her to feed him for a few weeks. Then he is given a bottle, which Bébéco will still be using at an age when other children are already eating with a fork and spoon: as soon as he wakes up, or whenever he wants it during the day, he shouts: *"Bibionico!"* and only calms down when the bottle appears. He might never have given up his *bibionico* if they had not weaned him by wiping the teat with some evil-tasting substance.

The child thrives and becomes chubby-faced, but at the slightest alarm, even the most minor bout of diarrhea, his father starts rooting about in his excrement with his fingers, and calls the doctor. This only child is fussed over and worried about incessantly.

He is circumcised on Friday, 13 July, at Vidal and Luna's home, 10, Rue Mayran. In a series of vulgar prunings, the ritual knife removes the foreskin of the new-born, who henceforth belongs to the people of the Alliance.

V

Frenchification: First Phase (1921–1931)

Just as Salonica had been the main attraction for the Sephardim when they left Spain, France would be the main attraction for the new diaspora of Sephardim from Salonica.

As we saw in Chapter 2, the first wave of would-be intellectuals and fortune-seekers had settled in France at the turn of the century; some began to practice as doctors, dentists or pharmacists, like two of David D. Nahum's nephews, while others went into business, like the Beressi brothers, whose father had died. The Beressis would be among those who succeeded in finding their fortune in France.

Vidal himself had felt very powerfully the drive to emigrate to France, which held the young Sephardim in thrall between 1900 and 1914. At the age of 19, in 1913, Vidal had tried his luck and failed. However, it was inevitable that the Nahum family would leave Salonica sooner or later, as the Beressi and Mosseri families had done. As it turned out, the catalyst for the entire family's emigration to France was the accident of Vidal's arrest. Indeed, the First World War concentrated and amplified the emigration of Salonicians towards France. Vienna had also been a center of attraction at the beginning of the century. But the route to Vienna was cut off between 1914 and 1918, when the frontier became a front; subsequently, with the dislocation of the Austro-Hungarian Empire, the great capital became an enormous swollen head on a dwarflike body, and the few Sephardic islands that had been established in Vienna were dispersed once again.

In 1917, the great fire of Salonica, which destroyed the Jewish city, further increased emigration to France, with which Salonica, where the Eastern Army had its base, was umbilically linked during the First World War.

Marseilles was the first place where the Beressis and the Nahums settled, and it eased their adjustment to the new culture, for Marseilles was at once French and Mediterranean, with both a national and a cosmopolitan identity. During the war, the Nahums in Marseilles continued to live in and on their relationship with Salonica, sending supplies for the Eastern army there. After the war, they attempted to redirect their exports from Marseilles to other countries. However, it became necessary for them to leave the Mediterranean for a capital city in order to continue in business. And so in 1919 the continentalization of the Nahums began: some settled in Paris (Vidal and part of his family), others in Brussels (Léon and his other brothers). Léon managed to maintain his business exporting Belgian metallurgical goods to the Balkans and the Middle East, and created a new incarnation of Nahum Steel, the firm the Nahums had founded in Salonica. But Vidal's import–export business was unsuccessful, and he was obliged to adapt to a new type of job, within the borders of what was not yet known as the Hexagon. In any event, the economic link with Salonica had been broken for good; what remained was the umbilical tie with Uncle Frances who had stayed on there, along with the enduringly vivid memory of the little lost homeland.

The rooting process had begun once again . . .

FAILURE IN GERMANY

The years 1920 and 1921 are marked for Vidal by his father's death, his marriage, the birth of his son, and his move into an apartment in which he will live for many years. These years also see his final attempt to establish and expand his import–export office. After Great Britain becomes inaccessible, and once he recognizes that Czechoslovakia, Yugoslavia and Romania cannot provide a wide enough client base, he tries his luck in Germany, along with Salomon and Samy Beressi, exporting textiles, clothing, and perhaps metals there. An exchange of letters with Samy Beressi dating from this time will be found among his papers, as well as postcards addressed from Germany to his new wife, and a passport that Luna obtains on December 11, 1920 to allow her to visit Germany. The document indicates that Luna has become a "Levantine Jew" like her husband (and thus belongs to the category of "special protégés"), and that the couple is already living at 10, Rue Mayran.

Being a Sephardi, Vidal is not affected by the hatred between the French and the Germans. If, at Frigolet, he had used the word "Boches," it was only by imitation, and he does not use it again. He does not see Germans as his hereditary enemies, nor does he consider them to be the scourge of the human race. He can speak German, which he learned at school, can recite the *King of the Alders*, and is fond of Germany, where he finds the food to his liking. Even after the Second World War, he will feel no hatred for Germans *per se*, and in the 1960s and 70s he enjoys boat trips on the Rhine.

After his engagement, Vidal begins to make expeditions to Germany, initially at the behest of his father-in-law. A letter from Salomon Beressi to Vidal dated October 7, 1920 shows that he is counting on Vidal to try and persuade French firms to purchase German goods, such as aluminum foil for chocolate manufacturers, or knives, forks and spoons, and to find cloth in France for him to export to Germany. The letter ends:

> Give my regards to dear Henri [Vidal's brother]. Kiss dear Luna for me and tell her that I am going to write her a separate letter.
>   A cordial handshake from your Papa.
>   Salomon[41]

Vidal makes several trips to Germany in 1920, and he may have planned to take Luna with him to Brussels and Frankfurt for the end-of-the-year festivities, where they were due to join Salomon Beressi. However, although she has obtained her passport on December 11, Luna remains in Paris (probably because she is three months pregnant and intends to take advantage of Vidal's absence to attempt an abortion). She writes to her father, who is staying at the Excelsior Hotel, in Frankfurt:

> Paris, December 16, 1920
> My dear Papa,
> I am writing you this card to give you some very good news. I want to let you know that my dear Vidal is leaving this evening via Brussels. He is taking the train at 10 something. I think he plans to stay in Brussels for a day and then go on to Frankfurt.
>   With all my love,
>   Luna

Salomon Beressi dies on March 31, 1921. Vidal continues to do business with Samy Beressi. On April 10, Vidal sends his wife two cards from Wiesbaden. He writes:

> Wiesbaden, 4 p.m.
> My darling Luna,
> I am leaving for Frankfurt at 4.30, and Samy is coming to join me tomorrow morning. We had lunch together, and I will write you this evening with all the details from Frankfurt. This is a magnificent city, and it was nice to have some company and see something beautiful. I wish I could have you with me so that you could see how pretty Wiesbaden is. I had a good journey and hope to do the same on my return. I especially hope to find news from you at the Excelsior Hotel when I get back. Stay well and take care of yourself, and all the best to my, to our, dear little son. With love,
>   Your Vidal

The card shows that Vidal is convinced that the child Luna is carrying will be a boy. The "take care of yourself" sounds like an entirely predictable expression of solicitude from a husband to his pregnant wife, and we may surmise that Vidal has not yet been told about Luna's heart problem.

The correspondence with Samy Beressi indicates that they are experi-

encing problems, including difficulties over bank transfers. Vidal, who has
returned to Paris on the 13th, writes to Samy on the 14th. He wants to know
if everything is in order with Sey and Hamm. There is mention of a request
from Sylvain (Benforado? Beressi?) that the sum of 515,025 marks be paid
into Samy's account at the Société Alsacienne in Cologne, and Vidal is
waiting for Samy's response to this request. He adds:

I'm also waiting to hear from you whether I should write to Angel to ask
him kindly to acknowledge Prinz's transfer of 176,136.10 marks, and send
him the letter of payment that Prinz gave me . . . I'm writing to the aluminum
manufacturer today.

On the same day (April 15), Samy writes a letter to Vidal informing him
that the Sey and Hamm firm has received 437 lengths of printed fabric
measuring 21,521.60 meters, and 130 lengths of shirting measuring 5,155.25
meters, and that there are 100 meters of printed fabric and 500 meters of
shirting less than expected. He wonders whether the mistake was made
before delivery or in measuring it once it arrived.

Telegrams and letters between Vidal and Samy cross in the mail. They
are trying to settle a very complex transfer of funds, and also to close an
account left in Germany by Salomon Beressi, who died the month before.

In a letter dated April 16, Samy indicates that things are not going very
smoothly:

> The three lengths of gabardine from my lot should have been delivered by Prinz to
> the Sey and Hamm firm; I am square with them, having had the payment for this mer-
> chandise as well as the others. Sales have been slow for these two gentlemen over
> the past couple of days, probably because of the trade fair closing . . . As for my stock,
> I have not managed to do anything with Sey and Hamm, nor with any other firm.

Samy then mentions that he will be in Cologne in the next few days.
Twenty days later (on May 6, 1921), the sum of German reparations to
the Allies is fixed at 132 billion gold marks. The mark begins to fall during
the summer of 1921, and finally collapses between 1922 and 1923. The
majority of Salomon Beressi's capital is in marks, and his widow finds herself
without resources. Pepo cannot manage the shop on the Boulevard Barbès
and is forced to give it up. However, the tradition of family solidarity means
that Myriam's brothers-in-law and her son-in-law will see to it that she is
not left destitute, and has enough money to raise her two young children.

PUTTING DOWN ROOTS

The Beressi family lives first in the Avenue Parmentier, then the Rue
Sedaine. David D. Nahum had taken lodgings on the Boulevard Voltaire
during his last visit to Paris. The first magnet for Salonicians settling in Paris,

before the First World War, was the Rue Sedaine and the neighboring area around the Place Voltaire, where their colonization of the area's residential buildings and diverse businesses has created a micro-Salonica.

The second magnet, the Sentier, is purely professional. In the years between 1910 and 1925, many Salonicians open stores there selling textiles or hosiery to the trade. Vidal opens a store in the neighborhood, in the Rue d'Aboukir, in 1922; he will stay there for nearly forty years, and for the rest of his life the Sentier will be the center of his professional activities.

The Salonicians who work together in the Sentier live scattered among different residential neighborhoods. Vidal's first homes are not far from the Sentier, first in the Rue Saint-Georges, then the Rue Clauzel, and afterwards, when he marries Luna Beressi, in the Rue Mayran, near the Square Montholon, in the 9th arrondissement. He continues to live there with Luna until 1931. Henriette, his sister, will make her home in a bourgeois street in the 17th arrondissement. There is, therefore, a residential concentration, a little clan of Salonicians, in the 11th arrondissement around the Rue Sedaine, where Myriam Beressi lives, and at the same time a residential dispersion of Salonicians all over Paris.

As time passes, Vidal becomes increasingly immersed in French life. The family's forenames were already translated into French in Marseilles, where Haïm became Henri, Jacob became Jacques, Elena Hélène, and Riquetta Henriette. Vidal remains Vidal, but he is known in the Sentier and in the neighborhood where he lives as Mr. Vidal, as if it were his family name. Although, at home and in his store, he immediately recreated a micro-environment originating in the Ottoman Empire, he did so with the help of a gentile couple: he employs a recent immigrant from Armenia, Wahram, as an assistant in his store, and his wife Macrue (Marie) as a domestic servant. The couple leave Alfortville (where most of the Armenians who came to France after the Turkish massacres had settled), and come to live in the maid's room at 10, Rue Mayran. Macrue, or "little Marie" (so-called not only because she is short, but also because Corinne has employed another Armenian Marie, Macrue Solovian, who is tall) looks after little Edgar when his parents go out in the evening. She is very loving towards the child. An affectionate relationship develops between the Sephardic couple and the Armenian couple; this friendship will continue in spite of Macrue's subsequent divorce, and Vidal's becoming a widower and remarrying. There is mutual trust, with loyalty and familiarity on both sides. A sort of common feeling, a common philosophy of life unites them. They are not conscious of having different religions, but rather of what they have in common: the fact that they are "foreigners" from the East.

Vidal is already completely Parisian, but at the beginning of the 1920s he does not yet feel French. When he is obliged to give up the identity of "Levantine Jew" (probably in about 1925), he does not consider asking for French nationality, but for the time being prefers to take Greek nationality, which is culturally and emotionally foreign to him, but to which the city of his birth now belongs.

VIDAL IN THE SENTIER

After the collapse of the mark, Hananel Beressi, brother of Salomon and uncle of Luna, a man for whom Vidal will feel respect and affection throughout his life, advises Vidal to give up the export business, and open a store instead:

"Don't waste your time in the export business, it's finished, it's dead. You must open a store, like all your . . . ." And as it turned out I bumped into a man I'd been at school with, a Mr. Baron: "Don't waste any time, look, we've opened a store, it was a grocer's, and we've started dealing in socks and stockings, and we're doing OK." He says to me: "In fact, my grocer has a brother-in-law who has a store in the Rue d'Aboukir, I'm going to introduce you to him." And I go to his place. And that's it, I buy the store in the Rue d'Aboukir, and then I make my start in the hosiery business.

Vidal takes the little store at 52, Rue d'Aboukir. The lease is signed on August 24, 1922, and the price is fixed at 2,700 francs for the first six years, 3,200 francs for the next three years, and 3,500 for the last three.

Vidal settles in to the Sentier; from now on, the export side of his business will be merely residual and sporadic, depending on the opportunities that are offered him. He specializes in socks and stockings, primarily aimed at traders and market stall holders in the French market.

The Sentier neighborhood is situated at the heart of Paris, in the 2nd arrondissement; the area that is primarily given over to textiles and hosiery consists of the Rue de Cléry, the Rue d'Aboukir, the little streets around the Place du Caire, and the Rue du Sentier.

To the West is the frantic temple of the Stock Market, where the banks have their head offices, lavish palaces dedicated to bureaucracy and money; to the North are the cafés, theatres and cinemas of the Grands Boulevards; to the East are the prostitutes of the Rue Saint-Denis, with their garish make-up and flesh for sale; to the South is the central market of Les Halles, where food for four million people is poured in and parcelled out again; at the heart of the neighborhood are the thundering rotary presses and the humming vans, motorcycles and bicycles belonging to the big newspapers.

It is a center of frenzied commercial endeavour, bordered by pleasure (the Rue Saint-Denis) and leisure (the Grands Boulevards), overlapped by the different centers that pump out the most powerful flows of money (the Stock Market and the banks), communications (the newspapers), food (Les Halles) and sex (the Rue Saint-Denis) in the capital; near to Les Halles, the belly and the underbelly of Paris are joined together, and their intense activity never slows down, becoming even more frantic at night.

Unlike the Rue des Rosiers, which at the time is colonized by Ashkenazim from Poland and Russia, there is no exoticism here, no fashion or lifestyle, and no external sign other than the names of the storekeepers and the graceless piling up of merchandise in store windows that would attest outwardly to the presence of a foreign community. In fact, the population is very diverse; a few blue-collar Parisians remain in the attic rooms and concierge's lodges, and the factory representatives who visit the neighborhood are French, while the storekeepers are mainly Sephardim. French customers are in the minority, and most customers are foreigners: North Africans, Armenians and Ashkenazim, stall holders and small storekeepers from the provinces or the suburbs.

When she records his oral autobiography, Vidal's granddaughter, Véronique, asks him why he chose the Sentier.

. . . *Already before the war, in 1910, before the European war, all the people from Turkey, whether from Istanbul or Salonica, who came to France, and especially to Paris, to work, all started out in the textile business, in cloth, hosiery, sweaters, and so on, and there were two centers: one over near the Place Voltaire, which was second-rate, where you'd find things that were more mediocre, much poorer quality, and another center that was a little more up-to-date, which was the Sentier, in Paris. So, we were concentrated there so to speak . . . , and at the end of the First World War, in 1920, for instance, it's no exaggeration to say that out of three hundred shops in the Sentier, a hundred belonged to Salonicians . . . We knew each other, we knew who was who, we often ran into each other in the street.*

Indeed, between 1920 and 1939 the Sentier becomes a little *agora*, with its hundreds of stores like cells in a honeycomb, where friends and colleagues meet, and, after exchanging a cheerful *Ke haber?* (What's up?), talk about anything and everything. One time, a Salonician friend of Vidal's came into his shop to bring him some very interesting news: "Did you know, Vidal, that one of our people was a very great philosopher? His name was Baruch Spinoza, he wrote a whole book about tics, it's called *Tics*." "I don't believe it, you're having me on . . . ."

Véronique: *"And why were you all in the hosiery business?"*

Ah! Because the job was easier . . . Fabric was more complicated, you had to have had some training, to be able to say: "That's wool, or it's a mixture, or it's cotton . . . ," whereas in hosiery it was easier. We would buy some socks. The socks cost 3 francs a dozen . . . we'd sell them for 3 francs 50. We'd buy stockings, the same thing, we'd buy cotton panties . . . There was no professional training, so to speak . . . Out of a hundred Salonician traders in the Sentier, eighty were in hosiery, the twenty who had received some training in other stores worked in textiles; there are three or four of them left in the Sentier, in the Rue d'Aboukir, and they're extremely well set-up, there's Mr. Broudo, for instance, in the Rue d'Aboukir, he owns a whole building . . . There's much more money in fabric than in hosiery, but in the end, in hosiery, we did OK, as you can see . . .

Vidal opens a business selling hosiery wholesale, at 52, Rue d'Aboukir.

He is on his own, and he needs capital: *I had some proposals from Mr. X and Mr. Y, to go into business with them, all that, I didn't want to, and finally my brother Léon told me: "Listen, our brother-in-law Élie has no more work in Marseilles, it would be better if he came to Paris and became your associate, that way you're not on your own . . . and if you need me, I'll come and back you up, if necessary."*

In fact, Élie brings a certain sum of money with him, which he invests in the store's business, and in return he receives a percentage of the profits. Every year, they do the accounts, and Élie is paid his share. Does Vidal lack faith in Élie's ability? Élie helps neither with the purchase nor with the sale of merchandise, he never attends to the customers, and never says a word when deals are being struck. Vidal makes him responsible for going to the post office and looking after the shop in his absence. He has much more confidence in his assistant Wahram, who is charged with sending and receiving goods, and various other errands. Élie will accept his status as figurehead with resignation, even satisfaction. In fact, the two brothers-in-law never become close. Vidal seems to have agreed to the solution of an "association" with Élie in order to defer to Léon's opinion, and out of solidarity with his sister. As long as he has the store, he never calls Élie's position there into question.

In the morning, I always opened the store at 8 o'clock. Élie came to work separately, and I came with my assistant Wahram who had the room on the sixth floor, with his wife, who in a manner of speaking raised Edgar . . . So, we were always there before 8 o'clock, and Uncle Élie was very punctual too . . . It wasn't his business, he didn't do the sales, he didn't do the buying, but he acted as a man of trust for me; for example, if I had gone out to see someone, and a customer came in: "Please wait, Mr. Nahum will be back in a few minutes." He knew how to make them wait. When I was traveling, it was the same.

I used to travel twice a week; I went to Troyes, to the factories, to buy oddments and ends of batches . . . I didn't work with the representatives; in fact, the representatives were annoyed with me because I did my business behind their backs, so to speak . . . I didn't buy at the regular price, that's why I had to go to the factories, to Troyes. And during the first few years of my career, it was very hard. I would leave Paris in the evening, I'd arrive at 11 o'clock at night, I slept in a hotel there if there was room, if not I stayed in the station waiting room. At 5 o'clock in the morning I took a coach or another train to go to the little villages nearby (where there were some factories) . . . But I was young enough, I was 30, 34, I could easily stand the traveling and the tiredness and all that . . .

Vidal works hard, from 8 in the morning until 6 in the evening, including Saturdays; he does not respect the Sabbath, he does not take weekends off in the English style, and sometimes goes to the store on Sundays as well, *because some customers who had done well on Saturday wanted to stock up again, so I was obliged to come in on Sunday morning myself.*

The Rue d'Aboukir was visited all the time by stall holders or small businessmen who had shops in Gennevilliers, Aubervilliers, or Noisy-le-Sec, and they would come to the Sentier to buy their stock. They'd go into a store: "Well, sir, I'm looking for black cotton stockings, show me what you have." We'd show him: "OK, such a price." "I'll take ten dozen, I'll take five dozen." In the beginning, in 1921, I used to sell combs and toothbrushes too, which I had left over from the time when I was in the export business, and I carried on with that line; and in fact I had some very good customers who came for example from Lille to buy combs. I would go off to the Ariège where the factories that make horn combs are, I would make my purchases and bring the merchandise back to Paris.

I've had some very good customers, and unfortunately I've also known maybe four or five crooks, people who were bad through and through. For instance, they'd buy eight dozen on a Friday morning, they'd pay and leave; the next day they'd come back: "Ah," they'd say, "you'll have to change them." "But why, my friend, when you've already opened all the packets?" "Yes, but I don't like them!" Well, to cut a long story short, there were some bad people. Luckily they were rare. Otherwise, people were nice. For instance, a customer who used to come from Poitiers. When he wasn't going to come, he'd phone me: "Send me twenty dozen more."

The store is in reality a narrow stall. In the display window, there are stockings and socks tied together in dozens, piled up higgledy-piggledy. A long rectangular table down the middle divides the shop into two narrow symmetrical corridors; Vidal usually stands on the left, and the customers usually stand on the right, but they come over to the left to look at, feel, and pick out socks or stockings, which are piled up in dozens in boxes on both sides, as high as the ceiling. At the back of the shop Vidal has a miniscule office, where he keeps his paperwork, his bills, and his typewriter; the office is screened off by a wooden partition rising to chest height that allows him to keep an eye on the shop. He can go out through the tradesman's entrance, which gives on to the corridor leading to the main door of the building. At the end of this corridor, there is a small yard, in which Vidal later rents storage space for his stock. On the first floor of the building lives the concierge, Mrs. Dauchel, with whom Vidal is on very friendly terms.

The shop is cluttered with boxes that have been sent in, and packages that are ready to leave. Vidal makes up his own parcels. He wraps up the merchandise in stiff brown paper, ties it with string, attaches a little wooden handle to carry it by, and gives it to the customer, or else he sends Wahram with the hand truck to have the packages dispatched by Calberson or some other transport company. The sound that the metallic wheels of the hand truck make on the floor tiles of the corridor, sidewalks and road surfaces is a source of great delight to Vidal's son, who is sometimes brought in to the shop on Thursdays.

Contrary to what Vidal will tell Véronique in his oral autobiography, probably because he finds it more dignified ("Did you talk to your customers much?" "No, *not usually.*"), every transaction is a bargaining process. Vidal haggles over the purchase price in the factories, and he haggles over the sales price with his customers. Since the merchandise in question always consists of oddments and reduced items, the price is subject to negotiation every time. Vidal varies his asking price according to his mood or the customer's appearance. The price that is finally agreed on differs from one customer to the next, and depends on how hard the bargaining has been, as well as a multitude of other factors, which vary according to the time of day and the psychological balance of power established during the negotiation. "Go on, you're my first customer today, I'll make a sacrifice to start the day with, it'll bring me luck and I'll make it up with the others." Or: "Well, you're my last customer of the day, too bad, I'll be eating up my profit."

The typical haggle unfolds in ritual fashion. A client walks in with a disdainful expression on his face, as if he were entering a sewage farm; he contemplates the merchandise with distaste, shrugs his shoulders, turns as if to leave, and then, absent-mindedly, picks up a dozen socks, pulls out a pair, and fingers it; grimacing disgustedly, he demands: "How much?" Vidal takes the pair of socks from him, and strokes them as if voluptuously: "Oh, these are very nice . . . I'll let you have them for 15 francs." "What!" cries the customer, laughing as if at something ludicrous, and immediately heads for the door. Just before he disappears from view, he calls: "6 francs." Vidal looks aghast. "But I pay 12 francs for them myself! I'll show you the bill! I can't do it! Look, I'll make an effort, thirteen francs, it's my last price."

Then the ferocious bargaining begins in earnest. The customer takes back the socks, offers a new price, and then, at Vidal's answer, throws them down as if they were filth. To bring the process to an end, he gives his last price, and Vidal, looking aggrieved, says: "No, no," puts the pair back in its packet, and the packet back in its box. However, neither man's last price is the real last price. Sometimes, the customer leaves and comes back five minutes later, and the discussion begins again; sometimes he does not come back at all; usually, an agreement is eventually made and Vidal, looking defeated, says: "I'm losing money on this deal, I assure you that I'm losing out, it's all right this once, but next time it won't be possible." And so, all day long, most of the sales end with "I'm making a loss on this deal, I'm losing money." At the end of one Thursday afternoon, his son says to him, horrified: "But Dad, you've lost a lot of money today." Vidal winks at him, and replies, with a sly smile: "Don't you worry, my Minou."

In fact, Vidal is not interested in socks and stockings, he is interested in his business. Although he puts all his energy into it, he still has not acquired a feel for textures, substances or colors, and relies on buyers' demands and suppliers' recommendations: "This is very popular at the moment." His lack of expertise makes him restrict himself to oddments, seconds, and reduced items, and the oddments, seconds, and reduced items make it impossible for him to gain any expertise. For more than a decade his inventory will include stockings in repulsive colors and hideous socks, and only the German occupation of 1940, and the resulting restrictions and scarcity of merchandise, will eventually allow him to get rid of what is unsellable, and even get a good price for it.

He is always obliged to bargain ferociously, because he sells very cheap merchandise to stall holders from poor suburbs, who need to sell as cheaply as possible themselves and consequently haggle over prices that are already very low, for reduced items and seconds, even thirds, pairs with mismatched colors, and all kinds of faults; it is over the lowest grade of merchandise that the bargaining is hardest.

Still, Vidal has one piece of luck, which he owes to his cheerful and pleasant personality. He is well-liked by some of the manufacturers, and most importantly he is a particular favorite with Mr. Doré, who owns the DD hosiery factory in Romilly, near Troyes. Because of his affection for Vidal, he gives him priority, in fact exclusivity, on the DD brand's entire stock of reduced items, oddments and seconds. At the time the brand is very well known and has a good reputation, and this gives Vidal a veritable monopoly in the Sentier on all cheap DD stockings and socks. Vidal reserves this merchandise for his best customers, and when haggling, always has the advantage of being able to point out: "But that's DD!"

In this way, exerting himself a great deal, earning a pittance on each item, but selling a fair amount, not suffering financially from his incompetence, continuing to put his polyvalence to good use by selling DMC thread to foreign customers, taking advantage of whichever business opportunities haphazardly and unexpectedly turn up (such as importing jute bags from India), Vidal prospers in the years between 1921 and 1930. However, he cannot expand his business; he still wants to do most of the work himself, and therefore cannot envisage taking on a bigger store, with responsible assistants or staff other than the faithful Wahram. He will never be a successful businessman like Samy, who becomes the owner of a department store in Paris. He achieves a moderate level of comfort, which allows him to go to good restaurants occasionally, such as the Grange-Batelière or the Reine-Pédauque, to go out in the evening, make excursions, take winter holidays in Sainte-Maxime, and summer holidays in Aix-les-Bains. By 1929 to 1930, he has saved enough money to buy some land in the suburbs and to begin building what ought to have been an attractive house; he passes his driving test at this time and acquires a little four-seater Fiat. Just then, however, he is hit by a crisis and a catastrophe, almost at the same time.[42]

THE RUE MAYRAN

Vidal becomes settled when in fall 1920 he rents the apartment at 10, Rue Mayran, where his son is born, and where he will remain for the next ten years. The Rue Mayran is at the foot of the slope that rises into the hill of Montmartre, and is only twenty or thirty minutes' walk from the Sentier. It is in a lower-middle class neighborhood, in which immigrants in general and Sephardim in particular are rare; in fact, in the Rue Mayran, the only Sephardim are Vidal and Luna.

Vidal's apartment is on the third floor and includes a little balcony from which Bébéco will one day drop a bottle of eau de Cologne, which breaks on the head of a passer-by. The living room and the bedroom look onto the street. In this bedroom, Bébéco's little iron bed with railings will remain in place for a long time; in the morning, after his father gets up, he loves to climb into his mother's bed and drink his *bibionico*. Later, Bébéco, by now known as Minou, sleeps in his little bedroom and spends most of his time there. The entrance hall divides the apartment in two; first the living room, then the bedroom are on the left; the dining room and the child's room are on the right, with windows looking out onto the yard; between the two is the kitchen, which is of average size. The family unit includes Marie or Macrue, who is nearly always there: Macrue is short, has quite dark skin and a subtle, gentle, beautiful Armenian face; she cooks, washes, cleans, and looks after the child. She baby-sits for him in the evening, with her husband Wahram when he gets back from work, whenever Vidal and Luna go out. The child protests when his parents leave, tries to go with them and beats with his fists on the closed door, screaming. However, Vidal and Luna's love for him does not stop them from going out regardless.

Bébéco becomes Minou. After a period of wearing his hair long and wavy like a little girl, they turn him into a little boy. He has frequent health problems, indigestion, diarrhea and bouts of urticaria, and old doctor Lehman is called out, prescribing Calomel for the child's weak liver, and Carabanas water, a vile salty solution, for indigestion. The child has the usual childhood ailments, including the sudden fevers that terrify parents, and are a particular source of anxiety to these parents of a child who will never have brothers and sisters.

After Dr. Lehman retires, Dr. Amar becomes the family doctor, or rather the child's doctor, for Vidal, apart from sore throats and pharyngitis, is never ill and hates taking medicine. It is because he feels powerless when faced with his son's fevers and illnesses that he calls Dr. Amar, who reassures him with his smiling face, his little goatee beard and his satisfied "good!" after each auscultation or taking of temperature. The child also suffers from a strange malaise, which sometimes comes over him when he is at table; he feels the urge to yawn widely, a need to take in air, as if he were suffocating, but he cannot yawn if anybody is looking at him, so he hides under the table, where he is protected by the cloth, and comes out again once he has recovered his composure. Is it related to his birth, when he was suffocated by the umbilical cord? Dr. Amar is not concerned about the symptom, and so Minou's bouts of suffocation are seen as normal and do not cause alarm.

The child grows. He learns to walk in Aix-les-Bains, where his parents like to go on holiday, and where they rent a little apartment. In 1925, Vidal opens a savings account for his son, then aged 4. It eventually reaches the sum of 480 francs, but, probably because of financial difficulties, Vidal is obliged to draw on this account, which is reduced to 4.20 francs by 1936. The child plays in his little room and has no playmates until he is old enough to go to school. He often sees his cousin Fredy, Corinne's son, but Fredy is two years younger, and the age difference only ceases to matter later. So he lives in the cocoon of his little room, enveloped in his mother's love, protected by his father's love, mothered in a different way by his Aunt Corinne, who plays the role of second mother, and Macrue, who plays the role of foster mother. He refuses to go to school when the time comes for him to join first grade infant's class. His parents do not insist on his going, until, after school has begun, a notice from the Town Hall arrives enjoining them to make their child fulfil his scholarly obligations, and they are forced to obey. Luna is very anxious that her son should go to the *lycée* and not to the neighborhood school, and she wants him to stay on in high school until graduation. Vidal, on the other hand, hopes that Edgar will be able to start business school as soon as possible, so that he can join his father's business in the Rue d'Aboukir, and eventually take it over. Vidal had worked for his father, and he sees Salonicians around him, in the Sentier, who are delighted to bring their sons into their businesses; he dreams of having Edgar at his side, and, in time, handing the store over to him (by then it will be "Nahoum and Son"), while he, Vidal, watches over him, advises him, enjoys some leisure, and thus grows old peacefully in the Sentier. By chance, there is a business school almost opposite the Lycée Rollin (now Decour), in the Avenue Trudaine. All his life, until the end, Vidal tells his son: "Ah! I got the wrong sidewalk, I should have taken you to the business school, but stupidly I took you to the Lycée Rollin instead," and, in this joke which becomes a ritual, there will always be some residual regret.

The day comes when Minou has to be taken to school. He refuses to get up, and is removed from his bed by force and cunning: his parents promise that his first day at school will be put off until later. By the same means, they slip on his uniform. He clings to the apartment door, screaming. Vidal prises him off and drags him down the stairs. The screams get louder in front of the concierge's lodge, and the concierge comes out, expecting some appalling spectacle, such as a piglet about to have its throat cut. Once he has been wrenched off the door of 10, Rue Mayran, the prostrate child, pulled along by his father, is taken up the Rue Rochechouart, then the Rue Turgot, and arrives at last in front of a huge and sinister building. School has already begun. Minou, weeping, again begs his father not to imprison him in this school. A monitor appears, accompanies the father and child as far as the door of Infants Class 3; the door opens, and the child stops screaming and cowers like a frightened animal when he sees about thirty other children who turn their heads and stare at him. The mistress, Miss Courbe, leads him to a seat at the back of the room; he runs to the door, but it is closed and locked, and his father has disappeared; the other pupils laugh at him, while he remains silent, trembling with fear, until the end of the morning. When school is over, his father is not in the visitor's room, and he thinks that he has been abandoned forever and bursts into tears; in fact, Vidal is busy with a customer and has sent Wahram, who arrives a little late. Student Nahoum thus makes his entry into civil life. He will gradually make some friends and will eventually get used to the *lycée*. In tenth grade,[43] he begins to read insatiably, at home and everywhere else, throughout the day. His enormous consumption of books earns him good marks in dictation; his tenth grade, then ninth grade, teacher, Mr. Marquand, gives his parents guidance in their choice of books for him. He confirms Luna in her intention to have him continue his studies. She wants him to have a professional career. Vidal puts up a feeble resistance, as a matter of principle. Finally, one year after Luna's death, at the end of Edgar's junior schooling, instead of sending his son to the business school he has him enter sixth grade at the same school, the Lycée Rollin. Edgar is not destined to follow the Sentier path.[44]

PARISIAN LIFE

Vidal's life in Paris, during the years between 1920 and 1930, still has various enclaves of the Orient and Mediterranean features, some of which are also Parisian ones. For many years, despite being a northern city, Paris was also an extraverted, Mediterranean-style one, with its café terraces, its people-watchers, and its leisure.

The apartment in the Rue Mayran is decorated like a French apartment, but contains two little fragments of the Ottoman Empire, which are on their way to becoming French: the Sephardic couple, who had already absorbed a good deal of French substance in Salonica, and the Armenian couple, whose cultural integration is quicker than it would have been if they had stayed in Alfortville.

Vidal gets up early in the mornings, at about 6.30 or 7. He starts singing and whistling the moment he wakes up, washes his face with soap, and splashes it vigorously with cold water; then, still singing and whistling, he approaches his son's little bed. The boy wakes up slowly and with difficulty, and Vidal sings, to the military tune for reveille:

*Minou, up you get, Minou, up you get
Minou, up you get now quick!*

He eventually manages to coax his son out of bed and leaves for the store, which he opens before 8 a.m.; he closes at around 6 or 6.30 in the evening, lowers his iron curtain, and puts on the padlock. Sometimes, Luna comes to collect him; Corinne also goes to pick up her husband, Joseph Pelosoff, who has a store in the Sentier like Vidal. The two couples go for an aperitif at a café in the Rue Favart, where they listen to an Italian singer who accompanies himself on the mandolin. Sometimes, they go to Poccardi's Italian restaurant, on the Boulevard des Italiens.

Who is Luna? Her son will remember an immense love, but will not be able to define her character. Edgar never speaks of Luna to his father, and Vidal never mentions her to his son. His granddaughter, Irène, is curious: "When the time was right, I asked him to talk to me, just between the two of us, about Luna, the family's painful ghost: 'What was she really like? Was she pretty? Did you really love her?' 'Yes, she was pretty, yes I loved her, she liked to enjoy herself, to go out, poor thing, but . . . ' 'But what?' 'She wasn't easily satisfied, she wanted . . . more, always more . . . .' ." When Edgar questions Macrue or Émy, they will say and repeat (but could they have said anything different?) that she was very kind, very loving: "She thought only of others"; she loved her mother and her sisters very much. She is discreet, "rather reserved" (Émy), does not confide her troubles or her worries. Who is Luna?

Luna leads the life of a housewife. In the morning, she buys her produce from the stalls and the greengrocers at the bottom of the Rue Rochechouart, and she takes her son along with her as soon as he is old enough to walk, before he goes to school. She often sees her mother and her sister Émy, who lives at Myriam Beressi's house, and especially her sister Corinne, with whom she goes on outings, and who looks after her son one day a week. That day is bath day, for Luna has no bath in her apartment. Corinne bathes, cleans, and dries her nephew and her own children in turn. Luna and Corinne often go to the Galeries Lafayette; after inspecting the goods on sale, they go for something to eat and drink at the tearoom. Luna likes to take her son with her, and is delighted when people exclaim, first: "Oh, what a lovely baby!" then, "Oh, what a beautiful little girl!," and finally, when he has short hair and is dressed in a little sailor suit: "Oh, what a lovely little boy!" She takes great care in dressing her son, and has suits made for him by the "little dressmaker" on the Boulevard de Ménilmontant where she and Corinne have their dresses copied from designs by fashionable couturiers. In the evenings, as we have said, she sometime joins Vidal for an aperitif, and she accompanies him on his dinners and outings in the evening.

What Luna loves most are Italian operas and *bel canto*, and she collects records by Tito Schipa. She enjoys the Argentinian tangos of Carlos Gardel and Bianco Bachicha, whose records she also has. Vidal and Luna both love the Spanish songs that Raquel Meller made fashionable in Paris in the twenties, particularly *La Violetera* and *El Relicuario*. The Salonicians' Spanish and Italian cultural backgrounds emerge very clearly in the Parisian environment: Corinne's husband, Joseph Pelosoff, particularly loves the anthem to Garibaldi, and has the record. Vidal's first and enduring love is for French *caf'conc'* and music-hall songs, from Mayol and Perchicot, which he always sings with feeling, to Georgius and Marie Dubas. Luna is particularly keen on opera and anything Italian, Vidal on popular songs and anything Spanish. These records, which Luna and Vidal often play (there is no radio yet), become the background music to their son's childhood. Before he knows how to read, he can recognize them by the design of their labels. When relatives, cousins and visitors come into the living room, and sit around the record player, they play a game in which they rearrange the order of the records, put them on at random, and then ask Minou for a particular song; Minou immediately finds the record, and is embarrassed and pleased when they applaud him delightedly. They ask him what his trick is, but he does not know how he recognizes them.

The couple enjoy both Eastern and Western cooking. Their everyday food is fairly westernized. However, when the family eats at Myriam Beressi's house or at Henriette Hassid's (where Vidal's mother does the cooking), Sephardic and Salonician cuisine takes precedence. The aperitif is usually raki, served with hard-boiled eggs, or better, oven-baked duck eggs (*uevose de baba ahaminados*), and fresh cucumber cut into strips and eaten with salt. The first course is the traditional *pastellico*, a big cheese, eggplant or spinach tart cooked in the baker's oven, followed by oven-baked mullet or Marseilles red mullet, tomatoes, eggplants or peppers stuffed with meat (lamb or a mixture of lamb and veal), chicken with spinach stalks, *arroz con fijones* (rice with haricot beans) to which everyone helps himself in the proportions he prefers, *cachcaval* (Balkan sheep's cheese), and *sotlach* (cream of milk and Maïzena flour baked in the oven). At Myriam Beressi's house, there is always some sweet treat, *rosquitas*, *charopes*, or *toupichtis*, which she makes herself. This Sephardic cuisine has its own originalities within the Balkan ensemble, and it retains traces of the Spanish past, such as *rosquitas*, or the delicious *bunuelos*, soaked in honey. It is a matricial cuisine,[45] which is found in its integrity in the homes of Vidal and Luna's parents, and it delights their son, who, as a small child, begins his lifelong love affair with the eggplant.

Family meals are cheerful, convivial and sociable. At Myriam Beressi's house, in the Rue Sedaine, where everyone speaks Spanish, they are more good-natured, free and easy, *Selanikli*. At the Rue Demours, Henriette Hassid's house, the atmosphere is more formal, and French and Spanish alternate. After dinner, at Henriette's, the family goes through to the living room, where the men sit on one side, the women on the other, and each group conducts its own conversation. Sometimes they set up a bridge table, but Vidal does not play cards. Sometimes, too, Liliane, Henriette's daughter, goes to the piano and plays whatever the guests want to hear.

The meals at the Grange-Batelière restaurant are group outings. Every time a member of the family from Brussels or Belgrade comes to Paris, there is a ceremonial meal there. Here Parisian cuisine predominates, with the luxury of caviar and smoked salmon to start the meal. Sometimes they also spend Christmas Eve at this restaurant. Another sign of Vidal and Luna's gradual Frenchification is their adoption of Christmas and Father Christmas. On the night before Christmas, they wait until their son is asleep, go out to a show, and come back on tiptoe to lay his toys on the floor beside the row of shoes; then they disappear again for their party. One Christmas Eve, Minou, who is curious to see what Father Christmas looks like, pretends to go to sleep, but forces himself to stay awake; he hears a noise, closes his eyes, senses through his eyelids that a light has been turned on, and hears his parents whispering. He catches a glimpse of their strange disguise, and sees them lay some toys down in the fireplace, which seem to have appeared from nowhere. The next day, he does not tell his parents that he has discovered their secret, preferring to leave them under the illusion that he remains under their illusion. But he reveals to his cousin Fredy that Father Christmas does not exist; in fact, the grown-ups go off on the night before Christmas to participate in some ceremony with strange rites, where they wear pointed cardboard hats and put little paper trumpets in their mouths, and thus disguised they bring back presents for the children, which they lay down in the fireplace. Fredy, who is two years younger, cannot believe this story, which is even stranger than the one about Father Christmas.

Vidal likes to have fun. Already, in Salonica, David Nahum, his father, had introduced the family to the strictly western custom of excursions, weekends and meals at good restaurants. Vidal spent his youth in Salonica having fun. He continues to have fun in Marseilles, while working at the same time. In Paris, in spite of his complete dedication to his work, Vidal retains and intensifies his Mediterranean sense of leisure. As we have said, the concerned attention that Luna and Vidal devote to their son does not prevent them from going out in the evenings, or going alone on holiday; they leave the child with Macrue in the evenings, and with Corinne when they go on short winter or spring vacations; since Edgar's birth Corinne has been a second mother to him. English influence is probably less important than the Mediterranean tropism in motivating Vidal and Luna's choice of Saint-Maxime, on the Mediterranean, as their destination in January or February. However, from the age of four onwards, Minou will accompany his parents, see the sea for the first time, and see his father in a striped, convict-style swimming costume. He will dip his feet in the water without daring to go any further, and delight in the scent and colors of the mimosas in bloom.

HOLIDAYS

In summertime, the couple prefers lakes and mountainous landscapes. Aix-les-Bains is a favorite destination for Luna and Vidal, who spend their summer holidays there from 1920 onwards, as we can see from the following postcard, which shows a panoramic view of the town, and is addressed by Luna to her mother, at 10, Boulevard Barbès:

> My dearest Mama,
> *Sûrement ya vérias Vidal esta maniana i te conto por nozotros que estamos muy buenos la caza que dormimos mutcho bueno i te estamos asperando un punto mas presto i estate segura que Vidal ya se va a ocupar de los ijos, mira ver de venir mas presto el tiempo aqui es muy bueno la caza la tomimos mutcho mas barata porque dechimos arkilas a otros dos camaradas vente presto te abrasso de todo corasson.*
> Luna

> (You must have seen Vidal this morning, and he will have told you that we are very comfortable in the house, that we slept very well and that we are expecting you a little earlier [than arranged]; don't worry, Vidal will look after the boys [Pepo and Benjamin]. Try and come as soon as you can, the weather here is beautiful, we got the house for much less because we asked two other friends to rent it, come soon, with all my love, Luna.)

Three other cards from Luna, written to her husband from Aix-les-Bains, were found among Vidal's papers, one from July 1922, addressed to 5, Rue Clauzel (before the Rue d'Aboukir), the two others from summer 1924. One of these is addressed to the Rue Mayran and the other to the Rue d'Aboukir:

> My dear Vidalico,
> We got back yesterday evening without any difficulty; Bébéco and I slept very well. Did you? I would very much like to know whether you are not too weary. Today, the weather is glorious, and darling Bébéco has already gone out for a walk with his dear Aunt Corinne. I shared a bed with Mama and I slept very well.
> Many kisses from your Luna

Two years later:

> Dear Vidal,
> How was the journey back, did you sleep well on the train? Or did you look at the scenery instead? We are all very well, we slept very well and ate well at breakfast, and here we are ready at 10 o'clock to go out for a walk, and Marie is going to do the cooking, she is in the middle of preparing us a delicious meal. Baby has been very sweet, he slept very well too. There's no more room, but I kiss you tenderly, and so does Baby.
> Luna

Probably a few weeks later:

Friday.

Dear Vidal,

I received your letter, and I was happy to have your good news. All of us are very well. Your letters are very short. I don't know why you have to dash them off like that, as if it were some onerous task.

Baby is very well, he is asking for his *semanahica* [or allowance, meaning the little present he receives once a week] and all his toys arrived in a dreadful state. See if you can buy him something without other [an Italianism: *senz altro*].

Love from us both.

Luna

On August 1 of the same year, having come to join Luna in Aix-les-Bains, Vidal sends the following card to Élie Hassid, his "partner," who has remained on guard in the Rue d'Aboukir:

Dear Élie,

Received your letter and look forward to hearing from you tomorrow as well, and on Sunday. On Monday I expect to be in Paris, tell Mama *ke estamoz passando magnifique* [that we are having a wonderful time].

Your Vidal

Thus, even in mid-summer, Vidal continues to work, traveling backwards and forwards between Paris and Aix-les-Bains, where Luna has settled into a Beressi *querencia* with her sister Corinne and her mother. Vidal is certainly less loving and less attentive these days, but the couple communicate in their love for Bébéco.

A card Luna sends to Vidal from Aix-les-Bains, on July 5, 1927, shows her posing playfully with her sister Corinne in front of a gothic window, surrounded by leafy branches (possibly a photographer's decor):

My dear husband,

Greetings from La Potinière where we had a very good supper. Admire my very ugly mug.

The next day, she sends him another card on which she is in a slightly different pose, again with her sister Corinne and in front of the same scenery:

Yesterday evening I sent you one picture, here's another, just as ugly as the first.

Luna

In a card Luna sends at the end of July 1927, during an excursion to the Sierroz gorges, the terseness of her style is softened by the sweet diminutive of the signature:

Greetings from Lunica.

105

Thus for years Aix-les-Bains almost becomes their fixed summer residence. Luna and Corinne like going for tea at La Potinière, and they walk as far as the lake, where Vidal remembers some lines from Lamartine, and declaims with pathos:

L'année à peine a fini sa carrière . . . [46]
He recites, sighing deeply:
O temps, suspends ton vol![47]

From Aix-les-Bains, they go for drives around the lake, they take the Mont Revard rack railway, and, when Mathilde and Bouchi, and Vidal's nieces Liliane and Aimée and their husbands arrive, expeditions are organized to the Lac d'Annecy, or Lake Geneva. They take boat trips on these lakes, and Vidal is happy, *kief,*[48] resting his head on Luna's shoulder.

It is in Aix-les-Bains that Edgar learns to walk, and, when he is about four, he wins the beautiful baby prize in a flower-decked competition, where he poses on his little tricycle, festooned with flowers. The first prize is a wheelbarrow, and the second is a ball. When he is given the wheelbarrow, he cries because he has not been given the ball; after deliberation, the jury decides to give him the ball instead, and he starts crying again because he has not been given the wheelbarrow.

In 1928 and 1929 Vidal, Luna, Corinne, Joseph and their children spend the summer at Challes-les-Eaux, a spa town reputed to cure sore throats and ear problems, which is situated not far from Chambéry, and is therefore also near to Aix-les-Bains. Vidal, who is susceptible to throat infections, takes a cure there, which entails visits to the pump-room, gargling, sprays and nose drops, under the supervision of Dr. Vincent, who prescribes a similar cure for his son. In 1928 or 1929, Edgar at last receives the present he has been longing for: a Peugeot bicycle, ordered for him in Chambéry. After his mother's death, this bicycle will be his friend, his escape companion and source of exhilaration when he flies along on it at high speed. In 1929 or 1930, Vidal decides to buy a car in preparation for his move to Rueil, in the suburbs, and he takes driving lessons. On a mountain road, he misjudges a turning and manages to stop the car, in which Luna and Edgar are sitting, with one wheel hanging over the edge of the cliff. He perseveres with his driving lessons, but finds them difficult, for he is excessively cautious, and feels afraid behind the wheel. Nobody knows how he manages to pass his driving test. He will not drive the little Fiat he buys second-hand for long; he will sell it, and will even forget everything that he had learned in order to be able to drive.

In 1929 or 1930, Vidal, Luna and Edgar make an excursion to the Vosges, around Lake Gérardmer. They admire a famous bearded woman, whom the coachload of tourists goes to visit at her home. All of a sudden comes a brutal shock, a warning sign: the flock of tourists has been following a path that leads to a well-known cave. After this walk, which may have been a little too steep for her, Luna feels faint, and sits down on a rock; the others surround her, put their arms around her, and give her alcohol or eau de Cologne to sniff. Vidal is anxious, her son is tearful. Luna comes round, rests a little, and then gets up and walks back to join the flock leaning on her husband's arm, with her son holding her other hand. "Death, that monster who knows neither law nor impediment," had spread "his wings" for the first time over its future victim.

THE NAHUMS (1920–1930)

Léon Nahum had moved to Brussels with his wife Julie and his daughter Chary, and he had a son, Edgard, in 1921. Under his management, Nahum Steel's business has prospered; in 1928 he receives the medal of the "Order of Leopold II," and it is probably at about this time that he acquires Belgian nationality for himself and his family.

His brother Jacques, who remains an Italian national, works with him: he continues to read, and collects his favorite authors' works in good editions. His two daughters, Régine and Hélène, are raised entirely in the French way.

Henri's job in Léon's company both protects him and allows him to be independent. His office communicates with that of Nahum Steel, and deals in a wide variety of transactions, including importing cheap Japanese products into Belgium. He has begun to live with a gentile, a Frenchwoman from Brittany, Gaby Coatsaliou. At first, she does not dare introduce him to her rather anti-Semitic family; Henri does not dare introduce her to his mother either, because he is living with her out of wedlock.

In 1930, Léon rents an apartment at, 49 Rue Demours for his wife to live in, since she is not happy in Brussels; Edgard's name is put down for the Lycée Carnot, and Chary becomes a boarder at the Lycée Victor-Duruy. Léon comes to Paris every weekend for over a year and a half, until the situation becomes unbearable and he repatriates his wife and his son.

Henriette, Vidal's older sister, lives at 18, Rue Demours, with her mother, her husband and her two daughters, Liliane and Aimée. Henriette feels no allegiance to religious prescriptions, and is very "up-to-date," but her husband Élie is still incapable of allowing a gentile to sit at his table.

The elder daughter, Liliane, is dark, intelligent like her mother, but less energetic, and very musical. In Marseilles, she won second prize from the Conservatory of Music for her piano-playing. She also met and fell in love with a young man from a poor family, who loved her in return. However, her mother would not contemplate allowing her daughter to marry beneath her, nor would she envisage her becoming a professional pianist. So Liliane is still waiting to be married. The younger daughter, Aimée, has blonde hair and very blue eyes, a pretty and appealing face, and a tiny waist, which she will retain all her life. She is very attractive. A gentleman accosts her in the tram one day, in her mother's presence, and offers to make her an actress. Her mother haughtily refuses this degrading proposition, but is nevertheless flattered at the idea that her daughter could have become a star like Mary Pickford.

Liliane, Aimée and Chary are of the generation who spent their child-hood in Salonica. They will get married in France during the 1920s. The eldest of them, Liliane, will follow the Salonician tradition: her marriage is eventually arranged by her parents, and her husband is a Salonician. Aimée is the first to break the rules and marry a man from Smyrna, with whom there is mutual attraction. None of the Nahums has yet married a gentile.

Vidal plays a role in Liliane's marriage. One of his friends in the Sentier is Mony Covo, Samuel Covo's son. Samuel had been Modiano's chief clerk in Salonica, and was an important representative for big Western firms, including Bayer. As we have seen in Chapter III, Mony was deported from Marseilles in 1917 to serve in the Greek army; his ship was torpedoed at Malta, and he escaped the war. On his return to France, he rented a shop in the Sentier, in the Rue d'Aboukir, about four hundred yards from Vidal's. Vidal and Mony are already in the habit of greeting one another and speaking in the street; during a train journey to Troyes they form a stronger bond.

Since he was in hosiery and I was in hosiery, we both went nearly twice a week to Troyes in the Aube, and on my way back one day I get into the carriage and I see Mony. So we talked a bit more, we chatted about this and that, and that was how (we became acquainted) . . . In the meantime, in Paris, Dr. Modiano, who was already a dignitary, meets my elder sister, Liliane's mother, and says: "You have a daughter and I have a young protégé, who I'm very fond of, his father is a friend of mine, let's introduce them to each other and see if anything comes of it."

The Oriental Association for Salonicians in Paris used to hold dances. About fifty families would attend. Of these fifty families, there were let's say fifteen young men and women; so Aunt Henriette, Uncle Élie [he is speaking to his granddaughter Véronique], *Liliane and Aimée went to the dance, but I think Aimée was more popular with the gentlemen than Liliane. So then comes this conversation with Dr. Modiano, who sings Mony's praises, and they consult me and I say: "I know him too; yes he's a boy from a good family, and yes, he's working in Paris as a store-keeper."*

An afternoon date is arranged at the Porte Dauphine, in the Bois de Boulogne. Henriette, Élie, Vidal and Luna accompany Liliane.

When they have finished eating their supper, Henriette invites young Mony to tea at her house, one evening the next week.

In the meantime, Dr. Modiano also gets involved, he comes back to see Aunt Henriette, he says to her: "Listen, you mustn't hesitate; I've spoken to the boy, he wants to get married, you're offering a good dowry, he has a good situation, his family in Salonica has a good situation, I've already written to his parents in Salonica, and the father has given his unreserved consent." So Dr. Modiano oiled the wheels a bit on one side and the other, and the engagement took place. And after the engagement came the wedding, and Covo's father, mother and brother, the whole family, came over from Salonica for the wedding.

Liliane's wedding to a Salonician, in 1926, is followed by Aimée's to a man from Smyrna, Isidore Benmayor. Isidore had come from Smyrna to study at a Parisian high school, between 1921 and 1922. Vidal was his "correspondent" in Paris, and Isidore would come to the Rue Mayran on his days off. He was on very cordial terms with Vidal and Luna. When he finished at the high school, his parents sent him to Liverpool, where they had business contacts, to set up an office there importing raisins and figs from Smyrna.

So it was 1928 or 29, and there I am one day in my store, the day before a holiday, and Isidore comes in — he was called Isidore then, now he's called Ben.

"Well, how are you?"

We embrace each other. "How is Luna?" he asks, "I've come to spend Christmas in Paris."

"Great."

"What are you doing for Christmas?" he says.

"Well, to tell the truth we have lots of plans, maybe we can have the Christmas meal together somewhere . . . "

"Ah!," he says, "see what you can do . . . Listen, shall I come back this afternoon?"

"Come back tomorrow so we can set something up."

And now, you see how strange fate can be, really peculiar: we used to go to a very good restaurant which has changed now, in the Rue de la Grange-Batelière, it was a marvelous restaurant, very good, not expensive, the owner was very nice, very cordial, and so on, and we had reservations for four for Christmas Eve, for me, your Dad's Mom [Luna], Aunt Corinne and her husband. I don't know what happened, but Aunt Corinne and her husband couldn't come. In the meantime, then, my friend Isidore comes back to the store. So I say: "Listen, we're going to have Christmas dinner in a restaurant, join us if you like . . . " I say: "But first we're going to my sister Henriette's house this afternoon, she wants to see you too, and she has invited you for an aperitif."

Vidal, who in later life will love arranging meetings that might lead to a match, may already have had a taste for it, and the invitation to his sister's house is not entirely innocent. During the aperitif, Henriette declares:

"Aimée will go with you."

And, indeed, we all met up on Christmas Eve, and off we went. And it was love at first sight! They started dancing together; we were all in high spirits. So the least we could do was say to him: "Listen, tonight we're going to dance until dawn, but tomorrow evening, come and have dinner at our house." So that was it, one thing led to another . . . How strange fate can be!

One year later, on Tuesday April 8, 1930, a big wedding was held for Aimée and Isidore. All the Nahums from Brussels and Belgrade, and all the Benmayors from Izmir were present. One wedding led to another. While he was at high school in Paris, the groom, Isidore, had become friendly with Hiddo Levi, the nephew of one of his family's correspondents, and so Hiddo was invited to Isidore's wedding and met Chary there. Chary was a beautiful young girl with a gentle, languorous face, always smiling and apparently serene, amiable and benevolent. Hiddo was himself an attractive and cheerful young man, who spoke with a Southern accent like the rest of his Avignon-based family. He was born in Smyrna in 1900, and his family was probably of Livornese origin, since he had Italian nationality. His relatives on his mother's side, the Amados, had already settled in France, and his sister Ruth had married a Naquet from Avignon. After graduating from the Lycée Lakanal in Paris, Hiddo attended the Ecole Polytechnique in Zurich, where he studied engineering. However, in 1920, at his sister Ruth's wedding, he was given an offer to join the Naquet family business, processing teasels from the garrigue for the wool-combing process, which was run by his brother-in-law. (Achille Naquet's father had founded the firm in around 1870, after the collapse of the market in madder dye.) So Hiddo specialized in teasels.

Hiddo and Chary liked each other and very soon married, in 1930. Chary left for Avignon with her husband and settled into life with a very likeable clan there.

Meanwhile, Mathilde, the Nahum's youngest sister, is far away in Belgrade. Bouchi is rich. They live a life of "high society." Bouchi even seems to have been governor of the Bank of Yugoslavia for a time. Mathilde writes very often to her sister Henriette and to her brothers, and complains that Vidal, whom she nicknames Coco and whom she often teases, does not write to her often enough. She frequently sends Belgrade sausage, which the family adores, by courier or by mail, and it is ritually shared out between them all by their mother, who cuts the biggest portion for Vidalico.

Every year, during the period between the wars, Mathilde and Bouchi come to Paris on the Orient Express. The Parisian contingent goes to wait on the platform at the Gare de Lyon for the fabulous arrival of the locomotive that has come all the way from the other side of Europe. It pulls in with a great plume of smoke, jets of steam, and squealing brakes, trailing the long blue centipede of sleeping cars behind. Vidal, Mony Covo, his wife Liliane, Henriette and Vidal's son, still a child, walk down the line of carriages, peering into the windows. As soon as Bouchi, who is a robust, stocky man with a moustache and a very Serbian face, and Mony catch a glimpse of one another, they both let out a great shout: Hooooooo! and everyone starts running. Mathilde brings sumptuous gifts for everybody. Their stay in Paris is the occasion for family gatherings and feasts, and daily outings. The couple invites the family to the best restaurants, the theater and the Opéra-Comique. Mathilde and Bouchi spend the summer in France, on the shores of Lake Léman or in Vittel; then it is time to go home, and the family gathers once again on the platform of the Gare de Lyon, to watch, with great emotion, the magical train depart.

Sometimes, Bouchi and Mathilde have Régine and Hélène to stay with them in Belgrade. The girls are nieces to both of them, since they are Sophie's daughters (she is Bouchi's sister) as well as Jacques's (Mathilde's brother), and they grow up in Brussels, where they spend their adolescence in the thirties.

Thus, during the decade between 1920 and 1930, the Nahum family gains three son-in-laws and simultaneously goes a little further into diaspora: Liliane and Mony remain in Paris, but Aimée settles in Liverpool, and Chary in Avignon. Bonds of affection are formed with the newcomers, and joint holidays bring together in particular Mathilde and Bouchi, Liliane and Mony, and Aimée and Isidore. Family solidarity remains strong, and the family is still entirely Sephardi. Although Henri is having a relationship with a gentile woman, it is out of wedlock and outside the family.

THE BERESSIS (1920–1930)

On the Beressi side, Corinne had married Joseph Pelosoff a year after Luna married Vidal. Joseph Pelosoff was Salomon Beressi's nephew, and worked for Hananel Beressi as his chief assistant. He often came to eat at Myriam and Salomon's house, and he was present at the Passover meal in 1920 when Vidal met Luna. He was in love with Corinne and, as he was sitting next to her, discreetly slipped the oyster attached to a piece of chicken he had been served onto the young girl's plate. When, much later, she told the story to her son Fredy, Corinne said: "My father saw him . . . After the meal, he said to me: 'Since when does Joseph allow himself to give you food off his plate?' I answered that it was the first time and that I hadn't asked him to."

Joseph has to wait for the elder sister, Luna, to be married before declaring himself. After Vidal and Luna's engagement, however, Vidal's brother Henri begins to court Corinne. Salomon Beressi invites him along with Vidal, and Henri follows Corinne into the kitchen, singing: "The bells are ringing for you and for me." Joseph then makes his marriage proposal in writing. Salomon replies that his daughter is still too young (although officially born in 1901, she is only 17 in 1920). Joseph replies that he will wait ten years if he must. Salomon Beressi would rather Corinne married Henri: Joseph's father had discredited himself in Salomon's eyes because in Salonica he had taken his mistress into the conjugal home. Joseph tells Hananel that he will kill himself if Corinne is refused him, and Hananel intervenes and speaks to his brother. When the latter tells him that the reason for his refusal is "Like father, like son," Hananel retorts: "You have two sons, are they so like you that they could be your twins?" This argument wins Salomon Beressi's grudging assent.

The wedding takes place three months after his death, amid an atmosphere of mourning and loss. Only family and intimate friends attend the ceremony. Corinne faints, thinking of her father. The couple goes on honeymoon to Vichy, to the Marquise de Sévigné Hotel, at the beginning of July 1921. While on her honeymoon, Corinne sends Luna a card from Vichy on July 5; that is, three days before her sister gives birth.

> My dearest Luna,
> I found some little coffee cups yesterday, they're not souvenirs, but decorative china like the service that Mouchico gave me. If you'd like them, write to me at once so that I can buy them for you. I am very pleased with my holiday in Vichy. We are enjoying ourselves very much, and we've been on some lovely coach trips. On Sunday, we went around Vichy, Châtelguyon, Royat, Mont-Dore, La Bourboule, Saint-Nectaire, you can't imagine what a fairytale it is, very picturesque. With all my love, stroke the bump for me, and say hello to Vidal.
> Corinne.
> Kind regards and greetings.
> Joseph

Three days later, Vidal telephoned to say that Luna had just given birth, and Corinne cut short her honeymoon, rushing home to be with her sister. Back in Paris, the Pelosoffs rented an apartment in the Rue Sorbier, in the 20th arrondissement, halfway up Ménilmontant, in a recently-built apartment block for middle-class families situated in the heart of a working-class neighborhood. Corinne had wanted to leave the neighborhood of the Rue Sedaine where Joseph lived. "Why do all the Salonicians have to live in a group like that as if it were a ghetto? I don't like it . . . They would always speak Spanish when they were together, and I wanted to speak French . . . I wanted to be more integrated, and more quickly than the others . . . I was careful how I spoke, I didn't roll my 'r's too much."

Luna and Corinne feel Parisian and want to be Parisians. They have the same tastes and the same interests. The two sisters communicate with one another constantly, and the two couples often get together for dinners, outings, restaurants and vacations. Corinne becomes very fond of Bébéco, and will continue to baby-sit for him even after Fredy is born in 1923, and Daisy in 1925; she bathes him and she looks after him when Luna and Vidal go away for a week or two on winter vacation.

Myriam Beressi, their mother, was 43 years old when her husband died. She receives a monthly "envelope" from her two brothers-in-law, who make sure that she has a decent standard of living. She remains very Salonician, living almost in isolation from the rest of the world in the little island near the Place Voltaire with its businesses, groceries, small restaurants and stores selling household linens, where everybody speaks Spanish.[49] In apartment buildings like the one she lives in, at 95, Rue Sedaine, the women call to each other in Spanish from one window to the next, do favors for one another, go to eat or have tea at each others' houses, and live together in an intimacy that is almost familial. Passover is celebrated at Myriam's house, where there is a great gathering of Besseris and Mosseris; Luna takes Vidal there, and rabbi Perahia, a family friend, comes to celebrate the Jews' deliverance from Egypt.

Myriam Beressi always has Oriental candies and treats to give her children and grandchildren. She does not love her children equally; her daughter Luna is her special favorite.

Pepo Beressi, the eldest brother, born in 1897, is a bachelor; he does not marry until 1930, when he falls in love at first sight. The store on the Boulevard Barbès has not been a success, and Pepo has become a sales clerk in a shop selling fabric. Benjamin, born in 1909, is still an adolescent, but he has had little schooling. They live with their mother at 95, Rue Sedaine, as does the youngest daughter, Émy, born in 1913. She goes to school on the Avenue Parmentier, where Luna occasionally goes to collect her.

Most of Salomon Beressi's brothers have settled in Paris, and Samy in particular has been successful there. He is now the owner of a department store in the city center, and he also has four stores in the Rue d'Aboukir. He lives with his wife, Gaby Lombard, his two sons, Alex and Roger, and his two daughters, Edith and Odette (the latter born in 1920), in a big and beautiful house at Villemomble, set in a landscaped garden. They have two Great Danes, which Vidal and his son are afraid of. The day after the Wall Street Crash, in 1929, Samy Beressi dies of a heart attack, at the age of 54.

Hananel has married a woman from Marseilles, born in Algeria, known to everyone as Nini, and he owns a store in the Sentier selling fabric, like his brother. Vidal is greatly impressed by him, and the two men like to take their aperitif together. One time, Hananel makes Vidal drink fourteen Bergers in a row, and Vidal has to make his way home on all fours and four hours late, while Hananel returns, upright and dignified, to his wife Nini. There are also many Beressis and relatives by marriage in Montpellier, Castres and Rouen.

The Mosseri family, into which Myriam Beressi was born, has also settled in France, and especially in Paris. Edouard Mosseri, Myriam's brother, who is reputed to be a confirmed bachelor, is a naturalized Frenchman; he has a little store-cum-office in the Rue d'Aboukir, very close to Vidal's, and they often meet to discuss the news. His favorite interjections are: "Haï Adonaï!" and "Merde, alors!" which he pronounces: "Merle, alors!" with a weak 'r'. He is very fond of cards and racing. He is also passionate about politics, and later acts as an electoral agent for Paul Reynaud in the Sentier. It is under his influence that Vidal puts his name down for Paul Reynaud's support committee, as soon as he becomes eligible to vote.

There is also *tia* Clara, Myriam's sister, who has a finger missing, and lives in a villa in Garches, where a small group of relatives who often visit Luna and Vidal also live.

Thus, with the exception of Myriam, who stays and will continue to stay in her fragment of Salonica in the Rue Sedaine, living and dying there, the Beressis and the Mosseris live scattered among the gentiles. It was a Beressi who, at the beginning of the century, had been the first to marry a gentile woman, thus creating the first mixed marriage; it produced four children. And while the Nahums have not suffered very violent blows of fate, nor known any sudden rise to the heights, the Beressis are very unequally distributed between great wealth, even fortune, and paid work as blue-collar employees, and they have experienced appalling tragedies and great reversals of fortune, beginning in Salonica with the murder of Joseph Beressi. Salomon Beressi's death at the age of 60 ruins his family, and Samy Beressi's death at 54 brings about the collapse of his empire.

FRIENDSHIP

Vidal's Salonician friends have scattered; some of them are in Paris, some in the Sentier; his dearest friend, Dr. Matarasso, who studied in Toulouse, has returned to Salonica. He has established himself as a specialist in diseases of the skin and scalp.[50] Vidal and his friend write to each other and send each other cards whenever they go on trips away from home. On June 25 1921, Matarasso sends Vidal a card from Portaria (Greece):

> My dear Vidal,
> I didn't manage to get to Chambéry, but here I am in Portaria instead. It's just the same, except that the geographers have left it off their maps. That's how absent-minded scientists are! The place where I am staying with Andrée is wonderful. There are mules instead of automobiles, but we drink icy water straight from the rocks, we pick flowers on our walks through the fields, and, in imitation of the French bourgeoisie, we are staying in a hotel with what you call modern amenities. I feel very much at home here, and if it were not for Salonica, I'd become a shepherd, and Andrée would be my Chloé. But we know more about life's constraints than Daphnis and his companion did, and so we'll be leaving Portaria soon.
> Your old friend.
> P.S. Have you left your libidinous youth and your venial thoughts behind you, in other words, have you married?

In another card from 1921, Matarasso expresses his nostalgia for Paris and asks Vidal to send him some songs. In 1921, a letter from Matarasso throws incidental light on the predicament of the young Hellenized Sephardim in the new Salonica.

> Heat, mosquitoes, the drachma falling (to subterranean levels), Jews obliged to do military service, despair, resentment leading to venereal diseases, overwork, profits in drachmas high, not so high in . . . , etc.

114

I don't think you want me to give you any more details, the heat and overwork which form the background to this list of facts are enough to excuse me from the task.

Well, my dear Vidal, the only good in the world is outside of Salonica. Satisfaction, profit and consideration count for nothing, compared with a more intelligent kind of life, which it is impossible to lead here.

Next year, I may come to see you for a few weeks. Do you need a hand moving any more cases of DMC? [An allusion to some manual help he gave Vidal during a goods transfer.] Send me some new songs. Write to me a little more often.

And how's business, is it going well?

Andrée sends her regards. Pay my respects to your wife and to your parents.

Your old friend.

Matarasso came to stay in Paris at least once before 1924, and, on his return from his 1924 visit, he sends a card:

Salonica, November 7, 1924
My dear Vidal,
Here we are at home in splendid peace and quiet: there are neither buses nor taxis, just three officers armed with white truncheons for the whole town. In Paris, pedestrians are crushed without a second thought, here it's *Yavach, Yavach.*

Vidalico, I was very glad to see you again in Paris, and one day I will be with you in Paris for good. My compliments to your lady wife. Greetings to Mr. Hassid. Send me a line from the towns or villages you pass through.

Your old friend.

Three years later:

February 17, 1927
My dear Vidal,
I am the father of a son, who was born on February 3. I've delayed in letting you know because the preparations for the *brit* and the *brit* itself took up a lot of time.

Andrée and my son Robert are doing well and send you and your charming wife their kind regards.

Write me a few lines so that I can place you in space and time. Are you still keeping your customers well-shod and combed? Keep it up.

With much love,
Your old friend.

Much later, Matarasso will come to live in France, in Cannes.

115

Diaspora, Again

The young Salonician generation of 1914 to 1918, who apart from a few exceptions scattered to live in different parts of France, are also dispersed at every level of the social hierarchy and in all the different urban professions and careers. Some begin almost at the bottom, but the smart ones, the survivors and the activists rise very high and sometimes make their fortunes. The idlers and the dreamers fall, even those from relatively wealthy backgrounds, but they never hit bottom, because family solidarity and the post-Salonician networks find jobs for them as commercial clerks or salesmen and usually, but not always, prevent them from having to become laborers. Vidal is resourceful, and a survivor, but although he has a good head for business he does not gain expertise, and is not inclined to delegate; as a result he never gets beyond low-priced items and oddments and cannot expand his small, one-man business. He is not really middle-class, but moves between the upper class and the lower, going from one to the other among his friends and his family without the slightest difficulty.

Whereas Dona Helena Nahum and Myriam Beressi keep up their Salonician lifestyle in Paris, their sons and daughters enter the Parisian world and become French, more or less rapidly, each in his or her own way. Léon and Vidal, both fathers of a son born in the new country, will take the decisive step of naturalization.

Naturalization

After 1926, Vidal feels settled and immersed in France, and he decides to request French nationality. The first step towards naturalization is the declaration, made on May 3, 1927, in front of the justice of the peace for the 9th arrondissement, that irrevocably guarantees French nationality for his son. Vidal and Luna probably set the naturalization process in motion after a special law is passed, on August 10, 1927. Léopold Belan, municipal councillor for the 2nd arrondissement, recommends Vidal to the Guardian of the Seals, who agrees to the councillor's request. Vidal and Luna finally become French citizens on February 18, 1931, by a decree signed by the President of the Republic, Gaston Doumerge, and countersigned by the Guardian of the Seals, Léon Berard. The *Journal officiel* of March 1, 1931 mentions the naturalization of Vidal Nahoum, a storekeeper born on March 14, 1894 in Salonica (Greece), in a list that includes the Italians Tomatis (boilermaker), Guariniello (carpenter), Serra (cement maker), Campenio (storekeeper), Goletto (retired), Ponsero (café owner) and Dalmasso (dairyman), the Spaniards Seas (cement maker) and Roset (farmer), the Belgians Breyne and Demanet (farmers), and the Russian Popoff (painter).

VI
Reuil and the Death of Luna

In October 1929, the crash on the New York Stock Exchange unleashes a massive economic crisis on the world, creating the storms and convulsions from which the Second World War will emerge. However, the shock wave has not yet reached France in 1930. This is the year that Vidal's business is at its peak. He buys some land and has a villa built on it. On December 11, 1928, he had already bought an apartment on the fourth floor of 51, Rue Demours, rented to Mrs. Clémence Doyen, for the sum of 81,000 francs, of which he paid 37,000 in cash, borrowing the rest. Did he envisage living in this apartment, which has a lift, at some point? Whether he did or not, the apartment is occupied, and Luna has increasing difficulty climbing the three flights of stairs without a lift in the Rue Mayran. Vidal starts looking for a new home.

So I was living at the Rue Mayran, on the third floor, but there was no lift, and poor Luna, my first wife, found it very tiring. And it was impossible to find a small apartment that was suitable, or else they were asking ridiculous sums of money! So in the end we decided to go and live in the suburbs. There was some land for sale in Rueil, it was for sale by auction, and I bought the land.

On Thursday July 10, 1930, there is a sale by office (*adjudication en l'étude*), executed by Maitre Radet, notary, of a piece of land situated in Rueil-Malmaison, in the Rue Cramail, with an area of 397 square meters, 8.73 meters wide and 51.05 meters long. The reserve price is 15,000 francs. Vidal seems to have purchased the land for 28,500 francs. The Rue Cramail is off the Avenue Paul-Doumer, which links the Gare de Rueil to the Avenue de Paris, the local name for the road running between the Porte Maillot and Saint-Germain-en-Laye, via Bougival. The land is at the civic limits of the street. Two houses already stand on either side of the plot, and there is also a beautiful villa almost opposite, set in a landscaped garden and hidden from view by a tall privet hedge. Planted fields begin immediately afterwards on the right-hand side of the street. On the left-hand side, there are more small houses, a huge building that houses the archives of the Crédit foncier,[51] a path, and then fields spreading into the distance.

In 1930, Vidal and Luna consult an architect in Challes-les-Eaux, who makes them plans for a house. The design of the house in the suburbs does not please Luna, who is dreaming of a dream house, for which she has a clearly formulated list of requirements: cast iron balconies, a painted fresco in the entrance hall, walls painted in gradations of color, a large and very bright kitchen, and most importantly a roof terrace. New plans are made in accordance with her wishes, and on October 27 of the same year, Vidal signs his consent to the plans drawn up by Mr. Isabel, a building contractor in the Avenue de Paris, at Rueil. The villa is to occupy the whole length of the land and to be distributed over three levels. The ground floor will be used for the storeroom, the garage, the laundry, and a little "maid's" bedroom with a window looking onto the garden; an Ideal Classic coal-fired central heating system will be installed beneath the inside staircase. On the front of the house there will be an outside staircase leading up to the front door. This will give onto an entrance hall; at the end of the hall will be a kitchen measuring 12.9 feet by 10.68 feet, with a staircase going down to the garden; to the right of the entrance hall, there will be a living room and dining room separated by a double glass door, which can be opened wide. Finally, on the floor above, there will be three bedrooms and a large bathroom. A third staircase leads to an open terrace, which covers the whole surface of this house with no roof.

The work begins in fall 1930, with the promise that it will be finished in time for the winter of 1930 to 1931. Vidal has no ideas of his own and takes no interest in what is supposed to be his future home. Luna, however, invests herself wholeheartedly in this villa. She does not want a house in the suburbs, but something that corresponds to her Mediterranean nostalgia for sun and light. This explains her insistence on having a terrace instead of a roof — something that at the time was even less common than it is today, especially since there was no method yet for making it completely water-tight, in the rainy climate of the Parisian Basin. She wants it to be spacious, with deep balconies bordered with cast iron, large windows, and big rooms, including the kitchen and the bathroom, and she wants all of them to have a lot of light. She has decided on the arrangement, dimension and decoration of every room. She wants oak floors throughout, good quality tiles for the kitchen and bathroom, moldings on the ceilings and on the bedroom walls, as well as in the living and dining rooms. She does not want wallpaper, she wants oil paint in gradated shades, with a different color for every room. She wants to decorate the upper part of the entrance hall with a small fresco, a painted trellis covered in flowering plants.

But then Vidal's business is hit by the economic crisis. He has had to borrow money to build the house; he has to make payments to the contractor as the work advances, and finds himself in difficulties. He starts gnawing away at the program of work planned for the house. Originally, it was to have been made of freestone; he has the first level built in buhrstone and the floors above in solid brick. He gives up the cast iron balconies, and has them built in brick instead. He has the second floor faced entirely in concrete. The consequences of all this cost-cutting displease Luna, who sees her dream villa turning into a monstrosity: the façade, with its bulky brick balconies over-laid with grayish concrete, offers a curious spectacle, and distresses her greatly when she sees the completed work.

The construction is behind schedule. When the end of their notice to leave the Rue Mayran is reached, the villa is still uninhabitable, and the couple, along with Edgar and Émy, Luna's younger sister, then aged 17, move temporarily into the Hotel Bohy-Lafayette,[52] in the Square Montholon, while they wait for the Rueil house to be ready. Edgar, then aged 9, witnesses his mother's displeasure and the arguments between his parents, whose causes he does not understand. Is it just because Luna is upset to see how the dream of her beautiful white villa has been betrayed? It is very likely that Vidal, who always prevaricates when he has bad news to announce, delays in letting her know about the modifications and suppres-sions, and only tells her when it has all already been done. His dissimulation will earn him further reproaches. Is there some other cause for the dissen-sion between them? Why did Luna bring her young sister with her to the hotel?

They decide not to wait for the work to be finished before moving into Rueil. They move at the end of May or beginning of June 1931. Vidal cannot help remembering Luna's exasperation, but he minimizes it in his oral autobiography:

We moved, and the poor thing, you know, she was very pleased, of course, but she had, how can I put it, some worries, some concerns, the door didn't close prop-erly, there was something wrong with the staircase, and so on, but those were just minor irritations . . . In the end, it all worked out fine, we had a rail pass, Edgar had his rail pass, he was still at the Lycée Rollin, he ate there at lunchtime, he came home in the evening, and so did I.

Macrue did not go with the family; she went back to Alfortville with Wahram, where she opened a grocery store. Luna found a maid in the Spanish shanty town of Saint-Ouen. This was before it was commonplace to have a Spanish maid: Luna simply employed someone she could speak a familiar and familial language with.

Émy stays at the villa with her sister. The last of the work is finally finished. A new routine begins for Vidal and Edgar.

Two weeks perhaps, a month at the most, have gone by since they moved in. June 26 arrives. Luna and Émy set off from the villa to go and have lunch in Paris at Corinne's house, where Vidal is due to join them. Rueil station is ten or fifteen minutes' walk from 29, Rue Cramail.

Vidal: *So I leave for work in the morning, your Dad goes off to school in the morning and . . . she was supposed to take the 11 o'clock train to meet me at Aunt Corinne's, and after lunch I had arranged to go and see a furniture salesman (with Luna), because we needed I can't remember what . . . So, we each went our separate ways.*

I'm in my store. Uncle Edouard, who had a store almost opposite mine, came rushing in. I'd gone out for a minute. So Uncle Élie, who had been waiting there in my store, says:

"Go quickly, Edouard's looking for you, something's happened . . . " "What?" "I don't know, hurry . . . "

He was in front of the . . .

"They've just phoned me from Saint-Lazare station, saying that Luna, poor thing, has passed away . . . Look, keep calm, I'm going with you."

Taxi, we arrive at Saint-Lazare station. Unfortunately, she was dead.

That's what happened. That morning, she'd been a bit flustered, in a bit of a rush to take . . . because of the timetable. She was with Émy and a little Spanish maid. And bad luck would have it that at Rueil, as well as the path you take, you remember, from the house to the station, there were also stairs to climb [to get on to the plat-forms], and as she saw that time was marching on and she was in danger of missing the train, she hurried up the stairs, which she was forbidden to do. The train arrives, she jumps on board the train, and sits down, with Émy next to her, the little maid opposite, or vice versa. Émy notices that the moment she sits down, her head slumps forwards, and Émy thinks she's resting. What did the little maid think? Well, they're chatting to each other, still thinking that she's resting. A few minutes later, they try to move her, it's a direct train from Rueil to Paris, which only stops once at Nanterre. But they still hadn't realized at that point, because if they had stopped the train at Nanterre, got her out, maybe she could have been saved. Well, anyway, when they arrive in Paris, the stationmaster and all that, she was already dead . . . Her sister didn't realize that, at the first sign she made of letting her head fall forwards, she should have stopped the train immediately, even if it was in the middle of the countryside, because the train would have stopped, they would have taken her out, they would have laid her on the ground, there was a chance, well, there was a chance of saving her, a chance . . .

MEDICO-LEGAL REPORT

I the undersigned Camille AUDISTERE, Doctor of medicine, residing in Paris in the Rue du Faubourg-Saint-Honoré (8th arrondissement), and requested by the special commissioner of Saint-Lazare station to examine the body of Mrs. Luna NAHOUM, aged 30, residing at 29, Rue Cramail, Rueil, declare and certify, on previously sworn oath, that I have observed: complete immobility. Purple marks on cheeks and lips. Oscillometer shows absence of pulse. Fingers stiff and cold, pupils dilated. The sister of the deceased indicates that in order to catch the train at Rueil, the deceased had run, had been out of breath on entering the carriage, and had slumped forwards immediately; that since an attack of "Spanish flu" a few years ago, she had suffered from heart trouble, with a weak heart, and severe attacks of palpitations.

It seems evident that Mrs. Nahoum died suddenly from a heart attack, after exertion.

Paris, June 26 1931

Signed: Dr. AUDISTERE
Appendix approved.
The representative special commissioner.
Signed: POCHON

On Thursday July 2 1931, *L'Indépendant*, a French-language evening paper published in Salonica, carries an account of the offenses committed by anti-Semites in the city on its front page, reports the appearance of two Bulgarian Comitadjis in Amatovo, and announces the end of a strike by bakers' boys. On page 3, its next-to-last page, is the following article:

A CRUEL BEREAVEMENT IN PARIS

Paris, June 29.
A bereavement of the cruelest kind has struck the Nahum and Beressi families, who are among the most notable members of the Judeo–Salonician colony in Paris. Mrs. Luna Vidal D. Nahum, daughter of the late Salomon Beressi and of Mrs. Myriam Beressi, née Mosseri, was torn away from her loving family, at the happy age of thirty-one, with shocking suddenness.

The unfortunate young woman, who lived in Rueil, one of the capital's most attractive suburbs, was due to join a family lunch party last Friday, June 26. As soon as the train moved off, Mrs. Nahum's head fell back against the headrest of the seat she was occupying. Her young sister, who accompanied her, and the other travelers in the compartment, thought that she had succumbed to a dizzy spell, and tried to relieve her. However, when they arrived at Saint-Lazare station, the doctors saw that the young woman had suffered a heart attack.

The Nahum and Beressi families were informed at once. The reader can imagine the agony suffered by the tearful husband, the unfortunate mother, the horrified brothers and sisters, and all the other relatives who rushed to the station. The tragic news, which was known at once in the city, caused the most painful shock within the colony, and in all of the Oriental and French circles linked to the Nahums, the Beressis and the Mosseris.

Mrs. Luna Vidal D. Nahum was a charming and beautiful young woman, with a ready smile, who wore her heart on her sleeve, and was always ready to do good. She was adored by her husband, worshipped by all of her relations, and radiated gaiety; everyone close to her was sincerely and deeply fond of her. Two weeks previously, she had gone to live in an attractive villa which her husband had just had built in Rueil, and she was busy working on the last modifications to the interior. This senseless death came and stole a young woman in full bloom away from life and happiness, and plunged her distraught husband, her inconsolable mother, her eight-year-old child, her sisters and brothers, and the families related to her into indescribable sorrow . . .

The funeral took place on Sunday, attended by a considerable throng of relatives, friends and noteworthy members of the Oriental colony.

To Mr. Vidal D. Nahum, to the widow Mrs. Salomon Beressi, and to her children, as well as to all the families afflicted by this terrible misfortune, we express our profound condolences and our intense sympathy.

S.L.

Edgar left early in the morning of Friday June 26, to go to the Lycée Rollin. He had become a day-boarder after leaving the Rue Mayran. He was in the 8th grade. He had recently written a novel, which was just six pages long, entitled *The Bandit's Love*, in a school exercise book. A rich and beautiful heiress is kidnapped by a bandit, who not only demands a ransom, but intends to abuse the young woman. Just as he is on the point of performing the ignoble deed (of which the novel's author had only the vaguest notion), the detective Max Vidal appears on the scene, frees the beauty and arrests the bandit. The novel had been passed around all the pupils in the class. The teacher had heard about it and had asked to read it. Naturally, she found it worthless, and returned it that day without comment to the author, who understood when no praise was given that the novel had not found favor, but was not upset, being entirely absorbed in his delight at being the class novelist.

He spent a very pleasant day; there was very little homework, and discipline was more lax than usual, as it was coming up to the vacation. During the afternoon study period, where he remained until 5 o'clock, he chatted gaily to his neighbor. Feeling very happy, he came out through the big gate onto the Avenue Trudaine, and saw his Uncle Jo, his Aunt Corinne's husband, standing waiting for him beside a taxi with its roof down. He was surprised, but not in the least alarmed. Uncle Jo explained to him at once that he was going to have dinner and spend the night at their house, because his parents had gone to take a cure at Vittel. The child was not particularly surprised by this sudden departure. He stood in the open taxi, his face whipped by the wind, and looked up at the overground métro which the car followed from Barbès-Rochechouart all the way until it sank back down underground at the approach to Combat métro station. He does not remember the two days he spent at his Aunt Corinne's house. Did he go back to school on Saturday? Did he play with his little cousins? He does not remember having seen his aunt. The servant, big Marie, looked after him and Corinne's children, and he had a sense of freedom.

On Sunday, in the afternoon, big Marie took the children to play in the Square Martin-Nadaud, which is next to Père-Lachaise cemetery. Edgar was sitting on the lawn when he caught sight of a pair of black trousers, which made him look up to see a tall man, dressed all in black. Vidal had come out of Père-Lachaise after the burial to see his son. He was displeased to see this carefree child playing on the grass, which was prohibited. When he saw the black suit, he instantly understood exactly what had happened, but pretended not to know anything. He did not get up to kiss his father, and this hurt Vidal, who said to him: "Come on, get off the grass." The child did not obey, and his father repeated harshly: "Don't stay on the grass, it's not allowed." The child moved off the lawn, pretending to sulk.

Afterwards, the child never asked for news of his mother. He did not ask any questions. One day, Corinne gathered her children and her nephew around her and announced that Aunt Lunica had gone on a journey to heaven; sometimes, people come back from these journeys, and sometimes they don't; you must never make your parents unhappy. Vidal was dismayed that his son had said nothing and had shown no emotion. He attributed this indifference to stupidity. Vidal did not understand why his son, although only ten years old, locked himself in bathrooms so often and for such a long time. Sometimes, he questioned him through the door: "Are you OK? Do you have a stomach-ache?" The son would stop his silent weeping, and answer that everything was fine. He would wait for his eyes to dry before coming out, and Vidal would look searchingly into his indifferent and tranquil face. Vidal did not realize that his son wept in silence in the evenings, in bed, when the light was out, nor that he awoke in despair every morning, when his mother disappeared from his dream. The following year, Vidal could not comprehend his son's refusal to go to the cemetery with his family for the anniversary of Luna's death.

Beforehand, Corinne had been very careful to inform her nephew that his mother, who had gone up to heaven, was dead on earth. Then she told him the most comforting thing she could think of, which turned out to be the most terrible thing he could have heard: "Think of me as your mother now, I'm your mother." Vidal was delighted that Corinne had said something so consoling to his son. He thought that the reason his son was so carefree was probably because Corinne had managed to replace his mother so perfectly. Much later, when he was past 80, Vidal would be very surprised when his son told him how much Corinne's words had hurt him. "But why?" said Vidal, "on the contrary, you should have been delighted . . . "

Vidal and Corinne were amazed at the child's indifference, and he heard them talking about this indifference without them realizing it. The child was indeed capable of playing, going for bicycle rides, and laughing. But he had cut himself off, forever, as he thought, from his family.

Vidal believed he had spared his son by failing to announce his mother's death immediately, and by excluding him from the mourning ceremonies and from the burial. Certainly, everything would have been different if the child had been able, with his father, to share in the sorrow, weep when the burial took place, and to embrace his Beressi grandmother, who had loved Luna so much. But the silence about this death and the dissimulation surrounding it caused the child to be silent and to dissimulate, and he found himself exiled and alone within the circle of his family. It was much, much later, almost thirty years afterwards, when Edgar wrote about Luna's death in a book published in 1959, that Vidal and Corinne would realize he had loved his mother.

So as not to leave Vidal and his son on their own, it was decided that Myriam Beressi, Émy, Corinne, Joseph and their children would come to Rueil for the summer of 1931. Edgar persuaded Fredy and Daisy to go on long bicycle rides with him, along the Seine, on the Île de Chatou. He listened to the records his mother had loved on a little record player, especially *El Relicario*, which spoke of love and death, but whose words he did not understand. He dug a big hole in the garden in which he wanted to make a kind of house.

The garden had a lawn, where an apricot and an almond tree had been planted; in its Northern exile, the Southern tree produced flowers at the end of February, but no almonds. At the bottom of the garden, which had been marked off as a vegetable patch, Vidal planted peas, green beans, tomatoes, and especially cucumbers, to which he was very partial. Unfortunately, he made a mistake with the seeds, and bitter apples grew instead of *pepinos*.

According to Sephardic tradition, Vidal should have married his single sister-in-law, Émy, now aged 18, since the Beressi family had incurred a debt for supplying a defective wife, and should now have replaced her with a new one. But Vidal's will to live, which at first was almost defeated by Luna's death, resulted in his beginning a secret relationship with a married woman, outside the family, and he convinced the heads of the family, presided over by Uncle Hananel Beressi, to find a husband for Émy elsewhere. They arranged for her to meet a young Sephardi with a "good situation," who may not have been a Salonician, called Victor Lerea. She did not like him, but she put up with him at first. Family outings with Victor Lerea took place in the neighborhood of Rueil, and then there was an engagement party in the house at the Rue Cramail. Meanwhile, Émy was having a clandestine but chaste relationship with a boy she liked; he demanded that she give him her engagement ring as proof of her love, and replaced it for her with a copper imitation, complete with fake diamond. In the end, Émy could not bear the idea of marrying against her will, and broke off her engagement. When Hananel asked her for the ring to give it back to the ex-fiancé, he discovered that it was a crude imitation of the original. Émy denied everything, wept, confessed, and gave him the seducer's name and address. Hananel, with his ivory-topped cane in his hand, and wearing his dapper suit and bow tie, told Vidal to come with him; they jumped into a taxi and ordered the driver to hurry to the young man's address. He lived with his father, who owned a garage. It was late morning. Hananel called out the garage-owner, and demanded to see his son. "But he's still asleep." "Wake him up." "But what's it about?" "Your son, sir, is a thief, a bandit, and a hooligan," cries Hananel, brandishing his cane. The son appears, denies everything, starts sniveling, and confesses. He has sold the ring to a jeweler. Hananel drags the address out of him and jumps with Vidal into the waiting taxi. Again, the driver puts his foot down and they head for the jeweler's. The jeweler feigns astonishment, but Hananel thunders, whirling his cane: "What? You yourself are a fence, a crook, and a thief. I demand that you restore this ring to me without recompense, otherwise I will register a complaint and create a scandal." The jeweler hands over the ring, and Hananel, appeased and smiling, says to Vidal as they get back into the taxi: "Now let's go and have a drink." Thus the matinee western comes to an end.

Then came October 1931. It was decided that Vidal and his son would go to live at Corinne and Joseph's house, so that the child would have a home. The apartment on the Rue Sorbier consisted of just three rooms: a bedroom, a dining room and a living room. The living room became a dormitory, in which Vidal, Edgar and Fredy slept, each on a day bed, while Daisy slept in her parents' room.

Edgar was supposed to have gone, to the Lycée Voltaire, as Fredy later did; it was fairly close to home, whereas it was a relatively long métro journey to the Lycée Rollin. After his mother's death, he wanted to go and be with his friends at his gloomy old school, even though he was bored to death during the long hour between lunch at the canteen and the two o'clock class. Every time they moved house subsequently, he lived further away from school, but he stayed on at the Lycée Rollin, which had become a protective cocoon, and where, despite occasional bullying, indifference, and moments of loneliness, he would find some warmth among his classmates. During the first year, so as not to leave Edgar on his own, Corinne sent her son Fredy to the Lycée Rollin with him.

Vidal was having difficulty with his debts and making payments, while Joseph was having serious difficulties in his business. The great economic crisis that raged through France had begun to shake up the Sentier.

In the summer of 1932, the new family returned to Rueil, which allowed them to save the money they would have spent on a vacation, without missing out on a vacation altogether.[53] In September, Edgar fell victim to a strange illness, which gave him ulcers in his throat that left him unable to breathe. Dr. Amar could not discern any known malady. He called in specialists. Lacking any other explanation, they diagnosed foot and mouth disease, the kind that affects cattle. Perhaps the child's will to live had cracked under the pressure of his immense sorrow, and allowed an incongruous virus to enter his organism. When the fever rose above 40 degrees, the doctors prescribed ice packs on the body, and Corinne stuck her fingers into the back of the child's throat to tear off the membranes that were suffocating him. Vidal was afraid he was going to see his son die a year after his wife. The fever gradually abated, and Edgar regained his strength. He was able to return to school and enter the sixth grade. Vidal had given up the idea of business school for good. He respected Luna's wishes and his son's desire; the boy had been advised to study Latin and Greek. They came to a compromise, and he was registered in an A stream, in which he would study Latin and a foreign language. When he arrived at the lycée, the classes had begun a week or two beforehand. He went to see the supervisor, Mr. Lorphelin, who asked him why he had failed to attend the first days of school.

"I was ill, sir."
"What was wrong with you, my boy?"
"Foot and mouth disease, sir."
"Hm! You know I don't like to be made fun of!"

So Vidal's son entered the sixth grade, taking his secret and his shameful fever with him.

VII
A New Life (1931–1939)

"Death, that monster who knows neither law nor impediment," of which Luna had written in her first letter to Vidal, had struck her down at the age of 30.

Her death caused a very violent but short-lived cataclysm in Vidal's life. For the first time, he began to suffer from a noisy kind of contraction in the esophagus, like a cross between a deep belch and the spasms of hiccups, which went on and on interminably. This discomfort faded, but it came back on several occasions for the remainder of his life, acting as a bizarre sign that misfortune had returned. A few years later, around 1934 to 1935, he suffered an even stranger malady. One evening, after a family dinner at the home of his sister-in-law Émy, who had married a man she loved in 1932, red marks began to appear on his face, which then turned dark purple; hard patches formed behind his ears, around his eyes, and on other parts of his body. An intense itching grew into terrible pain; his face looked hideous, disfigured, and he seemed to be on the point of dying. Then, very slowly, all the symptoms faded, and the sickness disappeared. It was a case of anaphylactic shock, whose cause was detected later, when it transpired that it always came on after he had eaten any food or dish containing sesame, whether in the form of seeds, oil, or tahini. He then took precautions, especially in Oriental restaurants, but sometimes, without realizing, he would ingest some sesame, and have the attack again, terrifying his son and those around him.

However, apart from these spasmodic or anaphylactic accidents, and apart from his tendency to pharyngitis, which had already led him to make two cures at Challes-les-Eaux, he remained in excellent health, and never consulted doctors. He had found female company and flesh to help him forget the gulf of death and absence in a secret relationship outside the family, and he was expending even more energy at work now that he was simultaneously confronted with the difficulties related to the crisis and the debts that he had incurred with the villa at Rueil. The inventory made after Luna's death gives some indication of his financial situation in 1933. Vidal has some bonds from the Crédit National and the City of Paris; he cashes in 30,000 francs' worth after Luna's death. He is 37,800 francs overdrawn at the Banque de France, and his various debts (in particular to the builders, painters, carpenters, etc., who worked on the villa at Rueil) amount to

202,000 francs. He has still not finished paying for the apartment in the Rue Demours, acquired in 1928.

The years between 1930 and 1936 are relentless ones for Vidal: he has to pay some of his debts, play for time on others, and find money to live on. The situation gets worse when Joseph Pelosoff falls victim to a crook, while Vidal and his son are living at his house, experiences serious financial difficulties, and has to give up his commercial assets. There are no vacations, except at Rueil, and Rueil will subsequently be rented out to bring in some money; there will be no more big outings, no more expensive restaurants. Life will become less difficult again after 1936, when the biggest debts have been absorbed, and there may have been a slight improvement in business.

For about three years, after Luna's death (in 1931) until 1934 or 1935, Vidal and his son live with Corinne and Joseph at 11, Rue Sorbier. The apartment is in a building dating from the turn of the century, overlooking a mixed neighborhood in Ménilmontant; this building is close to the pit that contains the circle line of the railroad, which is due to be covered over to build a school, a bathhouse and a public park. Immediately adjoining it is a rundown street, the Rue Juillet, that no-one seems to use. For years, some macaroni in tomato sauce is left sticking to the wall of the little house next door. A blue-collar lifestyle predominates in the neighborhood: couples can be heard arguing through open windows, there is drunken shouting, and the sound of crockery breaking; but people also talk to one another from their windows, and the family and the people who live on the same floor, Mr. and Mrs. Grucy, do favors for one another.

As in the Rue Mayran, Vidal wakens his son in the morning by whistling and singing. The room is not heated in winter, and so he orders: "Exercises, Minou," flinging his arms symmetrically apart and bringing them energetically back to his chest again several times, which according to him is what Breton sailors do. He goes to the sink and splashes his face with cold water (later, when he has the benefit of a water-heater, he will still disdain to wash in hot water). Half-awake, and bleary-eyed, the children and adults pass each another in the corridor of the apartment, as each gets ready for his or her day. Then Vidal goes out, catches the métro and goes to his store. His son is isolated by his secret, but he is not alone, and the presence of Corinne's children puts him at the center of another, smaller, children's world. Outside school, he spends all his time with his cousin Fredy; he plays with him, goes to the cinema with him, and takes him with him on his walks.

Edgar enjoys exploring the strange neighborhood with Fredy, and he draws up its map as if he were discovering an unknown kingdom. He also likes the Rue de Ménilmontant, which is lively and crowded, and which he goes down and up again every day, depending on the métro that takes him to school or brings him home. There are two cinemas in this street, the Phénix and the Ménil. He goes to the cinema with Fredy every Thursday, and on Sundays too, when he can escape from the relatives. An important part of his education will come from the street, and the cinema, and for the rest of his life he will retain a taste for working-class life, and a dislike for bourgeois neighborhoods, especially the 17th arrondissement, where his Aunt Henriette lives, and where Vidal will live later on.

Corinne's children are growing up, and her third son, Henri, who until now has been raised in the countryside, returns to the family home. There is not enough room, and so Vidal and his son leave. Henriette takes them in – she already has her mother living with her – and they sleep in her big apartment's little guestroom.

Hélène Nahum, who is a very sweet-natured, perpetually good-tempered woman, is delighted to have her Vidalico close to her. Every evening, before bedtime, she prepares some home-made yogurt for him. At meals, she serves him the tastiest bits and the biggest portions. Vidal is very happy to go back to being Vidalico, but his mother dies in 1936, of a blocked intestine. It was all right for Vidal to stay with his mother, but he cannot remain at his sister's house. The family will find a solution for him, as we will see later.

FATHER AND SON

Vidal is very gentle and patient with his son, who often feels impulses of affection for him, in spite of his secret grudge against his father and the fundamental misunderstanding between them. (Vidal thinks that his son is indifferent to his mother's death; Edgar thinks his father has betrayed his mother). The father is very rarely angry with his son; when he is, he will suddenly pronounce him an "idiot," with utter conviction. He slaps him even more rarely. He has never spanked him or imposed any form of punishment.

Vidal is extremely anxious about his son, although he is convinced that Corinne has given him an almost maternal protection. When they begin living on their own, just the two of them, and although the boy is now an adolescent, Vidal asks him constantly if he has slept and eaten well (and always wants to know what he has eaten at any meals taken in his absence), and he weighs him down with irrational worries: "Don't put too much butter on your bread," "Don't drink cold water." He believes cold, heat, dryness and damp to be bad for his son. In around 1934 or 1935, he writes to Edgar, who is staying with his Uncle Henri in Brussels, and is 13 or 14 at the time: "Last year, you left at 7 o'clock in the morning, *it's rather chilly at the moment, and I would rather you didn't go out so early.*" At about the same time, when his son is at Cayeux-sur-Mer, staying with the parents of his schoolfriend Henri Luce, Vidal writes: "I'm sure you are being very careful to dress properly, and keep your feet warm. If need be, put some newspaper in your shoes, because it is absolutely essential that your feet stay warm." If ever a letter fails to arrive on the expected day, Vidal worries, and sends telegrams:

Friday, 7 p.m.

My dear Edgar,

I came to the store very early this morning, hoping to have some news from you. The mailman comes at around 8 o'clock and brings me my mail, but no letters from Cayeux! I wasn't too anxious, but I did go and send you a telegram. At around 10 thirty, I received the letter you wrote on Thursday and at around midday received your telegram. I was very glad to read your letter and have your wire, but you don't say whether or not it is raining in Cayeux?? If it is, I am quite sure you must be taking the right precautions against the rain, and avoiding catching a chill or getting wet. I would be pleased to have your reassurance on these points by tomorrow morning . . .

In imitation, his son demonstrates the same anxious preoccupations in his letters: "Did you arrive safely in Paris? Wasn't it too hot on the train?"

He reassures his father in advance: "The wind only began to blow yesterday afternoon; of course I'm wearing both my pull-overs and sometimes my raincoat as well."

Vidal's paternal concern extends to the most bizarre things. He cannot bear the idea of his son using outside lavatories, at the bottom of a garden, and wiping himself with newspaper. When Edgar, who is already 16 or 17, is on vacation in Vert, near Mantes, at the house of a friend from the Coq-Héron group, Vidal comes to spend a Sunday there, and is horrified to discover that the lavatory is at the bottom of the garden. He pleads with his son to come back home, and sends him a telegram from Paris: "Uncle Élie very ill, come at once." Another time, when Edgar is at a different house in Vert, Vidal mails him some toilet paper. Later, in 1941, when he arrives in Toulouse to visit his son, who is then aged 20, and finds him staying in a room on the second floor of a café, with the lavatory at the end of the corridor, he insists that he change his lodging.

He will never cease to worry about trivial things, which will very fortunately prevent him from worrying about anything that is really worrying. He continues to fuss over his son when he is an adolescent, and when Edgar starts wanting to fend for himself, if only for the holidays, he will prevent him by using a form of blackmail which, until the summer of 1943, proves irresistible.

It works like this: whenever his son displeases him or refuses to renounce a desire that runs counter to his own wishes, Vidal collapses into an armchair, sighing heavily, and makes a noisy show of breathing his last. He will remain in his death-throes until his son, weeping, throws himself into his arms and begs his forgiveness. As soon as the son has submitted, the father ressuscitates. Of course, the son learns from these periodic paternal deaths and resurrections that his father's agony is somewhat exaggerated, and he attempts to resist this blackmail. Increasingly, he remains unmoved when the pseudo-moribund collapses into an armchair, bellowing Och! Och! Och! However, a point will always come when worry and then panic get the better of him, and he rushes to beg his father's forgiveness. (At heart, he feels guilty about his mother's death "because he had made her too unhappy," and he is haunted by the memory of seeing his father in the throes of anaphylactic shock with horror.) After each deathbed scene, Vidal informs his son that he has just lost two years of his life. Thus, by the time he reaches the age of 47 in 1939, his life will have been shortened by a century.

Vidal cannot understand why the teenage boy, once he is fifteen, wants to come out from under his father's wing a little, and live his own life. The first time he manages to spend his vacation away from his father is when he goes to Cayeux-sur-Mer, to the parents of his schoolfriend Henri Luce, where he is of course under their supervision. Then he and his friend Henri Salem decide to spend the 1936 summer vacation in Greece. They plan to sign up as ship's boys in Marseilles, and then travel around Greece after landing in Pireus. Contrary to his son's expectations, Vidal does not voice the slightest opposition to the plan, which his son tells him about in May, and Edgar makes joyful preparations. They are to embark on the *Théophile-Gautier*, and hatch a plan to get themselves employed as cook's assistants during the crossing. Then comes the time to apply for their passports and visas. Quite calmly, Vidal tells his son: "If you want to kill your father, then go to Greece." Edgar tries to harden himself against this blackmail, and insists that he is going, that he will keep in touch, that he will be very careful, and that he will not eat bad food. His father continues to lay down his law, not in the way of Moses exercising his authority, but like a Newton formulating the absolute determinism of the law of gravity: "All right, all right, if you want to kill me, all you have to do is leave." "I'm leaving!" The psychological battle goes on for several days, until the father, seeing that his son still firmly intends to leave, collapses into his armchair, stricken with the most appalling death throes, utters terrifying groans, and lets his head drop back, dead. The son cannot bear it; he weeps and sobs, not at his father's death, which he knows is only an act, but because he knows that he is about to give in, and to give up the greatest happiness he has ever been able to look forward to. His friend leaves alone, and sends him postcards. On his return, he tells the slave who has spent the whole summer in Paris, stuck in the Rue d'Aboukir, all about the marvelous trip he has had, the hospitality of the Greek peasants, and the experience of a life of freedom and adventure.

Vidal's is a cunning Oriental strategy. First, bide your time, wait, lull your opponent into a false sense of security, and then, at the right moment, announce imminent parricide: "If you want to kill your father . . ." and pretend to be dying. The strategy proves fail-safe for years. At the beginning of 1939, when the collapse of the republican armies in Catalonia brings a flood of 400,000 refugees into France, Edgar wants to take part in a commission for aid and investigation organized by the magazine *Esprit*, which would involve visiting the concentration camps on the borders in which the French authorities are interning the refugees. Again, Vidal makes no opposition at first, and then announces that he will die as soon as his son leaves for the Spanish border. Edgar is already 18 years old, but he gives in, and he will give in again the next year, when he is 19, and when his father, who has been drafted, and is at last leaving his son to his own devices, having accepted in principle that his son will go and stay in the university's hall of residence, announces that he will die unless Edgar goes to live with his sister Henriette. At 20, Edgar will give in again over the incident of the lavatory in Toulouse recounted above. He finally stops relenting when his father, learning belatedly that he has joined the Resistance, mobilizes a tribunal composed of his sister Henriette, his brother-in-law Élie, his nephew Mony, and his niece Liliane. The tribunal pleads with Edgar not to make his father die of grief, and when it fails, Vidal calls upon the supreme authority, Uncle Hananel, who commands his great-nephew to obey his father. Vidal is so astonished at his son's refusal that he forgets to die of it. Thus the sovereignty of parental authority, to which Vidal had bowed throughout his life, collapses.

Throughout his adolescence and until the age of 19, Edgar is successfully imprisoned by his father in a tightly knit web of precautions, protections, and physical and psychological constraints. However, Vidal has been completely negligent on the subject of manners, appearance and dress, as he is for himself. Vidal's wife used to chose his suits and shirts for him, make him change his underwear, give his trousers to be pressed; she took her son to her own dressmaker, who made him little suits to measure. At Corinne's Edgar was dressed with great care. Once Vidal and Edgar start living alone, however, things begin to slide. When they become desperate, Vidal takes his son to the Galeries Réaumur, near the Rue d'Aboukir, and buys him a cut-price suit which was too big for him and which creases as soon as he puts it on. The fly buttons that fall off the filial pants are not sewn back on, which causes the adolescent embarrassment in public places.

Although Vidal imposes a suffocating physical servitude on his son, he allows him the most complete mental freedom. He teaches him no manners, no principles, no ethics, no rule to live by or code of behavior.

Vidal does not vet his son's friends, or worry about their social or religious origins, nor does he exercise any form of exclusion, treating Jews and gentiles, boys from well-off families and those from poor families, alike. This negative moral philosophy is in fact the most positive moral philosophy he could have given his son.

Vidal is vaguely deist, but he feels no need to demonstrate the existence of the "dear Lord" to his son. He does not practise any religious ritual, and has not bothered to prepare his son for the *bar-mitzvah* nor have him practice for this initiation, which is the Jewish equivalent of first communion. It may have been at the urging of his sister Henriette (influenced by her religious husband Élie) and his mother, whom he respects, that he decides to correct this ommission. No less resourceful in religion than in business (as we will see later, on the occasion of his conversion to catholicism during the

Occupation), he succeeds in convincing the rabbi of the Rue Buffaut to give the *bar-mitzvah*, without prior initiation into the Bible or the Hebrew language, to a poor little orphan who has been deprived of his mother and is incapable of even the least demanding of studies. It is an extremely uncomfortable occasion for the child. He has been dressed in a sort of child's tuxedo, the whole family is present, and the rabbi prompts him, syllable by syllable, to repeat incomprehensible words, tells him when to sit down, get up, and make peculiar gestures; finally he makes him recite a text in French, and from his throne the boy thanks his dear family for having educated him in the ways of righteousness and virtue.

Vidal was the product of a process of secularization that had gradually been advancing for three generations, and the inheritance that survived from his ancestors was concentrated in the matricial foods that were served at family meals: hard-boiled duck eggs, salted cucumber, and *pastellicos* or *borekitas*. These dishes were served, and were as tasty as ever, at the weekly meals held at his sister Henriette's house, where his mother cooked Salonician food.

So Vidal had nothing to teach his son didactically. He would never have dreamed of formulating a general notion or a moral rule on the basis of the absolute and instinctive solidarity that he felt for every member of his family, his devotion to and sacrifice for his kin, or his generosity towards those close to him, all of which were things he felt naturally and which he in no way thought of as following a superior or external injunction. He did not need to teach him about Salonica, because the umbilical cord with the city had already been broken, and in Vidal's eyes was engulfed in the past (it is only much later that he wants to go there again, after he is 70); he has not tried to teach his son *djidio* Spanish, and Edgar never speaks it with his family (much later on, drawing on his memories of conversations between his parents and his grand-parents, and the Spanish servants, he will find himself speaking a crude form of Castilian when he is in Spain and Latin America).

Vidal did not even want to teach his son about business. He would simply have liked him to become a storekeeper, not out of any love of commerce (he had never felt any vocation for business himself and had wanted to be a doctor), but so that he would follow in his father's footsteps, be like him, and stay close to him.

In short, since Vidal had not been subject to any deep cultural "imprinting,"[54] other than that of the familial community, he had nothing to pass on.

His son therefore grows up in a cultural vacuum; moreover, as he is an only child and in secret inner dissidence with his paternal family, he is not even subject to the community-familial "imprinting" that was so profound in his father. Furthermore, the fundamental image of the Father has suffered terrible damage in his psyche, whereas the immense and faceless image of the Mother is dazzlingly radiant. Vidal's son experiences a triple lack during his teenage years: that of the Mythic Father, combined with the obsessive presence of his real father; that of his real mother, combined with the continual presence of the Mythic Mother; and finally that of a brother or sister. However, the cultural void of Sephardic secularization has been filled, in the son, by the cultural substance of French laicity: he has incorporated the glories and disasters of French history, adopting as his own Vercingétorix, Bouvines, Joan of Arc, Henri IV, the Revolution, Bonaparte, Napoleon, Alphonse Daudet's *La Dernière Classe* and Detaille's *Les Dernières Cartouches*, the miracle of the Marne and Victory *en chantant*. Moreover, perhaps under the influence of Fenimore Cooper and Gustave Aimard's novels, which exalt the American Indians, and Jack London's novels about the dogs of the far North, Edgar has discovered that Man was corrupted by civilization, and that he should return to the state of nature, like his ancestors who lived in caves and dressed in animal pelts. "That was all right in prehistoric times, but these are modern times," was Vidal's triumphant answer.

Encouraged by his hostility towards his family, Edgar convinces himself that commerce is theft. This notion grieves Vidal deeply, but he is unable to remove the poison from his son's mind. Vidal mobilizes his brother Henri, his sister Henriette and his nephew Mony, and during a family meal at the Rue Demours they struggle to convince the child that business is honest.

"But you sell goods that you bought for 10 francs for 15 francs!"

"Someone has to supply the customers with merchandise, they need it."

"Then they should go and get their supplies directly from the manufacturer."

"But it's too far away, too expensive, too much bother for them . . . "

"Then they should join together."

And so on.

To express all his ideas in concrete form, Edgar attempted to write an essay on "Man and animals." He bought a notebook, and began: "Man! Man."

That was as far as he got.

Vidal believes that his son is *bovo*, which might be translated in English as "a mooncalf." He has seen that his son is almost incapable of understanding what the death of a mother means, he has seen him respond to Luna's disappearance without emotion; his son even refused to go to the cemetery with him for the anniversary of her death. He considers him rather dim, and sees that he is often tongue-tied. Vidal, who is very lively himself, does not like dullards. At family meals at Corinne's house, Vidal tries to make his son understand him using only his finger and his eye; he points at something on the table, stares at it, and lightly snaps his finger and thumb to attract his son's attention; his son, baffled, fails to guess which object he is referring to: the salt? Bread? Oil? Wine? At a loss, he picks up the salt. Vidal responds with an impatient gesture, snaps his fingers again, and designates the thing imperiously. If his son fails this intelligence test a second time, he cries: "The wine!" "Why didn't you just say so?" "A son should not need words to understand his father." Vidal finds it distressing that his son pays no attention when he is with him in his store. He thinks that his lack of interest in business is due his listless intellect. Later, it worries him to see that, at an age when one is supposed to be developing intellectually, his son starts expressing ridiculous ideas, equating business with theft, declaring that animals are superior to humans, and wanting to imitate Diogenes, a madman from ancient times, who lived naked in a barrel. On numerous occasions, he confides to his sister Henriette how sad he is to observe that his son is so stupid, and that the most he will be capable of later on is working for some kind-hearted relation.

CITIZEN VIDAL

Vidal has been a French citizen since 1931. He retains an indefinable accent, which intrigues people: "Where exactly are you from?" "You tell me," answers Vidal, and people wonder, hazard a guess, and get it wrong. However, when the time comes to produce the answer, Vidal is at a loss: "I was born in Salonica." "That means your accent is Greek," they say, with astonishment. Vidal's accent has more of a Balkan flavor. Whereas his brother Henri has adopted the Marseillais accent, and Léon has a voice which seems to belong to him alone, not suggesting any particular foreign origin, and whereas neither Henriette nor Mathilde have the slightly whining, gently lilting accent typical of Salonician women, Vidal's voice, with its occasionally harsh resonances, is different from the high-pitched, hoarse tonality that many Selaniklis have when speaking French, but it never becomes entirely French and will always suggest foreignness.

Vidal has become a voter, and finds this new status almost as impressive as a decoration. Whereas, for every Frenchman born and bred, becoming a voter means becoming an adult, for Vidal it means rising to enjoy a dignity unknown for thousands of years, a privilege unheard of for an Oriental, who is completely dependent on those who govern him. True, Vidal is still too much of an Oriental to believe that the power that depends on his vote is also a result of it; however, precisely because he is an Oriental, he feels that he has been elevated to a higher sphere, in which one is in friendly communication with the authorities, and where one is courted by the powers that be, and solicited by them. Thus Vidal becomes comfortably accustomed to his acquaintance with his representative and municipal councillor, which for him are a source of great pleasure.

In Paris, Vidal has become politically aware to an extent. While Luna used to read *L'Excelsior*, a daily filled with photos and uniquely devoted to news, Vidal read and, until 1939, continues to read *L'Œuvre*, a leftist daily in the secular and antimilitarist tradition. He thinks of himself as a radical socialist, and when he becomes a voter in the 2nd arrondissement, he votes for the radical candidate – who only obtains a meagre share of the vote, since the Representative Paul Reynaud, from the party of social and national republican Union, is reelected every time. He is an influential politician, Minister of Finance in 1930, Minister of Colonies in 1931–1932 and Guardian of the Seals in 1932. In elections, Vidal behaves like an Oriental: he votes for the radical candidate in secret, and then addresses his congratulations to Paul Reynaud. Better still, under the influence of Edouard Mosseri, his uncle and neighbor in the Rue d'Aboukir, and a great agent of influence for Paul Reynaud in the Sentier, he joins Paul Reynaud's committee some time before the elections, in which he will secretly betray his chosen candidate, who will express his undeserved gratitude:

Paris, April 26, 1932

My dear fellow citizen,

You were kind enough to address a membership form to my committee. I would like to express my gratitude to you in person. Thanks to the energy of friends like yourself, we will win a decisive victory on Sunday.

Trust, my dear fellow citizen, in my devoted consideration,

Paul Reynaud

Thus, at each election, Vidal will congratulate Paul Reynaud, without ever actually voting for him. What is Oriental in this attitude is the concern to be thought well of by the man in power, the chief, the potentate. Undoubtedly, the fact that he essentially owes his liberation from Frigolet to the intervention of a representative and a minister has marked him, and he envisages seeking protection, if the need arises, from Representative and Minister Paul Reynaud. However, the specifically Vidalian element in this scenario is his skill in taking advantage of the Western system of the freedom to choose who to vote for, while simultaneously placing himself, Oriental fashion, beneath the protection of political power.

In the years 1935 and 1936, Vidal is integrated into a circle of friends, all of whom are gentiles. He has adopted the habit of having his lunch not far from his store in a restaurant called the Coq-Héron, in the Rue Coq-Héron, almost opposite the central post office in the Rue du Louvre. His son, who hates the food in the canteen (he has received a smack on the head from the supervisor, who caught him examining the unpalatable slice of meat he had been served with a magnifying glass), begins to join his father for lunch at the Coq-Héron. A table of regulars has formed there; they get to know one other and become friends. There is Mr. Lamouret, a short, vehement, leftist Christian, who is indignant about social iniquities; Mr. Perrin, who works at the post office, and is a one-eyed socialist; Mr. (name forgotten), a sales representative with a big pink chubby face, reddish hair, and a very grave expression that clashes with his round baby face; there is a very kindly fat lady, who works in a ready-to-wear clothes store in the Place des Victoires, and overwhelms the orphan with her affection. It is a period of unrest, and dramatic events follow in quick succession: Hitler takes power, there is rioting on February 6, 1934, and the Common Front, which will later become the Popular Front, is born. Around the table, they discuss these events endlessly; Vidal, ever the prudent Oriental, agrees with everyone. The fellow diners become increasingly intimate; Mr. Perrin invites Vidal's son to take a few days' vacation near his house, as a guest of Mrs. Copians, in Vert, near Mantes, where Mr. Lamouret is also spending the vacation with his wife and daughter. Naturally, the son has instructions to write every day to his father, and Mr. Perrin carries mail between them. A passage from one of these letters describes the ambiguous situation of a son whose father is known to most people as Mr. Vidal.

Mrs. Copians heated some water for my feet – it was boiling – [*Vidal is convinced of the benefits to health of footbaths in boiling water, and this information is intended to please his father.*] I had some coffee with milk and buttered bread. The lady talked to me about Belgium, and I told her that I'd only been to Brussels.

"But you're French?" she says to me.

"Yes . . . born in Paris," I say.

"S'funny, even so, s'mazing how foreign you look, whaddaya say, Paulot? Even more than your Dad, you look Basque or Spanish or something."

Silence . . .

"So you're not Basque, then" she says to me.

"No. But my grand-parents are from Salonica, in Greece."

"Ahh! Yes, yes, yes, I see! So that's it, whaddaya say, Paulot?" (Paulot nods).

So you can see I'm in a difficult position here, everyone thinks I'm Mr. Vidal junior. Imagine if Salem comes, or someone writes to me, they'll call me Nahoum. It'll be so embarassing! I'll have to make some hazy explanation, or say nothing at all, and the people in Vert will begin to view me with suspicion. I either want to be called Vidal or Nahoum. Since we've started with Vidal, let me stick to Vidal, but I don't want people to think that I was ashamed of being called Nahoum.

The regular lunch companions were pleased about the victory of the Popular Front. Vidal was certainly satisfied, but he was also worried that there would be disturbances. His experience in Salonica, where the great fraternizing celebrations that took place after the Young Turk revolution had not been followed by a radiant future, but by wars and convulsions, made him fearful. He was also afraid that Léon Blum's accession to the presidency of the Council would aggravate anti-Semitism. His son, on the other hand, was in paroxysms of delight, not because of the electoral victory, but because of

137

the great outpouring of joy in the streets, when the blue-collar workers and shop assistants believed they would be masters of their own destiny from now on. (He would experience the same joyous atmosphere again in May 1968, when people struck up conversations with one another, discussed the events, and the implacable Order that rules everyday life seemed to have been snuffed out.) Sales-girls from department stores, office clerks, old people, young people, everybody stood chatting on the sidewalks. Sometimes the discussions would turn into arguments, with some right-winger brandishing his ex-serviceman's card. "I fought in the war, sir!" "And so did I, sir," his contradictor would cry, raising his tricolored card for all to see.

It all blew over, summer came, and Edgar started buying newspapers and political magazines. The group of friends from the Coq-Héron saw no more of Vidal after the end of 1936. Vidal married again on December 26, 1936.

THE STRANGE MARRIAGE

Vidal had been subjected to increasingly powerful pressure from the family, who wanted him to marry again. One of their arguments was that since he could not continue to live at his sister's house after his mother's death, during the summer of 1936, he and his son needed a new home. But Vidal resisted, probably because he did not want to break off the secret affair he was having with a married woman. That made the family, who suspected the existence of this relationship, even more determined to bring it to an end. Vidal's mother must have nagged him affectionately before her death, and, whether in obedience to his mother's wishes, or because he was obliged to leave an apartment in which she was no longer living, or because he wanted to try and start a new life, or for all of these reasons together, he consented to a marriage arranged for him by the family.

Léon, the eldest brother and head of the family, played a decisive role in the affair. He found the fiancée. His wife Julie had a sister who had stayed in Salonica. Her name was Sara Menahem, she was 33 years old, and a beautiful woman, despite being rather buxom (which in principle suited Vidal's Oriental taste; he was never attracted to what he called skinny women). Sara was brought over to Paris, probably in September or October of 1936. It was all kept entirely secret from Vidal's son. Where did they arrange it? How did the first meeting go? How many meetings were there afterwards? In any event, Vidal broke off his secret relationship, but without letting his lover know he was about to get married. The wedding day was set for December 26, right in the middle of the Christmas vacation, which Edgar was being sent to spend in Brussels with Henri and Jacques, Vidal's brothers.

One December morning, Vidal takes the métro with his son to accompany him to the Gare du Nord. Out of the blue, as they are sitting in the carriage, he announces, with great embarrassment: "A lady is going to come to the station and give you a box of glazed chestnuts, say thank you nicely, because . . . she's going to be your new Mom." The boy, then aged 15, makes no reply, and there is no further mention of the lady. Edgar finds his seat in the carriage, stations himself at the window, and sees his father arriving with a rather attractive dark-haired woman with full lips, who offers him a box of glazed chestnuts, and says in a sing-song voice: "This is for you, dear Edgar." "Oh, thank you ma'am."

Then there is silence; a few stilted remarks are passed between them, the train starts to move off, they wave, and the train arrives in Brussels. There, Edgar forgets all about the woman; his father does not mention her in his letters, and he does not let his son know that he will be getting married during the vacation.

Letter from Vidal:

Saturday

My dear Edgar,

Yesterday, I had no news from you, and this morning I was very pleased to receive your first long letter which you sent on Thursday, telling me all about what happened with the lady crossing the border. I was rather upset to see that you were an hour and a half late when I think of dear Uncle Jacques having to wait such a long time in the cold of the Gare du Midi.

You must have been very hungry and cold too, my darling, having been so long in the carriage.

Is the weather good in Brussels at least? Luckily, the weather is fine here, and I hope it is the same where you are. How are you? I hope to have a long letter tomorrow full of precise details telling me how you have spent the first three days, and if you are all right, if . . . well, you are used to my questions and I look forward to your answers.

I will sign off with an affectionate hug and look forward to hearing from you soon.

Your Dad

Edgar is happy at his uncle Jacques's house. Jacques is very sweet-natured and likes to talk about literature, and his Aunt Sophie is very warm and expansive. Until now, he has only known his cousins Régine and Hélène very slightly. Régine is a little too old for him, but he becomes very fond of Hélène, who is two years his senior, and they go for walks together, talking about life and everything, except his mother, since he keeps his memory of her a secret. He is sad to leave Hélène at the end of the vacation. His father is waiting for him at the station, and takes him to a hotel in the Square Montholon, not far from the Rue Mayran; today it is called the Rue Pierre-Sémard.

A room has been taken for him, and it communicates with another room in which there is a double bed, and which is the newly-weds' room. Sara is affectionate and kisses the boy. He finds her pretty, but she has a pimple by her mouth. The next day, as he comes out of the lycée into the Place d'Anvers, he catches sight of the woman he has seen several times with his father (the secret lover). The woman comes up to him and takes him in her arms, crying: "My poor child!" She tells him that a family plot has succeeded in obliging his father to marry a stranger, and that she feels very sorry for Vidal and his son. Edgar starts crying stupidly, walks away from her, and, on his return to the hotel, begins to look upon the strange woman with suspicion. Vidal is not back yet. Sara calls Edgar and, in her sing-song voice, tells him that she knew his mother well, and that she wants to be a mother to him. He weeps again and allows the woman to embrace him.

A new routine begins. In the morning, Vidal and Edgar leave the hotel, one heading north and the other heading south; they return to the hotel to collect Sara and go and have lunch together in a little restaurant on the same street. In the evening, they eat a cold meal in Vidal and Sara's room, on a little table that she covers with a tablecloth. Every evening, they have *fontainebleaux*.[55] After dinner, Sara washes, dries and carefully folds the pieces of muslin used to wrap the *fontainebleaux*, and then stacks them no less carefully in one of the drawers. After a few days, Vidal begins raising his eyes to heaven whenever she is busy with this task, and he shakes his head forebodingly while looking at his son. The days go by, but still Vidal does not start looking for an apartment. However, he does begin to stay away increasingly often at night on "business trips." His son remains alone with Sara; after the meal and the ritual folding of the cheesecloths, each of them stays in their room, he doing his homework or reading, and she reading on her side.

Five months go by like this. One morning, July 1, 1937, Vidal returns from a "trip." Edgar hears Sara saying in her singsong voice:

"You really do spend a lot of time away, Vidal."

"What!" replies Vidal, as if unable to believe his ears. "What! Are you accusing me of something?"

"No, not at all, Vidal, I'm just saying that you spend a lot of time away."

"Ah, yes, but that means you suspect me of something, I understand it all perfectly now. Well, I refuse to live with a woman who is suspicious of me. Come, Edgar, get your things, we're leaving."

Flabbergasted, the boy puts his toothbrush and his schoolbooks into his satchel, Vidal picks up the suitcase he has not yet unpacked, and the two of them disappear from the hotel and from Sara's life forever. Vidal is probably not attracted to his new wife, and has gone back to his secret lover, who cannot bear him sharing another woman's bed. Sara waits in vain for her husband to return. Léon, being both brother-in-law to Sara and elder brother to Vidal, is obliged to intervene with severity. But nothing can persuade Vidal, and Sara, as the ruling by the civil tribunal of the first authority of the Seine region observes, "has no choice but to request a divorce from her husband, in support of which she offers to prove the following facts:

(1) From the beginning of the marriage, her husband treated his wife with coldness and reserve;

(2) After a time, Mrs. Nahoum realized that whenever he visited his first wife's family, he would return very late in the evening. Then he occasionally began to stay away at night;

(3) Finally, on July 1 1937, he abandoned his wife without warning and never reappeared;

(4) When his wife had him called and sounded out, he replied that he no longer wanted to return to her;

(5) That by means of a writ dated September 4, 1937, served by Maitre Lesage, bailiff in Paris, the applicant issued a warning to her husband Mr. Nahoum that he must come back and live with her, ensure her a living, and resume conjugal life. To this warning, Mr. Nahoum replied that "he refused categorically to live with her again, that he had organized his life with the intention of living alone with his son from his previous marriage, and that his decision was irrevocable."

On the grounds of all these grave affronts, the divorce was pronounced on April 25, 1938, with Vidal at fault.[56] Naturally, he had to pay all the expenses for the proceedings that she had begun. Sara was still in Paris in March 1938, and then she returned to Salonica. She would be arrested, deported and murdered by the Nazis, like most other Salonician Jews, in 1943.

THE RUE DES PLATRIÈRES

Vidal and his son find an apartment in the Rue des Platrières, downhill from the section of the Rue Sorbier where Joseph and Corinne live. This means that they are living independently for the first time, but Corinne continues to play the role of foster mother, every evening bringing or sending them a double portion of the hot main course that she has prepared for her own family. On his way back from school, Edgar does the shopping at the dairy in the Rue des Amandiers, taking the covered milk jug with him. He buys a liter of milk, some eggs, ham, yogurt, and cheese, and then, at the little grocer's in the Rue des Panoyaux, some Pelure d'oignon wine, to which Vidal is very partial. The only thing Vidal can cook is fried eggs. Father and son sit at their kitchen table to eat. Each has his own bedroom. In the son's room, there is a folding bookcase that his father has bought for him; it is soon filled with books. Edgar reads constantly, in the street, in the métro, in class, at table, in bed in the evening.

During Vidal's trips to his manufacturers, Corinne sends her son Fredy to spend the night in the apartment.

My dear Dad,

I hope you weren't too tired when you got back and that your headache has gone away.

My day went very well. Yesterday evening, Fredy and I went to the cinema, and when we got home the concierge was very quick to open the door for us. This morning, Aunt Corinne came at 7.30. We were both already awake, and she made us some coffee with milk and a croissant. She tidied the bedrooms, then I went to take a shower at 8.30, I didn't have to wait long there, then I worked and read until 12.30. I went to Aunt Corinne's house, where I had lunch: potato salad, fresh sardines, rice, lentils, steak and cake.

Then I came home to work on my recitation test. At 5 o'clock, I went to get Fredy and we went for a long walk. I didn't forget to buy the milk.

Tomorrow evening, we have been invited to grandmother's house for dinner, that way you won't have to prepare anything. I hope you will come back with good news.

With love.

Edgar.

P.S. It's not boiled milk.

With more or less difficulty, Edgar passes up from one school grade to the next. His father has not given up the idea that he might go into business after the baccalauréat. He takes advantage of Edgar's affectionate trust in his brother Jacques to ask him to suggest to his son that he studies commercial law. This explains the following passage from a long letter written by Jacques to his nephew, on November 16, 1936, shortly before the Christmas holidays, which Edgar spends in Brussels while Vidal and Sara are getting married:

As I have no idea what subjects are usually taught in Parisian schools, could you let me know if they teach commercial law? If the answer is no, or even if it is yes, you might think of consulting a book on commercial law for half an hour every Friday; I am sure you would enjoy it. I am making this suggestion because I think you want to acquire some general knowledge, which will put you in a position later on to decide what you need to do to choose your career in life . . . .

A new life begins in the Rue des Platrières. In the morning and in fact all the time, Vidal continues to sing the tunes he has loved since his youth: Mayol songs, Neapolitan melodies, tunes by Raquel Meller, songs about Paris. He and his son sing *Le rêve passe* together, and it moves them to tears, for they both love Napoleon:

The soldiers below are asleep on the plain
Where the evening breeze lulls them with its song.
The earth's breath is sweet with golden corn

142

Far off the sentinel passes with rhythmic step
Then suddenly, out of the sky, from the shadows it springs
[. . .]
The hydra with its pointed helmet stealthily advances
The child awakes, excited, but all around is silence, sleeping
And in his heart, hope has returned.
[. . .]
Do you see them
The hussars, the dragoons, and the guard
Still standing
From Austerlitz beneath the Eagle's gaze?
The men of Marceau and Kléber, singing their victory,
Giants of iron, who ride on Glory's back . . .

For Vidal, the thirties are the years of Georgius, Lys Gauty, Lucienne Boyer, and evenings at l'Européen, the music hall in the Place Clichy, where he takes his son who, like him, is very fond of Georgius and of Allibert's Marseillais operettas, especially *Trois de la Canebière*. One evening, in 1937 or 1938, his son takes him to see Marianne Oswold, whose renditions of Prévert and Kosma's songs (*A la belle étoile, L'Evadé*) have moved him deeply. Part of the audience whistles its disapproval, and Vidal thinks the songs are dreadful and is surprised at his son's strange taste.

Vidal's favorite actress is Marie Bell. She probably embodies his Mediterranean ideal of beauty, since she is dark and well-rounded, with an ardent expression, and is passionate in the more or less melodramatic films in which she stars. His son, on the other hand, is transfixed at the age of 12 or 13 by the sovereign Nordic beauty of Brigitte Helm in *L'Atlantide*.

THE FAMILY

Vidal's mother dies in 1936. Vidal will take the framed photographs of his mother and father with him to all his different homes, as if they were his *lares*. He frequently looks at them and talks to them. In fact, he feels very strongly that they are still alive somewhere and continue to protect him. He had remained little Vidalico, their youngest son and cherished child, until they died, and he will cherish them until his own death.

Léon is continuing to expand Nahum Steel, whose offices are in the Rue Antoine-Dansaert. He is the most prosperous and the most eminent of the brothers. After having been made a Knight of the Order of Leopold, he receives the Order of the Crown in 1938. His son Edgard feels more Belgian than the Flemish or Walloons, who feel divided in their identity. He is even fonder of military marches than his cousin Edgar, and is always humming them.

Léon continues to play the role of eldest brother and head of the family, and his opinions are decisive for his brothers. For instance, it is on his advice that Vidal remarries. But the demands of his own life lead him to break up this marriage. However, although familial authority suffers a first and powerful defeat at this time, fraternity is unaffected, and there is no cooling of relations between Léon and Vidal.

Chary, Léon's daughter, lives with her husband Hiddo in Avignon, in an attractive house in the Rue Banastérie, at the foot of the wall of the papal castle. They have two children, Jackie (born in 1932), and Nicole (in 1937). A boy, Jean-Loup, will be born in 1943. Hiddo is a partner in the family firm, which cuts teasel thistles to be used in wool processing all over the world. Chary and Hiddo are integrated into the vast Naquet tribe. They have become completely French through their connection with the family, and are very much at home in Avignon. Jacques and his wife Sophie live in Brussels. Sophie has retained her Serbian accent, her frank way of speaking, and her cordiality. Jacques works in Léon's firm, and remains interested in literature. Régine will be 20 in 1937 or 1938; Hélène is two years younger, and when Vidal's son gets to know her, he is amazed to discover that there is someone in his family he can talk to about what interests him.

Henri is living in Auderghem, a little suburb of Brussels, in a house set in woodland and surrounded by landscaped gardens, with his companion Gaby Coatsaliou; Gaby's brother, whose business has failed, is living with them. Gaby is now a member of the Nahum family, and Henri is one of the Coatsalious. The couple gets on well, though Henri is still something of a womanizer, always on the lookout for fresh conquests. Vidal continues to admire this trait in his brother, even when Henri makes advances to his own wife. A very close bond has remained between the two brothers since their youth in Marseilles and their shared memory of Frigolet. Henri's principal business is importing Japanese bazaar goods, which he does from a room next door to the offices occupied by Nahum Steel,

Henriette's daughters have nicknamed her "Maniouche belle" and "la babonette," who, according to a text they learned at school, "never went home with clean hands," because she picked up and kept everything she found along the way, thinking it might come in handy some day. She was very concerned about the situation of her brother Vidal and her nephew Edgar, and was happy to take them in after their departure from the Rue Sorbier; she has done everything she can to find a dignified solution to Vidal's widowerhood, and, as we will see, will later take in her nephew when Vidal is drafted. Her husband Élie continues to keep an eye on Vidal's store.

Henriette has become firmly established at 18, Rue Demours. At first, Liliane and Mony live in the Rue Laugier, very close to the Rue Demours; later, when Henriette's neighbor on the same landing leaves, she arranges for her daughter and son-in-law to rent the apartment. The couple do not seem to have been physically compatible; they have no children, and in private each lays the blame for this sterility on the other. (One of the uncles was apparently charged by a family council to find out whether Liliane is barren.) Liliane's unhappy marriage has brought mother and daughter closer, and the umbilical cord is further shortened when they become neighbors on the same floor. Henriette is very unhappy about her daughter's unhappy marriage, and enfolds her in her tenderness. They seem to confide in each other about everything and have complete confidence in one another. One day, Henriette tells Vidal's son that her Liliane is very unfortunate, because she has to pay herself for the jewelery she pretends to have received as a present from her husband. Her nephew does not understand why she has told him this.

Mony and Liliane go out often and they often invite friends into their home; on these evenings, Liliane takes her place at the piano. When she is alone, she plays Chopin; for friends, she plays popular songs and dance tunes. The couple goes regularly to the Salonicians' Club, but Vidal has not registered as a member, and is not particularly keen on going there. Mony and Liliane play bridge, but Vidal is not interested in card games. (However, ever since the National Lottery began, he has bought several tickets for each draw, and, probably after his situation improves and he has repaid his debts, he begins to dabble on the stock market again.)

Liliane and Mony often go on vacation, but never alone – either with Mathilde and Bouchi, or Aimée and Ben, and/or other couples who are friends, almost all of them businessmen in the Sentier or Salonicians, although there are also a few gentiles. Postcards from them show that they went to Dinard, La Baule, etc. In fact, Liliane is not lonely. Apparently, she has a confidant, a protector, perhaps a lover, within the couple's circle of friends. Liliane lives in two worlds: she is a woman in the traditional Salonician world, and has submitted to all of its constraints, and also a modern Parisian woman, all of whose aspirations she shares, including that of working professionally as an artist.

Mony is part of the Nahum family, but Henriette does not really like him. He is small, and sickly, but very quick and competent. He makes a much better success of his business in the Sentier than Vidal does. He sells better quality merchandise, for better prices. At home, Mony is mean with money, and keeps an eye on expenses (Liliane is just as parsimonious, but she is very generous when away from home, on outings and in restaurants). In around 1937, Mony takes great pride in installing a "picture gallery" in his apartment; he has been told it consists of works by well-known painters, and he shows it off to be admired by his visitors.

Aimée, Liliane's younger sister, lives in Liverpool with her husband Ben; they have one son, Pierre, known by the family as "little Pierre." The only French thing about him is his name: he is born English, raised English, will have an English accent, marry an Englishwoman and be naturally integrated among the gentiles on the other side of the Channel. Henriette and her husband, and Liliane and Mony, go to Aimée's house in Liverpool nearly every year, and she comes every year on vacation to France.

Mathilde and Bouchi continue to lead the high life in Belgrade. They still have no children, and never will. Every year, they come to spend the summer in France, and sometimes go to take a cure at Vittel. As we have said, their arrival is cause for celebration; they bring presents for everybody, and invite them to expensive restaurants where Bouchi and Mony argue about who will pay the check, sweeping the marveling family along in their wake. Mathilde dearly loves her brothers and sisters, especially Henriette, her elder sister, and although she is younger, she has an elder sister's affection for her brother Vidal, whom she calls Coco.

The scattered family does not lose touch. They write to each other regularly, and most importantly they make journeys to see one another, and meet either at one another's homes, in Brussels, Paris, Liverpool and Belgrade, or on vacation. Since the end of the Great War, the Nahums have become French, Belgian, English, or Serbian respectively. The Brussels and Paris Nahums have begun to think of themselves as westerners, as we can see from a letter written by Henriette from Belgrade in February 1937 (or 1939) to her nephew Edgar. Henriette was born and married in Salonica; her youth and early adult life were therefore influenced by the East. But when she returns to the East – not to Salonica, but to a city that has many characteristics in common with the Oriental city of her youth – she sees the Serbian city as exotic, with the eyes of a bourgeois Parisian; of course, the "Frenchness" of her vision is all the more pronounced because she wants to describe the Balkan city for and through the eyes of her Parisian nephew.

My darling Edgar,

I have been in Belgrade since January 9 and believe me, I don't know myself. Can you believe it, Aunt Henriette, "the hyperactive maniouche," always rushing around, last to bed, first up in the morning, me, the anxious one, the agitated one, spending whole days doing nothing! I really don't recognize myself. In fact, my vacation is exactly the proper kind of vacation that a woman my age ought to take, and that's what I'm doing. Aunt Mathilde and Uncle Bouchi are doing everything they can to make my stay with them as pleasant as possible, and I am very grateful to them.

Belgrade is an old city, and Uncle Bouchi tells me that it was only a very small town before the war. Since 1918, it has been expanding rapidly, with new buildings and new neighborhoods, and the population has tripled. There was a ghetto [sic] here until 1914, and you can still see some dilapidated cottages inhabited by poor Jews, which are a sorry sight. In town, the population is mixed, with various Slavs, Europeanized Greeks and others in Hungarian costume, as well as Slovenians, Czechs and Albanians. The Albanians are the poorest race of all, and some are even quite destitute. For one dinar, they carry loads weighing forty or fifty kilos on their heads, they work as woodcutters, and so on; in short, they are laborers. What do these poor people eat? Raw onions and bread; and on a feast day, when they have earned a little money, they treat themselves to a little glass of *chlivovitza*, which is a kind of plum liqueur. There are some fine houses in the new parts of town, near to the new royal palaces. There is also an old palace in the center, and the dramatic events that have happened there have made it a historic place. It has beautiful grounds sloping down to the river Danube and the river Save, and you can see their confluence there; the waters of the Danube are blue, while those of the Save are muddy, and there is a straight line, which looks as if it has been traced by human hand, marking their confluence. The park is called Kalemydan, a Turkish word meaning Tower Square, and the fortresses built by the Turks at the time of their conquest of Serbia still stand within it. So far, it's the only place I have seen that I find worthy of interest. The climate in Belgrade is harsh, with bitter winters and very hot summers. The food suits the climate, with fresh or preserved meats and sweets. There is nothing to drink apart from water, which does not taste very nice with meat. They eat a little fish, which is very expensive and comes from the rivers; salt water fish from the Adriatic and the Aegean is rare and expensive. You have to go to a special restaurant to eat it. I've forgotten to tell you that they never serve a meal without gherkins, chilis and all kinds of similar condiments. Everything is homemade, and all the housewives take pride in keeping their pantries well stocked with jams, bottled vegetables and salted meats like the pickel-fleisch sold in Alsatian delicatessens. Uncle Bouchi explained to me that the custom of having so many provisions at home began in the past; when the winters were especially harsh, the snow was often three or even six feet deep. Nowadays, they sweep the sidewalks and people can get around, but in those days they had to stay at home, and thanks to their provisions they were not afraid of starving to death. In October, they would make provisions of flour, cheese, and meat which they salted, etc., and they still do in spite of modern conveniences. Visitors may turn up hungry at any hour of the night, and there is always something to give even the fussiest guest: foie gras or their particular treat, cold meat with gherkins, well-cut and well-presented. I haven't told you that one still sees a fair number of Muslims, who have remained in the country and are still very religious; there is a mosque where the muezzin sings to call the faithful to prayer. I find it all very interesting, it reminds me a little of the country where I was born – only a very little, but still it brings me closer to the way of life in my homeland. Serbian is difficult for speakers of Latin languages, due to the succession of consonants, with hardly any vowels at all. Everybody speaks Serbian and German, plus a little French since the war, because many refugees lived in France. English has taken precedence over French at the moment, and the handful of English teachers cannot satisfy the great demand for private lessons. As far as entertainment goes, there are card games for adults, and sports for young people: skiing, tobogganing, and ice-skating right in the center of town; children learn to skate from the age of 5. There are not many classical concerts, only one or two per season. There is only one theater. The city's main street is about as long as the distance from the Place des Ternes to the Avenue Niel, and all of Belgrade's young people go walking there every evening; they call it the Corso. There are two lines on each sidewalk, going in different directions in Indian file, and the most agreeable entertainment in Belgrade for a young man or a young woman is to go to the Corso.

A New Life (1931–1939)

Well, there you are, a little summary of Yugoslavian life, not counting the provin-
cial-town gossip, which is never-ending.

We are well and I hope you are well too, my darling. What are you doing, are you
satisfied with your work? I expect you are right in the middle of a period of serious
study. You will certainly have earned your holidays by the time April comes. Write to
me when you have a moment, I would be very glad to have your news.

That's all, my darling, Aunt Mathilde and I send you all our love,

Aunt Henriette

Mony Covo is the only one who still has a father and mother in
Salonica. None of the Nahums remain there. Only one Frances is still living there, Dona Helena's brother, Azriel Frances, with whom the family
keeps in touch by letter. Nobody returns to Salonica, on vacation or on
pilgrimage, except for Mony and Liliane, and Léon and his wife Julie,
whose parents still live there. The reason is that Salonica is no longer
Salonica. The whole of the central district, which was destroyed by the
1917 fire, has been transformed; the city is now a Greek city with a
Sephardic minority, rather than a Sephardic one with Greek and Turkish
minorities, as it had been in the past. In 1931, there is an outbreak of violence against the Jews, which results in the emigration of 10,000
Salonicians to Tel Aviv. Henriette refers to Salonica as her homeland in the
letter we quoted above, but it is a homeland swallowed up in the past. The
Nahums' gradual Frenchification has been progressing since their mother's
death. She had prepared Salonician dishes for her family until the end of
her life. Subsequently, they go to eat this kind of food in restaurants, but
with the exception of *pastellico*, they only occasionally eat Salonician cuisine at home.

Vidal and his family sometimes go to a little Sephardic restaurant on the
second floor of a building in the Rue Cadet, and to Les Diamantaires, an
Armenian restaurant in the Rue Lafayette. Two or three Salonician restaurants remain in the Sentier, most of which are above stores, but they will
close during the war, as will the Salonician restaurants around the Rue
Sedaine. Henriette and Liliane, like Corinne, still sometimes make *pastellico*, a sheep's cheese tart, which they make with unsalted or half-salted soft
white cheese instead. The proximity of Diamand, the Alsatian delicatessen
in the Avenue des Ternes, means that ham on the bone, Strasbourg
sausages, pickel-fleisch and especially smoked tongue, to which Vidal is
very partial, become part of their Frenchified diet.

On the Beressi side, Myriam, Luna and Corinne's mother, continues to
run her home and prepare food in the Salonician way. The family still cele-
brates Passover there, in the presence of rabbi Perahia. Myriam has retained
her affection for Vidal in spite of his remarriage and his relationship outside
the family, which she is aware of but does not mention to him. Vidal
continues to pay her an allowance. Myriam is always overcome with

148

emotion whenever she sees Luna's son, saying, with tears in her eyes: "*La cara de su madre*" ("his mother's face"). Her children leave home when they marry. Émy, a spirited, dark-haired beauty, with a round face, brown eyes, and well-defined lips, had been a sales assistant at a very young age, working on the display at Bouchara, the fabric store on the Boulevard Haussman. Later, after breaking off her engagement with Victor Lerea, she "happens" to meet Maurice Cohen at her mother's house, falls passionately in love with him, and marries him. Maurice is from Istanbul. He has reddish-blond hair, blue eyes, and a powerful, muscular physique; he is tough and energetic. He has no money, and makes his living initially by going around the markets selling goods from a handcart, accompanied by his wife. They go to live in Le Havre, and work on the regional markets. To begin with, Vidal and Hananel supply merchandise to Maurice on credit.

However, when a payment does not arrive on time, Hananel gets angry, Maurice takes offense, and relations between them break down. Vidal continues to supply Maurice with merchandise, but seems to have been less generous than he had hoped. Even so, they remain on good terms.

Letter from Émy to Vidal:

Le Havre, October 20, 1932
My dear Vidal,
I've just received your letter and, as you can see, I'm answering it at once.

First, I want to thank you for all the trouble you have gone to on our behalf, and for being so kind as to store my furniture for me at Rueil, because as you know you're saving me a lot of expense, thank you . . .

I also want to ask you to thank Mama and Corinne very sincerely from me, because Maurice says they have been very kind. I really am lucky (as all riff-raff are). I'll be writing to them tomorrow in any case, I'm a little tired at present.

Secondly, as far as Bernard is concerned, carry on, whatever you decide will be fine.

Thirdly, anklets: difficult to sell, none at all yet, but if you don't need them right away, Maurice will go around the haberdasheries, and if you can send us wool stockings, especially if they're cheap, so we can undercut the competition, and wool socks too, BUT THEY HAVE TO BE CHEAP ONES, maybe we'll manage to sell the anklets at the same time.

Fourth: Soler, from Toulouse, wants to send a representative. Not a good idea, we're living in a furnished room and it will make a bad impression.

Fifth: you had an address for scarves. Could you ask for a sample in your name and send it on to me? . . . And most importantly, send me the prices.

Six: insurance? Get her to pay you the difference, I've paid it for a whole year. And not a cent less, because she's riff-raff.

Now, health, good for everyone, I hope. Business? Let's not talk about it! Better not. The only people here are sailors and dockers and they're all out of work, so they don't buy anything. That makes everything nice and simple, don't you think?

If business improves a bit, I'm going to come to Paname[57] at the end of November to learn the new dance, the yoyostep. Tell Corinne I'm going to buy myself some CLOGS like a fishwife.

Send everyone my love, and Maurice's,

Émy

Le Havre, October 24, 1932

Dearest Vidal,

I really hate doing this, but I have a favor to ask you and I don't know how to begin, it's very embarassing, I'm just going to say it straight out, here we go, I've got a big problem, I have a bill to pay at the end of the month for 4,000 francs, and another for 600 francs (furniture).

All I have is 600 francs and the 1,000 francs that you have.

I've written a letter to the manufacturer telling him that I can't pay him 4,000 francs, I offered either to pay 2,000 francs at the end of the month and 2,000 at the end of November, or take back the merchandise and I'll pay the difference.

The man wrote back saying he'll put a stop on the merchandise, which is still at the factory girl's, until I pay ... So I sent him a registered letter in which I pointed out that he had no right to stop it, seeing that none of his bills had been either refused or contested, and I proposed the same two options to him again.

As you can imagine, I'm not prepared to pay in full for merchandise that I only received in part, so I will only pay for the part that I have had.

But it hasn't stopped raining here all month, and I've had a lot of difficulties this month. It would be nice of you, dear Vidal, if you could send me that 1,000 francs on the 27th to Le Havre, because I am sending him 2,000 on the 28th ... and if you could also lend me 600 francs, which you would give to Mama on the 29th so that she can pay for my furniture on the 30th.

I will do everything in my power, dear Vidal, to pay you back on November 5 or 6. I hope you're not having any problems on your side and that you'll be able to do me this favor, by way of revenge, old buddy.

Thank you in advance and I look forward to your reply by return.

Lick everyone.

Émy and Maurice

Maurice and Émy, who have had their first son, Raymond, live a hard life in one small room. Later, when they have earned a little money, they go back to Paris, and move into a little apartment in the Rue des Mûriers, not far from the Rue Sorbier, very close to the Square Martin-Nadaud. Maurice opens a dressmaking shop over by the Place Voltaire, and then one in the Sentier, in the Rue Montmartre. His business begins to take off, but then the war begins. He signs up at once for the foreign legion, and Émy takes charge of what by now is a small business.

Pepo is 32 years old in 1930. His manner and his voice are Italian, and he has a typical Beressi face with well-defined features. He is jovial and easy-going, but also very strongly built, which has encouraged him to do some boxing. He never starts a fight, but does not think twice about laying out anyone who does him wrong. His character makes him unsuited to business, and he makes a living as a salesman or clerk. In 1933, after various affairs, he meets the love of his life, a young Sephardi girl called Margot Camhi, whose family had left Usküb (Skopje) for Salonica, and then Paris. Throughout their engagement, the two young people, who are very much in love, kiss constantly. After the wedding, they go to live in Besançon, where Margot becomes manager of the local branch of Au Muguet (selling women's lingerie and stockings). Their son André is born in Besançon in 1937.

Benjamin is good-natured, naïve, absent-minded, not very gifted academically and ill-suited for the "struggle for life." He is 30 in 1929, and works as a clerk. He will take up with a gentile woman, a Miss Jamot, who comes from Le Havre; they live together without marrying, and their daughter, Odette, is born in 1934. The young woman has a concierge's lodge, they live modestly, and the family does not see much of them.

Samy Beressi dies in 1929, at the age of 54, of a heart attack. His son Roger is obliged to give up his father's department store, and begins working in textiles. His second son, Alex, who studied law, becomes a lawyer or legal consultant. He is 28 in 1939. Edith is 23 at the same date. Odette, who is not yet known as Ana Beressi, is 19 years old, and graduates from high school.

Hananel Beressi continues to dominate things from his great height, and his reign as head of the family is uncontested. Hananel is like the tribe's "Godfather;" he even has the same muffled and slightly trailing voice that Marlon Brando uses in the film – a voice that is even more striking coming from such a tall, energetic-looking man. Vidal admires and respects Hananel, who despite his lack of schooling has the allure of an aristocrat. It was Hananel who advised him in 1921 to give up the export business and rent a store in the Sentier, and who, in 1931, came to the rescue of Émy's engagement ring. He also has an insatiable appetite for women, food and drink. Vidal often asks his advice and confides in him. Élie Beressi, the youngest of the brothers, has married a gentile woman from the Creuse, called Léonie. They do not have any children, and live in Clermont (in the Oise region).

On the Mosseri side, Edouard, Myriam's brother, continues to make a living from his business, bet on the horses, and head the election committee for Paul Reynaud in the Sentier. He always carries a cane, like Hananel, and wears spotless white gaiters over his shoes. He delights his nephews Fredy and Edgar by playing the musical saw, keeps a little device in his pocket that imitates birdsong, and calls everyone he knows, whatever their age, "*Mon p'tit.*" Towards the end of the thirties, he begins a relationship with Mrs. Dumontet, a gentile woman, who is a divorcee or a widow, and who will protect him during the Occupation.

On the Beressi and the Mosseri sides, family members are scattered in different parts of France. Although the Salonician household in the Rue Sedaine remains, the Beressis and Mosseris, like the Nahums, are becoming

French, and are being absorbed into the gentile world. There are already two mixed marriages among the generation that was born in Salonica.

During the 1930s, a revelation transforms the lives of two Salonicians Vidal knows. Both fall under the spell of a magical world, which they discover in something they read by chance. The first of these Salonicians, Henri Matarasso, had come to Paris in 1911, and had started working as clerk to a coffee and cocoa-broker whose authorized representative he became. He left for Spain during the First World War, perhaps in an attempt to avoid military service, and his son was born in Barcelona. Then he settled in Brussels, and continued to work as a broker until he was ruined by the crash of 1929. Being interested in literature, he opened a little bookstore for bibliophiles in Brussels, and it was then that he had a life-changing revelation: he discovered Arthur Rimbaud. He later opened a bookshop in Paris, in the Rue de Seine, specializing in original or rare editions from the 19th century; he acquired the manuscript of *Une saison en enfer*, and discovered an unknown portrait of Arthur Rimbaud. From then on he lived for books, and made his living from books.

The second conversion happens to a nephew of Élie Hassid's, Félix Gattegno, who starts out selling hosiery in a doorway. Reading the surrealists changes his life. He devotes himself to literature, joins the editorial committee of the Cahiers du Sud, translates Federico Garcia Lorca's *Romancero Gitano* into French, and introduces Vidal's son to Saint-John Perse, in 1940.

Thus, the Salonician diaspora infiltrates every milieu, and dares to contradict the sociological dictum that intellectual proletarians who possess no cultural capital are prohibited from pulling themselves up to the heights of the intelligentsia.

During the years between 1931 and 1939, Vidal has a great deal of work, many worries, many problems, almost no vacations, a stormy relationship, a failed marriage, a return to his former relationship, and possibly further unknown affairs. In spite of everything, he remains as cheerful as ever and continues to spend his life singing. No one knows that France is about to collapse, that Germany will occupy her, that night will fall.

VIII
The 1939 to 1945 War

THE PHONEY PEACE

Vidal and his son have settled in the Rue des Platrières for the duration, or so they think.

But terrible rumblings are rising from the heart of Europe. Hitler's Germany has embarked on a program of rearmament, dragging the other nations, who are far behind the Germans, into the great war machine. The screaming Führer is transmitted over the radio into the peaceful homes of France, and the cinema newsreels, which precede the main feature with its mouth-to-mouth kisses, depict the solemn, hysterical, mystical Nuremberg rallies, and the insane Moscow trials. The fighting in Spain, where the European war has already begun locally, with all the future allies and enemies taking part, is heard, seen and read about in France. So war has already broken the twilight peace of Europe. Then, in 1938, the process gathers speed. Hitler annexes Austria, entering Vienna in triumph on March 14 and, in April he demands that Czechoslovakia hands over the territory that lies between the mountains of the Sudetenland and the German border. Vidal tries to reassure himself. "No, no, there won't be a war," he keeps saying in his conversations. He also frequently says: "I'm optimistic." He thinks everything will turn out all right. He keeps himself informed about what is happening, but never thinks of intervening through political action. He does not understand why his son is attending meetings and briefing sessions.[58]

Whereas Vidal is confident, Edgar is anxious. They spend the summer of 1938 in Luchon, where both father and son take a cure, the first for his throat, the second for his nose.

By September 1938, the situation has become explosive. On September 4, Bernes accepts the demands made by the German population in the Sudetenland, but then Hitler begins to insist that these regions must be annexed by the Reich, and the Nazis launch terrorist attacks on Czechoslovakia. The tension mounts, and everyone thinks that war will break out. Some Parisian families do not return from their vacations. Others leave for the provinces, fearing massive poison gas bombardments, which everyone predicts will happen on the first day of hostilities.

Henriette, Élie, Liliane and Mony leave for Niort in Mony's van, and Mony returns to Paris for his business. Vidal takes his son with him to Niort one day in September, but since the threat of war seems to have frozen in its very intensity, Vidal goes back to Paris, accompanied by his son, who does not want to stay in Niort. On September 30, the Munich agreement is signed. Germany, Italy, Great Britain and France agree to let a third of Czechoslovakia's population and territory be amputated, along with 40 percent of her industrial potential, and, with the Sudeten mountains, her strategic borders. Vidal and his son feel relieved. Vidal goes back to his business, and Edgar, who has passed his first baccalauréat in June (to Vidal's great pride: the title of *bachélier* retains its Medieval dignity in his eyes), joins the philosophy class.

The year 1938 to 1939 passes, and the threat of war reappears in spring. In April 1939, Hitler lays claim to Dantzig and renounces the Germano-Polish agreement. Great Britain, France and the USSR negotiate on a treaty to protect Poland. The negotiations fail to make progress, and Edgar learns, either from *La Flèche* or from Bergery's assertions at a Frontist meeting, that secret negotiations are under way between the USSR and Hitler's Germany.

Summer comes. Vidal and Edgar leave to take a second cure in Luchon. The first cure has proved beneficial for the father's throat and the son's nose. There is a small group of teachers at their guesthouse, and father and son are incorporated into this group. Vidal is still very outgoing, very communicative, always laughing, and although he is an ousider in these teachers' world, they have no difficulty becoming friends. Father and son also like walking. They hike to the summit of Superbagnères; as they are going down through the forest, a tremendous storm takes them by surprise. Edgar, fearing that the trees will attract lightning, trembles during the descent. But Vidal, who is usually very fearful in such circumstances, behaves with courage and reassures his panic-stricken son.

Vidal is obliged to return to Paris for his commercial or romantic affairs, and leaves his son under the protection of the members of the teaching community. Edgar feels rather relieved, and has a taste of freedom; every evening he goes for a drink at the Allées d'Etigny, where there is music, with an English teacher, Mr. Desacher. Mr. Desacher continually requests the Genlis family band, which consists of Mr. Genlis on violin, Mrs. Genlis on piano, and Genlis junior on drums, to play *Tiger Rag*. Although their interpretation is lifeless in the extreme, more reminiscent of an apartment tomcat than a tiger, Mr. Desacher never fails to beat out the rhythm, beaming ecstatically. Vidal's son is adopted by a lady from Toulouse, Mrs. de Salvagnac, who is on vacation with her 14-year-old granddaughter, a charming and cheeky young girl, who also adopts the 18-year-old boy. The lady is glum, and strict with the adolescent girl, whose secret she reveals to the young man: her granddaughter is illegitimate, they do not know who her father is, and she has been abandoned by her mother. Edgar feels a strange bond with the little girl and her grandmother. They write to each other, and meet again one year later in Toulouse, then lose touch.

On August 7, 1939, Edgar sends a card announcing his return to Paris:

My dear Papa,
Everything is fine. I arrived Sunday morning. Don't need any money. Weather fantastic.
Love

On August 23, news breaks of the Germano-Soviet pact. Hitler's demands are increasingly vociferous. The German city of Dantzig is ready to erupt. Despite the apparently inevitable threat of war, some people reassure themselves by remembering the previous year, when an unhoped-for agreement prevented it at the last minute. Although Henriette and her family have returned to Niort, Vidal remains in Paris. On Sunday, the evening before September 1, completely by chance, he decides not to stay the night in Paris (he is still haunted by the idea that a massive bombardment will come and wipe out the city) and, with his gasmask slung over his shoulder, he takes his son with him to Chatou, to his cousin Murat's house. Murat is the brother of his cousins Paul, the dentist, and Saül, the pharmacist; he is a senior executive at a bank that is managed by Botton, a highly-placed relative. Murat lives in an old house standing in a garden that has half run wild, on a tributary of the Seine, opposite a dyke. He has taken a gentile wife, and has a daughter with an exciting bosom, who is about the same age as her cousin. That afternoon, the two young people are standing, leaning against each other, with their parents close by, when the radio announces that Germany has delivered an ultimatum to Poland.

Suddenly, the Chatou dyke, which is guarded by a soldier, begins to seem very dangerous. They spend the night in this mysterious house and then, in the morning, they learn that France and Great Britain have declared war on Germany. The Wehrmacht arrives outside Warsaw within eight hours, and Soviet troops enter Poland from their side; in one month, Poland has been occupied and divided up between them. The French troops have barely moved from their position beside the Sarre. The phoney war has begun.

Élie, Henriette and Liliane are stuck for a time in Niort. They want to go home but at the same time they are afraid to, and as foreigners (Greeks), they have trouble getting the safe-passes which would allow them to travel back and forth between Niort and Paris. A card from Élie to Vidal, which is incorrectly dated June 3, but must be from the end of September, communicates their uncertainties and their difficulties:

9, Rue de la Poste, Niort
My dear Vidal.
We have spent every one of the past few days trying to obtain our safe-passes. Henriette finally got hers yesterday, but they are unwilling to give me mine; they say I shouldn't waste their time asking for a permit and then staying put here. It has been impossible to get one for Liliane. In short, after having been to see all the people there are to see, the three of us went together to the office of the captain who is respon-

155

sible for signing passes. He told us he had received orders not to let any more foreigners travel between one town and another, and especially not to Paris. As a favor, he said he would permit one of us to go and bring back our winter things. Otherwise, we could ask to reinstate our residence as being in Paris, but then we could not come back. Of course, he did tell us that in case of some disaster that meant we had to stay at our Niort address, he would authorize me to return to Paris before the end of the hostilities. We have all three just made another request, which will probably be granted on Sunday, to let us return to our home.

Kind regards.

In another card dated October 15, Élie announces that he hopes to obtain a safe-conduct in the coming week. He adds:

So as soon as I get it, I will come back to work.

I have decided, if it's no bother to you, that I will come and stay at your place, bringing with me a little foldaway bed that Liliane has in her upstairs bedroom, and which Mony will bring over to the Rue des Platrières for me.

It is very likely that Henriette, being a meticulous housewife, did not want her husband to go to his apartment on his own, because he might "make a mess." This plan was never put into action (reticence on Vidal's part? Collective return of Élie, Henriette and Liliane?). In any case, Henriette, Liliane and Élie are back in Paris before the end of 1939. The exile to Niort, and other problems, may have made Henriette irritated with her husband and Vidal. Violent reproaches are exchanged, and there is a temporary break-off of relations. They make up again during the end-of-year festivities:

January 1, 1940

My dear Vidal,

I wish you a good and happy New Year. I hope 1940 will bring good things to you from every point of view, and health and happiness for you and the same for Edgar. Élie and I have made it up; pity got the better of me, and the remorse that came after. I have asked his forgiveness a thousand times, after seeing him cry like a child. Well, it's all over, he has forgiven me.

Now it's your turn to forgive me. I was so violent during those last few days that I wonder whether I wasn't mentally unbalanced. The anxiety that overwhelmed me was something unimaginable that I had never felt before in my life. So, my darling, you who are so kind, forgive me and tell me that you don't hold my violence against me.

With all my love.

Your depressed sister,

Henriette

Previously, on September 28, Vidal had obtained a temporary travel pass allowing him to go to Jeumont (in the Nord region) by train, and also to

Romilly and Troyes (in the Aube) by car (Mony will let him use his van to visit the manufacturers). The permit is renewed in December. Life apparently returns to normal again.

Vidal lunches in a Greek restaurant in the Rue Serpentine, where his son joins him, now that he is a student in the Quartier Latin. The student is trying to gather economic, sociological, historical and political information about Man and Society. But the science of economics is an enclave of legal studies, history is taught as part of a degree in history and geography, sociology is combined with ethics to make up one of the four certificates in the philosophy degree, and politics is taught at the École des Sciences Politiques. His father has left him entirely free in his choices, and observes without protest that he does not intend to orient himself towards business.

Edgar takes sociology classes with his friend Georges Delboy. Henri Macé, who has had to repeat a year, is still at the lycée. Henri Salem decides to flee the war and stows away aboard a boat in Marseilles bound for America. The bond of friendship with Henri Luce has weakened; he too has been held back in school, and Edgar's political preoccupations have driven them apart. However, Edgar is still in touch with the Barré family, who are always very hospitable towards the young man and very friendly to Vidal. Vidal may have been helped by Mr. Luce, who is highly-placed at police headquarters, in obtaining a safe-conduct or in assisting his sister who is stuck in Niort.

At the Sorbonne, Edgar is pleased to meet up with Claude Lalet, a former pupil of the Lycée Rollin like himself, from the class above. Lalet, who is a militant communist, has gone underground. Although for very different reasons (the reason for communist pacifism was the Germano–Soviet pact), they are both pacifists, and get on well together. Later, during the Occupation, Lalet will be arrested by the Nazis, and become one of the Châteaubriant martyrs.[59]

Around April, Henri Salem suddenly returns to Paris. He had successfully boarded a transatlantic liner in Marseilles, and emerged two days later from under the tarpaulin covering the canoe in which he had been hiding. He did not know that the ship was due to make a stop in Lisbon, where the stowaway was handed over to the police. The Portuguese police imprisoned him in a fortress, and he spent two or three months there, amusing himself by translating *Les Luisiades* into French, but he never finished his translation. When they sent him back to France, he was set free, and because he was not old enough to be drafted he was not considered a deserter. He would leave again for North Africa before the German invasion, intending to succeed this time in departing for America.

Edgar has begun his PMS (*préparation militaire supérieure*, the preparatory military service for students) with the alumni of the École des Sciences Politiques. At the end of the first semester of accelerated, non-specialized training, he chooses to enter the Service Corps, which seems to him much less bloodthirsty than the infantry, the cavalry or the artillery. To his great surprise, many of the students from Sciences Politiques, who come from well-known military, diplomatic and aristocratic families, also choose this section for "sissies." Nevertheless, after the rout of Dunkirk, their captain tells them that, amid the general distress, their Corps has become the heroes' section. Nearly 70 percent of Service Corps members died there, surpassing both foot soldiers and gunners in sacrifice.

VIDAL THE SOLDIER

Vidal could never have guessed that he would become a soldier at the age of 46, after managing, at 20, to come through the First World War without being drafted by the various enemy armies that might have called him up. When the nation-states had swallowed up all the territory and there was no longer any escape from nationalism, he had even succeeded in inventing the fictional nationality of "Salonician," and then in taking advantage of his position as a stateless person, conferred on him by the identity of Levantine Jew.

The general call-up of September 1939 also drafts men in his category. However, his incorporation is postponed, and for a while he thinks he has managed to escape, because at first he benefits from a reprieve, as a widower and the father of a dependent child.

He is nevertheless extremely alarmed; he is not just afraid of going to war, but of Nazi Germany. Vidal, who had learned German at school, had done business with Germans and generally found Germans and Germany to his liking, now saw Germany as the persecutor of the Jews, which, if it invaded France as it had Poland, would condemn them to a fate like that of his ancestors in Spain, who were forced to choose between leaving and conversion (at the time he did not realize that Nazi anti-Semitism was not the same as Christian anti-Judaism). What should he do? What escape route is open to him? He learns that some wealthy Jews from good neighborhoods are preparing to leave for the Americas. But he cannot contemplate going into exile himself. Not only because his business and romantic affairs keep him in Paris, but because he has absolutely no desire to leave. He has put down roots. He telephones his brothers in Brussels, who are just as worried as he is, and, like him, can think of nothing better to do than wait. And then, once the phoney war sets in, Vidal's optimism gets the upper hand again.

One day in March 1940, he receives a summons to report to the camp at Satory, near Versailles. He is worried: *I'd been asking around in the Sentier, among my colleagues, to see if there was anyone else in the same situation, but there wasn't really anybody. Anyway, I take the train, I turn up at the barracks, and at the barracks gate I present my piece of paper.*

"Ah yes," they say, "it's in the yard, the second building."

I go there, the man says:

"So, you've been called up to do military service."

But in 1940, I was already 46 years old.

No matter, he says:

"Men up to the age of 50 are eligible for the draft, sir."

So I say:

"I'm a widower, I have a dependent son."

"That may be, sir, but you'll have to come to the barracks tomorrow."

Vidal returns to the barracks the next day, and they send him for a preliminary medical: *I happen to meet a very nice sergeant, sergeant Worms. So he says to me:*

"What are you doing here?"

"Well, I'll tell you what I'm doing . . . I've been summoned . . . "

"Ah," he says, "but this part is for people working in administration, you're going to be sent to be a soldier; well, I'll tell you what you have to do, go back to your barrack-room, I'll give you a number."

And off I went, and I was given a very warm welcome by the other soldiers, my other colleagues, one was a maker of eyeglasses, another was a gardener, another a gravedigger, another an accountant. Anyway, we were all about the same age, all in about the same situation.

Two, three days went by, there was a medical inspection, ears, eyes, everything, and I'm pronounced fit for service . . .

And so I became a soldier," recounts Vidal, who, thirty-eight years later, at the age of 84, is still astonished at what happened to him.

He obtains passes to spend the night in Paris, but he learns that his company of munitions workers is to leave for an explosives factory. He leaves the store in Élie's hands for a time, but since Élie has always been kept away from the manufacturers and customers, he makes mistakes over the prices of the merchandise (which in fact vary according to the customer). Vidal decides to close his store. Indeed, many of the stores in the Sentier close because of the draft (numerous Sephardim having obtained French nationality), or because, like Maurice, Émy's husband, Hiddo, Chary's husband, and Benjamin, Luna's brother, they sign up for the foreign volunteers' infantry regiment.

Edgar is delighted at the prospect of staying alone in the apartment on the Rue des Platrières, but before leaving Vidal puts pressure on his son to go and live at Henriette's, and once again his son gives in.

We are ordered to leave for Bourges, and there they put us to work in a munitions factory, where they make shells; I and my colleagues, we all went to see the captain, we were already a company by then, and so two or three of us asked:

"Why have we been put here in the munitions factory, when we don't know the first thing about it?"

"You don't need to know anything, we'll explain everything that has to be done."

Well, anyway, they assigned us to a foundry, filling shells. What a crazy idea that was, you can imagine how good we were at filling them, well, we had foremen who taught us what we needed to know; some of us were in one room filling the shells with powder, the others were in another room keeping guard, half the team worked during the day from 6 in the morning until 6 in the evening, and the other half from 6 in the evening until 6 in the morning. It was a very, very tough assignment . . . a job that didn't require any intelligence but which was absolutely vital, they needed to produce munitions.

The work is dangerous, since there is a permanent risk of explosion, and it is unhealthy; the men all turn yellow, and neither showers nor washing can get rid of the color; they are nicknamed "yellows." Vidal's success in adapting to these conditions is helped by his feeing very much at home in his group: *I had some very good friends down there; there was a deputy bank manager, the manager of a fabric store in the Sentier, a gravedigger, a street peddler, and a market stall-holder, a Mr. Corman, a tough guy who had done some crazy things in his time.*

Vidal admires Corman, who speaks underworld slang, and claims with pride that he used to be a pimp, just as much as he admires the deputy bank manager. He admires all smart people, no matter what they do. For his part, Corman is astonished that Vidal doesn't "gabble away in Yiddish:" "You're Jewish, you should be gabbling away in Yiddish." "No, I speak Spanish," Vidal tells the incredulous Corman. "You're kidding me, buddy!"

An important step forward in Vidal's process of Frenchification takes place when his friends introduce him to Beaujolais.

It is announced that they will be given leave for the Whitsun festivities: *We were very happy, we each paid our share to buy the rail tickets, and on the morning of May 10 we arrive at the barracks . . . but then no-one was allowed to leave. The Germans had entered Belgium and were invading France.*

Vidal is stuck, so his son goes to spend a day in Bourges, on May 31. He is amazed to see that his father is all yellow, and surrounded by other yellow men. Insistently, Corman asks him: "Do you gabble away in Yiddish?" and is very displeased when he answers in the negative. Edgar eats at the canteen with his father's friends, a group photo is taken, and the son leaves again in the evening.

When he talks about Bourges thirty-eight years later, Vidal will always say: "I'm not saying it was enjoyable, but . . . "

Vidal would meet up with all his friends again after the defeat, when he returned to Paris. Many of them would come and visit him in his store, at closing time, and they would go for an aperitif together.

THE RETREAT

By May 15, 1940, it is clear that disaster is imminent. The Dutch armies lay down their weapons, and German tanks literally blow holes in the French army at Sedan and rush on towards the Channel. On May 27, the Belgian

King surrenders. Between May 28 and June 3, the German vice tightens around Dunkirk, and the Anglo-French forces bale out, leaving all their equipment behind them. Great Britain refuses to intervene in France from now on, not even using fighter planes. On June 6, the French front, which has been more or less reassembled by Weygand, collapses at the Somme, and on June 9, at the Aisne. The much-anticipated repetition of the miracle of the Marne does not take place, and, on June 10, the French government leaves Paris, while Mussolini "stabs France in the back" by declaring war. By June 12, the mass retreat has become mass panic.

On June 16, Paul Reynaud, who is head of the government and Vidal's representative, resigns; Pétain replaces him and asks the Germans for an armistice on June 18; on the same day, in London, de Gaulle calls upon the French to resist. The armistice is signed at Rethondes on June 22, in the same train carriage in which the German army had surrendered in 1918, and the war comes to an end on the 25th, when German troops reach Biarritz, Montluçon and Chambéry.

Vidal and his friends from Bourges are caught up in the retreat. Shortly afterwards, on June 10, the 15th company's officers announced that they would be departing for the Italian front, and guns and equipment were distributed. However, before there was time to assemble all the equipment intended to transform the munitions workers into foot soldiers, they were obliged to retreat.

The whole French army was in retreat, and we could already see columns of trucks passing through Bourges, and armored vehicles and all that, all these people leaving. We didn't see any sign of the French airforce, unfortunately, nothing but German planes.

One afternoon, the captain gives the order:

"Right, men, assemble in the barracks. We're leaving."

"How are we leaving?"

"On foot, for the time being, on foot . . . "

It was impossible to get hold of any trucks, impossible to get a train . . . Our captain organizes our departure, heading South.

A few hours before we are due to leave, a sergeant comes to tell me:

"Nahoum, you're wanted at the gate of the barracks."

"By whom?"

"I don't know."

And there is Fredy.

"What's going on?"

"Well, I've left . . . "

Poor Fredy, it was an incredible stroke of luck. When the Germans were approaching Paris, there was a rumor going round that the Germans were picking up all the boys aged between 16 and 20 and sending them to Germany. So Corinne at once sent Fredy south on his bicycle, she gave him the road maps and off he went.

Fredy is only just 17, and his mother has told him to go and find Vidal in

Bourges. Vidal introduces Fredy to his captain and asks if he can go along with the company.

I say:

"He's my nephew, he's just arrived from Paris on his bicycle, he's spent two nights sleeping rough."

"Ah," he says, "OK, we'll adopt him . . . "

While we went to see the captian, Fredy had left his bicycle at the barracks gate, with all his things. We went back to get it, because we were ready to leave, but no bicycle. So I had some very good friends who took pity on me, they were very kind:

"What's happened?" "Well, my nephew has just arrived, and someone has stolen his bicycle."

There was this little guy, a very smart carpenter, and he says to Fredy: "Don't worry, here you are, son, take this bicycle and follow us." He follows us, and we're marching in Indian file, one hundred and fifty guys. And suddenly, behind us, we hear someone shout: "Stop thief!" It was a guy from the barracks, a sergeant. He says: "It belongs to an Italian, it was his bicycle. Why did you steal his bicycle?" I say:

"But we didn't steal it."

"What do you mean," he says, "you didn't steal it?"

"He has come all the way from Paris, he left his bicycle in front of the gate, it wasn't there when he went back, and as we were in a hurry to leave, we took this one."

"But that's stealing!"

"No it's not, it's not stealing."

And then the guys all joined in.

They have to give up the bicycle. The march on foot continues. Vidal has two suitcases, two boxes of clothes. What does he take with him?

During the night, we camp on some ground. Luckily we were fairly organized: we still had a cook, and there was a car carrying a cooking stove. In the morning, they served us coffee out in the open, in the middle of the countryside, and the captain, well, I don't know, there was the telephone and all that, he receives orders to continue the journey on foot, there was no other way, and to stop at noon for lunch at a water tower, you know, in the countryside they have those water towers.

We were already settled in comfortably, we were getting ready for lunch, everybody lent a hand to peel the potatoes, to do this and that, the cook had already made the food and all of a sudden: "It's an air raid, we've got to run!" Some German planes were coming towards us, and we start running across the fields; less than a quarter of an hour later, the water tower exploded. I think there must have been spies who had signalled that there was a gathering of French soldiers, because there were two hundred of us, all the same . . . Luckily we had made some distance . . .

And in the evening, we arrive at a farm . . . our captain tries to make a deal with the farmer, to see if he will take us in for the night. The farmer says:

"I can't, but there's a barn, you can all sleep in there."

"But what about food supplies, coffee?"

"I haven't got anything."

"Listen, we can give you some bags of coffee, we have some in the army, although it's green coffee. Give us some bread, some potatoes and some bacon."

They made a deal, which meant that in the morning we had something to eat, and afterwards, hup! off we go again. There were hordes of refugees on this road, heading south. On the road, we meet another company on its way, I don't know where from, from another region, they had twenty horse-drawn cars, carts with them. So they said: "Look, there are three or four guys in each cart, eight or ten of you can fit in." So that meant we no longer had to march on foot. We spent one or two more days on the road, I can't remember, and we arrived at Argenton-sur-Creuse. There, the captain, and all that, thanks to some phone calls, had got a train ready for us, and the train was bound for Toulouse.

In fact, as Fredy clearly remembers, Vidal and four of his friends, who had found out how quickly the Germans were advancing by listening to the radio, decided to abandon the convoy and were given a lift on a military bus bound for Argenton-sur-Creuse; there, in a café, they heard Marshal Pétain's message on the radio announcing that he had asked for an honorable armistice. Vidal burst into joyful applause, and then stopped clapping when he became aware of the frosty silence surrounding him. The little group then went to the station at Argenton and boarded a train that was about to leave for Toulouse, where Vidal knew that his brothers had taken refuge.

Between Argenton-sur-Creuse and Toulouse, it's maybe four hours by train, and we took four days. But anyway, we were on the train, we had just about enough to eat, the captain always managed to find a way to feed us . . .

In fact, the captain is no longer with them, and everyone gets by more or less by looting (a friend of Vidal's, the tax inspector, is caught stealing a keg of wine, and an officer threatens him with the firing squad). Shortly before the train arrives in Toulouse station, Vidal becomes a temporary deserter, jumping from the train with Fredy to go and join his brothers.

All the people caught up in the military and civilian panic fleeing from the North, East and West converge on Toulouse. Vidal's brothers, Léon and Jacques, had managed to leave Brussels the day before the Germans arrived, on May 11, and, after a stopover in Paris, have taken refuge in Toulouse with their families (Henri has stayed in Brussels with his Breton companion, who is confident that she can protect him). Vidal's son takes the train for Toulouse on June 9, when he hears on the radio that the Parisian Academy has suspended its examinations. Henriette, Élie, Liliane and Mony leave on June 10 or 11 by car, first for Niort, and then, as the German army advances, they flee to Toulouse. Vidal has the address of the hotel where his brother Léon has been staying for over a month, and once there he gets in touch with his son. Edgar is having a wonderful time; he is in charge of a reception center for student refugees, which has been set up by Professor Faucher. After a special session of examinations, he has also passed his first two history certificates and his first year in law.

Once he feels reassured about his family, Vidal puts his military situation in order and obtains permission to sleep in town at his son's lodging, 8, Rue des Arts. On July 6, the demobilization center in Toulouse permits him to return "to his home," and to the question: Address to which the forementioned will return? Vidal answers 10, Rue Pisançon, Marseilles. Why? Some Vidalian mystery is afoot here. In any case, he will make at least one trip to Marseilles at the beginning of August, while residing temporarily in Toulouse.

A large section of the family is reunited in Toulouse and begins living there. Jacques, Sophie and their daughters rent an apartment, as do Léon, Julie and their son Edgard. Henriette, Élie, Mony and Liliane rent a house by the Pont des Demoiselles tram terminus.

Vidal never even considers staying in Toulouse. His idea, from the beginning of July, is to return to Paris, which is in the occupied zone, whereas the South of France, which is directly governed by Vichy, is a "free zone." But he is worried about the risk of living under German authority: *So I go and see my captain: "Well," I say, "I would really like to go back to Paris, but the Jewish question is bothering me." He says to me: "Nahoum, don't worry. You are a French soldier, go back home to Paris, it's not written on your face that you're Jewish, don't worry, you go back with your head held high."* Vidal also sends a letter to his friend Jean Golaudin, who is a legal counsel in Paris, asking for his opinion. The latter sends his reply to Léon's address, 96, Boulevard Anatole-France:

30 July 1940
Dear Sir,
I thank you for your letter of July 27.
    Here, everything is calm, the Germans are behaving correctly, and supplies are fairly well-maintained.   Yours

That makes up Vidal's mind. In fact, he is actually in a hurry to return, for financial reasons (unlike his brothers, he has not brought along enough money to survive on, because the retreat took him by surprise at Bourges), and probably for romantic reasons as well. He is in a hurry, and as the German authorities take a very long time to issue return permits, he manages to obtain a mission order in Marseilles from the Ministry of Finance, signed by the president of the chamber of commerce in Marseilles, enjoining him to go to Paris. He returns to Toulouse, insists that his son leaves his room and goes back to live with his sister Henriette, and takes the train for Paris on August 16 1940.

He returns to the Rue des Plâtrières, reopens his store in the Rue d'Aboukir, and then, in October, via a small black market network, he manages to buy a German pass to go to Toulouse. He finds his son living in a room above a café, with a shared lavatory at the end of a corridor, and once again he obliges him to move out and into the house of Mrs. Marie, a woman of Greek origin, the widow of a Frenchman from Toulouse, who had lived in Constantinople and had a son there. Vidal is delighted with all this, and he leaves Edgar there.

In Toulouse, Edgar is free and happy; he is responsible for the student refugees, he has made friends of all kinds and all nationalities, he meets his first girlfriends, and he meets writers whose articles he has read in the *Nouvelle Revue Française*. He also adopts a family who adopt him, and offer him everything he loves and admires. When Mrs. Henri arrived in Toulouse with her four children she was completely destitute; their father, a well-known physicist, had died during the exodus. Some university teachers from Toulouse found her a lodging, and Mrs. Henri, who is of Russian origin, serves tea and shares her food with everyone who visits her. Edgar is friendly with her daughter Hélène, who is the same age as him, and he will later become friendly with her second son, Victor, with whom he will take part in the Resistance. Young Alex accepts him as a member of the family, and little Vera, who likes to sit on his knee, loves him tenderly. He begins to feel alive. The disaster has delivered him from his father's constant supervision, and the Occupation will be his liberation.

A HARSH WINTER

Supply shortages suddenly hit Toulouse at the end of summer 1940. The winter of 1940 to 1941 turns bitterly cold, and wood and coal are distributed parsimoniously. The Southern zone is peaceful, but the war goes on. Great Britain stands alone in resisting German bombardments, but all relations with France have been broken off after Mers el-Kébir.[60] In Dakar, De Gaulle fails in his attempt to rally French West Africa to help him liberate France (September 24). Vichy begins officially collaborating with Nazi Germany (after the interview between Pétain and Hitler at Montoire, on October 24). The first exclusionary measures are applied to Jewish civil servants and to freemasons. The Pétainist Legion is created. Night grows darker and spreads over the whole of Europe: between April and May 1941, first Yugoslavia and then Greece are invaded by Germany; Germany attacks the USSR on June 21, 1941, and makes a rapid advance on Leningrad, Moscow, and the Caucasus.

Edgar lives a student's life with a group of friends, and occasionally goes to see his aunts and uncles. There is a drama in the Nahum family. Henriette decides to find a fiancé for her niece Régine, and organizes a meeting with a Salonician businessman who has taken refuge in Toulouse. After this introduction, someone tells Sophie, Régine's mother, that the businessman is Liliane's lover. A stormy interview takes place in a café between Henriette and Sophie, and the two women end up saying all the nastiest things they can think of about the other's daughter. On her return, Henriette relates what has happened, and Mony is furious: "Oh, so I'm a cuckold! Well, if I'm a cuckold, you just wait and see!" "No, no, darling, you're not, you're not" they soothe him, assuring him that it is all slander. Henceforth, relations are broken off between these two branches of the family, although Léon acts as the relay for discreet contact between Jacques and his sister. In fact, Régine had only agreed to meet the businessman because she did not want to upset her family; she was already having a relationship with a military airman, Paul M., whose base had retreated to Toulouse. Between them, it is love, joy, passion; it was Régine who found Edgar his room, which is above the café she frequents with her lover. Meanwhile, Edgar, who by now knows all the student refugees living in Toulouse, introduces his cousin Hélène, who wants to meet a boy, to a boy who wants to meet a girl. At her first meeting with the Austrian student Schrecker, there are embraces, kisses, and then, very quickly, engagement and marriage, with his father in attendance. Professor Schrecker is a university teacher specializing in Leibniz, and he soon leaves for New York.

The situation worsens. Vichy's first anti–Semitic measures apply to foreign Jews, and Jacques and Sophie are sent in forced residence to a Pyrenean village, Sierp, not far from Luchon. Their daughters, who are French, stay behind, but Paul M. has to leave Toulouse. His base is initially transferred to Istres. His superior officers refuse him permission to marry Régine. Régine takes advantage of a trip to see her cousin Chary in Avignon, and makes a stop at Istres on her return journey. She goes home pregnant. Then Paul's squadron is posted to North Africa. Régine has to have a painful abortion on her own; this terrible experience leaves her with asthma, which she will have for the rest of her life.

Vidal returns to Paris on August 16, 1940, and moves back into the Rue des Platrières. Fredy, who took his first baccalauréat exam in Toulouse, has returned to Paris, where his parents have remained with their other two children. They are still living in the Rue Sorbier. Then, when Vidal sees that the big apartment he had bought in the Rue Demours is unoccupied, he suggests that Corinne and Joseph share it with him; however, they will only live in the apartment for a very short time. Émy, Corinne's sister has also remained in Paris; her husband Maurice, who has been demobilized from the foreign legion, comes to join her there and starts running his garment-making shop in the Rue d'Alexandrie again. He meets his second son, Maurice-Gérard, born in June 1940 while he was at the front.

Vidal has met up with his friends from the regiment who live in Paris, and he sees them every day for an aperitif. He has reopened his store; the absence of most of the other wholesalers, who have taken refuge in the Southern zone, and the fact that hosiery products are in short supply, are good for his business: he sells the old stock that has been gathering dust for years, manages to get hold of a small supply of hosiery from the manufacturers, and becomes prosperous again for a time.

In September 1940, all the Jews in Paris are ordered to register at the local police stations, to have their identity cards stamped "Jewish."

Well, then there was a debate among all our compatriots, all the businessmen in the neighborhood: "What should we do?" So I say: "We'll have to obey, because suppose they check our papers in the street . . . what happens if we haven't obeyed the order to get them stamped?" So we went, me, everybody, we all went to the police station to get our identity cards stamped . . .

Meanwhile my brother Henri, who had stayed in Brussels, came to see me because he was allowed to travel [taking advantage of his Italian nationality, which at the time protects him, since Italy is Germany's ally]. *He had already obtained permits from the Germans in Brussels, and he really encouraged me. He told me: "You did exactly the right thing coming back to Paris, you did the right thing reopening your store, now don't worry, they can't bother us, there is no reason to, especially since we aren't young any more, we aren't soldiers and you've already been a soldier."*

Vidal is very optimistic during the fall of 1940. His business is doing well, and the "Jewish" stamp on his identity card reassures him more than it worries him, because he feels that he has his papers in order with the law; he even hopes to bring his son back to Paris. He is happy with his friends, and hardly suffers at all from the restrictions. He feels safe. He lives among the gentiles. The war has entirely Frenchified him, but this has happened simultaneously with the activation of the machine that wants to reject him from France and divide him forever from the gentiles.

In January 1941, the occupying authorities reveal their plan to Aryanize Jewish businesses in order to "exclude the Jews from French economic life definitively, and in the briefest possible time." The Jews will not have their property taken away from them, but they will be forbidden to reinvest their liquid assets in a commercial enterprise, and their businesses are to be inspected by administrative supervisors. Harsher measures are still to come. The ordinance of April 26, 1941 prevents Jews from practising numerous economic activities, prohibits any contact between the public and Jewish employees or executives, and appoints provisional administrators to take the place of Jewish owners.[61] Among his papers, Vidal will keep the small yellow poster with black lettering that reads *Jüdisches Geschaeft*, "Jewish business," which he was obliged to display in his store window.

Vidal is taken by surprise when in December 1940, an Aryan provisional administrator, Mr. Freulon, of 150, Rue de Rivoli, is nominated to take charge of his business. In January 27, 1940 he hands over his balance sheet, his business accounts, and his end-of-the-year inventory. He notifies Mr. Freulon that Mr. and Mrs. Lezot have made an offer to purchase his business. This is an attempt by Vidal to make a more or less fictional transfer of his business to Georges Lezot, his friend from the regiment. His friend and legal counsel Mr. Golaudin draws up the document, but it is not signed, due to the opposition of the administration.

On July 12, 1941, Vidal is obliged, by the application of the law of June

2, 1941 targeting all Jews, to declare his assets. He declares the house in Rueil–Malmaison (value about 150,000 francs), the apartment at 51, Rue Demours (value 81,000 francs), bonds with the Crédit National worth 400,000 francs deposited in a bank account on which he owes 160,000 francs, an annuity of 1,500 francs deposited at the Comptoir National d'Escompte de Paris, 1,680 francs in his bank account, 17,000 francs in cash, and his furniture: two divan beds, a bookshelf, a chest of drawers, a writing desk, a pedestal table, an armchair, six chairs, and one small statue.

The administrative supervisor comes twice to inspect Vidal, obliges him to deposit the money from his sales at the bank, verifies his accounts, and so on. After the ordinance concerning the Jews of April 26 Vidal realizes that *"it was all over, the atmosphere was ruined."*

Circulation between the Southern zone and the Northern zone is prohibited, except for bearers of special permits issued by German headquarters. *Thanks to a friend I was able to get hold of German papers, a pass that was real but not official, not registered in the records, which I got from a guy who took bribes, and made permits . . .* Thus, Vidal obtains a permit in his name, which is valid from May 1 to August 1, 1941. He crosses the demarcation line at Vierzon by train on May 14, showing his passport, which is not stamped "Jewish," and arrives in Toulouse where he stays for ten days.

He is happy to see his son, his brothers and his sister. All of them urge him not to return to Paris, but Vidal goes back anyway. One month later, he decides to make another journey to Toulouse; he is thinking of opening a store there, as a colleague from the Sentier has done. He leaves Paris on June 24 and returns on July 9, after his son's birthday. His son urges him to stay in the Southern zone, but Vidal still wants to play for time, and perhaps has romantic reasons as well.

On July 23, 1941, he leaves for Toulouse again. His store seems to have been closed on June 30, as indicated in the report that Mr. Baumgartner, the business's new provisional administrator, makes on June 8 to the provisional administrators' Inspection Service. Vidal still wants to go back to Paris one last time before his pass expires; it is working perfectly, getting him back and forth across the demarcation line at Vierzon.

I catch my train, not in the least bit worried. There were four of us in the compartment. We arrive in Vierzon. There's a loudspeaker announcement, first in French, then in German: "Clear the corridors, have your identity papers ready, have your Ausweis ready, prepare for inspection." Well, that was OK . . .

A few minutes later, two German police officers board the train in my compartment, there were four of us there: "Papers, papers." The first gentleman produces his; then he asks me, I'm sitting opposite, I hand them over; he doesn't give them back to me, he keeps them. He asks another man, and he hands them over, he asks the last one, and he hands them over. I am a bit taken aback. He says to me: "Luggage." "Yes, I've got one suitcase." He gabbles away in German to his colleague, I could understand German, but I couldn't hear them properly. "OK, fine," he says, and they leave. They carry on with their inspection of the other compartments. A few minutes later, they both come back. They tell me: "Come on, get your suitcase down, open it!" There was nothing illegal in there, so that was OK. "Hat?" "No." I had a beret, because at that time we were all Pétain's legionnaires. He takes the beret, and tears out its lining. I had no idea what was going on, and nor did the other three, poor things. "Overcoat?" "Yes, yes, I have an overcoat." He rips out the whole lining. "Shoes, take them off!" I take off my shoes, he starts knocking on the heels, to see if they can be dismantled. I say nothing, I wait. "Well," he says to me, "you'll have to get off the train." "No, no, I'm French, I'm not getting off, I'm a businessman, my managers have sent me to Toulouse, I have to be in Toulouse, I can't get off." And they both go away, but they still have my papers. Ten minutes later, and they have been anxious minutes for me, I see them coming back. So in the end, one of the other passengers, who is calmer and more courageous than me, goes up to the policeman, he speaks good German. The German says, "Yes, we have been told to look out for a passenger whose age and physical description correspond to those of that gentleman, he smuggles cash around, he hides it in his beret or he puts it in the linings of his clothes." Well, anyway . . . When the train set off again, one of my neighbors asked me: "Would you like some cognac?" "I'd love some, I could do with it."

When I arrived in Toulouse, the next morning, I decided not to go back to Paris again.

Vidal had left Paris without enough money to rent a store, as he had envisaged. *Well, never mind, I say, and life begins again.*

On his son's advice, he immediately has a new identity card made up, without mentioning that he is Jewish. He moves into the Rue de Fleurance with Edgar; he finds some restaurants he likes, especially the Conti, in the Place du Capitole, where the portions are big. He rushes to get there as soon as it opens, and is served first. He eats very fast, with enormous appetite, and the minute he has finished his own plate, attacks his son's plate with his fork – he often invites Edgar and his girlfriend Violette Chapellaubeau out to eat. He also drinks the wine from his son's glass when he is not looking. In favor of the Conti, he has stopped attending a regulars' restaurant above a store, whose owner and cashier, a provocative woman with a faceful of makeup, goes around the tables with a little pair of scissors for cutting out food coupons. "What do you want?" Vidal asks her on the first day. And the beauty clicks her little scissors and says, in a lubricious voice: "Everything, everything and everything."

The anti-Semitic measures make people flee Paris. The arrests begin in 1942. Vidal's neighbor in the Rue d'Aboukir, although born French, is arrested and deported. Raids on a larger scale begin. People flee in increasing numbers. Most of them are obliged to pay smugglers to help them. Corinne urges Fredy to leave for the Southern zone before the rest of them, and Fredy goes to Toulouse, where he is able to take the second part of his baccalauréat exam. At the beginning of 1941, Corinne seems to have made a first clandestine crossing over the demarcation line, wading across the river Cher in water up to her waist. She finds a place to rent in Lyon, and then probably returns to Paris (since she writes to her nephew on July 29, 1941). What is certain, in any case, is that during the summer of 1941 the whole Pelosoff family decides to make a clandestine crossing of the Cher, with the help of a smuggler. Joseph goes first and, from the bank on the free side of the river, watches his children cross one by one, followed by his wife. The family goes to live in Lyon, where Fredy joins them, and where he prepares for a degree in philosophy and law. He will meet up with his cousin Edgar again at university, and then he will be conscripted into a youth work scheme, a sort of civil service created by Pétain.

Corinne and Joseph settle in Lyon. Joseph works with Émy and Maurice (who crossed the Cher in the same circumstances as the others and at about the same time), and a Mr. Désiré Herr. They found the Lanchère firm, which has a garment-making shop. They all live together in a villa in the Rue Saint-Fulbert. Daisy goes to La Martinière high school, and graduates from there in 1944. Henri has also gone back to school. Until March 1942, however, Corinne, who is very courageous, still hopes to make return journeys to Paris. She sends a card to cousin Paul Nahum: "Corinne would very much like to go and see Paul. What do you think? In her condition, is it wise?" Cousin Paul dissuades her. In fact, he is himself arrested and sent to Drancy, where he stays for only three days. Raids and arrests are increasing in the Northern zone. Corinne's brother, Benjamin, is arrested in 1942, but his "Aryan" wife and his little 8-year-old daughter are not. The German police come to arrest Pepo, Margot and their children, who miraculously escape deportation. Henriette's, Vidal's and Corinne's apartments are emptied and ransacked by the Gestapo. Only Liliane's apartment, where the seals of the Argentinian government have been posted, is spared.[62]

In the Southern zone, Laval's return as Prime Minister in April 1942 and, most importantly, the occupation of the Southern zone by German troops in November 1942, make all Jews fear the raids, arrests and deportations that continue unchecked in the Northern zone. In September, Paul Schrecker and his wife Hélène, daughter of Jacques and Sophie (who are still in forced residence in Sierp), are lucky enough to obtain American visas, thanks to Schrecker's father, who is now teaching at an American university. They leave from Port-Vendres aboard the last ship for New York, accompanied by Mrs. Vera Henri, who has been invited to America by some of her deceased husband's colleagues, and is taking her children Hélène, Vera and Alex with her. Her eldest son, Victor, who has not managed or wanted to obtain permission to leave, stays behind and goes to Lyon to live in the student residence with Edgar. When German troops enter the Southern zone, Vidal's son is in Toulouse with his friend Jacques Francis Rolland, who has come to persuade him to go and live at the student residence in Lyon, where they will be able to lead a life that is both Rimbaldian and Marxist. Rolland has come up with what he calls "the synthetic conception of life," a combination of the uncompromising life of the bolshevik militant, the scholarly life of the Marxist student, and the adolescent's life of partying. The two friends meet up again in December at the student residence in Lyon; they share a room, and Victor Henri is their neighbor on the same corridor.

After German troops enter Pétainist France, Italian troops occupy Nice and Savoy. The exodus from the Northern zone to the Southern zone is followed by the exodus from the German zone to the Italian zone. Henriette and her family leave for Nice, now occupied by easy-going Italian troops. Most of the Nahums and the Beressis in the Southern zone are reunited for a time in Nice.

NOVEMBER 1942 TO SEPTEMBER 1943

November 1942 is the turning point in the Second World War. The Americans arrive in North Africa, and the Pétainist admiral Darlan rallies to their side. German troops invade Vichy France, and scuttle the fleet in Toulon. At the same time, Stalingrad resists the German attack, and this resistance turns into a resounding victory after von Paulus's troops are surrounded and forced to surrender, on February 2, 1943. Beginning in spring 1943, Soviet troops take the offensive and win back Koursk, Bielgorod and Kharkov.

During the period between November 1942 (occupation of the Southern zone) and September 1943 (occupation of Italy and the Italian zone by German troops), Nice is a magnet for Jewish refugees. Then it becomes an enormous trap.

The first Nahums to settle in Nice – Henriette, Élie, Liliane and Mony – stay at the Hotel Splendid, 50, Boulevard Victor-Hugo. On the Beressi side, Émy and Maurice have left Lyon and moved to Nice, probably after German troops enter the Southern zone. Corinne and Joseph join them there in spring 1943.

Before the entry of the German troops, Vidal has been thinking of settling in Lyon (an identity card issued on September 8, 1942 shows him apparently residing in this city, at 92, Chemin Villon); he moves to Nice at the end of 1942. He stays for a time at the Hotel Splendid, then rents an apartment in January or February 1943, at 16, Rue Guglia, and buys some furniture. In fall 1942, he makes numerous journeys, some for romantic reasons, others to visit relatives and his son. He feels safe in Nice, but he is not getting enough to eat. He goes to two restaurants, one after the other, for lunch.

In Nice, Vidal continues to send letters worrying about his son's health, nutrition, warmth, cold, and tiredness:

My dear Edgar,

I got back safely yesterday evening, and was very pleased to find your telegram saying you had arrived safely.

Now I will just wait every day (demanding father) (but-you-wouldn't-want-him-any-different) for your good news.

Write to me in Nice, at the Hotel Splendid, because I'm leaving today.

Write and tell me what you need in the way of underwear, and as soon as you receive this letter, telegraph me in Nice, at the Splendid, the hotel address, and I will have some handkerchieves and socks sent to you.

So, my darling, I am expecting a telegram in Nice first, and then letters . . . Be very sensible and don't go up any mountains, don't do any climbing, look after yourself, eat well and think of your Dad by writing to him often every day, even if it's only a little card in between long letters. With love,

Your Dad Vidal[63]

Vidal thinks that his son is safe at the student residence in Lyon, with his two friends. He does not know anything about their clandestine activities with the communist students and the patriotic youth movement's United Front. He does know that Edgar goes every evening to his Aunt Corinne's house, not far from the student residence; she gives him and his two friends a share of the family's dinner.

Towards the end of spring 1943, Vidal's son arrives in Nice in the company of Jacques Francis Rolland, Victor Henri and another friend from the resistance, Henri Pozzo di Borgo. They have managed to obtain false *Urlaubsschein*, the repatriation papers issued to sick French prisoners, bearing the names of real prisoners from the forbidden cities of the North. These will allow them to have real identity papers made up in a town hall on the coast, along with ration cards, tobacco and clothing coupons, and so on. They have changed their identities out of necessity, because their class has been called up for the STO (*service du travail obligatoire*, or forced labor service, in Germany), and the prisoners' resistance movement of which they are now members has supplied them with the fake *Urlaubsschein*. So Vidal finds out that his son is in the resistance. He entreats him to give up this madness, begs him not to accept false papers, and insists that he can get him a job in the Italian military organization working on the construction of the Mediterranean wall. As mentioned earlier, he calls a gathering of every last member of the family in exile in Nice, and then arranges the ultimate interview, with Uncle Hananel, to no avail. After a few scenes of melodramatic despair in which he declares that he will die of grief and worry, Vidal philosophically admits defeat. A contributing factor is his preoccupation with problems in his love life, where a break-up, a new relationship, and a reconciliation are intermingled. He is also extremely preoccupied with food. Although he has two lunches one after the other in two different restaurants in Nice, it is not enough for him. However, in the area around Nice, in

Roanne and Tarare, he finds the copious, rich food that satisfies him. In her letters to Mathilde, his sister Henriette makes fun of her brother's obsession with finding a "good table."

Henriette has had news of her brother Henri, who is still living in Belgium, protected by his "Aryan" companion and by his Italian nationality. She receives some letters from Raymonde Coatsaliou, the sister of Henri's partner: "Raymonde writes that she is leaving on the 25th and will go to Henri's house for the vacation. I am writing her by this mail to ask her to write me a nice long letter on her return telling me about our dear brother" (letter from Henriette to her sister Mathilde, dated July 19, 1943). "We have had a long letter from Henri. Thank God, he is very happy and tells us so. His garden is full of flowers, his home is unharmed, and his health is good. Well, thank goodness at least one of us has been spared by this dreadful war" (letter to Mathilde dated August 19, 1943). Henriette has not seen her daughter Aimée, who lives in Liverpool, since June 1940. Indirectly, Mony has received some very worrying news about his family, all of whom are still in Salonica. "My dear husband is doing his best not to show us his quite understandable anxiety about his family. Unfortunately, bad news gets confirmed every day, and it is awful" (letter from Liliane to Mathilde, dated August 19, 1943).

In fall 1942, Jacques is still in forced residence in the Pyrenees, and Léon is still in Toulouse. As we will see, they manage to take refuge in Italy before September 1943, thus benefiting almost a century later from the fortunate initiative taken by their father David in Salonica, when, after the Russo-Turkish war, he obtained Italian nationality for his whole family.

VIDAL HIDES LIKE A HERMIT CRAB FROM PERSECUTION

Vidal and his brothers have been slow to understand the nature of the threat, which becomes clearer and worsens between the beginning of 1941 and spring 1942. At first, they think the new Nazi anti-Semistism is purely and simply a continuation of the old Christian anti-Judaism. They react to it initially as if it were a new version of the persecution under Isabella the Catholic, which had forced their ancestors either to camouflage themselves as Christians, or go into exile. Seeing no other way out, they spontaneously choose to act like neo-Marranos, and seek their salvation in conversion and apparent devotion. Léon, Julie and Edgard, their son, convert to Protestantism (obtaining a pre-dated baptismal certificate from the pastor) and go regularly to sing hymns on Sunday at the Calvinist church in Toulouse. Vidal, for his part, rushes to the diocese of Toulouse, has himself baptized, and begs his son to convert. As a safety measure, he obtains further baptismal certificates, each pre-dating the one before. There is even one from the parish of Notre-Dame-de-Bon-Voyage, in the diocese of Nice, which states that he was baptized on June 20, 1913, and that Georges and Marie Lezot are his godparents (extract from the "true replica" made on January 16, 1943).

At the same time, he believes that being a French army veteran will protect him, and in March and April 1942 he writes to the national Veterans' Office and to the army headquarters at Vichy to obtain a certificate proving that he is a veteran of the 1939 to 1940 war. They reply that the text of application allowing this certificate to be issued has not yet been published. In the absence of a certificate, he registers with the Legion of Combatants and Volunteers of the National Revolution, which the Vichy regime has created in order to unite the veterans of both world wars under the Pétainist banner. He receives his summons at the Rue de Fleurance, his son's home, which he shares during his trips to Toulouse. Moreover, since 1940, and apparently even in Paris, he has taken to wearing a Basque beret, like the Marshal's legionnaires, which has become a symbol of Pétainism. As soon as he acquires his own lodging, he tacks images of the Holy Virgin, a medal of the Pope and portraits of the Marshal to his bedroom walls. Thus furnished with Catholic and Pétainist symbols, he tries to protect himself from the threatening environment in the manner of a hermit crab.

Like so many others – who ended up being deported for that very reason – Vidal believes at first that he will be safer if he abides by the law than if he tries to escape from it. He is not afraid of cheating within a framework of legality, as he did when he obtained his German pass, but he still retains his legal identity. He recognizes the risk involved in giving it up and becoming illegal, but does not recognize the opportunity to save himself. He reacts in a typically Oriental fashion: he believes the powers that be will be grateful to him for his submission.

He eventually agrees to change his identity when his son begs him to. First of all, his son has to convince him not to declare himself Jewish when applying for a new identity card, but for a long time Vidal continues to resist the idea of assuming a false identity. He finally consents in 1943, in Lyon. The Resistance makes up false papers, and Edgar gives him the cards he needs for his new identities.

Previously, Vidal has considered reverting to Italian nationality, like his brothers. Indeed, at the beginning of 1943 he obtains a certificate of Italian nationality, issued by the Italian consul in Salonica, declaring that he features on the register of nationals under number 47a, letter N, and gives his residence as Livorno (as we have said, Nice will remain under Italian occupation until September 1943, and therefore until then letters can easily be sent between Nice, where Vidal and Henriette are living, and Italy). Does he change his mind? In any case, he decides to stay in France. He has known since spring 1943 that his son is in the French resistance, and he has too many ties in France to think of leaving, even with his brothers, for Italy.

Thus, Vidal's first self-preservation strategy is that of a neo-Marrano Sephardi (conversion, false devotion) and an Oriental (obedience to power). He reacts like a "Salonician," although during the Second World War he can no longer take advantage of the urban "nationality" that he managed to have recognized during the First. Certainly, in 1943 he could have reverted to Italian nationality like his brothers. This providential umbrella was to save all three of them, one in Brussels, and the other two in Italy; but unlike Léon and Jacques, Vidal cannot take his loved ones with him, and he is able to benefit directly from a different type of protection, namely the false papers provided by the Resistance.

ITALIAN PROTECTION

After Germany's invasion and partition of Yugoslavia, Mathilde takes refuge on May 25, 1941 in Abbazia (Opatija), in Istria, which at that time is in Italy. Her husband Bouchi, who falls ill during the retreat, and is cared for by Dr. Paolo Nogara, dies there on February 27, 1942 at the age of 54. The couple has been coming to Abbazia on vacation since the twenties, and they meet up with old friends and make new ones there. Probably after Bouchi's death, Mathilde, who speaks perfect Italian, manages to revert to the nationality she had as a teenager: Italy continues to recognize her nationals, even if they have acquired another nationality. Bouchi, who is very far-sighted, has made bank deposits in different countries, and must certainly have had some funds in Italy. Mathilde's beauty and seductive charm will help her find influential friends, including a *monsignore* from the Vatican. These friends not only make sure that her Italian nationality is completely restored to her, and that she is allowed to travel; they also help her in her efforts to bring to Italy the members of her family who are in danger in France. Although Fascist Italy has adopted some anti-Semitic measures, they do not have the legal or effective rigor of the German measures, and, in any case, now that she is a Nahum again, Mathilde no longer has the Jewish stamp on her Italian papers.

She resumes contact with her sister and her brothers at the beginning of 1942, and she begins to work energetically to get them to Italy when German troops enter the Pétainist zone and put them in danger. Her brother Jacques is the one in the worst and the best situation. The worst, because as a foreign Jew he is subject to forced residence in a small town in the Pyrenees (Sierp), but also the best, because he has retained his Italian nationality (to be on the safe side, he even took his wife's jewelry to the Italian consulate in Brussels, when Fascist Italy asked for this "spontaneous" donation to help fight the war in Ethiopia).

In April or May 1943, Italian Jews living in France are given permission to repatriate to Italy. Jacques, who reverts to being Giaccomo, accordingly requests repatriation for himself, his wife and his daughter Régine to their homeland. Mathilde goes to work in Rome and successfully uses the protection she enjoys to her advantage. Léon's daughter and son-in-law, Chary and Hiddo, also benefit from this measure. The Italian consul in Avignon strongly advises them to "return" to Italy as soon as possible, and they leave with their three children. Jacques, Sophie and Régine join them in the special repatriation train. Mathilde is waiting for all of them in Modena, where they decide to settle.

Do Léon, his wife and his son Edgard still think they are safe in Toulouse? Henriette talks about the "deep sleep" they have succumbed to in a letter to Mathilde dated July 16, 1943: "in March, they were sound asleep, and I almost had to use force to wake them all up."

She urges them to leave Toulouse, which is in the German zone, and where raids have started arresting many foreign Jews, and come to Nice, in the Italian zone. It is a dangerous journey, because Léon's identity papers, and those of his wife and son, bear the fatal stamp; they leave without their identity cards, on the night bus, and finally arrive in Nice, where they move in with Henriette at the Hotel Splendid. While awaiting their hoped-for repatriation to Italy, they need a permit allowing them to stay in Nice. They do not have the slightest chance of getting one, since they lack the necessary documents. However, Mony has a friend who knows a police commissioner; the man accepts a bribe, and Léon obtains his temporary residence permit.

They wait for their Italian papers. Their case is a difficult one, because Léon has not been an Italian national for a very long time, and neither Julie nor Edgard have ever been Italian. But Mathilde's ingenuity or her charm go to work in Rome, and she succeeds in re-Italianizing her brother and Italianizing his family. Léon must first have obtained the same document that Vidal received (but didn't use), a certificate from the Italian consulate in Salonica confirming his Italian nationality. Using this as a starting point, Mathilde takes steps to obtain Italian nationality for his wife and son. Léon, Julie and Edgard wait in Nice for the promised repatriation papers. Henriette describes their wavering: "Our Léon still cannot make up his mind about his journey, in spite of your express letter. It's true that it is very difficult at the moment to know whether to advise someone to do one thing or another" (letter dated July 16, 1943). On July 19, Henriette writes to Mathilde: "He [*Léon*], the person principally concerned, does not want to go to Godmother's [*Italy*], Julie definitely doesn't want to go, and Edgard is the only one who thinks they should go there."

On July 25, 1943, the Fascist grand council disavows Mussolini, and he is dismissed by the King of Italy, arrested and handed over to Marshal Badoglio, who begins armistice negotiations with the Americans. Thus, Italy seems to offer not only a refuge for the Nahums, but their possible liberation. The permits for Léon and his family arrive at the end of July or beginning of August. Unfortunately, the Italian papers are in Menton, which has been annexed by Italy, and a border now separates it from Nice. How does Léon manage to cross the border with his Belgian passport? He turns up at the Italian customs post laden with heavy suitcases, and, leaving his wife and son standing some way back, asks for permission to spend an hour or so in Menton, so that he can take his daughter and his grand-children their things, which, he explains, due to a mistake made by the rail organization, have not followed them to Italy. He finally makes the customs officer relent by giving him a large box of cigars. Then Léon beckons to Julie and Edgard: "*Ma que!*" cries the Italian police officer, "you don't need your wife and son to take these suitcases to your daughter!" But Léon, who has not become Italian again for nothing, asks him to imagine the disappointment of a mother and a brother who long to embrace their daughter and sister once again. The Italian does not have the heart to exclude a *mamma* and a *fratello* from this occasion for familial embracing, and lets all three Nahums through. They rush to Menton, collect the papers that declare them Italian, catch the train, and meet up in Modena with Chary, Hiddo, Mathilde, and Jacques and his family. Thus, on August 4, 1943, a large fragment of the Nahum family is reunited in Modena, where they benefit from the help of a friend of Mathilde's, Mr. Benassati.

Léon to Henriette:
Modena, August 4
My darlings,
Thanks be to God, we had a very pleasant journey, and found all our dear ones very well. All that I hope for now, my dears, is to know that you are all in perfect health and have no worries, God willing. We are very glad that we were able to join our dear children.
Our dear sister says that she sent her registered letter on Monday and will do all she can for the four of you.

In the same letter Mathilde confirms:

My darling sister,
Dear Léon and his family arrived safely. They're thinner, well, they are here now.
I will do all I can for the rest of you; in the meantime, see what you can do on your side.
I love and embrace you all,
Your Math

There is an intense exchange of letters between Henriette and Mathilde in July and August of 1943. From now on, the plan is to get Henriette, Élie, Mony and Liliane to Italy. The problem is much more complex because Henriette had adopted her husband's Greek nationality before they even left Salonica, and because Mony and Liliane are also Greek citizens. Mathilde puts Henriette in touch with an Italian (In the army? A civilian?) posted to Nice who will help her in her efforts, while she continues to work tirelessly in Rome. There is an attempt to speed things up using the pretext of a surgical operation that must be performed in Italy. However, the repatriation procedure fails to make headway. Henriette's letters express alternating hope and discouragement. In every letter, there is an account of days spent in an oasis, in an almost holiday atmosphere,[64] along with evocations of a time of anxious waiting.

July 13:
I went straight to the consulate; they still haven't received anything; they promised me they will let me know it has been accepted as soon as they have news: *vediamo*! We really have to be very sensible and not get our hopes up: only what if it *is* meant to be! What joy, what happiness! If it turns out to be impossible, we'll just tell ourselves again that the Good Lord did not want it that way . . . I am very pleased to know that you have spent some pleasant days at the magical villa and that you visited Saint Peter's, that extraordinary place . . .

July 16:
Every day I wait for a sign from the consulate regarding the enquiry about us, but nothing comes.

July 26:
I don't know where this letter will find you, if you will still be in Abbazia, or if you have gone home, or if the application has been accepted and you can come and see me. The most important thing is to wait very patiently and then the happy day when we embrace each other again will not be long in coming.

August 5 (letter to her brother Jacques):
Since Léon's departure, our health continues the same here, and yesterday Dr. Bachicat gaves us a slight hope that a cure will be found. What we are hoping for is a rapid recovery, and then we will go and convalesce at my niece Régine's house.

August 9 (to Mathilde):
The doctor is still promising us a cure and convalescence at Fernande's house: we're waiting. We are also waiting for the little presents from my nephew [*meaning some money sent by Mathilde*] which should arrive soon. I hope that you have seen our brother, and will read this letter to him. He knows all about what is happening with our patient's illness. On no account must you worry, everything will be all right and he will get better, as he has after all his previous illnesses. The place of his convalescence will be chosen

and indicated to us by the doctor, which means there will be no likelihood of our going to stay with Godmother. Godmother will have to come to him, if she wants to see him. God grant that this day will come, it will be such a happy one for us . . .

August 10:
My nephew has sent us some lovely presents, which will allow us to go on vacation. We haven't yet decided where we'll go, perhaps to stay with our friends the Parents, who are at a charming little place not too far from here. However, as I wrote to you yesterday, Dr. Bachicat assures us that our patient will be convalescing soon, and that the whole of our family will be able to come to Fernande's. We are ready to leave. Here or there, it's all the same. The preparations will take very little time.

I have been to see our cousin at Terbes [?], and he gave me the certificate your friend had kept for me at his house. I have it in my pocket, and if I go to Fernande's it may help me if [?] the others do not have it [?]. [*Perhaps she is talking about a certificate from the Italian consul in Salonica confirming her Italian nationality.*]

Well, be cheerful; even if we do go and spend a few days with the Parents, we will got to Fernande's afterwards, as soon as we can.

A few keys are missing here. There seems to be someone in Nice who can help Henriette and her family leave France. Is it the same person as the one at the Italian consulate who is looking after Henriette's file? Is it another Italian, someone with influence? Whom does she mean by Bachicat, which is a disguised form of the *djidio* word *Bachica*? The word refers to a short female, who is the person who will choose the place of convalescence, in other words, where they will go to live outside of France. Does Fernande stand for some other country than the Godmother's (Italy), which might be Switzerland, or does it refer to another place in Italy where the Hassids and the Covos have been assigned to live?

August 13 1943:
We're not worried, because the doctor is still promising to take us with him for the convalescence. All of our friends and acquaintances are waiting too; they would all like to go on vacation with us. I cannot begin to do anything here in the way of preparations; it will be all of us together, unless it is in the same exceptional circumstances, I mean those of our eldest. We also have the presents from our nephew, and when the time is right, and when it's possible, we will take advantage of them and use them. For the time being, we can wait, they have promised to let us know if we have to make a little journey to see Mrs. Escumière [*escumler:* hide? escape?]. If that happens, we will go to Suzanne's or to the Parents'. Yesterday my friend Isabelle came to see me and we went for an ice cream. She is quite prepared

to come with us to see Fernande; she advises me to take all our winter clothing, because it will be cold up in the mountains.

Again, there are many terms in code here that we cannot decipher. Fernande seems to be mountainous and cold, despite the fact that this is the month of August: is it Switzerland, or a part of the French Alps occupied by Italians, or does it refer to a secret passage through the mountains? If it does, to go where?

August 20 1943:

I am so sorry that you are worried on our account, but I absolutely promise you that everything has changed and that our patient is much better; his cousins have left, and he feels less tired. The doctor has also confirmed this, and we're not worried about him . . . If you can get a return pass, come and see us . . . It's all enough to make me wonder where is best for us; we trust in the Good Lord, who has protected us until now and will continue to do so.

After this letter, Henriette mentions the three hypotheses again:

- either they obtain an authorization to go to Italy;
- Mathilde will make a return journey to Nice;
- or they will leave for a place of refuge (to some friends' house, the Parents'? In Switzerland?).

On August 22, Henriette writes to her brother Jacques; she seems to be increasingly convinced that the best idea is to stay with Suzanne and then leave from there for Fernande. She is no longer counting on the friends from Terbes. Nevertheless, in a letter dated August 24, she reports that various tall stories are circulating (probably rumors concerning the confused events in Italy, and the danger of Germany's intervening against her former ally), and writes: "I am going to see the friends in Terbes at once, because that will reassure me." However, she has envisaged the worst, for she writes: "All the arrangements have been made, I repeat, so that if his temperature rises, we will have what we need at hand to relieve him, and we will take to our heels." Henriette is very happy to have finally received some indirect news (probably via Spain or Portugal, which are neutral) of her daughter Aimée, who is in Liverpool: "I was overjoyed yesterday to receive a card from Pinto telling me that he has had a telegram from my darling little Aimée. All three of them are very well; she received a letter from me dated June 10, through Pinto. The only way of getting letters to her is through him."

On August 28, Henriette asks her sister: "Have you got the pass so you can come and help me? I know that the application was accepted on this side and the answer has been sent off."

Then Mathilde stops receiving letters. Communications have broken down. On September 3, the Americans land in Salerno. Marshal Badoglio signs the armistice with the Allies on September 8. But the German armies immediately surge towards Italy, occupy it, disband the Italian army, and, of course, occupy Nice and Savoy. Henriette, Élie, Mony and Liliane are caught in the hoop net, but they manage to get out of Nice in time; they go first to Roanne, and then to Caliure, near Lyon. The Hassids change their name to Acide, the Covos to Coveau. Caliure's parish priest has their false ration cards validated and protects them.

However, in Nice, Corinne's husband Joseph is arrested on board a train leaving for Lyon. His identity card is not stamped "Jewish," but the Germans make him go into the lavatory and confirm that he is circumcised. Corinne, who has accompanied him to the station, stands by, helpless, as her husband is taken away in a German police van.

SEPTEMBER 1943 TO SEPTEMBER 1944

Vidal is still traveling between Nice and Lyon, and Roanne and Tarare, where Myriam Beressi's brother, Edouard Mosseri, is living. Edouard's companion, Mrs. Dumontet, comes from the region. She protects him, and subsequently helps his whole family. In the Southern zone, Vidal has been reunited with his former lover from Paris, but their relationship has become very stormy, and every reconciliation is followed by another break-up. He has met a widow in Lyon, Mrs. Blanc, who runs a hairdressing salon. He probably goes to live with Mrs. Blanc when the German troops enter Nice.

Vidal lives at Mrs. Blanc's place for a while. At the time, hairdressers enjoy a privileged position; she is given all kinds of Lyonnais foodstuffs by her customers, women with businesses selling meat, charcuterie, dairy products and groceries. Vidal has found a "good table", eats well, and takes pleasure in Mrs. Blanc's voluptuous figure. He has Edgar and his girlfriend Violette invited to lunch there, and asks them to bring a "spontaneous" gift of flowers. But his former lover, with whom he has had so many break-ups, tracks him down and declares that she will commit suicide if he does not leave the hairdresser at once. So Vidal goes to see Mrs. Blanc and says, more or less in the following words: "Darling, I've been keeping a secret from you, but now I have no choice but to confess it to you. I am a member of the secret army of the Resistance. My superiors have given me orders to go to Algiers, and so I have to make a clandestine crossing over the Spanish border. I must leave at once. Farewell, my love, we will meet again beneath the great sun of Victory."

Mrs. Blanc grieves and laments, but is eventually obliged to yield to such heroism. She takes some sausage, butter, cans and provisions out of her store, and fills a huge backpack with them. Staggering under this great weight,

Vidal leaves for the Spanish border, gets on the tram, and arrives at the end of his journey in another district of Lyon. A month later, Mrs. Blanc spies him queuing in front of a baker's shop: "Vidal! You! Here!"

Vidal leaves the queue, takes her arm, and looks around him in all directions. "Sshh," he whispers, assuming the expression of a hunted man, and leads her to a deserted embankment of the Saône, where he gradually begins to relax. He tells Mrs. Blanc that he did leave for the Spanish border, but when he got there he discovered that a traitor had informed on his network. He was obliged to wait in the snow and the cold of the Pyrenees until he received orders from his superiors to return to Lyon without letting anyone know, even the woman dearest to him, and to wait there for further instructions before setting off for Spain again. Mrs. Blanc listens to the story, incredulous at first, then moved by all the dangers he has faced, and she asks him to come home with her for a moment so that she can give him some more supplies. In spite of the orders from his superiors, Vidal returns to Mrs. Blanc's, and leaves a second time loaded with cans, sausage and provisions. Then he breaks up with his lover again. He goes to Caliure, where he will receive providential protection from the local priest. Afterwards, he looks for lodgings for Corinne, who is completely destitute after her husband's arrest, and they end up living together in La Rochetaillée.

From now on, Vidal, who refused to entertain the idea in 1942, lives entirely under a false identity. His son has been able to obtain numerous false identity cards for his father and his family, and Vidal has four himself. The first, which is stamped with the seal of Belmont town hall (in Isère), is in the name of Nicolas Vidal, businessman, born March 14, 1892 in Castres, Tarn. The second is in the name of Georges Lezot, his friend who lives in Paris. The third, in the name of Eugène Barré, accountant, born July 26, 1899 in Charny (Meuse), and residing at 14, Rue Denfert, Sucy-en-Brie, is intended to serve for possible journeys to Paris. The fourth belongs to Louis Blanc (Mrs. Blanc's deceased husband), born on April 8, 1894 in Maltat (Saône et Loire), residing at 12, Rue d'Algérie, in Lyon; it is stamped by police headquarters in Lyon. Vidal also has two (false) demobilization certificates, one in the name of Nicolas Vidal, the other in the name of Louis Blanc. He has a false work certificate in the name of Louis Blanc, who since June 1935 has been employed as an agent by Georges Lezot, insurance broker, with offices at 23, Rue Terme, in Lyon. He has also kept the extract from the parish records which certifies that his marriage was blessed on July 6, 1920, when he married Miss Anne Marie Françoise Bechard. Finally, he has rent receipts for an apartment rented by Nicolas Vidal from Louis Blanc (in other words, by himself from himself), at 12, Rue d'Algérie, in Lyon. In the end, he will live in Rochetaillée under the name of Blanc, and at the same time he will keep lodgings in Lyon, under the name of Nicolas Vidal. In this way, he ensures that he has a refuge if he needs it.

Vidal is very worried about his son during the summer of 1943. Having no news of him, he turns up one day in the cul-de-sac at the top of La Croix-Russe, at the house where Edgar, now known as Gaston Poncet, is lodging. The landlords start shouting at him, saying that his son is a jewelry thief and a gangster, and that the German police came looking for him the night before. Vidal is horrified. Has Edgar been arrested? No, he did not go home, but the minute he gets back his landlords will denounce him. At the time, a torrent of arrests in Lyon is ravaging the resistance movements, and Edgar has narrowly escaped capture several times. Vidal probably resumes contact with his son through Corinne, who sheltered her nephew on the night he didn't go home. Mrs. Dumontet will obtain a few days' refuge for Edgar at the home of a couple of peasants, near to Tarare, before he returns to Toulouse and picks up the thread that had been broken with the resistance. He finally settles in Paris at the end of 1943 or beginning of 1944.

Fall 1943 sees the advance of the Russian offensive, which captures Kiev in November. To the West, in the aftermath of the Allied landings in Sicily, in July 1943, and in Salerno, on September 3, followed by the fall of Mussolini and Badoglio's request for an armistice (September 8), thirty German divisions rush into the peninsula and immobilize the Allies at the Volturne. Far away in the Pacific, the United States take the offensive. In France, resistance is growing, and repression is intensifying, as is the hunt of the Jews.

In fall 1943, Vidal goes to lie low at La Rochetaillée under the name of Louis Blanc. However, he still makes a couple of trips to Paris using the identity of René Barré, the stepfather of his son's high school friend Henri Luce. Henri is enduring the STO (forced labor service) in Germany, along with his brother Georges. Edgar addresses his letters to Louis Blanc and signs Errol Pastel. Vidal also receives letters from Mr. René Barré. Mr. and Mrs. Barré have had Edgar to stay during his trips to Paris, and later often invite him to lunch when he goes to live in the city in the winter of 1943 to 1944. Mr. Barré is a Lorrainian patriot; as an inspector at the SNCF (the French national rail service), he has been able to provide Edgar with contacts in the rail service's management, who supply precious information about the trains requisitioned by the Germans. Vidal hopes that Mr. Barré will put pressure on his son to stop his dangerous activities. We have part of the correspondance they exchanged between April 25 and August 10. Since it is subject to the Nazi's censorship of the mail, this correspondence takes great pains not to express the writers' true feelings. Letter from René Barré to Louis Blanc (Vidal):

Paris, April 25, 1944
My dear friend,
Received your letter dated the 19th of this month. Since you were here, we have had quite a fright, as you probably know, and our neighborhood has suffered cruelly from the Anglo-American bombings. The worst affected area is between Montmartre and

the Rue de la Chapelle, on one side, and the Rue Ordener and Saint-Denis, on the other. The station, depots, workshops, etc., in the Nord area have been completely destroyed (La Chapelle, Le Landy, the Pont de Soissons, etc.).

The bombs that fell closest to us hit the Rue Custine and the Boulevard Barbès.

Like you, I hope ardently for the end of this horrible war, whose effects are increasingly demoralizing and disastrous.

Your goddaughter [he is referring to Vidal's son] came to see us on Sunday. She is in excellent health. I showed her your letter and once again urged her to follow the path I would very much like to see her take. However, she does not seem to like the proposed solution; she is probably expecting she will get the job that she wants. She is coming to see us again on Thursday at noon, and I will have another word with her, since you have given me permission to do so.

May 6 or 7 would be fine, Mrs. Barré and I are always very happy of the chance to shake your hand. We would be delighted to help you in any way we can, and in particular to buy the lease of your store.

That way, once peace is restored, you will have the great joy of seeing the business in hands that are certainly not those of strangers, and who will restore to you what you say has been "half of your life."

I hope that you are in the best of health.

We have heard good news from Henri and Georges, who are waiting in Berlin to return to Paris. We still do not know when. It seems that their leave has been stopped again or at least delayed for the time being.

I am sure that they will be glad to work with you when they come home.

I look forward to the pleasure of seeing you once again, my very dear friend.

Yours affectionately.

The letter indicates that Vidal is already preparing for the Liberation; he wants René Barré to pretend to take over his business, and René Barré confirms his agreement with his allusion that he will give him back "half of his life." The Barrés, like Mr. Luce, would like Henri or Georges to be employed in Vidal's business and thus find work when they return from the STO. Vidal answers this letter:

Lyon, May 3, 1944

My dear friend,

I was delighted to receive on Monday your letter of the 25th, which very fortunately told me your news. I have been worried about you, knowing that you live close to the Nord and Est stations, and also to the 18th arrondissement, which has been so hard hit. Since these unfortunate attacks show no sign of ending, I hope always to have good news from you, and I also hope to see the end of all our misfortunes.

Thank you very much for thinking of my goddaughter. I would be pleased if she were willing to forgo her own preferences a little, and follow my advice [So Vidal does not despair of making his son give up his resistance activity]. At the moment, I think that she is away from Paris. I am impatient for news from her, and I am extremely

184

worried when I hear about the bombings that are taking place almost everywhere.

I am pleased to read that you have had good news of the dear children in Berlin, and I hope that they will be fortunate enough to obtain their leave soon.

The journey I had planned to make at the end of this week will have to be delayed; I hope to make it on May 20 or 21. I thank you kindly for your answer to my offer to sell, and will give you all the details in person when I next come to Paris.

I look forward to hearing your good news, and send you my warmest regards, dear Mr. Barré, and to Mrs. Barré.

Louis Blanc.

Rochetaillée-sur-Saône.

A letter dated May 8 is missing, to which René Barré replies:

Paris, May 15

My dear friend,

We received your letters dated the 3rd and 8th of this month.

You must not allow yourself to be demoralized by this depression which, you say, has a relentless grip on you. What good can come of being demoralized? Yesterday, we had a visit from your goddaughter, who is in excellent health. She had already been to see us on Friday and is due to come back this afternoon. She is absolutely fine, and is very far from giving in to sadness. Cheer up, for goodness' sake! I beg you to remember that we are coming to the end of the race, and that we will soon cross the finishing line, by which I mean see an end to this terrible war. Admit, therefore, that this is not the time to let oneself be influenced by sadness. Cheer up, I say! Cheer up, I will never cease repeating to you. We are coming to the end of all our troubles.

We will certainly enjoy the calm that follows the storm!

You will see, my dear Monsieur Blanc, that we still have wonderful days ahead of us, and we will appreciate them all the more because of the suffering, anxiety and sadness we have been through.

We have had no news from Henri and Georges during the past few days. The last we heard was on April 29. But the mail comes in fits and starts: we often have ten letters in two or three days, then nothing for two weeks.

Agreed for your visit of May 20 or 21. We and your goddaughter will always be happy to see you again.

So once again, cheer up! The trials will not last much longer now.

I hope that your health is still flourishing. I look forward to seeing you soon, and Mrs. Barré and Mr. Luce join me in sending you our kindest regards.

(What was the cause of the fit of "depression" that Vidal confessed to in a letter to René Barré?)

The next letter from René Barré is dated June 15. In the interim, the Allies have landed in Normandy. Despite the capture of Caen on July 9, there is no clear outcome until the breakthrough at Avranches on July 31.

Paris, June 15 1944.

My dear friend,

We received your letter of May 31 at the appointed time. I apologize for not having answered earlier; the events are the reason for my delay.

I will not tell you anything new about what is happening, you must know as much about it as I do. I will therefore tell you instead about matters close to our hearts.

Your young goddaughter is well. We had a visit from her this morning and she expects to come back next Sunday as usual. She is happy, and is waiting bravely for the end of our torments. However, she is worried not to have had any news from you. We think this is due to a problem with the mail. While we are on that subject, I suggest we make a plan. If the mail ceases to function properly through the post office, hand your letter in a sealed envelope to Lyon station or whichever station is nearest, addressed as follows: "Mr. Barré, inspector of transport, responsible for technical inspection of the South-Eastern region at the Lyon station in Paris."

Simply ask the manager of the postal service to accept your letter and send it to me in a service envelope.

As far as my business is concerned, I have telephoned Mr. Baumgartner [the provisional administrator of Vidal's store] who, very kindly, asked me to confirm our conversation. However, I have the impression that the events have put a stop to everything and that the status quo will prevail. I can only feel very pleased about this.

That is all our news. However, I have something very painful to tell you. Paris is starving. The markets are closed and so is the central food market. I do not know what the outcome of all this will be.

I dare to hope that you are still in very good health and that soon we will have the pleasure of seeing one another again, when peace has been completely restored.

I look forward to hearing from you. Mrs. Barré and Mr. Luce join me in sending you their very best regards.

See you soon, and above all be cheerful.

On June 26, Soviet troops enter German territory. On July 20, there is an attempt on Hitler's life; the rumor of the Führer's death circulates for a while, as the following letter from René Barré attests.

Paris, July 22, 1944

My dear friend,

On July 11, I received your letter of the 3rd, which delighted us. On the 12th I also received your first parcel and the second on the 13th. Everything arrived in fairly good condition, although a few apples were a little bruised on arrival. But it was wonderful all the same and your god-daughter took possession of her presents the next day on the 14th and the following Sunday 16th. She came back again this week and we are expecting her tomorrow, the 23rd.

(Here, the letter reports that negotiations with Mr. Baumgartner over buying back Vidal's store have come to a standstill.)

For the time being, supplies, although very difficult to get hold of, are not too bad. We can get some greens and a few new vegetables. I have ordered some new potatoes. God knows when I will receive them. To change the subject, I think it is probably unnecessary to give you news of the events. We all know about them and frankly deplore the passing of that good man A. Hitler!! But it must have been an accident in the course of events against which men, even men of State, are powerless. As for me, I continue to believe that by August 15 the war will have virtually ended, with the obliteration of our enemies . . . I refer of course to the Bolsheviks and the Anglo-Americans.

René Barré then deplores the lack of news from the children in Berlin, but only in order to express even greater pleasure at the prospect of an imminent reunion. He repeats his encouragements to Vidal.

Have faith, then, my dear Friend! Let's hold tight, the war is on the wane.

He ends:

Mrs. Barré and Mr. Luce ask me to tell you that you are often in our thoughts and our conversations, and they send you their affectionate regards. I will be sure to join them, and assure you of my whole-hearted and indissoluble friendship.
    A very cordial embrace.
    René Barré

Letter from René Barré dated July 30:

My dear friend,
Yesterday I received your letter of the 25th of this month, which gave us much pleasure. Your little goddaughter came this morning to us and was delighted with your letter. She has taken it with her so that she can reply to you herself. I am also in a hurry to do so, taking advantage of the fact that it is Sunday, which "for the time being" is our weekly day of rest. I see that our two letters crossed in the mail, for I had replied in the meantime to your letter of the 3rd and to acknowledge the safe arrival of the two parcels . . . As usual, I let you know my great hope of seeing an end to this horrible war very soon, and in seeing you comfortably at home with your little god-daughter beside you. Most of all, I look forward to meeting you again in my little store . . . You will soon have the joy of taking back this store, which to a certain extent is your life. You will find it intact and in the same condition in which you left it, since you were kept away from it because of the current transport problems. You will understand why I prefer to see you in this store, which is really yours rather than mine, and which you had to leave in order to devote all your energies to working as our representative. So have faith, we will celebrate your return very soon.
    However, this is not the only object of my letter. And now I have an enormous favor to ask of you in return. This is what it entails.

187

The Industrial Society of Oil-Producers, of which, as you know, my brother-in-law is the manager, has received an order from the Ministry of Agriculture to hydrogenize oils in order to transform them into edible fats, which Paris needs urgently. However, this firm obviously lacks the means to do so; nevertheless, they sent an order at once for the raw materials they need for processing. I am going to come to the point straight away. The materials in question are an aluminium and nickel alloy, for which an order has been sent by the aforementioned Society to the Alais-Froges et Camargues company, in Chedde (Haute-Savoie). The order was countersigned by the Minister, following order no 5625 CD of March 31, 1944 to the French aluminium company. Now the great difficulty is transport. There are about 800 kilos of this alloy to be brought from Chedde to Paris. It is impossible to envisage rail transport, because the Savoy and Haute-Savoie lines are systematically cut off. The only option is by road.

I thought your friend Mr. Besson, at 18 Rue du Caire, might be able to look after the transport from Lyon to Paris. I think he will agree to bring the merchandise back to Paris if necessary. But will he be prepared to go and pick it up in Chedde? I doubt it! So could you please try to find a reliable transporter who would agree to take responsibility for getting it as far as Lyon, through "the maquis" if necessary, and, if need be, by agreement with them, paying a fee to the maquis?

As for the cost of transportation, it is not very important. The real value of the merchandise is such that the cost of transporting it is secondary. Moreover, transport costs will be reimbursed by the State. The merchandise is ready to be collected, in fact the only thing missing is the transporter. Do you need money to organize this, that is of course if you don't mind doing it? Naturally, you would charge your commerical rate. I would appreciate a rapid reply from you, since the matter is so urgent. Paris must live, in short.

I end my letter by assuring you of my friendship, which is easy to say, because as always I make my assurances of friendship with a true and sincere heart. Mrs. Barré sends you her warmest regards, as does Mr. Luce; I will go one better, and send you my fraternal and spontaneous embrace.

René Barré

Answer from Vidal dated August 10:

My dear friend,

I received your letter dated July 30 the day before yesterday, dear Mr. Barré, and was very pleased to hear from you. I confess that your letter heartened me, and has given me the strength and courage to look after myself and wait for relief. Very pleased to hear about my little goddaughter, and thank you for everything that you are doing for her.

In respect of your query about transporting the order for the Society of oil-producers to Paris, I at once set about finding a transporter for the journey from Savoy to Lyon and from Lyon to Paris. I went to see several firms, who have promised to give me an answer today, and so I have not made much progress yet. Trucks occasionally travel the Savoy–Lyon route, picking up freight on either their outward or return journey, depending on whether they themselves need to leave or return without freight. In order to get the job done, your friends should have told the Alais firm to help them, and find a truck going to Lyon. Once the merchandise is here, I hope that it will be possible, either through Mr. Besson, or through another road transport company, to bring it to Paris. It is impossible to get to Haute-Savoie without a special permit from police headquarters, and only the sender would be able to find a way of transporting the merchandise as far as Lyon.

I regret very much that, as you can see, I cannot give you the answer you were hoping for. Even the simplest transport is so complicated nowadays! If your brother-in-law gives instructions to get the goods transported to Lyon, he can give them the following address in Lyon: Mr. Nicolas, c/o Maison Lancher, 12 Rue d'Algérie, Lyon. If need be, I can store the merchandise at this address until it is sent to Paris; the main difficulty is getting it to Lyon in the first place. I await your news and remain entirely at your disposal.

Events come thick and fast: Paris rebels, the Resistance comes out into the open, and Leclerc's tanks enter the city on August 26. The city rejoices. The resistants are indifferent to the fact that Warsaw has begun its insurrection almost simultaneously, on August 1, and that Soviet troops are allowing the Nazi troops to crush the city, eventually annihilating all resistance there on September 10.

The allied offensive continues, and, in September, Rouen, Brussels and Anvers are liberated. In the meantime, the Allies land in Provence on August 15 and make their way North to Lyon, which is liberated by the French troops on about September 15.

Vidal's oral autobiography:

Right away, two or three days later, as your Dad [Edgar] had my address, a friend of his, I don't know how he made his way out from among the soldiers, but he comes up and touches me, and says: "I'm going back to Paris in a Jeep on an army mission, so I can give you a lift if you like." And I left with him and I arrived in Paris.

Indeed, Vidal obtains an FFI ("Forces françaises de l'intérieur"), the French Resistance forces pass, on September 19. He immediately joins the MNPGD (the National Movement of Prisoners of War and Deportees, the resistance movement in which his son had a position of responsibility). In Paris, his son will have a false mission order made up for him on October 12, so that Vidal can go and see his family in Lyon and Nice.

National Movement of Prisoners of War and Deportees
Paris region
22, Rue de la Paix
Paris, 2nd arrondissement
MISSION ORDER
MR. VIDAL NAHOUM, HOLDER OF IDENTITY CARD NO. 217874, HAS BEEN

SENT ON A MISSION BY THE AFOREMENTIONED MOVEMENT TO THE
LYON, MARSEILLES AND NICE REGIONS, TO MAKE URGENT CONTACT
WITH FAMILIES OF DEPORTEES. THE MILITARY AND CIVIL AUTHORITIES ARE
REQUESTED TO ALLOW HIM TO MOVE ABOUT FREELY USING ALL AVAIL-
ABLE MEANS OF TRANSPORT
Officer: Morin

Afterwards, Vidal has no trouble getting back his store, which has been
under provisional administration. It will not be so easy for him to get back
his apartment, which has been sold.

I went to see the gentleman who had bought it, he was a manager at La
Samaritaine. He said to me:

"But what do you want me to do sir, I bought it because it was for sale, it was
legal."

"Yes, I know, I'm not accusing you of anything, but it wasn't me who sold it
to you; now I'm back you'll have to return it to me."

"But who's going to reimburse me?"

"Ah well, you'll have to go to Jewish affairs."

Reappropriation had to wait until an act of Parliament was passed
annulling all sales made under the authority of the occupying force, and the
legal formalities were only completed in fall 1945. However, the buyer, Mr.
Dubessay, was obliged to let Vidal have the apartment before then. Corinne
came to live in this apartment with her children. Fredy would study law, and
Henri would be encouraged to attend the business school in the Rue
Trudaine. Vidal was also concerned about settling his wife Luna's estate, now
that his son had come of age, and he put the Rueil villa into Edgar's name,
although it was occupied by a tenant who refused to vacate it.

Vidal had not forgotten the camaraderie he had experienced at Bourges.
He managed to get in touch with some of his comrades from the 15th
company of military workers, and wrote the following summons on his typewriter, on the day of the German surrender:

Paris, May 8, 1945
Dear friend,
Victory has come.

A group of friends, who were drafted to Bourges in 1940, would like to revive the
camaraderie that united us during our ordeal.

In a spirit of cordial friendship, we have decided to organize a reunion, with the aim
of supporting and helping one another with the practical aspects of life.

If, in spite of your business and your occupations, you can spare us a few minutes
of your time, please come on Saturday May 12 between 5 p.m. and 6.30 p.m. to the
café-tabac at 72, Rue Jean-Jacques Rousseau.

We are counting on you, dear friend, and send you our most cordial regards.
Your friends from the 15th company in Bourges.

THE SURVIVORS AND THE DEAD

Vidal is the first to get back home to Paris. Henriette, Élie, Liliane and Mony will come and join him. Mony and Liliane return to their apartment, which has been protected by the Argentinian embassy. As we have said, the couple are now psychologically united; all the ordeals they have been through together have forged an almost organic bond between them, although they did not love each other in the early days of their relationship; a different kind of love now unites them very powerfully. At the end of the war, Mony learns that his parents, as well as his brothers, sisters and cousins, Samuel Covo, Reyna Covo, Peppo Covo, Renée Covo, Sam Covo, Oscar Hassid, Daisy Hassid, Ida Angel, Sam Angel and Juda Saltiel have all died at Auschwitz.

Henriette cannot get her apartment back immediately. It has been looted, and then let. She does not go to stay with her daughter, although Liliane has enough room: Mony has found it very hard, having to live with his parents-in-law for five years without a break, and Henriette herself insists, not only that she does not want to be a nuisance to her daughter, but that her cohabitation with her son-in-law must come to an end. While waiting for her applications to achieve the desired result, she moves into the Hotel du Grand Veneur, in the Rue Demours, near her home. She learns that her daughter Aimée, her husband Ben and their son Pierre have survived the war without incident in Liverpool. She will die in hospital of a heart attack in 1947, before managing to get her apartment back.

The Italian and re-Italianized Nahums lived in freedom at first in Modena. Indeed, they felt so free there that one day, on the terrace of a big café on the Via Independenza, Mathilde told some people at the neighboring table, who had complimented her on her beauty and that of her nieces: "*Siamo tutti belli e ebrei*" ("We're all beautiful and Jewish"). When the German troops arrived in Modena in September 1943, the family fled the city, fearing the possible effect of these words. Thanks to the kindly *monsignore* from the Vatican who protected her, Mathilde obtained authentic documents for the whole family under false names. Chary, Hiddo and their children took refuge in Zecca, a little village in the Apennines, where they were protected by the priest and by a Marquis from Bologna. Mathilde stayed in Rome, near her protectors. Léon and Jacques moved to Florence. Jacques died during the Florence uprising in September 1944. He had fallen ill during the fighting, when the inhabitants were destitute because of the state of siege, and had not been able to get medical care in time. He is buried in the little Jewish cemetery in Florence, where the tombs are well looked-after and decorated with flowers.

Florence is liberated by the Anglo-Americans; Edgard announces that he is a Belgian national and joins the English army, which posts him to Austria in May 1945. Léon and his wife return to Brussels as quickly as they can, revert to their Belgian nationality and take back Nahum Steel. They are reunited with Henri, who has survived thanks to his companion's protection. Their daughter Chary and their son-in-law Hiddo have returned to Avignon and will take French nationality.

After the German surrender, Jacques's wife and daughter return to Brussels. Jacques's brothers club together to pay them an annuity. Hélène Schrecker, Jacques's younger daughter, is in Washington, where her husband has found a research post, and she is teaching French. Mathilde stays in Italy. She has settled there, and has many friends and connections. The family network is back in action.

How did Vidal and his family manage to survive in exile without working? Léon and Jacques had time to take some money and their jewelry with them when they left Brussels, and they lived, first on their savings, and then, especially in Italy, from the sale of their jewelry, rings, gold chains, etc. Bouchi and Mathilde were able to take some money and some jewelry with them in their escape from Yugoslavaia, and they also drew on the savings accounts that Bouchi had opened. Mathilde sent money to her sister Henriette in Nice, and she was probably able to give financial assitance to her brothers in Italy as well. Vidal was not short of money at any point during the period between his departure from Paris and the end of the Occupation. Nevertheless, he had brought neither gold nor cash with him on the journey to Toulouse; the German inspectors at Vierzon could find nothing on him. How did he manage to live for three more years without working? Had he opened an account in the Southern zone before taking refuge there? He probably managed to make withdrawals from his Parisian bank account, since an envelope was found among his papers from the Banque de France, addressed to him at the Rue Guglia, in Nice. Was that enough? The powerful solidarity that existed between the Nahum brothers would have come into play, if ever one of them was in need. As in the past, and in the future, there were probably loans by one brother to another, and by other relations on the Beressi side. In any case, although they all stopped working during the Occupation, none of the Nahums became destitute.

On the Beressi side, Myriam Beressi stayed on in Paris for a long time, before her daughter Émy had her come to Lyon using a false identity card, obtained by François Robert and brought to her by his wife, Maryse. She was not arrested. Joseph Pelosoff, Corinne's husband, who was arrested in Nice, was deported to Auschwitz, and would not return.

Benjamin, Corinne's youngest brother, joined up in 1939, and, like Maurice, entered the 1st foot regiment of foreign volunteers. After being demobilized in Aix-en-Provence in 1941, he returned to Paris, declared himself Jewish, and was arrested at his home in 1942. He died, in unknown circumstances, in the transit camp at Compiègne, where deportees were imprisoned before being sent to Auschwitz. His ashes were repatriated after the war, and placed in the Beressi family tomb, at Père-Lachaise cemetery.

Pepo and Margot managed to leave Besançon, which had become part of the forbidden zone after the German invasion, and moved into 39, Rue de Chanzy, in 1940. Pepo found work in a factory in the suburbs manufacturing chemical products, where they were not too scrupulous in checking the identity of employees who were to handle toxic materials. The couple declared themselves Jewish and wore the yellow star. Their second son, Jean-Marc, was born in 1941. Margot began to camouflage her yellow star underneath a shawl, the lapel of her coat, or her purse. Pepo went to work on foot, not wearing his yellow star, in order to avoid the raids in the métro. He came home after the curfew, hiding in doorways whenever he heard the footsteps of a German patrol. The Gestapo came to their apartment one evening, accompanied by some French policemen. They hammered several times on the door. Pepo, Margot and their children held their breath. The policemen went to question the concierge, and she said that she had not seen the Beressis for several days, thus saving their lives. After that, the children were placed in foster homes in Normandy. Pepo sub-let the apartment above theirs, which was only rarely occupied by a sales representative who travelled all over France with his *Ausweis*. At nightfall, the couple would sneak upstairs and sleep in the representative's apartment. Margot worked at home on her sewing machine and the couple survived on what she earned until the Liberation. Mimo, Margot's young brother, was deported and never returned. Her older brother, who was in the army in 1940, had been taken prisoner; he was saved by his captain, who destroyed his company's archives and declared that private Camhi was henceforth to be known as Camille. At the Liberation, Margot would become manageress of a branch of the Au Muguet chain, at 24 Rue Faubourg-du-Temple, and later of the branch at 83, Boulevard Saint-Martin. Pepo would work on the Porte de Montreuil markets and would eventually be employed by Vidal.

Maurice and Émy were able to settle in Monte-Carlo, where they opened a garment-making workshop using their false identities. Maurice took part in a resistance group, and he was protected by a police inspector friend, François Robert, who would afterwards work with him.

Apart from the Nahum and Beressi brothers and sisters, other relatives or allies were deported. Cousin Paul Nahum was arrested and sent to Drancy, but providential intervention saw to it that he was liberated before being deported. His sister Marcelle was deported to Auschwitz. Élie Beressi was arrested for hiding English parachutists. He too returned from deportation, settled in Paris and retired from business. Many of the Salonicians from the Sentier died during deportation. But Salonica itself suffered a veritable hecatomb. Of the 56,500 Sephardim living there in 1940, 46,091 were deported to Auschwitz and almost all of them died there; a census of 1947 counted only 1,900 Jews. Mony's family was wiped out at Auschwitz. Vidal's maternal family was also wiped out, with the exception of two female cousins.

As soon as the war ends, Vidal increases his efforts to resume contact with family members scattered in different countries. He works determinedly, like a sheepdog rounding up lost ewes. He writes to the newspapers in Salonica looking for what remains of the Frances family. The survivor, Régine Frances, reads his appeal and writes to her cousin Vidal on February 19, 1946:

Régine Frances
Rue Georges-Stavrou, no. 7.

My dear Vidal,

I am writing to tell you that I learned from the newspaper about the enquiries you are making, to find out what has become of our relatives. More than once, I have thought of writing to you in order to ask for news of you all, but I had no address.

Unfortunately, my dear Vidal, Papa and Mama were deported to Poland, as was Jacques, along with his wife and two children, a boy and a girl; the boy was called Azriel, and was 5 years old, the girl was 13. Henri was also deported with his wife and his little girl, who was 5 years old.

Jeanne, being married to a Greek, was lucky enough to escape, as you know, and I, being a Spanish citizen, also managed to escape. But we were not spared. As Spanish citizens, we were a little more privileged than the Greeks, but they still made our lives very difficult. They told us they would send us to Spain; in the end, the Germans gathered all the Spanish together to send them to Poland. Fortunately, we had the presence of mind to run away beforehand. By five o'clock, we were far away from Salonica. A few days later, we learned that the Spanish had been deported to Poland . . .

Now, to return to Papa and Mama and my brothers. They could not escape, first because all the Jews who were Greek subjects had to stay in special neighborhoods, which were guarded by Jewish and Greek policemen, and then because they were not allowed outside after 5 o'clock in the evening, in the neighborhood they were forced to stay in.

Jeanne's husband did what he could to keep Henri safe, but once Henri saw that his wife and his child had gone, he gave himself up as well. Jacques also did what he could to escape with his family, but unfortunately he was betrayed at the last minute. As for Papa and Mama, I was quite prepared to take them in to live with me, since we were still free, but my husband was afraid, he convinced me that we would be lost ourselves if we were denounced. And in fact the Germans did come to make enquiries at my house a few days later, accusing me of sheltering a Jewish girl; since my conscience was clear, I faced them quite courageously. So there was a very grave danger.

Then afterwards, they couldn't escape because they didn't have a guide [to cross the border].

And now, as you see, my dear Vidal, I am unfortunately the only surviving member of the Frances family. Me, who was always so spoiled by all of them, Papa, Mama, Jacques and Henri.

How I wept when I went to the association and saw the letter that you wrote: at least there is one person who is interested in finding out what happened to my family, the Frances. For the time being, I am suffering from a great loss of affection, I am still praying to the blessed Lord to let me see them come home again.

To go back to my situation, as I told you, we went to a place five hours away from Salonica. Before leaving, we had entrusted the small amount of jewelry and money that we had to a certain Greek, an acquaintance of my husband's, who advised us to go to that village.

For a time, we had enough money to cover our needs; when we saw that we were about to run out, we wrote a letter to the Greek, but there was no reply. Seeing that the situation was impossible, and in spite of all the dangers he was running, my husband was obliged to return to Salonica. There, he was advised not to return to the village. So, from that time onwards, we were separated. He was sheltered in a Greek house, and our separation lasted a year.

During that time, I had to work as the village doctor in order to be able to feed my children, the youngest of whom is called Vidal. Mama and Papa gave him his name. He was born on the day that Germany declared war on Russia . . .

Well, afterwards, as soon as we were liberated, I returned to Salonica, but my husband had changed completely. He did not want me any more, because he was in love with the married woman at the house that had sheltered him; this went on for another year, and today our relationship is almost cold. The fact is that, because of the way he behaved, I can no longer bear him. Today, I consider him a complete stranger to me. I am very proud. I bear the name of the Frances family, and that is why I no longer want to have anything to do with him. Many times, I have thought of leaving our home, but where could I go with no money? Well, forget all that for a moment. I am very worried, my dear Vidal, and want to have news of all of your family. Léon and his family, Jacques and his family, Henri, my Aunt Henriette, whom I have been told to call Aunt ever since I was little, and her family, and my dear Mathilde, sadly a widow at such a young age.

Will you let me know about everything and everyone, please? How is your dear son? From the letter that you addressed to the community, I understand that you want to do something as soon as postal communications are viable. There is no point, my dear Vidal; you see, my dear Vidal, enough clothing has been sent from America; well, they took quite a long time to distribute it; they [the Greeks?] kept the best items and only gave away the rags.

Well, my dear Vidal, I have no right to stop you, you must do whatever you think is best, I only wrote you this to give you an example.

Write to me very soon [. . .]

Then, after Vidal's reply:

Salonica, March 5, 1946
My dearest Vidal,
I cannot describe the joy and emotion I felt when I heard the mailman call out my name. Immediately, I had a presentiment that it was a letter from you, because I also

have my son in Palestine from whom I regularly receive letters. He is 14 years old, and was in quite a high grade at school, but seeing that the situation in Salonica is very bad, I decided to send him to Palestine, because they were asking for children aged between 12 and 18. Now he is learning Hebrew, and he came first in the exams. I would also have sent my daughter, but after having received the permit I changed my mind, because I would have been left all alone with no-one to console me. I told you in my first letter that I am on bad terms with my husband. We are still living under the same roof, but . . . I am determined to be separated from him. What a great joy it was to know that all of your family are fortunately safe and sound. But I was very sad to hear about the death of your dear Jacques. I am pleased to hear about your dear David [Edgar]'s wedding. I wish them good luck. I am also pleased to hear that you intend to marry again, you really should, enough time has gone by with no-one to look after you. I think that your sister-in-law is called Corinne, I know her slightly, we used to live almost next door to one another.

You ask me if anyone has come back from the camps; a few have, and I keep asking them for information about my parents. Unfortunately, nobody can tell me anything about them. I am still hoping to see them come home, that would be my greatest joy. Ever since we were liberated, I feel that my life has no meaning, it is entirely empty. Now I no longer have my dear Papa and Mama, or my brothers to come and see me, I am all alone. I have plenty of acquaintances, but it is not the same. You wrote to me about Dr. Isaac Matarasso. I will go and see him today, and I will tell him what you wrote me about him. He is the best of friends; I have consulted him more than once, to find out some information, and he is very kind.

I don't have very much to write to you. I am still waiting for greetings from you all. I thank you for your kindness in taking an interest in my family. Send my best wishes to your dear son, and his wife. To you, I send my love.
Your cousin Régine

In a third letter dated April 18, 1946, Régine mentions the dear friend Vidal had enquired about, Dr. Matarasso:

I went to tell him what you had said about him. He told me he would answer you the very same day and that he was pleased that you remembered him.

Thessaloniki, March 15, 1946
Mr. Vidal Nahoum.
Paris.

Dear Sir,
In response to your esteemed letter of November 19, 1945, we regret to inform you that the people mentioned in your letter do not figure on the registers of the members of our community who have returned to our city since the Liberation. In spite of our posters and publications in the Jewish newspapers of our city, nobody has come forward to provide any information about their fate.

IX

After the War (1945–1960)

VIDAL AT FIFTY

Vidal managed to get through the Second World War like a fish escaping between the holes in a net. But he did not survive it in the same way as he had the First World War, which was of a different nature: 1914 to 18 was a war between nations. It did not specifically concern the Jews, and especially not the Sephardim living in the imperial cities. The second war specifically threatened the Jews themselves. Nevertheless, Vidal never felt any need to make a personal stance against Hitlerism, and he even hoped to avoid the draft, although he was called up at the beginning of 1940; afterwards, his only thought was to flee from the persecution that represented a constant threat to his life.

So, although he naturally hoped that the Nazis would be defeated, he did not understand why his son was taking pointless risks, by engaging in the war instead of avoiding it. He tried every means possible, including the intervention of family and friends, to dissuade him. After the Liberation, Vidal was of course relieved, but his feelings about his son's attitude did not change. "Your son is a hero, Vidal, " Corinne would tell him, in an exalted tone. And Vidal would pull a face, expressing both incredulity and lack of belief in the very meaning of the word.

The period between the wars, and during the war, had made a Frenchman of him; the Occupation completed the process. He might have felt rejected by this homeland which had suddenly stripped him of all his human and citizen's rights, and withdrawn his French nationality, making him a pariah and a victim of persecution. However, he never felt himself to be a foreigner. Although it may seem paradoxical, his relationships with the gentiles became both more intimate and more numerous; many gentiles in France helped him and protected him, from Georges Lezot to René Barré, not to mention Mrs. Blanc (who realized that Vidal had abandoned her, and went to see his son to let him know she was looking for him, that she forgave him and hoped he would come back to her); he was never personally insulted by a Frenchman. Even when the worst measures of exclusion came in to force, he did not feel excluded from France, but included by those French people who helped him and loved him. However, the French Jews who had been integrated for generations suffered terribly, as if from a personal attack, from the Pétainist measures of rejection that were taken by "France." But Vidal did not think of France as a nation-state, he saw it as a new, different kind of Sepharad, with a different way of doing things. In the same way that his ancestors had become acclimatized to the old one, he had become acclimatized and had made his descendants a part of the new one. This was his way of becoming French; it did not turn him into a patriot.

Moreover, he did not feel that anti-Semitism was specifically French. It was a sort of natural menace that existed in the gentile world, like earthquakes and eruptions in the physical world. At the same time, this persecution came from a higher power, which was arbitrary, mysterious and capricious by nature.

So, in is view, Nazi anti-Semitism came from above, as a result of Hitler's insane resolution, and not from the Germans. Even under the occupation, Vidal did not really see anti-Semitism as a German affliction. He had learned German in Salonica, frequented Austrians in Vienna, and got to know Germans in 1920 and 1921 through his business. Unlike the Frenchmen who were "anti-*Boche*," he did not think the Germans were marked by some hereditary flaw.

Essentially, it was because he had no real conception of the nation-state that he didn't feel himself to be an enemy of Germany and the "Boches," any more than he felt rejected by France and the French people.

He had remained ignorant of post-Christian anti-Semitism, which emerged in the West and in Russia, and was based on the belief that the Jews were involved in an international plot for global domination. This strain of anti-Semitism survived in spite of Hitler's propaganda, which had been hammering out the theme of a Jewish-plutocratic-Bolshevik conspiracy for four years. Thus, Vidal was unaware of the very existence of the pseudo-Protocol of the Elders of Zion, and he wrote on Fenruary 27, 1947 to Mr. Sam Levy, a cultivated Salonician who was editor of the *Sephardi Notebooks*:

Dear Sir and friend,

In spite of your numerous occupations and although the Notebooks must make considerable demands on your time and energy, I am writing you an SOS.

A good friend of mine, who is from an old French family from the east, is well-read and cultured, and has Church dignitaries in his family, tells me a heap of incredible stories, which he swears are true, about the ambitions, plans for domination, etc., of our people of Israel.

His only sources for these accusations are the Protocols of the Elders of Zion, and he believes these protocols to be true. Could you tell me something about them?

If you can, I would be very grateful to you, and I ask you to forgive me for the bother that I am causing you.

With cordial regards.

Similarly, during the war and in its aftermath, Vidal was not interested in

Zionism, precisely because Zionism was a form of nationalism that had been created as a response to anti-Semitism; he never dreamed of Palestine as a refuge, nor, once the Jewish State had been founded, of Israel as a homeland. He belonged to the Jewish people, but in a tribal fashion, as a *ben amenou*, a son of the people, and not "a child of the fatherland."[65]

Thus, in November 1947, when the Jewish Resistance is attacking the British in Palestine, there are confrontations between Zionists and Arabs, the State of Israel is in gestation, and the United Nations have adopted a plan for the partition of Palestine, Vidal, who is now fifty, is more interested in his Salonician roots. He does all he can to retrace the history of the Nahum family in Salonica's Sephardi community. In order to acquire information about his ancestors, he writes to his cousin Paul Nahum, the non-religious dentist and socialist, thanks to whom he was liberated from the Frigolet camp in 1916. But Paul Nahum is irritated by this interest in such a "minor thing":

> I haven't read Mr. Sam Levi's Notebooks, and they could be of no interest to me now. Great events make us forget petty things. However, for my Uncle David I will make an exception. My uncle deserves a place of honor in the history of Salonica's Jewish community. So I am going to send you some information about him. I hope you will be pleased with everything my memory has retained. You can add to it what you know yourself. After two wars, and with a third on its way, I'm afraid stories about Salonica are trivial matters!
>
> Thousands of people are dead, burned, murdered, and poverty is everywhere. And now there is the ultimate Event, the beautiful hope, of a free Palestine, a Jewish State . . . Well! . . . Do you really think that Salonica counts for much in comparison?

It is only very gradually, and years later, that Vidal begins to feel a bond with Israel. Even then, as we will see, he does not think of it as his fatherland. Although the word "compatriot" comes to him naturally when referring to a Salonician Sephardi, he never uses the word "fatherland," not even for Salonica. However, although he has no fatherland, Vidal has several motherlands. Later, we will see him make journeys to Spain, Salonica, Israel and Livorno, to his multiple matricial origins. And the motherland he dreams of most in his old age, the place he would like to die, is Livorno, the city where he feels instinctively that the Nahums' modern identity was formed.

The war has not really made him political either. Before the war, as we have seen, he felt most sympathy with the radical-socialists, no doubt because this party stood for the Republic, liberty, and the absence of nationalism and xenophobia. But that did not prevent him from being a member of the support committee for Paul Reynaud, the "national," that is right-wing (but in no way anti-Semitic) representative of the 2nd arrondissement in Paris. Reynaud was several times a Minister, and an eminent political personality, and Vidal congratulated him at every election, despite the fact that he voted radical until 1936. He felt no attraction to socialism, and was even among those who, during Léon Blum's government, thought it very imprudent for a Prime Minister to be Jewish. He felt, in a viscerally Oriental fashion, based on the ancient wisdom, that Jews should protect themselves from politics, rather than taking part, and that fighting anti-Semitism was more likely to aggravate persecuting wrath than to uproot the pernicious idea. The war confirmed him in his feeling that the Jews' only recourse was to camouflage themselves and take cover when the gentile world became enraged. He did not realize that the new Nazi anti-Semitism was not a return to the old Christian anti-Judaism, and so he automatically reacted as a neo–Marrano, believing that the icon of Pétain combined with that of the Virgin would afford him a tutelary protection. Then, after having conformed to the decrees of power for a time (although this did not stop him cheating to obtain a travel permit), he camouflaged himself completely and waited for the Plague to end.

Thus, Vidal does not acquire what was known at the time as "political consciousness." True, he votes communist after the Liberation, as does Corinne, influenced by his son, who had been a "sub-marine" (or a sub-Marrano) for the party within the non-Communist resistance movement. At the end of the war, and especially by those who have little involvement with politics, the USSR is seen as the Archangel that truly vanquished Hitler's dragon, crushing him in his Berlin lair. The Communists represent freedom. Nevertheless, two or three years later, when his son becomes disenchanted with the party, Vidal will lose his illusions. Since by this time radical-socialism has almost died out, he focuses on Paul Reynaud's successor, Michel Junot, and in the last instance on Jacques Dominati, whom he will not only congratulate, but will actually vote for.

FATHER AND SON (CONTINUED)

After the war, Vidal continues to worry about his son's health, eating habits, and tiredness, and asks him to send telegrams and letters every time he travels. In Paris, there is inevitably a telephone call every morning between father and son, to "hear the news," and the son accentuates his filial status by calling his father "P'pa." Nevertheless, something about the relationship between Vidal and his son has changed. The change is of course a result of the emancipation permitted by their separation in 1940, the son's independent life in Toulouse while Vidal was in Paris, and then the fact that Vidal had been obliged to accept his son's decision to choose his own destiny. When he saw that all his Oriental despair had ceased to obtain the desired result, Vidal accepted the new situation without a fuss, although he continued to hope in a routine fashion that his son would follow his wise advice and distance himself from active resistance. Shortly afterwards, it was his son who had been able to give him useful advice and who had ensured a certain protection for him by providing him with false papers. It was thanks to his son that the father had been able to return quickly to Paris from Lyon, and then to obtain mission orders. Thus the son has naturally begun to feel that he is a father to his father and, in the card that he sends him in May 1945, when rejoining the staff headquarters of the 1st army at Lindau, he calls him "My dear old son." This reversal will be accentuated with time, without in any way lessening the son's filiality, but making it more complete, and allowing the son to express his increasing fondness for his father through this game. One day, when the father is growing old, he will ask for a blessing from his son-father, who was originally to have been called David like his own father, in the form of a kiss on the forehead.

The father has also stopped thinking his son is a *bovo*. Although he does not admire him in the least for his action against the occupying force, he is pleased that his son has frequented "celebrities." In any case, Vidal no longer feels that there is any opposition of judgments or values between his son and himself. Since his son is no longer *bovo*, he thinks that he must naturally share all his own ideas and feelings.

Whenever his son protests or criticizes him, Vidal always diverts his divergence by means of the same joke. When Edgar was a child, Vidal had taken out a subscription for him to *Benjamin*, the children's paper, which contained personal ads for the exchange of stamps or games. Vidal tells his now adult son: "You should have put an ad in *Benjamin* while you had the chance: 'Would like to swap unbearable father for nice father.' It's too late now, you'll have to take your father as he is."

Vidal is not at all offended that his son continues to use the last of his resistance pseudonyms after the Liberation, and that he has considered changing his name legally. Vidal himself is known as Mr. Vidal by his neighbors, and he understands the reasons for wanting to camouflage the name Nahoum. But he will certainly be glad when his son decides against changing his name legally and, by living under and taking on a double identity, becomes something of a Marrano, something of a *deunmè* himself.

Edgar now shares his life with Violette, the woman who had been his companion during his time underground, and he marries her the day before leaving for Germany with the 1st army. Family and friends celebrate at the Greek restaurant in the Rue Serpente, which the son now loves as much as his father. The son will often have money troubles in the next few years, and for a long time he will earn only a meagre salary. Vidal will be sad that his son has not proved capable of earning a proper living, but he will always be there to make up for the shortfalls in his budget, to help him out at the end of the month, and to respond to all his requests for help.

HALF HIS LIFE

Vidal is 50 years old in 1944. He recuperated his store at 52, Rue d'Aboukir, immediately after the Liberation. He has reverted to being Mr. Vidal. His new concierge is Mrs. Dauchel's daughter, and his relationship with her is as affectionate as the one with her mother. He is reunited with his surviving Salonician friends from the Sentier. But he is no longer the sole supplier of DD stockings and socks; he no longer has the energy to go once or twice a week to Troyes and Romilly and persuade the manufacturers to let him have batch-ends and seconds, and increasingly he does his buying through representatives, who do not give him good prices because he only takes small quantities. Only a few of his former customers come back to him; some are dead, others have retired, and as time goes by things will only get worse, because small businesses like his will be eradicated by the big supermarkets. Vidal no longer has his assistant Wahram to run his errands for him, and Élie is too old now. So he exerts himself physically much more than he did before the war, undoing and making his own parcels and taking his packages to the mail with the handcart.

A spring has broken, as a result of both the new economic situation and his age (he is not worn out, but he no longer has the youthful energy that in the past had always allowed him to readapt and start again from nothing; in fact, as we will see, he will fail in his attempt to start working in the fabric business). As we have already said, Vidal is a good businessman, because he is resourceful, but also a bad one, because he is not competent. When he was in direct contact with the manufacturers, and bargaining with customers, he did very well, but once he only has indirect contact, through representatives, and bargaining gives way to selling at fixed prices, he has neither the competence to assess qualities, nor the taste, nor the sense for predicting fashions that would enable him to adapt to the new conditions.

Although he is viscerally attached to his store, which as we will see, is his *querencia,* he no longer goes there as regularly or as punctually, and he closes it when he has an errand to run. His cousin Paul, in his letter of November 26, 1947, writes: "I've been to see you twice at 52, Rue d'Aboukir and found the store closed. Aren't you working any more? Not on Thursday nor on Wednesday at 2 o'clock?"

Vidal tries in vain to export pipes, paraffin, glue and gelatine to unknown customers, but there is a quota on gelatine, the refineries cannot even supply the domestic market with paraffin, and the stock of pipes runs out.

The store scrapes by. Vidal must certainly have had savings in the bank that he could use again after the Liberation. But he fails to prosper, either during the period of restrictions that continues until about 1950, or during the great economic boom that begins in about 1955. Corinne, who has a feeling for fabrics, urges him to try his luck in wholesale textiles. He gives up 52 Rue d'Aboukir and in 1949 takes over a big store in the Rue de Mulhouse (also in the Sentier), which he runs with Corinne; he employs his brother-in-law Pepo there, but the business does not get off the ground. He does not have a wide enough range, and he has no customers. He gives up the Rue Mulhouse in 1952 or 1953, returns to the Rue d'Aboukir, and opens a store at number 45, near his old store, calling it the "Maison Vène" (he thinks that using his initails VN to make "veine"[66] will bring him luck). Now he has a catalogue with a price list, and in addition to stockings and socks, he sells bathing suits, underpants, shirts, panties, slips, table napkins, pillowcases, and so on. Business fails to prosper here either. He sells the lease and, around 1958 or 1960, buys a cheaper one on the periphery of the Sentier, at 26, Rue Beauregard, near to the Porte de Saint-Denis, where he will lose more money than he earns. However, he still manages to find a way of keeping afloat. In 1955 he sells his attractive apartment in the Rue Demours and buys a smaller one that he will also sell later. He takes on a few bits of business here and there, and he dabbles prudently on the Stock Market. We do not know whether he has any luck or not, perhaps he has good and bad luck alternately. He seems not to have taken any risks, because apart from his bonds at the Crédit National, he has shares in metallurgy and textiles, especially DMC, which remain "safe" for a long time, as well as a few shares in Bénédictine, his favorite liqueur.

Nevertheless, he continues to run his store, not for profit, since his outgoings there are greater than his income, but in order to retain his autonomy. As he wrote to René Barré, his business is "half of his life." That does not only mean that half of his life is occupied with work, it means that his life is made up of two parts, and that this part is the life that belongs to him alone.

His business is much more than a business, it is an activity which allows him to use all his intellectual abilities. It is also what makes him part of the Sentier's little Salonician community. Of course, the neighborhood has lost much of its Salonician population, and new faces from unknown regions have settled there. But the little islands that remain of the former *agora* are even more intimate, and visits between stores are even more cordial. The less Vidal works, the more precious he finds these conversations between old colleagues, with whom he talks about the past, friends who have moved away or died, and Salonica . . .

This "half of his life" is also the independent half of his life. During his marriage with Luna, he submitted to his wife's moods and desires at home. In his store, however, he is captain of the ship. Moreover, during his first marriage, he already used his business address for his personal correspondence, and he continues to do so. Thus, he addresses his letters to his granddaughters Irène and Véronique from his store, and asks them to write to him there. Paradoxically, he finds privacy not at home, but in his place and life of work.

During the fluctuations that followed Luna's death, his store had remained his anchor. He missed it when he was in exile in the Southern zone, and even at the height of the Occupation he planned to recuperate it, with the help of René Barré. Later, when his business is in a state of collapse, he is even more reluctant to give up his store because life in his new marriage is more difficult. The more dependent and submissive he becomes at home, the more he needs this place where he can be free and independent: increasingly, the store becomes his *querencia*.

THE OTHER HALF

After the Liberation, Vidal moved in to 51, Rue Demours with Corinne and her children. Fredy was studying law, and Henri, who was interested in film-making, was persuaded to attend the business school in the Rue Trudaine to study accountancy. Corinne waited for the deportees to return, but her husband Joseph did not come back from Auschwitz, and was among the legions of the disappeared whose death was certified by a special law.

The relationship between Vidal and Corinne became a conjugal one. Her daughter Daisy could not reconcile herself to this arrangement, and she accepted her aunt Émy's offer to go and work with her in Monaco. Maurice, Émy's husband, had considerably expanded his garment-making shop, and Émy was in charge of the retail stores. They were rich now, and lived in a beautiful mansion. They had become personalities in the principality. Maurice was a tribal chieftain, imperious, but very generous, with a profound sense of honor and justice. His wife Émy continued to adore him ("I adored my husband, it was an uncontrolled passion"), and he inspired feelings of loyalty in his collaborators. Despite the cordiality of their relations, there was a kind of antinomy between Maurice and Vidal, because Maurice was force-fully direct and Vidal was evasive. Neither was there much warmth between Corinne and Émy, and that had been the case for a very long time. Corinne was secretly mortified by the fact that her daughter had gone to join the Monaco tribe, although nothing offensive had either been said or done: Daisy had simply found a job in a family firm. A year later, she married Maurice's young brother, Sam, who had come over from Turkey to study law in France, and had joined his brother's firm. The invitation to the wedding, which took place on June 5, 1948 at Monaco town hall, was announced on the bride's side by Mrs. and Mr. Vidal Nahoum (although they were not actually officially married), and on the groom's, by Mrs. and Mr. Maurice Cohen.

Vidal and Corinne are married on 29 September 1951 at the town hall of the 17th arrondissement, with a contract stipulating that their property remains separate.

They are alike in that they are both very receptive to everything: the world, family, and friends. Corinne's children and Vidal's son and daughter-in-law come to eat at their table. They do not only enjoy the company of people of their own generation, but also that of children, first Edgar's daughters, Irène and Véronique, and then Corinne and Marianne, Daisy's daughters, and they take pleasure in seeing elderly relatives, like cousin Paul and Uncle Hananel. During the period between 1945 and 1960, before death has begun to strike all around them, there are numerous meetings between the scattered but still communicating Nahums and Beressis. Vidal and Corinne are at the crossroads and see all of them, when those who live far away make trips to Paris, or when they themselves go to visit those who live far away. So they see Mathilde from Italy, Henri, Gaby, Léon, Julie, Edgard, Sophie (there is a strong reciprocal friendship between Sophie and Corinne) and Régine from Brussels, Chary and Hiddo from Avignon, Aimée and Ben from Liverpool, and Liliane and Mony who live close by. They also see relatives and allies on the Beressi side, Marguerite, née Beressi, Élie Cohen's wife, Ana Beressi, an actress, married to the manager of the Galeries Lafayette, her brothers Alex and Roger, Émy, Maurice and the tribe from Monaco. They meet other distant relatives, cousin Esterina Hasson from Nice, and Jo and Daisy Angel, who had been a friend of Luna's at the Alliance in Salonica, as well as many others.

They take a great interest in current events. Vidal reads *L'Aurore* and *Le Monde*, which Corinne also reads. They argue, because Corinne gets indignant about injustices and abuses, whereas Vidal views them with Oriental resignation. He always takes the government's side, and then that of the President of the Republic, whoever he may be, while she passionately criticizes the leaders, whom she finds inadequate. Vidal is quick to rally to de Gaulle, in 1958, whereas Corinne finds his putsch against the Republic unacceptable. The persecutions and misfortunes of the world move her deeply, and he approves her distractedly: "Yes, Poulette."[67]

Vidal still loves traveling, and so does Corinne. They go to the Côte d'Azur, or take cures at Dax, Montecatini, or Abbano-Terme, and they go on excursions, especially along the Rhine. They are both sociable, and very easily strike up friendships with strangers in trains, guesthouses, or at their restaurant table; they admire nature and monuments, and are always ready to look at the world with wonder. Vidal remains very poetically childlike. Thus, arriving one day at the little piece of land that Corinne buys at Vaux-sur-Seine in 1954, he hears chirping and exclaims: "Listen, Poulette, the little bird is singing to you to say hello."

The piece of land on the hills at Vaux-sur-Seine looks down over a great expanse of countryside. For two years, Vidal and Corinne take picnics there, then they have a platform built for a little prefabricated house, to which they plan to add annexes later on. They go there at weekends, asking Henri or Fredy to drive them, and they invite their children and friends there. Corinne, who is passionate in her friendships, has formed a bond with a lady from Vaux, Mrs. Bernard, and they sleep at her house until theirs is built.

Vidal is jealous of the complicity between them and teases Corinne. In fact, easy-going Vidal secretly feels Orientally jealous of everyone who shows too much interest in her.

His humorous and teasing nature is fully expressed in his conversations with her. Like his father, who in Salonica used to tease his wife Dona Helena about her family, he teases Corinne about the Beressis' "meanness," especially that of Corinne's grandmother, which never fails to arouse Corinne's passionate indignation. "How can you say that, Vidal! It's the Nahums who are mean." Indeed, the Beressis are more extravagant than thrifty, as Vidal knows, but it amuses him to keep up the joke. He brings up some obscure neighborhood gossip from Salonica, which he interprets viciously, arousing further protestations from Corinne. Or else he tells her: "You're as mean as you grandmother," which he knows to be doubly false and which arouses double indignation. He sets off Corinne's counter-offensives with joy, exulting in the sensitivity, sincerity and uprightness of the Beressis: "Me, I'm frank, like my father, but as for you lot . . . " "We are diplomatic, Corinne," answers Vidal with dignity. These pseudo-quarrels always end up as a tournament between the virtues of the Nahums and those of the Beressis, those of Vidal and those of Corinne. The moments of greatest pleasure for Vidal are when Corinne explodes with irritation. Then his long drawn-out laugh rings out: "Heh heh heh heh heh." For him, this represents joy in a couple, to tease and keep on teasing, and his joy is increased by the fact that although Corinne knows he is only joking, she takes his attacks very seriously and treats them as injustices. When Irène is about 10 or 12, she joins in the game on a third level. She declaims: "The Beressis are very sensitive, but the Nahums are tyrannical brutes." Papou, delighted, feigns indignation: "Ah, now wait a minute! It's the other way around." Then, claiming that "his blood" is making him do it, he lets fly with a volley of curses in Spanish that scandalize Corinne.

In the same way, Vidal likes to tease his son and be teased by him. Edgar teases him about the putative Nahum ancestor, a minor prophet in the Bible, from whom Vidal claims to have inherited a gift for prophecy. "He may have been minor, but he was still a prophet," Vidal insists. His son announces that the latest historical research has confirmed that Nahum did indeed predict the fall of Nineveh – only it was after the event, and not before it. "Lies, lies, all lies!" Vidal exclaims melodramatically.

In the same way, Vidal, who never fasts for Kippur, claims that he obtained a dispensation from the rabbi of Salonica when he was a little boy, because he was ill and needed to eat. "But that ran out a long time ago," Corinne always cries. "Ah, no, I consider his dispensation to be still valid." "You're forgetting, Dad, that the rabbi actually prescribed you a double ration for Kippur."

Vidal is increasingly fond of the food that Corinne prepares for him, and he expects his Poulette to serve him his hot meal whenever his appetite demands. At first, he has lunch at around twelve thirty, then at twelve, and finally, in the nineteen-seventies, eleven thirty, then eleven o'clock. As soon as he gets home from the Sentier, he pesters Corinne to heat up the dishes, starts by stealing a hard-boiled egg out of the refrigerator, and little cucumbers, when in season, which he eats with salt.

During the first period, when she is still willing and able-bodied, Corinne prepares Salonician dishes as well as western dishes: *pastellicos, sfongatticos* (gratins) of spinach, cheese or eggplants, and meatballs made of a mixture of veal and lamb. She always puts some aside for Edgar, in case he comes by or wants to take them home with him.

The regulating marriage between Vidal and Corinne ends up deregulating their relationship. Although Vidal is an anxious but calm type, with no tormenting conscience or feelings of guilt, Corinne feels increasingly ashamed about having taken her sister's place and about Vidal having taken that of her husband who died in deportation. She feels the need to exalt her virtue as an exemplary wife and mother, who has given the best upbringing and healthiest start in life to her children, including Edgar, her "fourth child." At the same time, she often suffers from oppression, anxiety and insomnia, which will get worse with time, and be "somatized" to become a variety of physical ailments; she feels that she is very gravely ill "with her nerves," and she will frequently consult her physician, Dr. Milanolo.

Although his son does his best to interpret them to him, Vidal remains characteristically dissociated from Corinne's torments. As long as Fredy and Henri, Corinne's sons, are still living in their apartment, he convinces himself that her problems are caused by the fatigue and worry that her sons give her, and he tries to persuade them to leave the apartment in order to relieve their mother. However, she begs Fredy to stay with her until he is married; she had been secretly hurt by Daisy leaving home and would have interpreted Fredy's leaving as disowning her.

She becomes increasingly irritable towards Vidal, especially after they move into the Rue Laugier, when Fredy and Henri leave the apartment to live in attic rooms on the same block. It is increasingly clear to her that Vidal is the incarnation of what she is suffering from obscurely and unconsciously, namely guilt about her sister and her husband. He prostrates himself beneath the storm, answering her bitter criticisms with mawkish endearments: "Yes, my little chicken," "Yes, chicken," "Yes, chicky." Even when she is in a paroxysm of rage, when she cries: "I've had enough, I can't take it any more," he automatically replies: "Yes, chicky." Very rarely, in sudden exasperation, he explodes in a terrifying rage. Then she stops, dumbfounded.

With time, it will all get worse, but in the years between 1945 and 1960, there is still more harmony than dissonance. Their all-pervading receptivity to other people, family, friends, acquaintances and the world in general, maintains the harmony between them. Things will degenerate gradually, in fits and starts.

LOVE OF FAMILY

As Vidal grows old, he feels increasingly childishly attached to his parents. He often looks at and talks to their portrait photographs, which he has had framed like paintings, and they play the role of comforting *lares* that greet him whenever he enters the apartment.

The events have made him even more devoted to his family. He had paid a pension to Myriam Beressi, his mother-in-law, until her death in 1946. He and his brothers provide a pension for Sophie, the widow of their brother Jacques, who died during the liberation of Florence.

Léon and Vidal also persuade Mathilde to remarry. Mathilde had left for Argentina with a relative of Bouchi's, and then returned, disappointed, to move back to Italy for good in around 1948. She lives alone. Somebody, I do not know who, introduces her to a gentleman who, although short and fat, is a very rich tobacco merchant, called Mr. Salem. Vidal had been obstinately persuaded to marry again, and now he obstinately persuades Mathilde to make this marriage, which takes place in Milan in 1949. A few days later, she leaves her husband. She explains to her nephew Edgar that when she first saw her new husband's naked body on their wedding night, she discovered that "his whole body was covered with boils, like a toad." So, being unable to live with a man whose skin repulses her, she divorces him. Vidal never ceases to watch over his sister and, as we will see, rescues her on her deathbed in 1969.

Vidal continues to assist members of his family, even distant ones, who are in need, as this letter from his relative Djentil attests:

Petit-Quevilly, June 19, 1957
Dear Vidal,
I apologize for my long delay in replying to you and thanking you for the 100,000 francs that you were kind enough to send me via Jo Angel. He gave me the money at once, and it has been a great help to me.
I hope that you are all well, you, Corinne and the children. My health is very precarious, due to fatigue, and I have moments of weakness. Of course, I am no longer very young, there is no getting away from it.
I also thank you for your kind invitation. I will sign off by sending you a loving embrace.
All the best.
Djentil

Vidal has remained curious about everything. He even continues, as he did as a child in Salonica, not really to collect postage stamps, since he has no album to store and classify them in, but to accumulate them. He even continues sporadically to exchange stamps:

26, Rue Beauregard, Paris 2nd.
Paris, February 9, 1959.
Mrs. Marianne Burges
Mainzer str, 71
Cologne

Dear Madam or Miss,
I saw your advertisement in *Le Monde* newspaper and am writing to inform you that
I would be very interested in making some exchanges.
    Please could you let me know which stamps you would be interested in? And also
tell me what you can, on your side, provide in exchange.
    I look forward to hearing from you.
    Yours faithfully.

There is something else that has never ceased to intrigue him. One of
President Roosevelt's secretaries of state is called Frances Perkins. Although
his son has told him that Frances is an American forename, Vidal imagines
some flattering and mysterious family relationship with his maternal family,
the Frances. He writes between 1950 and 1960 to Frances Perkins and
receives a very kind reply, which naturally confirms that Frances is a forename and not a patronym. Although the letter denies that they are related,
in Vidal's eyes it puts him on familiar, almost familial, terms with Frances
Perkins.

PAPOU

Vidal stays young, even childlike in his character, feelings, and ideas, but a
new circumstance, without making him lose his youthfulness, turns him into
Papou. Papou is the *djidio* equivalent of Pop or Grandpa, but with less
senilizing and more ancestralizing connotations. His two granddaughters,
Irène and Véronique, are born in 1947 and 1948. When they are almost
babies, their parents leave them with Vidal and Corinne while they travel in
Italy and elsewhere. Then Véronique becomes the special favorite of Liliane
and Mony, who have no children. Liliane adopts the little dark-haired girl,
who might be the reincarnation of her mother. Mony, who has lost his whole
family in the Sephardi hecatomb in Salonica, becomes attached to the little
girl who becomes his own daughter. Vidal is enchanted with Irène, and
Corinne, whose children have not had children yet, becomes even more
attached to her first grand-child because she loves babies, and because Irène
soon begins to love her "Nona" in return. The grandmother begins an inten-
sive grooming session as soon as the little girl arrives at her house: she combs
her, dresses her in pretty little outfits, washes her hair, puts it in ringlets with
a curling iron, and scolds her if she ever says a rude word.

Vidal and Corinne are convinced that it was on her own initiative, all by herself, that baby Irène, looking at Corinne, called her "Nona" ("grand-mother" in Italian and in *djidio*), and looking at Vidal, called him "Papou," as if the voice of her Sephardic blood had spoken through her mouth.

Edgar and Violette also leave their daughters with Violette's parents, Joseph and Christine Chapellaubeau, in Hautefort, in the Dordogne. Joseph Chappellaubeau comes from a family of landowners. He is self-educated; when very young, he became a socialist; he introduced the first car to Hautefort, and owned land that was worked by a sharecropper; he is a very sociable and communicative man; he became a bailiff, and then, late in life, a jam manufacturer. After his first car, a big Talbot, which he had around 1935, he runs around the Dordogne in his little 1920s Citroën, in theory for his work, in fact so that he can talk to people. Christine Entraygues's family is from Corrèzes and has lived for generations on an isolated farm, Russac, not far from Turenne; she was appointed to teach at the infant school in Hautefort, after she married Joseph Chapellaubeau.

Joseph Chapellaubeau would have preferred his daughter to stay at Hautefort and look after her parents, especially him. He is bitterly disap-pointed that she has married a Parisian. He is not remotely anti–Semitic, and protected some Jewish intellectuals from Toulouse under the Occupation, whom his daughter had hidden in Hautefort and the surrounding area. However, since there is no smoke without fire, the Nazis' hatred of the Jews suggests to him that the Jews must have committed some great crime against the Germans. Moreover, he has heard that the Jews hop while praying in their synagogues, and he is continually asking his son-in-law: "So why do you hop when you're praying?" His son-in-law replies that he does not frequent synagogues, which in Joseph Chapellaubeau's view makes him an even more curious Jew.

Thus, both Chapellaubeau and Nahoum grandparents take in the little girls while their parents are "rushing about the place," as Joseph Chapellaubeau puts it. Vidal imagines that the Périgord is inhabited by starving peasants, and sends his granddaughters parcels of gingerbread, chocolates, cookies and honey. He writes very frequently to Joseph Chapellaubeau to inquire about Irène and Véronique. Mr. Chapellaubeau (who is 75 years old in 1952) replies:

Contentious Recoveries
J. Chapellaubeau
Ex-bailiff
Hautefort, August 4, 1952

My dear Sir,
In reply to your letter of August 2, received this day Monday 4, I am delighted to tell you that both of the little ones are in good health, Irène seems to be cured of her

210

whooping-cough, and Véronique's cough is beginning to go away. Irène is wonderful, but she will not stand for any opposition or annoyance, "or I'll tell my Papou"; if anyone has forgotten you, it is not Irène.

Today we received a card from our two traveling pigeons, from La Spezia or Naples or Rome, I couldn't understand a word of it, and even if they were in Vesuvius, I wouldn't go looking for them. Since I am unable to leave my wife night or day, they could have given her the pleasure of staying at her side.

Well, they can just drift around as they like, I think I will see them again as soon as their wallet is empty; money burns a hole in both of their pockets . . . you should give them a talking-to about being more economical . . .

At the end of this letter, Irène adds in clumsy handwriting: "Farewell to Papou and Nona."

Hautefort, August 12, 1952
Dear Mr. Nahoum and friend,
Yesterday, when I received your letter, I was unable to answer it, although I should have done, in view of your curiosity about the health of our granddaughters. Irène is wonderful, of course she eats her soup, and does chabrol with gusto (perhaps you do not know the word "chabrol," you can ask someone to explain it[68]), she sleeps and plays without a worry in the world.

My wife and I very much hope that the air of the Landes will do Mrs. Nahoum good [Corinne had gone on a cure to Dax, but when she came back she had difficulty breathing], and hope you both have a good rest during your holidays.

The two nomads wrote today, they are two wretches who have no idea what tomorrow will bring, they know that you are close to them, and that is enough for them.

Hautefort, August 17, 1952
Dear Mr. and Mrs. Nahoum,
Friends, today is Sunday, and as I know that you are curious to have news of your granddaughters, I am writing to you in their absence, as they have gone for a walk, to let you know that they have been running around like hares all over the place, especially in the garden where the plums and pears are ripe. When they are there, they don't have a worry in the world, they are in the best of health, and Irène's response to the slightest annoyance is always to declare: "When I go back to Paris, I'll tell my Papou." You are her truly her protector, and capable of punishing all her enemies . .
.

A year later, he writes the same type of letter, with the same good news about Papou's granddaughters and the same complaints about the two "nomads."

A few years later, the little girls themselves write directly to Papou and Nona. The following is a letter from Véronique, dated August 9, 1953:

Dear Papou, dear Nona,

I was very pleesed to receve your letter yesterday, so I am ansering you. Yesterday and the day before it was teribly hot, but today it is raining and nobody can go out. Fanfan came yesterday evening, Irène was scared of him, now he is scrayping away paper, he wants to go hunting insted, but because it is raining he cant hunt. He has a gun for hunting and one of those cowboy belts with bullets in it. When Fanfan has scrayped everything down he will put up some more very beautiful paper and the house will be very beutiful. Jean-François is pretending to be a mechanic with his tricycle if you could see his hand it is all black!

All my love to you and to Nona from all the family.

Véronique

The years pass, the little girls grow up, and one goes to Papou and Nona's, the other to Liliane and Mony's, every time their parents want or have to travel. On vacation at Hautefort, they answer letters from Papou, who wants to know everything and worries about everything. They are now roller-skating and riding bicycles; they are 13 and 12 in 1960.

Wednesday, June 6, 1960
Dear Papou,

How are you? I hope that you are having fun. Irène is very pleased that you want to buy her a bicycle. We are having a great time, little Goumet isn't here, but he is going to come. Mom had her bicycle fixed for me and now it is mine. I go on long rides to the neighboring villages. Until she gets her bicycle, Irène is riding on my luggage rack. The weather is quite nice. Our neighbor Mrs. Latour's fruit is not ripe yet, but it soon will be and we will take advantage of that.

Tell Liliane that I am thinking of her, that I am very fond of her . . .

Guess what, one day we laughed so much, we saw some lovers who were kissing . . . .

Véronique.

P.S. Answer us quickly and excuse the horrible handwriting and innumerable spelling mistakes.

Irène:

Dear Papou,

We are well. We eat well. We sleep well. We play well. We are still little.

As for the bicycle, here is the price. The man in the bicycle shop wrote it down. He showed me three bicycles, one was blood red, the other two navy blue. I would prefer a yellow or pale blue one (very pale). Since as everybody knows I am so subtle, I said to myself: "If I'm getting a nice bicycle, it ought to be one I like."

We are having good fun. We go on long rides. The sky is blue, Hélène takes good care of us . . . ..

Whereupon, I billion kisses.

P.S. Sorry about the mistakes, but it's the vacation, it doesn't mean I love you any less.

Answer:

Paris, Friday July 8
(Your Dad's birthday)
My dear Irène,
My dear Véronique,
Very glad to receive your letters yesterday, my little darlings, and thank you. I paid no attention to the mistakes or the handwriting, because when a person is on vacation she can't worry about all that.

Write to me again, both of you, tomorrow or the day after, it will give me a great deal of pleasure.

As for your bicycle, dear Irène, please be patient for a few more days. I will see if I can buy you one in Paris (now that I know which color you prefer) and have it sent to you. Otherwise, I will send you a postal order and you can buy it in Hautefort.

In the meantime, ask Mrs. Hélène her surname, and let me know, because I will send the postal order in her name and then she will be able to go with you to the bicycle shop to pay the man.

In the meantime, I am worried to read that you have been riding on Véronique's luggage rack. It is not safe, for either of you.

Liliane is already back at the Rue Demours, her house is indeed number 18. I look forward to having your news soon, and Nona and I send you our love.

After a joint letter from Irène and Véronique, giving Mrs. Hélène's surname:

Paris, July 11, 1960
Mrs. Hélène Dominguez.
Hautefort.
Dear Madam,
Today I sent you a postal order for 196 new francs (19 600 francs), asking you kindly to accompany my little Irène to the bicycle shop and buy her the bicycle with derailleur gears that she has chosen, and which costs 20,000 francs, less 2 percent which is 400, that is 19,600.

I hope that the merchant is trustworthy, and will supply a good bicycle. I enclose the price list that he gave Irène, and which she sent me last week. Please see if the seller will bring the price down a little for you; if he does, you can buy Irène and Véronique whatever they would like with the money.

I look forward to hearing from you.

Yours faithfully.

213

Dear Papou,

It's fantastic, at last I have the bicycle of my dreams, it's super. It is a blue and white Peugeot. You are amazingly nice.

We will run errands. There is a little bag on the back, with glue, repair patches and tools in it.

We have put up a swing in the garden. We are having fun. I haven't got anything more to say, I told you everything in the other letters.

You are a Papou in a million.

I OOOOOOOOOOOOOOOOOOOOOOOOOOOOOOOOOOOOOOOOOOOOOOOOOOOOOOOOOOOOOOOOOOO
OOOOOOOOOOOOOOOOOOOOOOOOOOOOOOOOOOOOOOOOOOOOOOOOOOOOOOOOOOOOOOOOOOO
OOOOOOOOOOOOOOOOOOOOOOOOOOOOOOOOOOOOOOOOOOOOOOOOOOO kisses.   Irène.

The next year, Irène and Véronique go to stay with different English families in Bristol. Véronique is very happy and describes English food to her Papou:

In the morning I have cornflakes with milk and a cup of tea, then it's time for coffee with cake, then (at 1 o'clock in the afternoon) it's lunch, the pudding is delicious, then (at 5) it's tea with sandwiches and cake and pudding, and then (9 in the evening) coffee with cake . . . And of course I haven't even mentioned all the candy, ice creams and drinks I have during the day.

But Irène is very unhappy:

My dear Papou,

You wanted a long letter, you're going to get it, I am too bored to refuse you that pleasure. I would even say that this letter is a future novel.

Let's see, the house is small and gray, my room is small and gray, it looks onto the garden (because there is a "little garden") where the widow I'm staying with sunbathes at night. The bed is a bit small, but the sheets are quite nice. I have only seen Véronique once, I will see her maybe twice during our stay.

What do I do during the day? No need to search my memory to answer you: NOTHING.

It's a real nightmare, perhaps I'm dreaming right now, I don't know, it's all a gray mist like the one that surrounds me. I sit in the dead husband's armchair and only leave it to eat (in the morning: I fried egg and some cold milk; at midday: raw peas, parsley, I piece of fruit; 4 o'clock: salad, bread and butter, no dinner; I'm starving and don't dare ask for more), and I go around the department stores (pathetic) and accompany the little kid (6 years old) to school, I have to do whatever she takes it into her head to ask. She is always nosing about in my things.

Home, sweet home, I would be much happier in Hautefort!! The widow is nice, but she doesn't talk much, she is a widow and Catholic; the only member of the household I like is a big dog, but he doesn't speak English. Well, with the food here you wouldn't survive for two days. When I think that I have to stay here until the 5th, and there's something else, listen, I'm going to tell you a secret. Two days after I got here, I said to myself: "I can't possibly stay in this miserable royalist country;" I slipped off to the neighbor's who has a telephone, giving an excuse to the widow about something to do with my passport, and then, what d'you think she does, Réréne, all by herself she telephones the woman who runs the organization to ask her if Véro and I can go back on the 28th. In the afternoon, the old woman goes to the airport, and when I ring again the next day, she tells me it's impossible (which proves that she's English, because impossible isn't a word in French) . . .

My darling Papou, write to me every day, I'm so bored, that way with your letters, and Mom's (while we're on the subject, what rotten luck I had being born to her, it's her fault that we're stuck in this hole). Quick, hurry, rush over to your machine, and it's not Halle Grove but Hill Grave.

I kiss for Papou, I million for Nona.

Vidal reacts at once and writes to his niece in Liverpool, to Irène's land-lady, and to Irène.

My dear Aimée, my dear Isidore,

I am writing to ask a favor of you, dear Aimée. Violette tells me that Irène is very depressed about her stay in Bristol, and she has been begging her mother to let her come home early, on July 28th instead of August 5th. Apparently, the poor little thing is so depressed that she told her Mom: if you don't let me I'll die, or something of the sort. I know Irène is at an awkward stage, and what's more she is still a child, although mentally she is quite advanced for her age, and knows (or thinks she knows) every-thing about everything; being in the habit at home of listening in attentively to her parents' conversations and arguments, she is, in my opinion, very sensitive at the moment. That is why I am writing to beg you to write to her, to find out her news, and tell her that as you are in Liverpool she can write to you or telephone you. See if there is a telephone where she is staying, have a chat with her. Véronique is more stable, Violette told me that she's not worried about her at all, but as for Irène . . . Irène's address: c/o Mrs. Nation, 14 Halle Grove, Henlaze, Bristol. And Véronique's: c/o Mrs. Reeves, 11 Manor Park, Bristol 61.

I look forward to hearing from you. All the best from Corinne and me.

Your uncle,   Vidal

Madame Nation,

I have pleasure to write you, for my little daughter Irène, I am his grand' father.

Irène is a charming girl, but very "timide," and I beg you very much to care Irène, the most possible, and I thank you sincerely in advance. Ask please Irène what she wish best in preference for meat, and Irène must take every day many fromage (cheese), bacon and fruits.

With all my heart, I thank you and remain very sincerely,

Vidal Nahoum.

Excuse, please, my "english."[69]

My dear little Irène,

Very pleased to get your four-page letter, and have read everything that you wrote to me carefully. I'm going to read it again later with Nona at home.

Carry on writing to me like this, my little darling, make your letters as long as possible, and Nona and I will be very glad to hear how your vacation is going.

I wish and I hope that you are enjoying it a little more, that you are not too bored and that you are on more friendly terms with Mrs. Nation.

As far as food is concerned, it is bound to be different from what we have at home in France, but they don't have a bad system in England. Just try and eat what you like, ask for a bit more cheese, honey, jam, fruit, and I am sure that Mrs. Nation will do her best to satisfy you. I have written a little note to her asking her to look after you as well as she can.

Write to me about BEA, is there any hope of changing your departure date? Answer me quickly and write me a long letter.

Your Papou.

Dear Papou, dear Nona,

Some unexpected and catastrophic events have prevented me from answering you earlier. I realized very quickly, right at the beginning, that the widow was only taking me for the money, and that's why she is trying to get me off her hands any way she can. The latest way she has found is to send me to a private CATHOLIC school (where everybody looks down their noses at me, because I'm not religious); and I sit all day long in my corner, it's enough to give me a sore backside, the English girls make fun of me and ask me questions very quickly so I can't understand them, and I just whistle with a distracted look on my face, and pretend to be indifferent, although I am far from feeling it. I stay there all day long, and what's more I have to make do with just a miserable little tomato sandwich to eat. I am staying in this hateful school until term ends, which coincides more or less with my leaving. So, you see, just when I had made some resolutions: "Such is the life!"[70]

It is still raining. I watch time go by with a microscope. I've written a letter to Dad. I want to cry all the time!

Well, there you are! Tell me everything you're all doing in your letters, that will make them longer.

I kiss for Papou, 100,000 for Nona.

Irène.

Paris, Tuesday July 18

My dear little Irène,

Very glad to receive your letter of the (you didn't write the date) this morning, but not at all glad, in fact sad, to read everything that you wrote me, my darling little Irène.

I can picture you sitting there, sulking and very sad in your corner, and it upsets me. I have also seen your letter to your Mom, and I understand the state you are in, and why you feel like crying. Mom is coming back at the end of this week and she will find your letter waiting for her at the Rue Soufflot.

In the meantime, Irène, I beg of you: re-act. Pull yourself together and show what you're made of, Irène, and prove that you are worthy of the name Nahoum. If you are going to school, it's for your own good. I add: "maybe." Maybe it's for your own good, to let you practice your English more, and be with girls of your own age.

The fact that the school is Catholic doesn't matter in the least, because all religions are good and honorable. If people look down their noses at you, take your time and answer them very politely, and very nicely. That will show them that a young French girl (religious or not) deserves respect, and is intelligent enough not to waste time with childish nonsense.

Why is Mrs. Nation making you go to school? Did she give you any explanation when she told you about it?

Cheer up, Irène, I beg you. Don't be sad. Don't cry. Pull yourself together and make your Papou happy by writing him quickly that things are a little better. Please ask for food, and eat well, my little darling. Véro has written to me, she is happy, she's lucky. I expect a speedy reply from you, and Nona and I send you our love,

Your Papou Vidal.

Start your letters with My dear Nona and dear Papou, because your Nona is very sensitive (like you).

In a subsequent letter, Irène winks at her Papou by beginning: "*My dear Nona, my dear Papou.*" She is happy at the school now: the headmistress, sister Ursula, gives her private English lessons and brings her comic books in secret; she likes the school dinners, is no longer bored, has made some friends, and "is having a great laugh," goes to the cinema and to tennis matches, sings, goes to parties were there are fab records, and expresses her regret at having to leave: "It's the last day, worse luck!" She asks him not to show her letter to her father (who is probably in Santiago de Chile at the time, where Violette will join him in August).

Answer from Papou:
Paris, Thursday July 27.
26, Rue Beauregard.
My dear little Irène,
Very glad to receive and read your letter, telling me that you are enjoying your time at school, and about the friends you have made, and all the details you gave me point by point, it's nice of you my dear little Irène, and I am proud and pleased about it.

The fact that you had a moment of discouragement is natural, understandable and absolutely normal; then you pulled yourself together, you got over it, and you have been quite energetic and understanding in your efforts to adapt yourself to English life. I congratulate you my darling.

Mom is worried that she hasn't had a letter from you; please write to her very, very quickly.

I agree not to send your letter to your Dad, and am waiting for your promised explanations why.

Stormy weather here, and Corinne and Marianne [Daisy's two daughters] are
staying with us; they've come from Vaux for a change of scenery, because they both
have whooping-cough, and they are having a terrible time of it. So is Nona.

Answer me quickly, my darling, and tell me if you have already written to Mom.
Looking forward to seeing each other on the 5th. Which airport are you arriving at?
Nona and I send you our love.

Your Papou.

My warm regards to Mrs. Nation.

As Vidal's letter indicates, he is now Papou to two other little girls,
Corinne and Marianne, who are born a few years after Irène and Véronique,
and send their grandparents exquisite childish letters from Monaco. Irène
and Véronique are 14 and 13 respectively in 1961. Irène preferred her Nona
to her mother as a little girl, but soon distances herself emotionally from
Corinne when she begins to perceive her hostility towards her mother, and
now prefers Violette. She will always remain strongly attached to her Papou,
to whom she will become very close. When Irène is a teenager and a woman,
Papou will confide things to her that he keeps from his son. He is delighted
with the mutual teasing in their relationship, which Irène enjoys as much as
he does, and they will keep it up until the end. Already, as a little girl, Irène
had joined in the game by ending her letters with millions of kisses for Nona
and just one for Papou. She will delight in teasing him about Wilhelmine,
with whom Vidal had fallen in love in Vienna when he was 18 years old,
and whom he remembers with exagerrated sighs. One day, years later, during
a family meal at Violette's place the teasing about Wilhelmine starts again,
and someone asks: "What did this Wilhelmine look like, anyway?" Vidal,
his mouth full, and a glint in his eye, points silently at his granddaughter
Irène.

FAMILY

On the Nahum side, Nahum Steel's business has taken off again and has
benefited, first from the reconstruction, then from the economic boom in
the period between 1945 and 1960. Léon has taken on his son Edgard to
help manage the business. Edgard has married; he has taken a gentile as his
wife. Léon has found his brother Henri a job in Nahum Steel, now that he
can no longer get hold of the Japanese imports from which he had earned a
living before the war. The Nahum brothers take care of Sophie's livelihood.
Her daughter Régine works as a secretary. She is subject to serious asthma
attacks, which often immobilize her. She remains present and devoted at her
mother's side, and keeps herself alive, without joy. Her unhappiness is very
great, and she has nobody close to her to whom she can talk about it.

These days, Liliane and Mony are a very affectionate and united couple.

They have practically adopted their niece Véronique, Vidal's granddaughter, who finds a home with them during her parents' frequent absences. They have Liliane's father, Élie, living with them.

On the Beressi side, Fredy and Henri, Corinne's children, have left the family apartment. Fredy, who began working for the Crédit National in 1948, and then finished his law degree, now occupies a position of responsibility there. In 1958, he marries a young gentile girl called Germaine Sibilli, who is a teacher, and whose family come from Piedmont.

On November 31, 1956, Élie Cohen dies of a stroke at the age of 49. He was born of the union between the Cohens and Beressis of Salonica, and his family had persuaded him to marry his first cousin, Marguerite Beressi, with whom he had five daughters. He was extremely successful in business; he owned the Grande linen company and the Burma jewelery company, among others. Henri, Corinne's son, worked as an accountant in one of them. Élie Cohen was a very generous man, and helped subsidize all the artistic or literary activities in which members of his family were involved. He left his wife Marguerite in 1952, which strengthened the bond of friendship and intimacy between Corinne and Marguerite.

Vidal still thinks it best to spare his family any brutal announcements when someone dies; in 1946, when his son was with the French military government in Germany, he had not informed him of the death of his beloved grandmother Myriam. Vidal is even more inclined to dissimulate with respect to Corinne, because she is extremely emotional. Every time somebody dies, he does his best to hide it from her, and breaks the news to her gradually, so that the final revelation comes after the funeral has taken place. He might begin by saying: "Hananel has caught a cold," or "Élie Cohen has been told to rest on doctor's orders." Then, when Corinne, alarmed, presses him, he gives less reassuring bulletins every day, until Corinne, who always believes him at first, suddenly discovers the truth, often after the burial. Vidal then mobilizes either Edgar or Fredy to soften the blow. Corinne suffers a great deal anyway, and heaps reproaches on Vidal. He has still not understood, and will never understand, that the worst thing to do is prevent someone from taking part in the joint farewell to the person they have loved, and that tears and outpourings of sorrow serve a necessary purpose.

X

The Nineteen-Sixties

TRIALS

Vidal is 66 in 1960. He is still fit and healthy, and takes no medicine. When Corinne presses him to see a doctor about his bladder or his heart, he goes from one doctor to the next until he finds one who does not prescribe any dietary restrictions. He avoids taking the medicine prescribed to him, in spite of Corinne's exhortations. Corinne has faith in the competence of her general practitioner, Dr. Milanolo, and respects the "important professors" whom she insists on consulting whenever her illness seems to come under their specialty.

Although Vidal remains in good health, his son falls seriously ill in 1962. After a fever lasting several days, which rises to 104 degrees during a flight between California and New York, he is belatedly diagnosed with hepatitis and is admitted to Mount Sinai Hospital, in New York. Violette, who is obliged to return to Paris, informs Vidal. The news also upsets Corinne terribly, and on the same day she falls in the métro, and is taken into hospital for a few hours to have stitches and be given an anti-tetanus injection. Vidal is distraught. Although he has never taken an airplane and is terrified of doing so, he wants to fly to the aid of his son, but he cannot abandon Corinne. For two weeks, Vidal is in a torment of anxiety, because his son, who is in a state of continual drowsiness, is incapable of sending him any news. Vidal alerts Léon, who has a correspondent in New York. Léon sends a telex to this correspondent:

> Please do me the following favour: a relative of mine, Edgar Nahoum Morin, has been hospitalized at the Mount Sinai hospital, 5th Av – 100th St, New York with a case of infectious hepatitis. As his father who is in Paris is worrying, because of lack of news, could you inquire about the conditions of the patient . . . [71]

The correspondent, Mr. Hick, immediately goes to see the patient in hospital, finds him asleep, and is told that the patient is recovering from the infection, but that he must stay in hospital for another two or three weeks. In the meantime, Vidal receives a telegram from his son: "Everything is fine." This good news worries him:

[October 62]

Paris, Wednesday afternoon.

My dear Léon, my dear Edgard,

I don't know how to thank you both. Received your letter of Monday yesterday, my dear Léon. I admit that I am still worried, because it was very bad luck that the correspondent who was supposed to see Edgar found him asleep. The telegram I received here yesterday morning, signed Edgar, tells me EVERYTHING IS FINE. I find that incredible from someone who is in hospital receiving treatment.

I really have nothing to reassure me. That's why I asked you for your advice, if I decide to leave. I feel as if I'm drunk, or sleep-walking. See if you can ask your correspondent, if it is no bother to him, to make another visit to see Edgar, and perhaps let him know in advance that he is coming.

I am sorry not to write a longer letter, I remain in sending all of you my love.

Corinne fell in the stairway of the métro last Friday. She was very upset to hear the news about Edgar. She was taken to hospital, but thank God, with our doctor's intervention, she was back at home by the evening. She is getting better, and the doctor is coming to see her this evening to take out the stitches he put in her head. I had a hell of a Friday!! In the morning, hearing about Edgar, and in the afternoon, the hospital calling about Corinne.

However, Vidal is soon reassured. A writer, Claude Mauriac, who has visited his son in Mount Sinai Hospital, brings him good news. Finally, Edgar escapes from hospital before he is due to be released, is repatriated, and arrives at Orly, where he is delighted to be given a wheelchair.

In 1965, Vidal writes to his cousin Régine Saporta Frances, who, as we have seen, is the sole survivor of the Frances family in Salonica, and lets her know that the last few years have been difficult for him:

26, Rue Beauregard, Paris 2nd arrondissement.

Paris, November 5, 1965

Dear Régine,

I have just received your address through Mr. Revah, and am writing to ask for your news and that of your sons and daughters.

These last few years, I have had a mountain of complications of all kinds, but thank God, I am beginning to see light at the end of the tunnel now. My wife has also had many worries about her health. Tell me if your sister is in Salonica, and who remains there of our Frances family.

I remain most cordially.

Your cousin.

Régine Frances answers Vidal at the end of November 1965. The letter is short; she tells nothing about her life, and wishes all the best to the Nahums.

The "complications" that Vidal mentions are of all kinds. First, business is dwindling and his store in the Rue Beauregard is eating up his money. He is often bored, waiting on his own for customers to come in. Luckily, he receives visits from a few old friends, of the same age as him, who are often already retired. He no longer obeys strict timetables. He puts a sign up saying when he will be back, and off he goes, running around here and there. He needs to keep himself busy, and, during the 1960s, with Fredy's help, he devotes himself to the interminable complications related to Hananel's estate, going from one heir to the next to work out a compromise. However, Corinne's arguments and opinions, and perhaps the advice of his brothers, persuade him to close down his store. He resigns himself to selling his business in 1966, at the age of 72, but he is unwilling to retire, which would mean, most importantly, losing his *querencia* in the Sentier, and he will rent a new store, which is even smaller and more peripheral, in the Rue de la Lune.

He also worries about his son's marriage. After his return from Mount Sinai Hospital, his son spends a long convalescence in the South of France, being looked after by Émy and Maurice in their son Maurice-Gérard's apartment in Monte-Carlo, and afterwards he does not return to his marital home. The fate of his granddaughters, deprived of their father, torments him. Worse, his son has been living with a Black woman since 1964, something that horrifies and worries Vidal.

New domestic complications have arisen. Vidal had managed to get the money to meet the needs of his household by selling his nice apartment at 51, Rue Demours in around 1955; he had bought a much cheaper apartment, smaller and more modest, overlooking a yard, at number 32 in the same street. When Corinne gets back the apartment she owns at 39, Rue Laugier, after the tenant's departure, Vidal sells his apartment after some difficulties (a buyer withdraws his offer although he has signed the contract) and he moves with her to the Rue Laugier.

The problems related to the move create upset and agitation for Corinne. She would like Vidal to spend the money from the sale of the apartment that he owned in the Rue Demours to set up and renovate the apartment that she owns in the Rue Laugier.

Vidal wants to reduce spending on the apartment, and fights every step of the way to consume his capital as slowly as possible. He wants to keep a little money of his own in reserve, if only to leave an inheritance for his son. Corinne, and no less secretly, also has a psychological need to acquire an inheritance that she can leave her children, not because they need it, but so that she can make them the gift of an exemplary mother. Edgar encourages his father to spend the money as his wife wishes in order to avoid scenes and quarrels. (Vidal's resistance to save his inheritance and Corinne's offensive to acquire an inheritance are all the more tragic because Edgar continually tells his father not to worry about his future, which is taken care of, and because Corinne, for her part, has no intention of injuring his rights, and frequently tells her children that she wants them to include Edgar in the division of her estate.) In the end, the move into the big and sunny apartment in the Rue Laugier, on the fourth floor with an elevator, does not bring the hoped-for peace. Corinne steps up her requests for money, for curtains, etc. Vidal is even more parsimonious than usual because he is sending money orders to his brother Henri, who is ill in Brussels, has been admitted to hospital several times, and is entirely without funds. Worst of all, the move to the Rue Laugier is followed for Corinne by an attack of depression and weeping. To add to her problems, she has cataract surgery in 1965. Vidal is therefore worried about Corinne's illnesses, about the operation she has to undergo, and about her fits of depression; he is the target of her growing irritability and her frequent reproaches, which increasingly concern the mess he makes at home. Although they often go on weekends to their piece of land in Vaux-sur-Seine, situated on high ground overlooking the river, and both relax there, the peace is broken as soon as they are back in the apartment. It is only at the end of 1965 that Dr. Milanolo, who has become Corinne's guardian angel, finds a temporary remedy for her depressions by encouraging the couple to leave Paris, seek a change of scenery, and travel as often as they can. Accordingly, they go to Locarno, and then make more frequent visits and vacations to Italy, Germany and France.

HENRI'S DEATH

Before all this, however, during the summer of 1965, death has struck very near to Vidal: it has taken Henri, the brother to whom he was closest. Vidal kept the numerous letters that Henri sent him between August 1964 and August 1965. The letters from 1964 reveal that he has had a remission, following a year of urinary problems, medical care and bouts in hospital. In the summer of 1964, Henri is recovering after a period in hospital; he confides his money troubles, his continually renewed hope of winning the jackpot, and on several occasions, expresses his nostalgia for Salonica. The first two letters describe his happiness about his recent stay in Paris with his brother; then, in his letters written in September 1964, he remembers their dead relatives. Henri, like Vidal, is non-religious, does not obey the prescriptions of the Law, and lives with his partner Gaby's gentile family; however, late in life, when death is approaching, his cult of the family encourages him to return to the synagogue.

[Letter of September 9]
Yesterday, my dear Vidal, I went to the prayer service, and I went to say a prayer for our dear departed, but I'll tell you I got very emotional; I wept in front of the hazan, and he held my hand to repeat the names of our dear Papa and Mama, poor Henriette and dear Jacques, and Bouki too, as Math asked me. I don't know why I was so upset. May the Good Lord hear my prayer and may we always stay healthy, and have no

illnesses, *i todo bueno che nos venga presto* [and may all good things come to us quickly]. Luckily, when I went to sit down I found myself next to an acquaintance from Salonica who again urged me to be calm, and that consoled me and helped me get over my emotion. For you, my dear Vidal, I wish with all my heart *saloud buena i todo bueno presto che tengas* [good health and all good things quickly], and that everything works out as you desire, and that you are not tiring yourself too much. I hope so with all my heart.

I enclose the winning 3-franc ticket so that you can put it in for me again and send me another for the draw next Wednesday evening. Thank you a thousand times in advance.

I am sending you a little flask that Gaby promised dear Corinne to put her salts in; she should ask for them at the drugstore and keep them in her purse at all times . . .

I thank you in advance for the 600 francs you promised me.

Stay well, my dear Vidal, and may in these days of *Nissim i Nihaflot* the Good Lord *mos escriva a todos nosotros en livros de vidas buenas i presto oun trocamiento bueno che venga* [May the Good Lord write all of our names in his books of good lives and let a change for the good come soon], because when I think of the future, my heart sinks.

I'm sorry for this rather melancholy letter, but I can't manage to calm my nerves, and writing this to you has been a great relief to me . . .

In the following letter, dated September 17, Henri thanks his brother for the money order for 600 francs, tells him that he has won nothing on the latest lottery ticket, and ends: "Still doing no business, and still counting on the lottery, although it hasn't come to anything yet." The following letter shows that Vidal has told him about his own preoccupations:

[October 15]

My dear Vidal,

I received your letter of October 15th, and was very glad to hear from you, although your letter saddens me because of all the troubles and worries that you are having, my dearest Vidal, and I pray to the Good Lord that you are still in good health and keeping your spirits up to help you through these difficult times. On top of the Rue Laugier, now your Edgar is homeless, how did that happen? Is there no way of reconciling him with his wife? When he had happiness in the palm of his hand, a nice apartment, a wife, well-brought up children, to just give everything up like that, it's a pity all the same . . .

I imagine that you must be losing sleep and that all these worries must make you want to urinate very often. Moreover, I can understand that dear Corinne must be very tense, what with the bother she is having because of the Rue Laugier, which will do her health no good at all. May the Good Lord watch over her and may everything work out for the best.

As far as my pension is concerned, I'm still waiting . . . they told me that my file is in order, but that I will have to wait for my pension to be fixed.

As for my hospital bills and x-rays, I still owe nearly 6,000 francs and I'm paying 600 francs per month . . . I've worked out that you have sent me 600 francs three times for the hospital, and now, if you can see your way to sending me more, you will be doing me a very great favor; I am very ashamed and sorry to beg in this way, but the situation is not of the best and I have not managed to do any business at all with the teasels . . .

In a letter dated November 14, Henri writes that he has just heard that Corinne has fallen and suffered bruising in the métro.

From Math, I have no news, I know that there are strikes going on in Italy, the trains, mail, etc. I am expecting her letter in the next few days, for my rent which is payable on the 20th of this month, and so I am very worried about the delay . . . Apart from that, my *dear Vidal, I'm still waiting for the blessed jackpot, para quittar el pied del lodo* [to get my foot out of the mud], it is high time it came, *presto che sea* [let it be soon].

The letter of November 30 repeats his hope of winning the lottery:

Next Tuesday, I will celebrate my birthday, 76 *chanims*, and in the evening, it's the draw for the lottery: who knows? A nice present on my birthday. May the Good Lord will it. Amen.

There are four more letters before February 25. Henri's health is good; Gaby, on the other hand, is suffering from severe headaches. He again confides his money problems, asks his brother for help, and is still putting his hopes on the elusive jackpot:

Quick, may the Good Lord allow me to have a little win, how happy I will be to have peace of mind and be able to sleep without pills.

But on February 25, Henri writes:

I thank you, my dear Vidal, for the present of 1,000 francs that you made me, and it came just at the right time. You see, since last Thursday I have been at home with the beginnings of bronchitis and the doctor has advised me to stay in bed for ten days . . . This latest illness which is keeping me at home frightens me, I don't know why, I don't feel very confident about it.

March 3
My dear Vidal,
I received your letter dated March 1st, and thank you for your *buen couidado* [good care]. Thank God, I am a little better, but not yet completely recovered. I still have pains in my lower back, I think it's my kidneys. I telephoned the doctor, and he told me to keep applying balm to the sore parts, and I will go and see him next Monday. I read the details that you wrote me about the sale of the Rue Demours attentively, and *todo lo che es bueno che te rija el Buen Dio* [May the Good Lord give you all that is good].

Because of the delay I've had with the pension, I've had other debts and also quite a high gas bill, I'm using gas heating at the moment, because coal is impossible, it's too exhausting, and neither Gaby nor I can cope with that any more. We are getting older, my dear Vidal, especially this winter, and Gaby and I have aged a good deal. Perhaps the fine weather will give us better health. That's why my old debts from the hospitals haven't been paid yet. Well, if you can, a little money order would help me out. Now the fine weather is back; today you would think we were on the Côte d'Azur . . . I am thinking of going out tomorrow for a little walk, it is already ten days since I last left the house, and on Friday I have a meeting with Léon, I don't want to miss it. Well, *saloud buena che tengammos i todo bueno che venga presto* [let us enjoy good health, and let all good things come quickly] because it's urgent and I haven't got much time to wait.

The letter of March 15 brings some very bad news. Henri has to change the belt for his hernia, he has broken his dentures, and, worst of all, he is having pains in his kidneys again.

There's no point, my dear Vidal, in writing anything at all about that to our dear Math, she is so far away, and so alone, that it is not worth worrying her. In her last letter, she wasn't very happy that the management had taken away her percentage, so let's not cause her any new bother and may the Good Lord protect me *presto che sea saloud buena che aiga* [let me have good health soon]. Amen.

On March 18, Henri replies to a letter dated March 16 in which Vidal has told him that he has had to keep to his bed for ten days.

In any case, my dear Vidal, when you don't feel well, try not to be difficult; on the contrary, be very calm, and then the fever will go down more quickly and above all the person with you won't be irritated.

As for me, my dear Vidal, the pains in my kidneys have moved elsewhere, right at the bottom of my back, all around the belt. These pains bother me and frighten me, I don't know where these pains come from, and my doctor wants to find out the cause with x-rays, analyses, etc. [. . .]

Henri thanks Vidal for offering to pay half of the fees for his x-rays and analyses, and he hopes that Léon, their elder brother, will agree to pay for the other half.

Well, my dear Vidal, today is Purim, *donde estan los foulares*[72] of the old days, and the colored candy, do you remember?? We should have won the jackpot and gone and celebrated el seder in Paris, all of us together for this *zahoud*, maybe for the last time, because time is passing and I am growing old, my dear Vidal, and so is Gaby, she feels tired, and all the medicine that she has to take may be making her ill, but it soothes her headaches.

On March 25, Henri announces that he is leaving the hospital, and mentions that he will have to make more payments.

But next Monday, it's the lottery, and who knows? The Good Lord will decide to perform a miracle and let me win a prize. Let it be so.

In the same letter, he describes his stay in hospital, in a big room, with fourteen patients:

It's not very cheerful. *Que se fase???* *Fine sea de todos los males* [What can you do?? May all our ills come to an end.]

The letter of March 30 tells Vidal that, according to the doctor, the kidney examination has show nothing serious, but that he has anemia in his blood, nephritis and a second hernia (the real illness he is suffering from seems to have been concealed from him). All of this requires costly treatment. He thanks Vidal, who has invited him to Paris for Seder:

I think that if I can arrange my departure for before April 8, we should manage to get the seats . . . Thank you again, my dear Vidal, for your *buen couidado* and your invitation and may the Good Lord let me come to Paris and take part in Seder, it's on my mind and I think about it every day.

But the letter of April 8 puts an end to these hopes:

In spite of my very great DESIRE and the great JOY that I was promising myself in coming to Paris for Seder, which I want to do so much, and also, of course, to see you both and embrace you, I am sorry to tell you that I will not be able to make the journey. I have nephritis, which is causing me a good deal of pain in my kidneys, and I have to have injections from a nurse every other day, not to mention the medicine for my anemia [. . .]

The pains get worse (letter of April 15). Vidal has suggested to him that he change doctors, but:

If I go to see a new doctor who doesn't know me, he'll want to make blood and urine tests, x-rays etc. And to think that today I was due to take the train for Paris . . . I see, my dear Vidal, that you are not going to Seder either since you have your grand-daughter from Monte-Carlo staying. We will do it *con bueno* [with luck] next year [. . .] I see, my dear Vidal, that you also have a lot of worries with your Edgar, *El Buen Dio che te lo en presente* [may the Good Lord prevent it], he is giving you a lot of trouble, my dear Vidal, and I am very sorry for the worries that you keep having, from one quarter or another. *Presto oun trocamiento bueno* [a change for the better soon]. In any case, I will ask you to send me a money order as soon as you can, for about 1,500–2,000 Belgian francs, which will be to cover my hospital expenses . . . Let's pray to the Good Lord that He will let us live until next year to celebrate Passover with joy.

Henri is taken into hospital shortly after this letter, and returns home on May 5. Vidal asks him for the laboratory's analyses so that he can show them to a young relative who practices medicine (and whom he would rather consult for his health problems than Dr. Milanolo), but Henri answers him on May 10 that they will not give him this information. His letter continues as follows:

I see, my dear Vidal, that you are short of breath, have dizzy spells, and have trouble climbing stairs . . . Don't you think you should retire, it seems to me that it's time, after more than fifty-five years of work. The stairs in the métro are especially tiring. I hope that you can quickly find a buyer for your store and that you can enjoy the years to come.

I see, my dear Vidal, that you were thinking of coming to see me, and that perhaps you will one of these days. I am very happy to think that I will see you. But I want to warn you that I have aged and grown thinner, and you mustn't be frightened when you see me, because I have difficulty walking, and getting up and sitting down in my chair is painful . . .

On the financial side, since you asked me, things are not too rosy. I had a little extra that Matica [Mathilde] sent me, and Léon gave me 1,000 francs. Also, when I was in hospital, I had the Rabbi come, and first I asked him to say a little prayer. *Ressivido che sea* [may it be received]. He asked me if I wanted help from the charitable society and I accepted, and I received a certain sum. I told Léon about it afterwards, and he was not pleased: "How does that make us look?" he said. And so that's where I stand, my dear Vidal, reduced to begging for help???? . . .

I pray to Almighty God to allow me to live a little longer and especially to let my pains go away.

The letter of May 20 describes terrible suffering:

When I lie down, the pains lessen, but when standing, I have pains everywhere . . . it's unbearable to suffer in this way or else to spend the whole day lying down. I go out for a while every morning and evening, I rest on a bench in the sun and then I come home, but I still couldn't go far, or take a tram.

He hopes that Vidal will come and see him the following week with Corinne, as he has announced, and ends:

And the win on the lottery still doesn't come, it would have been a relief to pay my debts and have some peace of mind. Perhaps on the next draw if the Good Lord so wishes, let it be so. Amen.

Two days later, Henri advises Vidal against coming to Brussels. The journey might weary him, and moreover Gaby is tired, also suffering from rheumatic pains.

It means, my dear Vidal, that the house is looking a little neglected, which is quite understandable when someone is ill and especially when the other person is obliged to see him suffer. So, my dear Vidal, you had better put off your journey until later, con bueno [with luck].

In his letter of May 31, Henri is alarmed that Corinne is having to undergo surgery on her eyes. As for him:

My doctor . . . is pleased because I have lost no more weight during the past two weeks and also because the pains move around. But for the past two weeks, I have had pains in my spine and my right shoulder-blade, and these pains are even more atrocious . . . I never thought I would have to suffer so much in my old age???

Letter of June 8:

My dear Vidal,
Received your letter of June 1st and am very glad to hear that dear Corinne is much better and I hope that you are also in very good health.

I hope that in spite of the uncertain weather you have taken advantage of the weekend to go and take some fresh air at Vaux.

Through Sophie and Régine, who come and see me often, I know that Edgar is writing articles in *Le Monde*, surely that must bring him in a fair amount of money, along with his trip to N.Y. and Montreal for the congress, enough to pay his taxes. Which one does he travel with, the lawful one or the other . . . ?

Last Sunday, it was Shavuot, and I remembered el *Moulino del ayrre* – l'*inkioussa de 7 escaleras* [the windmill with its seven flights of stairs] – in the mévlané where we ate alichouah that had been cooled in the pool, and so many other things besides. How far away it all is, my dear Vidal, and now my legs are half-paralyzed, it's too painful to walk, and for the past two weeks I haven't left the house, except to go to the doctor's, leaning on Gaby's arm and an umbrella. Last Wednesday, I felt terribly depressed all day, very pessimistic, and Gaby was frightened and called the doctor.

The doctor suggests that Henri should either return to hospital, or go to take a cure at a spa town, or else see a specialist in rheumatic illnesses. But Henri does not want to go back to hospital: "I would have gone mad," and can't afford to take a cure; he consults a specialist, who will examine his analyses and x-rays.

And to think that this year I wanted so much to take a little break, by which I mean leave Brussels, go to the sea, that would have made such a change for me, and for Gaby, even if it were only for eighteen days, and here I am stuck in Auderghem, and what's worse in an armchair. How the Good Lord is punishing me, my dear Vidal, to make me suffer in this way, it's quite atrocious. The only time when I'm not in pain is at night in my bed, under two blankets and an eiderdown; after half an hour in bed, in the warmth, all my pains disappear, but in the morning, as soon as I put a foot on the floor, it starts again.

And so all my money is slipping through my fingers to pay for hospitals and doctors. Every consultation with the doctor, in addition to the medicine, costs me 400–500 francs. You can imagine. Léon was very kind last week and sent me 1,000 francs, plus the monthly allowance. *Todo para las medecinas* [it all went on medicine], and without seeing any improvement, that's the worst of it . . . I had put a bit of money aside to buy myself a suit, but the money went on medicine!

I would so much like to give you better news, my dear Vidal, I am very sorry for maybe bothering you with my illness, but I write to you as if you were near to me, and it consoles me that you are thinking of me in these difficult moments . . . I have a great need to pour out my heart, because I know that you share in my sorrows.

This letter has alarmed Vidal, and he is thinking of leaving for Brussels to arrange meetings with the doctors, so Henri tries to calm him by assuring him that he is not suffering from an illness but rather from a rheumatic condition from which recovery is very slow. He asks him to reassure Mathilde and tells of his hope for a speedy improvement. He adds that he will be seeing his doctor the next day. The following day, June 16, he writes to Vidal, no longer on his typewriter as he had on previous occasions (his machine is is need of repair), but in very shaky handwriting. He informs him that the doctor has told him he will need to wait at least fifteen days before seeing the effects of his treatment.

When my pains have almost disappeared and I can walk more easily, then we will see if it's necessary to go and take a cure . . . So, be patient, my dear Vidal, *e el Buen Dio va se apiedar de mi* [and the Good Lord will take pity on me] and I will soon be relieved.

But Henri has to be admitted to hospital again. He writes to his brother on July 18 from his hospital bed. He is in great pain, he is praying a good deal, he is hopeful:

Nothing serious, says the doctor, but it takes time to cure rheumatism.

The last letter, written on July 18, is in extremely shaky handwriting and is incoherent in places:

My dear Vidal,

I got your last letter and my bed and I thank you for your encouragement. May the Good Lord let me recover a little sooner.

Unfortunately, the analyses aren't giving any good results yet. God willing I will give you better news as soon as possible and we will have the joy of seeing each other again *con bueno*. I embrace you, my dear Vidal, with all my heart, as well as dear Corinne.

Your poor brother.

M.C. has not sent the promised dispatch. Do me a favor and write a note saying that I am in hospital.

During this tragic period, Vidal is kept in Paris by Corinne's health and his own health problems, and he does not realize that his brother is incurably ill. Henri dies in August 1965. It hits Vidal very hard. So many intimate memories and secrets bind him to Henri, from their youth in Salonica, Frigolet and Marseilles. He was the closest to him of his brothers, had long been his model, and had always remained his confidant. Vidal goes to Henri's funeral alone. Corinne is suffering from an ingrown toenail, and cannot accompany him. His son Edgar has been living since the spring in a village in a remote part of Britanny, where he is making a sociological study. At the time of Henri's death, he is in Rio de Janeiro. Edgar's daughters are on holiday. Vidal is also very upset not to have received condolences from Violette, the wife with whom his son is no longer living. He pours out his heart to his granddaughter Irène on the telephone, and she writes to him shortly afterwards:

If Mom has not sent her condolences, she will very soon. A delay isn't necessarily a sign of forgetting or indifference . . . in any case, my darling little Papou, my Mom never does anything wrong and I don't want you to be unkind about her or bear a grudge against her (because I sensed your understandable anger on the telephone). She had a very sad time herself, at the beginning of this month.

Vidal faces his brother's death alone. His son has failed to perceive his immense sorrow.

During the 1960s, death strikes several times. Élie, Vidal's brother-in-law and former associate, dies in 1963, at the age of 87. Cousin Esterina Hassoun, in Nice, dies in December 1964. Vidal is unable to go to Nice for the funeral. His brother Henri writes to him:

I see, my dear Vidal, that our poor cousin in Nice has gone to heaven. Peche comeremos [we will eat fish, to exorcize the death] and I hope she will pray for us, that we should have good health i todo bueno presto [and all good things soon]. Poor cousin, no-one from her family could accompany her to her final resting-place.

In 1968, death comes for Sophie, the widow of his brother Jacques, whose daughter Régine remains alone. On the Beressi side, Maurice Cohen, Émy's husband dies suddenly of a heart attack, at the age of 63, on November 4 1967. His business collapses. However, the tribe formed by Maurice's relatives and friends will remain united. Émy, who has never ceased to love her husband passionately, will worship his memory.

TAKING ACTION

In 1966, when he is 72 years old, Vidal sells the business at 26, Rue Beauregard, which he had purchased between 1958 and 1960. However, he cannot make up his mind to retire and rents one last little store, which is even more peripheral, at 11, Rue de la Lune; he goes there on an irregular basis, depending on his meetings with irregular customers. Corinne criticizes him for his obstinacy, since his efforts bring no success, and advises him to close his store. But he does not want to let go.

Being less and less occupied by his business, Vidal needs to keep himself busy elsewhere. In 1964, he applies for his veteran's card. His request is refused, because he did not serve in a fighting unit. Nevertheless, he returns to the attack, appeals the decision, and adds a touching consideration to his request:

> Dear Sirs,
>
> I am writing you this letter as an appeal, to ask you kindly to re-consider the request for a VETERAN'S CARD that I made to your departmental service, in the Rue Réaumur. In a letter dated December 16, 1964, this service informed me that I had been rejected, the reason given being that I "was not part of a fighting unit."
>
> However, I want to let you know that when I was assigned as a military worker to the BOURGES EXPLOSIVES FACTORY (Cher), we were informed in May 1940, at the start of the enemy offensive, that the MILITARY EXPLOSIVES FACTORY in Bourges had been declared a combat zone, due to its particular activity as well as the continual air bombardments that the enemy made on the explosives factory.
>
> I was effectively present there for a period of more than ninety days, between March 24 and July 6.
>
> Being over 70 years old, I would very much like to obtain my veteran's card and hope that you will respond favorably to my request.

Despite the mockery of his son, who suggests that he ask for his First World War veteran's card at the same time, and Corinne's "come on, Vidal, you weren't really a soldier," Vidal is stubborn, and writes on March 31 to enquire about the fate of his request for an appeal. On April 20 he receives a letter telling him that his file has been transmitted by the departmental service to the director of the national Veteran's Bureau. Vidal writes on April 27 to the national Bureau: "I hope that a favorable reply will arrive and give comfort to the last years of my life, for I am now in my seventy-second year."

But bureaucracy is not moved by his old age, and finally, on June 12, 1966, Vidal receives a final confirmation of his rejection.

At the same time, Vidal has begun to fight for another hopeless cause. After reading a news report issued by a committee for the defense of the despoiled that appeared in *Le Monde* in 1962, Vidal writes to this committee on November 18, 1962, asking for an indemnity for "injuries suffered to my health, liberty, and the pursuit of my profession during the German occupation of France." The reply he receives tells him that as a French national, his case comes under French law, and that he should therefore have addressed his request to the Ministry of War Veterans and Victims before February 28 1962. (It is very likely that Vidal had in fact made an application at the appropriate time and that he had received some compensation.) Vidal launches a second attack from a different direction, writing to the Minister to obtain an indemnity for which the Franco-German agreement of July 15, 1960 had made provison, in favor of French nationals who had been victims of Nazi oppression. He points out that he was obliged to live in hiding during the last war because of the prohibitions of all kinds targeting "persons of the Hebrew faith." But the Ministry replies that the right to an indemnity to which he is referring is subject to prior recognition as a deportee or prisoner, resistant or political activist.[73]

Vidal makes his next attack on another front, launching a campaign to obtain what has always been the object of his admiration and fascination, namely a decoration.

His obsession began, as we have seen, when his father, David Nahum, was awarded the Belgian decoration of the "Order of Léopold" in December 1902. In 1921, after his father's death, Vidal wrote to the Ministry of Foreign Affairs in Brussels to obtain a duplicate of the diploma, and as we have also seen, Vidal then framed the diploma and the medal under glass. In spite of his many moves, they never left him.

As a young boy, in Salonica, Vidal had sought out medals, and he had once received one from Constantinople as a birthday present from his brother Léon. Throughout his life in France, Vidal collected the bronze medals struck by the Mint, from those which bore the effigy of Napoleon (whom he had worshipped since childhood) to those celebrating various centenaries, including that of the Crédit National (at the Liberation, he had bought some bonds which could not have been less profitable, bonds at 3 percent, and he kept them until his death, not just because it was impossible to sell them, but because he kept hoping for a lucky draw).

In 1969, he will ask the Crédit National to award him the medal given to those who have been with the institution for fifty years. In his capacity as a "long-term and faithful bond-owner," he receives this medal in January 1970.

Vidal writes on October 24, 1963 to the municipal councillor for his arrondissement, Jean Legaret, to find out if he is eligible for the veteran workers' medal. The councillor answers on October 29, telling him that he must make his application to the prefect for the Seine region, and sending him a duplicate letter in support of this request. Letter from Vidal, October 31, 1963:

Monsieur le Préfet de la Seine,
I am writing to ask you kindly to let me know if I am entitled to make a request to receive the veteran workers' medal.

As a small businessman, I have worked for forty years in the 2nd arrondissement, I have been a voter for the last thirty years, and as I am approaching my 70th birthday, I would very much like to know if I have the right to make this request.

I look forward . . .

After his request is refused, Vidal sends two letters to the Prefecture, one to the Department for economic affairs, the second to the Service for honorary distinctions. The second (February 17, 1964) reads:

Dear Sirs,
As I am about to turn 70, and have been a businessman and a voter in the 2nd arrondissement for over forty years, I am writing to ask you if I may be entitled to an honorary distinction.

If so, please let me know, and send me the appropriate forms that I need to present to you to that end.

I look forward . . .

Vidal has also written to Mr. Legaret, on February 14, to ask him if another distinction might be accorded to him, "after these long years of diligent work as a small businessman."

Edgar and Corinne's laughter and mockery accompany every step, which Vidal enjoys, since he loves being made fun of as much as he loves teasing others. Soon, on February 17, he receives the following letter from Jean Legaret:

Dear Sir,
I received your letter dated February 14. Since you are not eligible, as a businessman, for the veteran workers' medal, I am asking the President of the municipal council to examine, with particularly favorable consideration, the possibility of awarding you the medal of the City of Paris.

I will keep you informed . . .

On March 11, 1964, Mr. Legaret tells Vidal that the medal of the City of Paris has been awarded him by the president of the municipal council and that it is waiting for him in his office in the Rue des Prouvaires. Joy: March 14 is Vidal's 70th birthday, and he bounds over to the Rue des Prouvaires.

Dear Sir,
I received with pleasure your letter of the 11th and thank you very sincerely. Your letter concerning the award of the medal of the City of Paris arrived on the day when I had arranged a family party in my home for my seventieth birthday, and I wanted to

let them know the good news, by going on the same day to the Rue des Prouvaires to collect it.

I expect and I hope to meet you before long, so that I can express all my gratitude to you again, in person.

Until then, I remain [. . .]

Vidal is impatient to wear the ribbon that goes with his decoration. But which ribbon?

Paris, April 22, 1964
President,
Municipal Council of Paris

Dear Sir,
Thank you for your letter of April 17.
Unfortunately, the award of the medal of the City of Paris does not entitle the bearer to wear any kind of ribbon.

Yours [. . .]
Jean Auburtin

The medal of the City of Paris thus turns out to be an incomplete decoration. Vidal is incompletely satisfied. From now on, he will endeavor to obtain a real medal. And, as we will see, he will eventually have the merit of acquiring, through his persistence, the decoration of the Order of Merit.

VIDAL SAVES MATHILDE

Mathilde, Vidal's younger sister, falls ill in Turin in spring 1969. As we have said, she had arrived in Italy in 1941, during the collapse of Yugoslavia, had reverted to the Italian identity of her youth, and, after the war, had put down roots there, after a disappointing trip to Argentina, possibly followed by a trial period living in Paris in 1953. She had entered into a marriage that she broke off as soon as she discovered that her husband, who had the virtue of being very rich, had the fault of possessing a body covered in boils. She had moved to Bologna, to be near her sister-in-law Manon (sister of Bouchi, her deceased husband), who had married an Italian doctor practicing in that city. Her funds were beginning to run out. It was, of course, impossible to retrieve the real estate and other capital that they had left behind in Yugoslavia, which was now a people's republic. She nevertheless managed to visit Bouchi's grave, in Abbazia, now known as Opatija, in the province of Istria, which had been Italian at the time of Bouchi's death, and became Yugoslavian after the war. Afterwards, she regularly sent money to maintain his grave.

Mathilde was fluent in English, French, German, Serbian, Italian and

Spanish, and had no difficulty finding employment as an interpreter. But the development of simultaneous translation and the training of qualified interpreters meant that requests for her services dwindled. Around 1959 or 1960, she found another job managing the Roman branch of the Prémaman[74] chain, in the Via Fratina. She reigned as a benevolent tyrant over a handful of staff, and remained a great lady, in spite of her exile in the world of paid employment. She took her meals at a modest restaurant frequented by state employees or office workers. She would survey the menu with disillusioned disdain, finding nothing on it to her liking, in spite of the waiter's recommendation of various delicacies, and would end up asking for a special seasoning to be added to a certain appetizer, a different sauce to the pasta, and some particular refinement for the *secondo piatto*. Then she would change her mind, and make further demands, amid the roomful of solitary regulars reading their newspapers. She often went to see Manon and her husband in Bologna, but she was increasingly isolated.

She was very disappointed and displeased to be transferred to Turin in 1964. She felt this move to be an exile and an abasement, but she could not refuse, since she was obliged to earn her living. Officially, she was 61 years old, but in reality she was seven years older, having taken advantage of her migrations without return to take a few years off her age on two occasions. However, even with her gray hair she remained a tall and beautiful woman, with the same regal posture, and a haughty expression in her blue eyes.

In Turin, she moved into a residential apartment building, where she had a devoted employee, Carlo Rolle, and a friend, Mrs. Ortona. She had more or less resigned herself to this life, but after a fall at the beginning of 1969, she broke her hip and had to go into hospital in San Giovanni. They put her entire body in plaster, and once she had been immobilized in this way, she fell into a kind of coma. Her family was informed that she was expected to die. Léon, Chary, Liliane and Vidal rushed to her bedside. Vidal was alone in refusing to believe the fatal diagnosis, and wanted to take Mathilde to Paris and have her cared for by the best specialists there. The hospital would not allow her to leave. By chance, Vidal's son had kept up a very affectionate friendship with a woman from Turin, Magda Talamo, whose brother was a hospital doctor. Vidal went to find Dr. Talamo; the doctor gave her emergency treatment, and when the patient remained prostrate, he prescribed exploratory examinations. He thought it medically pointless and legally impossible for Mathilde to leave the hospital in Turin. But Vidal bombarded Dr. Talamo with telephone calls day and night, and convinced him to act. He managed to raise the legal obstacles to the transfer. Vidal chartered an ambulance, speeded up the formalities, went to collect Mathilde's passport, organized her reception in hospital in Paris by telephone, and, in the presence of Dr. Talamo, whom he had mobilized,[75] he left with his sister at four thirty in the morning by ambulance for France. They crossed the border on May 5, 1969. Mathilde was in a desperate state when she arrived at the surgery in Fontenay-aux-Roses. However, contrary to all expectations apart from Vidal's, she was convalescing by the beginning of June. Mathilde then reproached Vidal for having saved her life, thanking him effusively all the while. The brother whom as a child she called "all-powerful chief" (doubtless at his own insistence), and who had later been demoted to "coco," was reinstated, this time with reason, "all-powerful chief."

Mathilde stayed on in Paris and rented an apartment at 87, avenue Niel, not very far from Vidal's home. Nevertheless, she was careful not to go and see him too often, for fear of imposing on Corinne; but every morning, on his way to or from his store, Vidal would go and visit his sister.

The sixties came to an end. Vidal had shown very little interest in the events of 1968. On the personal front, 1969, the year of the expedition to Turin to save Mathilde and that of Maurice Cohen's death in Monte-Carlo, ended sadly for Vidal and Corinne. She was suffering increasingly from her ailments, oppressions and depressions. Vidal had received a warning sign regarding his bladder; he had found himself unable to urinate, and then made a very rapid recovery. He wore a hernia belt, but refused to have surgery. His sight had weakened, but he did not want to have a cataract operation, which Corinne had trustingly agreed to herself as soon as the "important professor" Offret advised it. He was beginning to feel very weary at times.

THE JOURNEY TO CALIFORNIA

Vidal's son had been invited to join the Salk Institute in La Jolla, Southern California, very near to San Diego. In September 1969, he and Johanne had moved into a big and beautiful Californian villa made of wood and glass, right next to the ocean.

Back in Paris, Vidal and Corinne were not well. Corinne was suffering from an attack of depression and Vidal felt extremely tired. He was 75 years old. Although ordinarily he concealed his troubles and his illnesses from his son, who was away overseas, he wrote him a letter in January 1970 asking him to come back to France as soon as possible and to give up his plans to return via Asia. He expressed his desire that all four of them should to go to Ravello, where Johanne and Edgar had in vain tried to persuade Vidal and Corinne to come and join them two years earlier. It was the first time he had ever asked his son for help, and it was the first time the son had felt that his father was old. As he wrote at the time: "The realization of his father's mortality represented a huge leap forward." As soon as he read the letter, Edgar called Paris and found Vidal morose and anxious, and Corinne depressed and oppressed on the telephone. At that moment, Johanne suddenly had an idea: "Invite your parents to come out here," which Edgar immediately did. When Vidal, stunned by the unthinkable suggestion that he make a plane journey (he was 75 years old and had never flown before), began to say that it was impossible, Corinne, who was holding the receiver, could be heard crying: "Yes, yes, yes." Vidal then raised the problem of how to pay for the ticket. Edgar replied that there were special deals with TWA and that, in any case, he could cover the expenses of their journey. "So give me the money to go to Ravello," said Vidal, in a final attempt at escape. "No way, old man!" Corinne, who was holding the receiver, was still exclaiming: "Yes, yes, come on, let's go." Vidal kept fighting: "We'll see, let me think about it." His son did not manage to get a definite promise from him. But as soon as he hung up the telephone, Corinne mounted her attack, nagged Vidal without respite, finally wrung an agreement out of him, lost no time in dragging him to the American consulate for the visas, and then to Air France (which he preferred to TWA) to reserve the two return tickets from Paris to Los Angeles. Two days later, he telegraphed his son announcing the day and time of their flight. With another telephone call, Edgar learned that Corinne had recovered from her problems and her insomina. The day was approaching, and Vidal did not know how to get out of the horror of the airplane. Corinne (not knowing that it was forbidden to take any foreign food into the United States) had prepared a *pastellico* and an eggplant gratin for Edgar. The great day came. In the passengers' waiting room, Vidal started muttering strangely; when Corinne leaned closer she realized he was reciting the prayers he had learned in his childhood. When the passengers were called, he headed for the airplane with his hat on, chanting like a rabbi. Although they had arranged that his son would collect him by car in Los Angeles, Vidal had also informed a distant relative in Los Angeles, Mrs. Faraggi, whose address he had. Once inside the airplane, before and during take-off, and for a long time afterwards, he kept up his chanting, and only stopped when they started serving the meal, which delighted him. During the flight, fearing that neither his son nor his relative would be there when he arrived, he managed to persuade the pilot of the Boeing 747 to telephone Mrs. Faraggi at home, remind her of the plane's arrival time and ask for confirmation of her presence at the airport. Then Vidal began to get used to the plane, while Corinne found her first experience of air travel enchanting.

Of course, Vidal began to feel very anxious again when the plane prepared to land, and he prayed ardently until the plane touched the ground. At customs, the officials tried to confiscate Corinne's *pastellico* and eggplant gratin. "It is prohibited!" "But it's for my son, my son, my son," implored Corinne, who eventually made the customs officer relent.

Vidal had not lived under the same roof as his son since his son's emancipation. Vidal and Corinne had never been invited to a house lived in by Edgar, who had never before lived in a big house with several bedrooms and bathrooms. They were very happy in this ephemeral family home; staying with them at the same time was Alanys Obomsawin, Johanne's and Edgar's American Indian friend, whom they loved dearly, and who had great fun with Vidal and Corinne.

On the first day, fearing that he would feel lost in an unknown world, Vidal went to the synagogue in La Jolla, where he was received with great cordiality and invited to a party. But he did not really need the "Jewish connection." Vidal and Corinne were naturally included within the great flow of warm and joyful friendships, and they enjoyed the jubilant atmosphere of that year, the last when the words peace and love held sway. They were practically adopted by Colette Neagle, a Frenchwoman married to a Californian architect, who invited them to stay at her house the following year. They were pleased to meet the inventor of the polio vaccine, and scientists who had won Nobel prizes. They also enjoyed tender, intoxicated, exuberant parties where everyone danced. Everything was good, or almost everything, because Vidal received a wound that he kept secret from his son.

Since an irresistible hunger took hold of Vidal as early as 11 in the morning and 5 in the evening, and made him press Corinne insistently to hurry up the evening meal, it had been decided that at La Jolla he would respect the collective timetables. Moreover, although he felt like going to bed as early as 9 in the evening, and very much wanted Corinne to accompany him, Edgar and Johanne had made him agree to let Corinne stay up with them after his bedtime. He had accepted, with apparent resignation. As far as meals were concerned, he coped by making himself a snack before mealtimes, at about ten-thirty in the morning and five in the evening. But, after dinner, when he was about to go to his bedroom, he would ask Corinne: "Are you coming, Poulette?" "No I'm not, Vidal." "Leave her alone, Dad." "Yes, leave her alone, Dad." Off he would go, dragging his feet, while the others remained in the living room, talking or watching television. He would reappear a quarter of an hour later: "Poulette!" Everybody would protest, and off he would go again, defeated, only to reappear a few minutes later, go away, and come back, until Corinne, sighing, would get up and follow him.

After a discussion in which Johanne and Edgar had disputed his right to impose his timetables and desires on others, Johanne exclaimed to Edgar: "Oh, how lucky I am to be an orphan!" Vidal said nothing, but he felt one of the greatest offenses of his life. Johanne had touched what was most sacred to him: she had dared to imagine that Edgar could and should have done without his father, and by the same token that Vidal could and should have done without his son.

Nevertheless, Johanne had been constantly affectionate and attentive towards Vidal and Corinne, always thinking of presents to make them, and it was also she who had had the idea of inviting them in the first place. But none of this did anything to eradicate the offense, and Vidal retained a mortal rancor towards Johanne ever afterwards.

This wound did not spoil their visit. All of Corinne's problems had disappeared. Vidal was happy. The couple had found, in December and January, a Mediterranean climate that reminded them of Salonica, Marseilles . . . Their appetite for socializing was satisfied; they met a great many different kinds of people, all of whom were cordial, and some truly friendly and affectionate. Most of all, they were part of a happy spiral, where, especially in the relationship between Corinne, Vidal, Edgar and Johanne, each person's happiness enriched that of the others in an uninterrupted loop.

XI

The Nineteen-Seventies

PILGRIMAGES

The visit to La Jolla had regenerated them. It had created a home, albeit a temporary and peripheral one, in which Vidal, his son, Corinne and his son's wife could live together. They reconstructed this external and temporary home afterwards in Castiglioncello de Bolgheri, in 1976, and in Saint-Antonin and Ménerbes, in 1977 and 1978. There were also stays under neighboring roofs at various times, in particular the next year, in La Jolla.

The memory of their first stay in La Jolla was so compelling that Edgar and Johanne went back in 1971, after a university conference in Mexico City, and Vidal and Corinne came to join them there. This time, Edgar and Johanne were staying with friends, the Foresters, while Vidal and Corinne were guests with the family of Colette Neagle, for whom they had become adoptive parents. The second stay in La Jolla was very pleasant, but did not rekindle the magic of the first one. Vidal and Corinne revived ties and friendships they had made there, which were prolonged into visits to France and lasting correspondences, especially with Mrs. Faraggi in Los Angeles, and her children.

It was arranged that Corinne and Vidal would join Edgar in New York, in fall 1973. The son would have them to stay with him in a very big apartment on the twenty-seventh floor of a tower on Bleeker Street, which had a superb view over southern Manhattan. But Vidal had a great fear of New York, and of the twenty-seventh floor. Corinne pressed him, but he resisted, and in the end health problems prevented them from discovering the city, although they had forewarned Charles Mallah, a Salonician who was some kind of relative or friend, of their arrival there.

Despite the New York failure, the precedent for long air journeys had been set, and accordingly Vidal and Corinne set out on pilgrimages to Salonica and to discover Israel.

Since the end of the war, Vidal had been thinking about Salonica incessantly; he wanted to find out about his family's past, and had been interested and surprised to learn through his son, who had begun a correspondence with the scholar Joseph Nehama, author of a *History of the Jews of Salonica*, that the Nahums were originally from Aragon. On his side, Vidal was corresponding with Mr. Revah, another scholar who was planning to write a book

241

about Salonician families, and he had sent him a photo of the Léon Gattegno Franco-German school, where he had studied.

The initial plan to spend Passover in Salonica had aborted in 1966:

26, rue Beauregard
Paris, April 5, 1966
Dear Mr. Revah,
First of all, *"enveranada boena i saloud boena,"*[76] *i el Dio ke moz de zahou* to go and celebrate next Passover in Salonica. Yesterday evening, at Seder here, Mr. Nino Barsilaï told me that he had been in Salonica last year, and that Seder had been a great success for the circle, with photos published in the newspapers . . .

As I told you, I was intending to come to Salonica with my wife this year, accompanied by my brother-in-law, Mr. Maurice Cohen, who is due to leave Monaco by car this weekend for Salonica and Istanbul. Since my wife has been ill, the doctor advised her against traveling by car, but we have promised ourselves that we will come next year, God willing, by airplane.

It would give me great pleasure to hear your news, and also to know whether you have been successful in your plan to write a book about Salonician families. I look forward to hearing from you . . . .

Actually, Vidal had no intention of going by airplane to Salonica at that time; he wanted to travel by boat, but Corinne, with Edgar's encouragement, wanted to take the airplane. So Vidal put it off, trying, in his usual way, to play for time. He managed to avoid taking the airplane, but consequently he did not manage to get to Salonica, either in 1967 or the following year.

In fact, as we have seen, Vidal did not take an airplane until the beginning of 1970, to go to La Jolla. Although he was still afraid, he flew to California again the next year.

This meant that the trip by plane to Salonica could be seriously envisaged, and it was decided that they would go in April 1973.

And now, in addition to his desire to see Salonica again, he felt the desire to see Israel. Vidal had begun to take a sympathetic interest in Israel's fate at the time of the Six Day war, in 1967.[77] Vidal thought of as Israel not as a homeland, as we have said, but essentially as exemplary proof of the merit of the Jews in peace as in war; then, little by little, he began to see Israel as an ancestral matrix. So the journey to Israel was combined with the voyage to Salonica. But it was in Salonica that he decided to spend the Passover Seder. He wrote to the headquarters of the Israelite Club to make his reservation at the Hotel Electra, to arrange his reunion with former acquaintances, and above all to take part in Seder. They spent ten days in Salonica from April 14 to 23, 1973. Vidal had has his 79th birthday on March 14. They celebrated Passover with great emotion at the association reuniting the survivors from the Sephardic community. Did Vidal meet up with his cousin

Régine Frances in Salonica? Was she still alive? Did he meet Mr. Revah, was he still alive? Was his friend Dr. Matarasso still in Athens, or was he already established in Cannes? In any event, Vidal did see a cousin of his, Vital (Saporta?), and some childhood and school friends. His son remembers Vidal's joy at being back in his little homeland, with its climate and its food, but at the same time his sorrowful observation that, physically and biologically, it had been completely destroyed. The Salonica of wooden buildings that he had known, the whole of the formerly Sephardic city center, had been destroyed in the fire of 1917; a new city with a new outline had replaced them, and Vidal could find neither the street in which his family's house had stood, nor the configuration of his neighborhood. What he found instead was an integrally Greek city, which had retained only a few rare vestiges of the Sephardic population that had first dispersed, and then been exterminated.

Vidal and Corinne were both moved and delighted, in a different way, by their journey to Israel, which also lasted ten days, from April 24 to May 3. They were impressed by the way that the remains of the ancestral past coexisted with modern achievements. Vidal wanted to see Kfar-Nahoum, which he declared to be his family's place of origin, and he brought back a color photo of it that he framed and put up in his living room. In Tel Aviv, they met some Salonicians who had been established there for a long time, including Mr. Aelion, who for many years was the editor of the only French-language Israeli newspaper. But there was no Salonician club in Israel, even in Tel Aviv.

The decade that began in 1970 was one of pilgrimage. Before the pilgrimage to Salonica, there was the pilgrimage to the ancestral Sepharad, Spain.

It was winter, and his son had advised him to go to Malaga. Vidal and Corinne arrived there speaking the language of Cervantes, but they had no difficulty understanding people and making themselves understood. One day, while they were speaking in *djidio* in the sitting room of their hotel, a man started looking at them; then he approached them, murmuring: *"Soch ben amenou?"* ("Are you a son of our people?"). It was a phrase to be spoken softly, almost inaudibly, to the stranger whom one believes to be a coreligionary, and which one lets pass or modifies if the person shows surprise or fails to understand. This phrase must have been exchanged by the Marranos, in the seventeenth century, as a secret sign of recognition. And now, in the same country, a few centuries later, two possible descendants of Marranos had recognized one another in Malaga by using the same coded language as their ancestors. In response to the question, Vidal nodded, and the man introduced himself. He had been born in Salonica and owned the hotel. During the German occupation, he had fled with his mother, on foot, over the mountains to Turkey. From there, they had left for Palestine, but, not feeling at home in Ashkenazi society, had migrated to Egypt, then to Spanish

Morocco; there, he had been successful in business, and had made the crossing to Malaga, where he had become the owner of the hotel. Vidal and Corinne were delighted with their stay, where thanks to the hotelier, Salonica and the Sepharad were tangibly reunited.

In Malaga, Vidal was very conscious of bearing within him a piece of Spain's historical memory: *In Malaga, they* [the Spanish] *loved it when I spoke my Spanish and sometimes I would tell them a joke in Spanish, and use words that they themselves had forgotten, but they knew they were the original ones.*

After the pilgrimage to Salonica and to Israel, there was the pilgrimage to Livorno, in 1975. Vidal and Corinne had been invited by Edgar to join him at the dilapidated castle of Castiglioncello de Bolgheri, situated on top of an unfarmed hill looking down over the "five lakes" and the island of Elba. The sole occupants of the castle were the caretakers, Mr. and Mrs. Pagni, who maintained it for the owner, Baron Mario Incisa. The Baron had allowed Edgar to stay at his castle so that he could work on a long book that he was writing. Edgar occupied a small apartment. The Pagnis offered a room in their apartment to Vidal and Corinne. Mr. Pagni was a worker and went every day to the Monte Edison chemicals factory, twenty kilometers away. Mrs. Pagni did the housework and looked after her little garden. The food was rustic and Mediterranean, and delighted Vidal and Corinne as much as Edgar. They stayed for about two weeks, after which Vidal wanted to go on to Livorno. Edgar drove them there and they stayed for two or three days. Vidal contacted the consistory, and asked the rabbi to consult the archives to look for any traces of the Nahums and Beressis. But the old tombs in the Jewish cemetery had been dispersed, and the community's archives had been destroyed by the Germans. Vidal found nothing, but he projected and focused all his love on Livorno, and often imagined and fantasized about retiring to Livorno, and sometimes strongly desired to do so, as we will see.

There was a further, shorter pilgrimage to Frigolet, on the occasion of a visit to his niece Chary, in Avignon. Vidal brought back a botle of the elixir made by the monks of the abbey, which had become a historic monument.

Finally, after this succession of pilgrimages, Vidal planned to make another trip to Salonica; this time he would rent a room with its own kitchen. A letter indicates that he was still envisaging this plan in 1978. Later, as we will see, Vidal thinks of ending his days near to his ancestors, either in Salonica or in Livorno.

Vidal has even more reason to turn towards the past and his roots because death has been striking cruelly around him: it has taken his last living brother, Léon, and the last of his sisters, Mathilde.

THE DEATHS OF LÉON AND MATHILDE

Léon, the eldest brother, would leave the estate of Nahum Steel to his son

Edgard. In 1964 he had acquired a third decoration, the "Order of Léopold I," and Edgard had been decorated with the "Order of Léopold II." At the end of 1970, Léon is suffering from a pulmonary illness whose cancerous nature is concealed from him. He has to make a succession of stays in clinics where they tap his lungs. Then he has a fall, breaks his hip, and is confined to bed. Vidal is unaware of the seriousness of his condition. Still preoccupied with Salonica, Vidal questions his elder brother about the layout of the rooms in their father's house in the Dzinaneria; worse, since he is not particularly worried about his brother, he leaves on his second trip to La Jolla, in February 1971. When he returns from California, Vidal and his son go to visit his brother. Léon, in bed, continues to hold himself very upright, and still has the same courteous smile. The news of his death, in April 1971, sends Vidal, accompanied by his son, rushing to Brussels. Léon had never ceased to advise Vidal, up until the last years of his life, and he often reprimanded him for his "childish behavior." As far as Vidal was concerned, he had remained the head of the family, his father's proxy.

Edgard would continue to run Nahum Steel, until he sold it to a Germano-Belgian financial group. He had taken a gentile wife, and had two daughters, Michèle and Anne-Marie, and a son, Robert. Their Sephardic inheritance would be diluted by their Belgian identity.

Mathilde is taken into hospital in Beaujon in 1974 or 1975. The doctors think she is still young enough to have surgery, being 72 years old. But Vidal knows that Mathilde has made herself younger by seven years, and that the 1903 birth date on her identity papers is false. Before telling the doctors, he goes to consult his sister, but he does so very carefully, because his son is with him. Mathilde is lying there, lifeless, on her hospital bed, and hardly has the strength to speak.

"Mathilde, my darling," says Vidal gently, "the doctors want you to have a little operation, seeing as according to your papers you are only seventy-two years old."

Mathilde opens one eye, she murmurs:

"And?"

Vidal whispers:

"It's a question of your age . . . "

All of a sudden Mathilde sits up, her eyes flashing, and bursts out:

"What! You dare to slander me in front of your son? You dare to claim that I am not the age that I am?"

"Oh no, my darling, no, I never meant to say that!"

"Yes you did, Vidal! You implied it!"

"Me? How could I have implied such a thing?"

Mathilde calms down. In the end, Vidal asks to speak to the head doctor, and confesses the secret to him in order to prevent an operation which would be too dangerous for someone who is nearly eighty, and makes him swear not to reveal Mathilde's true age, even to his close collaborators.

Mathilde dies at the Hôtel–Dieu on December 14, 1976 "*doppo due anni di dolore incredible in hospitali*" ("after two years of terrible pain in hospital"), as Vidal writes, in sketchy Italian, to Carlo Rolle, who had served Mathilde devotedly in Turin. Mathilde had made Vidal her universal heir, but all he inherited was an account overdrawn by 76.20 francs. Finally, in 1977, Carlo would tell him to resign himself: "Just think, Mr. Vidal, for my part I am still waiting for the social fund to pay a backdated pension for my sister who died on September 2, 1972. Year after year, they keep stringing me along, but I haven't had a single cent." Carlo Rolle feels justified in concluding that "it's a uniquely Italian custom!" but then, he has never been to France.

Régine, Jacques and Sophie's eldest daughter, dies in Brussels, almost at the same time as Mathilde. Vidal had kept in touch with her, and had recently invited her to Paris. Always very discreet and secretive, she had remained alone after her mother's death, and she died in discretion and silence, having maintained no close relationship with anyone apart from her cousin Chary, in Avignon.

During the same period, other relatives of Vidal's die, in particular his niece Liliane, Henriette's daughter, who passes away in hospital in 1979, almost at the same time as her husband Mony. They are buried at Bagneux, in the "Hassid-Covo" family tomb, in which the coffins of Henriette, Élie and Mathilde are already present, and where Mony has erected a stone to the memory of his murdered Salonician relatives. Liliane's sister, Aimée, comes from Liverpool to Paris for the funeral. Perhaps artificially, she has kept her blonde hair, but she has also kept her extraordinary blue eyes, small waist and perfect figure. She will die shortly after 1980.

The family had now shrunk considerably, from the top down. All of Vidal's brothers and sisters were dead, as were three of his nieces. The fourth, Hélène, Régine's sister, was very far away. Hélène was now calling herself Nahum again after her divorce from Paul Schrecker. She had found a job teaching French at Athens University (Georgia), and then a post as translator in the Canadian parliament in Ottawa. Vidal and Hélène wrote to one another, and on one occasion Vidal sent her some information about her Nahum ancestors in Salonica. From Ottawa, she wrote a very emotional letter to Vidal, after Mathilde's death.

December 23, 1976

Your letter, which I opened a moment ago when I got home, caused me great sorrow. How much I regret not having seen her before she passed away – that's another one I have missed. Now I see that all my family are scattered and dying, and here I am very much alone, so far from everyone.

I am so sad that she had to suffer so much: why didn't they find out what was wrong with her earlier? It's truly incredible. I must have had something like a presentiment, because last week I went to the synagogue, something made me go, and now I know what it was that pushed me to do something that is fairly unusual for me. May God give her peace . . . I dare to hope that you and Corinne do not feel too alone. My dear uncle, you are my last remaining relative on my father's side.

However, their relationship broke down in 1978, after Hélène came on a visit to Paris. Her visit happened to coincide with one of Corinne's depressive periods, when she had stopped inviting people to lunch. Hélène, who was absolutely mortified not to have been invited to a single meal, was also offended that her cousin Edgar had not invited her, although she was staying right opposite his home. She did not know that relations between Johanne and Edgar had become difficult, and that Edgar had more or less incarcerated himself in his room in order to finish writing a book. And so she broke off her relations with this selfish and discourteous family, only keeping in touch with her cousin Chary. There was a last exchange of correspondence between Hélène and Vidal, after Liliane's death:

March 6, 1979
Dearest Vidal,
It was with great sadness that I learned that Mony and Liliane had unexpectedly passed away in January. I am very sad about it, but even sadder that the family did not think fit to tell me, and left me in total ignorance. If the family no longer wishes to include me in it, then I will stay out of everything.

Paris, March 12, 1979
My dear Hélène,
Very upset by your letter; I'd like you to read it again! Who do you mean by the family? Do you think that Aimée, Corinne or I were in any condition to write to you? Or your cousins? I put your name in the announcement in *Le Figaro*, because you are part of the family.
    If you want to take back your very threatening terms, write to me, and I'll write you, I hope, and tell you everything I can about Liliane's cruel illness. I say I hope, because since Corinne has been ill for over two months, and has severe anemia, which has given her a zona virus, we are having a very sad time, and it is making us very weary. Let's hope I hold out! God willing.
I look forward to hearing from you.
With love,
Your UNCLE.

Hélène did not reply. Edgar would try to meet her in Ottawa three or four years later, but would not find her at her home or see her name in the telephone directory. By then she had married a Canadian meteorologist, Joseph Calvert, and had taken Canadian nationality.
    During the seventies, Vidal began to play the role of shepherd to his dead. Not only did he talk about them incessantly when reminiscing, but he also thought about reuniting in Paris the members of the flock who were scat-

tered in cemeteries abroad. Increasingly, he had begun seriously to envisage bringing Bouchi's remains to lie next to those of his wife Mathilde, buried with her sister Henriette in Bagneux cemetery. He would also have liked to have his brother Jacques emigrate from the cemetery in Florence to Bagneux. In 1977, he wrote to the Borniol firm with a view to disinterring Henri's body from Auderghem cemetery and transporting it to Bagneux. He even found out about the capacity of the vault that contained Samy Beressi, deceased in 1929, with some unknown intention.

With his whole being, in the years between 1975 and 1980, he therefore battled against dispersion and forgetting. Not only did he want to find his relatives who were scattered throughout the world, he also wanted to get back in touch with former correspondents from his days in Salonica, like Cornelia Monday in Canada, Wilhelmine in Austria, and other lost friends. Who was the person he wrote to, and who replied with this note from the graveside?

Dear Mr. Vidal Nahoum,

My son forwarded me your letter. I realize that your retirement has not always been carefree. That is generally the case for all of us. At the age of 77, I have retired to a senior citizens' club, and have more or less ceased all outside relationships as I await the inevitable.

Wishing you better luck for the future, I present you with my best wishes.
[Signature illegible]
July 8, 1975

"QUERENCIA"

The other half of Vidal's life was now residual. Vidal closed his store in the Rue de la Lune before 1980, for want of customers. He no longer owned any real estate, but still had shares and bonds. He wanted to carry on selling and buying securities, according to his inspiration or on the advice of his broker in the Rue de l'Opéra. However, he did not understand that what had once been the most reliable choices, such as textiles or iron and steel, had now become the most risky. Nevertheless, Vidal and Corinne were able to live and travel not only on Vidal's pension and his savings, but also thanks to the sale of their piece of land in Vaux.

After the closure of his store, Vidal continued to use the address of the Rue de la Lune for his mail. Nearly every morning, he went there directly; with a pang of anguish he would pass the building where his sister Mathilde had lived, in the Avenue Niel, get on the métro at Pereire, change, slowly mount the stairs at Bonne-Nouvelle, stop at a gaming arcade where he would play one or two rounds of roulette, go and pick up his mail, visit a few friends in the neighborhood, including Mr. Saltiel, a fellow wholesaler, in the Rue

Saint-Denis, perhaps glance at the beautiful prostitutes in the street, possibly drop into his bank, the Banque de France, or go and see his stockbroker to find out how the market was doing, and then, weak with hunger, go home early and persuade Poulette to heat up the dishes for lunch.

He had found a little apartment above his store for his granddaughter Véronique, and he would call up to her from the street when he wanted to speak to her. He avoided stairs, but when Véronique undertook to record his oral biography, he climbed up to the second floor, and in 1978 they had the conversations which are almost all contained in this book.

His granddaughter Irène also went to meet him in the Rue de la Lune. Although she had adored "her Nona" when she was little, she had begun to avoid her. Ever since her parents had separated, she could not bear it when Corinne, without fail, praised her father to the skies while disparaging her mother; as a result, Corinne complained of the forgetfulness and ingratitude of a child for whom she had cared so devotedly. So Irène would go and see her Papou where they could be alone together. When a customer came in, Vidal would introduce her: "This is my granddaughter, my son's elder daughter, she's at the lycée, she's like my son, she doesn't want to work with me in the store when she grows up either." Vidal and Irène would joke and tease one another. Irène pretended to shame her grandfather about her father Edgar: "You know how badly I've turned out, what a traumatized, unbalanced teenager I am, I'll end up a criminal on the front pages of the newspapers, the name of Nahoum will be tarnished for good, and your little prophet will be erased from the Bible." And Vidal would begin laughing his interminable laugh, although it would eventually stop long enough to let him sigh, in one breath: "Ah, Rirènou, how you hurt your Papou!"

They would sometimes go and have lunch together at a little restaurant where, after devouring his food, "he would swallow his coffee scalding hot ('Coffee's not good unless it's scalding,' he'd say), and then he'd go to sleep, sitting up in his chair; he'd take his five-minute nap wherever he happened to be. He'd wake up from this Napoleonic doze all fresh and perky."

It was during these lunches that Vidal confessed to Irène some of the secrets he would never have revealed to his son. He wanted to give her a collection of old love letters which he had deposited with a trusted friend, but in the end he thought it unwise, and must have destroyed the letters.

Vidal had an ever-greater need to see his son, to confide his worries and his problems to him, seek his advice, and, increasingly often, ask him to intervene in his quarrels with Corinne. When Edgar was in Paris, he would telephone him every morning, to hear his news and receive a broad account of his activities. He would come and see him at his place, in the Rue des Blancs-Manteaux, or he would have him come to the Sentier. Sometimes, Vidal would tell his son that he could not to carry on living with Corinne, and confided his dreams of other women to him (he could not bear the idea of living without a woman); from time to time, his son advised him to leave

Corinne for a while, and he fiercely resisted the idea, arguing that she needed him and that he could not leave her on her own. Occasionally, Edgar would question him about the past and ask him if he had had a mistress before his mother's death. Vidal swore that he had not, but his son knew that he was an Oriental, meaning that he was a master in the art of feigned sincerity, and he was not absolutely convinced. Vidal was always very tender, a maternal father to his son, but his son was sometimes irritable and would rebuff his father, who was saddened to see the character of the Beressi sisters repeated in him. Nevertheless, the time when the son had thought only of freeing himself from his father was far away. In fact, it was this liberation that had brought them together; more than ever they were umbilically linked in a circular relationship where each was simultaneously father and son to the other.

THE DOMESTIC TRAGEDY

During the seventies, the store in the Rue de la Lune was closed, and then the business was sold. The small, semi-prefabricated house in Vaux-sur-Seine, which had been a place where Corinne could relax once a week, had gradually been abandoned, and then sold. At first, Vidal and Corinne had taken the train and walked up the hill to get to their plot of land, but they found the walk more and more tiring, and it was usually Henri, Corinne's youngest son, who drove them there and brought them back by car. Finally, Corinne sold her land in 1976.

Vidal still leaves every morning to go and roam freely on his way to the Sentier, but in the afternoon he stays in the apartment. After the customary ten-minute Vidalian snore in an armchair, Vidal and Corinne watch television, read, talk, or argue. Vidal waits for dinner time, looks at his watch, makes up his mind a little after 5 o'clock to alert Poulette; she resists indignantly, and then, defeated, goes off to the kitchen as 6 o'clock approaches. After watching the news, he is quick to go to bed. He still sleeps extremely well and falls asleep almost as soon as he gets into bed. Corinne's insomnia is worse and worse, she reads *Le Monde* almost from cover to cover, takes up a book, gets out of bed, goes to the sitting room, stands at the window, and sometimes stays up or awake until very late in the night, finally falling asleep exhausted at about 4 o'clock in the morning.

She is increasingly irritable, reprimanding and rebuking him about the dirt and the mess he makes in the apartment, which she cleans frantically, and the jokey replies Vidal makes in an attempt to calm her irritate Corinne even more. She is less and less willing to join in with his playful teasing, and laughs increasingly rarely at his jokes.

Meals have become a permanent source of conflict. Not only does he constantly urge her to prepare them sooner, but she keeps a constant eye on him to make sure he sticks to his diet. Vidal has had a few bouts of high blood pressure, and the cardiologist has prescribed a salt-free diet, a limited quantity of wine, etc. He does what he can to cheat, helps himself to more wine furtively, and provokes her nagging. Vidal steals food from the refrigerator, makes himself bread and butter, eats candy and crystallized fruit in secret; he has hidden a bottle of Benedictine on the highest shelf of a closet, by the toilet. After his very weak cup of coffee, he goes to the bathroom to urinate; while Corinne is busy with the washing up, he takes down the bottle of Benedictine and has a good slug or two from the bottle, which fills him with immense satisfaction. One time, he is caught by his son: "Dad!" "I'm only wetting my lips," replies Vidal smoothly.

Corinne's suffocations, oppressions and ailments have become more frequent. She has had an operation on her other eye, and she has dental problems. She wants Vidal to recognize the seriousness of her ills and the intensity of her suffering. Whenever he complains of a pain or some minor injury, she explodes. "But that's nothing, Vidal, compared to what I suffer!" She consults Dr. Milanolo very frequently; the examinations do not reveal any heart problem or lesion of the organs, but Milanolo recognizes that she nevertheless suffers terribly "from her nerves." He recommends outings and vacations. But the trips and vacations only calm her for a time, and are less and less effective.

The crises of depression have become crises of her rejection of Vidal. She can no longer bear him. He makes the situation worse when he tries to calm her: either he says, "But Poulette, you ought to be the happiest woman in the world," which exasperates her, or else he answers all her reproaches mechanically: "Yes, Poulette." His son tells him again and again that Corinne is suffering from unconscious guilt feelings, as a direct result of their marriage, but Vidal, who has never felt any guilt in his life, would rather believe that she is trying to get rid of him now that he is old and has no more money. During the worst crises, when he is as ever preoccupied with the meal, and she has less and less appetite, and less and less desire to cook, she shouts at him: "Oh, go to a restaurant, Vidal!" Vidal doesn't like going to restaurants on his own, and he is too fond of Corinne's cooking, because she makes what he likes and what agrees with him.

When things get too bad, Vidal telephones Edgar and begs him to come over. Edgar understands the problem that Corinne is suffering from. He rebukes Vidal, and Vidal is all the more willing to accept this reprimand because its aim is to soothe Corinne by satisfying her. Vidal then makes a solemn promise in front of his son never to make Corinne suffer again, and the whole scenario is repeated the following day. Sometimes, Corinne asks Vidal to leave the apartment. Edgar advises him, in these cases, to leave for a few days, to give things time to settle down. But Vidal cannot bear this idea and says: "She needs me, I can't leave her." After an especially serious crisis, Edgar succeeds in convincing his father to go to a hotel, and to ask for news of Corinne only through his intermediary. The next day, however, Vidal wants to go back home, and his son manages to dissuade him. Vidal has his niece Liliane phone Edgar: "How can you encourage your father to let himself be turned out of his home?" Corinne, for her part, is beginning to calm down, and Edgar thinks that the situation is evolving favorably. He thinks that his father should let his presence be desired rather than imposing himself. But, during their morning phone call on the third day, Vidal is at the end of his tether, and explodes. "You idiot!" he shouts, seeing again in his fifty-year old son the dim-witted child of 10 to 15. He goes back home, and the drama begins again. His son is suddenly afflicted by a digestive blockage, he feels like vomiting and succumbs to a high fever. He knows that he can do nothing to prevent the tragedy: Vidal wants to stay, when he ought to leave; he needs to escape, but his chains will not let him.

When Vidal and Corinne are alone, the apartment in the Rue Laugier is even more reminiscent of a mortuary because everything in it is clean, tidy, and polished to a shine. Visits from the children and grandchildren have become less frequent. Edgar is often away from Paris. Only Henri comes regularly, does odd jobs for them, shops, and drives them around in his car. Corinne has gradually abandoned the Salonician custom of preparing several dishes in advance in case of unexpected visitors. Little by little, she has also stopped making the *sfongatticos* of spinach or eggplant, the cheese *pastellicos*, and the veal and lamb *keftes*, of which she always used to keep a portion in reserve for her children and Edgar. The ritual games in which Vidal would pretend to want some of the portion kept for his son, eliciting Corinne's indignant protests, are a thing of the past.

MOMENTS OF RESPITE

And yet there are still moments, indeed periods, of respite, receptivity, communication and pleasure. The outside world comes into the apartment via a thorough reading of *Le Monde* and watching the televised news. They argue and take opposing sides; Vidal is a fatalist, and continues to approve and congratulate all the successive Presidents of the Republic, whereas Corinne feels close to the people, and becomes indignant about the privileges, abuses and prodigious spending of the State. On one occasion, she even writes to Giscard d'Estaing, telling him that if he wants to balance the French budget, all he has to do is stop holdng receptions at the Elysée.

There are also outings to restaurants, at the invitation of one of their children. On these days, Vidal is very happy, becomes impatient, and starts waiting for the host's car long before it is due to arrive at the door of his building. At the restaurant, he hastily consults the menu, asks for bread while he waits, is in a hurry to order, makes his order first, asks that he be served as quickly as possible, and then, once the order has been taken, keeps his eyes on the waiter, and, at the first opportunity, calls him over to ask for his dish. As soon as his food arrives, he lowers his face over the plate and eats voraciously, as if suffering from starvation, with the total concentration of an animal. He no longer hears or sees anything, but, from time to time, obeying the same instinct as his hominid ancestors two million years before, prior to the invention of fire, his eyes scan the visual field, as if to check that there is no enemy present who might come and snatch his meal from him, and continue to do so until he has devoured every scrap. Although by now he has begun to relax a little, he still waits impatiently for the main dish. Only when this dish is finished does he lift up his head again, beaming, and look around him, first at the others' plates, to see if there is anything left to steal here or there; he drinks down a big mouthful of wine, and joins in the conversation, taking advantage of a moment's distraction on the part of Corinne or his son to steal something from their plates. With his eyes, he repeatedly indicates his empty glass and the bottle of wine, and, when Corinne and Edgar tell him to stop drinking, declares with dignity: "But this is a Republic, after all." If anyone reproaches him for having thrown himself on his food, forgetting everything else, he gravely recites a Turkish proverb: "The eye sees, the soul desires." If his son tells him off, he recites an old Salonician proverb: "*Se alevantaron los pepinos i aharvaron a los bagtchavanes*": up rose the cucumbers and beat their gardeners.

There are also big parties; he reigns as joyful patriarch over the wedding banquets of Irène and Véronique, at Violette's house, where some of his birthdays are also celebrated. A month in advance, Vidal starts reminding his son that it is his birthday on March 14, so that he will make preparations for the meal and presents. Edgar is not someone who remembers birthdays, but Johanne, who adores birthdays and presents, never forgets. There is a wonderful seventy-ninth birthday in a restaurant, in 1973, and a big party for his eightieth birthday at Edgar's place in the Rue des Blancs-Manteaux; the party after the meal is recorded, and on the tape Nona's joyful laughter can be heard, intermingled with that of Vidal, Irène, her husband Daniel, Véronique, Johanne and Edgar. Vidal sings *Les Volets clos* [Closed shutters] with great emotion:

Comme aux beaux jours de nos 20 ans
[Like in those happy days when we were 20],

in which the narrator, as an older man, comes back to the house where his love affair had taken place *Sur la place Où s'efface Quoi qu'on fasse Toute trace* . . . [Nothing there In the square Every trace

Has been effaced]
and where
Je croyais presque entendre
Ta voix tendre
Murmurer:
"*Viens plus près.*"

[I could almost hear
Your voice so dear
Murmuring to me
"Come closer."

He sings the song again, and this time everyone joins in; then Vidal, followed by the others, sings *Les Feuilles mortes*. More songs follow; there are some fairly recent ones that Vidal loves, like *Zon, zon, zon*, or *Elle avait des bagues à chaque doigt*. Vidal asks Irène to sing *La Complainte des amants infidèles*, which she has been singing since she was six years old, always repeating the same childish mistake.

Bonnes gens
Ecoutez la triste ritourné-et-leu
Des amants errants
En proie à leurs tourments
Parce qu'ils ont aimé
Des femmes infidé-et-leus
Qui les ont trompés
Mignomininieusement . . . [78]
[Good people
Hear the sad refrain
Of lovers who roam
Consumed with pain
Because they loved
Unfaithful women
Who deceived them
Mignonminiously . . .]

They go back in time, and do *Sombreros et Mantilles*, then songs from the turn of the century, including *Tout nu*, which Perchicot used to sing:

On m'a trouvé tout nu
Auprès de Notre-Dame
Dans la rue Saint-Martin
[I was naked when they found me
Over by Notre-Dame
In the Rue Saint-Martin]

Then there is a glorious joint rendition of *Le rêve passe*. Vidal and Edgar sing a pathetic version of *Les Deux Ménétriers*, which Pepo Beressi had taught them:

Sur des noirs chevaux sans mors
Sans selle sans étriers
Par le royaume des morts
Vont les deux ménétriers . . .
[On black horses without bridles
Without saddles, without stirrups
Through the kingdom of the dead

Ride the two minstrels . . .]

The two minstrels ask the dead if they would like to live again, and they all answer in unison with an enthusiastic: "YES!" But, say the two minstrels, "if you want to live again, you will have to love again." And the dead, unanimously, cry with horror: "NOOOOOO!"

They follow this with Italian songs, like *Les Papaveri*, and then Vidal digs up *La Bella Gigudi* from his past:

Andeva a piedi de Lodi a Milano
Per encontrare la bella Gigudi . . .
[I walked all the way from Lodi to Milan
To see the lovely Gigudi . . .]

Then comes another song from before the First World War, *Sur la route de Florence*:

Mirela, Mirela, ma jolie,
Je reviens pour te retrouver.
Tu es la plus belle d'Italie.
Je reviens t'apporter le bonheur.
Mais toi, m'as-tu gardé ton cœur?
[Mirela, Mirela, my pretty one,
I'm coming back for you.
You're the loveliest girl in Italy,
I'm coming back to make you happy.
But tell me, do you still love me?]

Vidal goes on to the "second catastrophe," in which the poor exile learns that Mirela died six years before. Then he recites Flambeau's speech, from *L'Aiglon*:

Jean-Pierre Séraphin Flambeau, dit Flambart,
Né de papa breton et de maman picarde . . .
[Jean-Pierre Séraphin Flambeau, Flambart they call me,
Father was a Breton, Mother was from Picardy . . .]

At Irène's request, he sings a Turkish song of nostalgic beauty, whose lyrics he translates:

The river has overflowed
Into my garden.
I have seen so many troubles.
The telegraph wires could not take my troubles away.
A pen could not take them away.

Then he goes on to *Jul on para*, an Ottoman version of *La Violettera*:

Ten cents a rose
A little girl is selling her roses
Come buy my roses . . .

And finally, the Turkish story about an illiterate soldier, who asks the hodja to read him the letter that his fiancée Eminen has sent him. The hodja says:

Baban salam edior
Aman salam edior
Hodja salam Edior
Vidal translates line by line, with emphasis:
Your father salutes you
Your mother salutes you
The hodja salutes you . . . .
The soldier then says to the hodja: "I beg you, don't deceive me, tell me about my Eminem." The hodja doesn't know what to say, because he has read that Eminem is dead; all he can do is repeat that his father, his mother and the hodja salute him, and the soldier realizes what has happened.

"But that's dreadfully sad!" shudder Irène and Véronique, laughing uproariously.

And the party goes on, they laugh, become emotional, laugh because they are emotional, become emotional because they are laughing together. Thus, there are some wonderful parties with Vidal the patriarch and super-Papou at their center.

Whenever Corinne begins to sink into her depressive cycle, Vidal, obeying Dr. Milanolo's prescription, persuades her to travel. It is increasingly difficult for him to convince Corinne, who, afflicted by the atony of depression, no longer has an appetite for anything. However, eventually, after everybody has played his part in the effort to persuade her, she agrees to go, and he makes train and hotel reservations. Then they leave for Monte-Carlo to stay with Daisy and Sam, or for country guesthouses, including one in Normandy that they are very fond of, or on a cruise on the Rhine, or to take a cure in Italy, or to Switzerland, to Lake Leman, or to a hotel or seniors' residence in Alsace or the South of France. They have no trouble getting to know their dinner companions, they make friends, and they receive cards in German and Italian asking to see them again. They charm everyone they meet with their gaiety, their curiosity about everything, their warmth and their mutual teasing. They also go and stay with Edgar in the house that he has rented in Ménerbes. On one occasion, Edgar and Johanne take Corinne with them to Naples and Salerno, obliging Vidal to allow her to go alone. She immediately comes back to life, just as she had come back to life in California, and this time she has a chance to go out in the evening and stay up late. She spends a rapturous night in Naples, watching Edgar and Johanne dancing until the early morning at a friend's apartment.

During the good times, when they show their bright side, they inspire an almost filial affection in the people they meet. It was like this for Colette Neagle, in La Jolla; she lovingly adopted them as parents ("I love you as if you were my Mom and Dad," she wrote to them). It was the same for Jean Récanati and his wife Suzanne. Jean Récanati was the younger brother of a high-school friend of Edgar's, whom Edgar had recruited at the beginning of 1943 into his resistance movement; he was arrested and deported, and he died in Mauthausen. The boys' parents, of Salonician origin, were deported and killed in Auschwitz. Jean was the sole survivor of his family. At the Liberation, he had joined the communist party, had become deputy editor-in-chief of *L'Humanité*, had left the party, married, and had two sons who came of age in the seventies; one was a militant in the communist League, the other a university professor.

However, two crises of misery brought an end to their friendships with Colette and with the Récanatis. Every time she came to France, Colette was invited to lunch or dinner at Vidal and Corinne's. One of these trips, towards the end of the seventies, coincided with a period of deep depression for Corinne, and Vidal told Colette on the telephone that he was sorry but they could neither receive her nor see her. Colette felt rejected and broke off the relationship. Shortly afterwards, Edgar organized a meal at a restaurant with his parents and the Récanatis. All the way through the meal, the Récanatis looked gloomy and said nothing. Vidal and Edgar wondered what had offended them. In fact, their son Michel had just brutally disowned them, and declared that he was going to kill himself; he had then disappeared without a trace. Two years later, Jean Récanati died of a heart attack and his wife belatedly discovered that Michel had also died.

Lastly, and towards the end, two young female relatives from Grenoble, Danielle and Nicole Angel, whose grandmother was first cousin to the Beressi sisters, also fell in love with Vidal and Corinne, and took great delight in their company.

Vidal was still always ready to turn into super-Papou and Corinne to turn into super-Nona. They could be radiant, and inspire spontaneous admiration and feelings of filiality. Sometimes, Corinne's joie de vivre would return in the midst of her torments, while Vidal's joie de vivre, which had never gone away, was only temporarily darkened by his domestic torments. Thus, through so many years of trials and suffering, he remained paradoxically happy. And the more he advanced into his eighties, the more his unchanged youthfulness amazed people. Danielle Angel writes, "there was nothing ponderous or methodical about him, but he gave the impression that he understood everything, and had a profound knowledge of things . . . and he had retained an immense capacity to find wonder in the world. What enthusiasm he had! I often felt old compared to him."

DREAM

Vidal had a visceral attachment to Corinne, and was incapable of tearing himself away from her. Although he dreamed of freeing himself from his domestic hell, he would not consider living alone. He even refused his son's offer to go and move in with him. He was only willing to make his escape if another woman had already accepted him beforehand. On one occasion, he had made advances to a lady who was widowed or divorced, but when she found out that he was married, the scrupulous woman refused to go any further until he obtained a divorce, whereas Vidal was only prepared to consider the opposite procedure.

He also had designs on Corinne's cousin Marguerite, who had been a widow since 1956, and was 62 years old at the time that he began to make his advances. In spite of the fact that Corinne and Marguerite were very close, he suggested to Marguerite that they could live together. Marguerite's first reaction was one of shocked incredulity; she told him that she could not take her cousin's husband, and then she said that she could not consider such a thing unless he and Corinne were already separated. Vidal did not give up. Irène was taken into her grandfather's confidence, and he asked for her encouragement: "I remember how moved I felt when I looked at my young eighty-year-old Papou, with his luminous blue eyes, his beautiful hair, his playful expectations of life."

Shortly after sharing this secret, Vidal saw a forty-five entitled *I'd do anything for a turn in your bed*. He sent it by mail to Marguerite and waited. When after five days he had received no reply, he called her: "So, what do you say?" "How dare you, Vidal!" cried Marguerite indignantly, and hung up. Irène told him off: "For God's sake, Papou, you only need to look at cousin Marguerite to see that she's the last person you should send something like that to, you should've asked me first, we'd have gone for something classical, sophisticated." Vidal was not discouraged: perhaps he thought his tenacity would make Marguerite give in. In 1975, she told him on the telephone: "Let me think about it for a few days." She died before having had time to think about it, of coronary thrombosis, at the age of 65. Vidal was 81.

At around the same time, he was advancing on the Turin front. His sister had introduced him to a close friend of hers there, a widow called Mrs. Ortona. When Mathilde had come to live in Paris, Vidal had gone to Turin to sort out her affairs for her, and he had invited Mrs. Ortona to lunch. Afterwards, he had written to Mrs. Ortona saying that he wanted to come to Turin and meet her again on a more intimate footing. Mrs. Ortona was scandalized, and wrote to Mathilde; she said that she was very offended to have been treated as if she were a loose woman, when she was a respectable widow. Mathilde reprimanded her brother, who was very annoyed that Mrs. Ortona had betrayed him in this way, and things went no further until Mathilde's death, in December 1976.

At that time, Vidal wrote a very dignified letter to Mrs. Ortona to let her know the sad news, and to tell her that he hoped to see her, so that he could speak to her about his sister, during a trip he was due to make to Turin in the near future. Mrs. Ortona replied that she was very sad and would have been glad to meet Vidal when he was in Turin at the time that he had mentioned, but informed him that she had already made plans to go and visit one of her sons, who was married to an Israeli woman, on a kibbutz in Rehovot. Vidal replied that he would like to meet her anyway, even in Rehovot. Mrs. Ortona's reply to him was very distant and evasive:

Dear Mr. Vidal,
I regret that I will not be able to meet you in Turin between the dates of 15 and 20 February, nor in Rehovot. I do not yet have any precise plans: when I leave Rehovot, I may go to Switzerland. Before planning your trip to Israel, I would advise you to consult your family first, since I regret that I cannot be of service to you.
   Please accept my most cordial regards.
   Silvia Ortona

In March 1977, another crisis flared up with Corinne, and for the first time Vidal resolved to leave and never come back. At the time, his son was staying for two weeks with a friend in Camogli, a little Ligurian port near Genoa. Vidal left for Turin, with the pretext that he needed to deal with the unresolved question of the backpayment of Mathilde's pension. In Turin, he learned at Mrs. Ortona's house that she planned to celebrate Passover at the kibbutz where her son was living, and he managed to get hold of the kibbutz's telephone number. He telephoned his son at once, from Turin, saying that he needed to see him urgently. This childlike father wanted his son to play the paternal role of making a marriage proposal on his son's behalf. Edgar invited his father to come to Camogli at once. Vidal arrived, having quite made up his mind that he would not return to the Rue Laugier. Edgar, who for the first time saw his father leaving on his own initiative, and not because he had been turned out, believed in the firmness of his decision. Vidal wanted to move either to Livorno or to Cannes, where he would be near to his friend Matarasso. But he had not quite given up his dream of La Ortona yet, and wanted his son to telephone the kibbutz at lunchtime, in order to attest to the seriousness and honorability of his intentions. Edgar did not feel able to make this pre-matrimonial advance; he argued to his father that Mrs. Ortona's letter and behavior did not leave any room for hope. But Vidal did not like to be beaten, even though it was clearly a lost cause, and he telephoned the kibbutz himself. Mrs. Ortona was not available, and he could not explain what he wanted to people who spoke neither French nor Italian. And so he gave up his dream of Mrs. Ortona (although afterwards he continued to fantasize about bringing the matter to a happy conclusion, until he learned that she had married a Dutchman). Nevertheless, at least for the time being, he stuck to his decision not to go home. The second day went by peacefully. Vidal was still planning to live in Livorno or perhaps Cannes. Edgar advised him not to settle in Livorno, where he knew nobody; it would be better for him to move to Cannes, because it was closer to Paris, and his friend lived there. Vidal reserved a seat on the train from Genoa to Cannes two days later. However, on the third morning, Edgar found his father calling Corinne on the telephone, "Poulette, Poulette," he was saying, in a voice full of emotion, with tears streaming down his face, "I'm with Edgar, he doesn't want me to leave you all alone, he wants me to come home to you tomorrow." "But you can stay longer in Italy if you need to, Vidal, take your time, I'm coping very well on my own." "No, no, Poulette . . . ."

His son reproached him for his lack of willpower, for having made up another story, and so forth. Vidal let this Beressi storm pass in silence, since his *bovo* son was incapable of understanding the changeful nature of love. Edgar drove him to Genoa station. There was a very long line in front of the counter where Vidal had to change his reservation and his ticket. He pushed his way through the crowd, brandishing his cane, and shouting at the top of his voice: "*sono vecchio, sono vecchio*" ("I'm an old man, I'm an old man"): the crowd parted like the Red Sea before the Jews, and Vidal arrived in front of the counter where the change was made for him.

Would Vidal have left Corinne if one of the three ladies he had designs on had accepted his propositions? Or was he merely pretending to imagine that he was capable of leaving her? What is certain is that he did not want to live alone, and would not entertain the idea. As Danielle Angel said, "he was a man who loved being married." He needed a woman at home; even as a widower, he had never been without a home, and had never really been without a woman either.

THE MEDAL, AT LAST

All the torments of the seventies could not discourage Vidal from stubbornly pursuing his efforts to obtain a decoration. The medal of the City of Paris had disappointed him: it did not have a ribbon with it, which meant that he could not wear it. So Vidal began the quest for a real decoration with a ribbon and a medal. The very absence of any full-time business occupation encouraged him to devote himself to this quest. He did not spend all his time working on it, of course, but he did apply himself to the task with perseverance.

At the beginning of 1972, Vidal writes to his representative, Jacques Dominati; since he never misses either a movie screening or a buffet when Dominati offers one to his esteemed voters, he has made himself known to the representative, has drawn attention to his long years of loyalty to Paul Reynaud, and is seen by Dominati as a patriarchal voter, a veritable burgrave of the 2nd arrondissement's electoral offices. In this letter, Vidal is hoping for a decoration. Since Dominati does not know (Vidal did not want to tell him for fear of weakening his position) that he already has the medal of the City of Paris, he suggests it to him as a well-earned tribute, for "there are not so many citizens of your merit that we should be prevented from making the effort, on the occasion that you mention of your fifty years in business, to honor you as you deserve."

Vidal informs him that he has already been decorated with the medal of the City of Paris, and in a letter dated April 19, 1972, Jacques Dominati undertakes to support Vidal's promotion to the Order of Merit. He calls the prefect's attention to "Mr. Vidal Nahoum's merits and qualities as a partic- ipant in the growth of the French economy," and describes him as "assiduous in attending the social functions at the 2nd arrondissement's local council." Moreover, Vidal's virtues are proven by the fact that he has already obtained the medal of the City of Paris.

An intense correspondence now begins. On April 28, 1972, the prefect intends to give "more particular attention" to the representative's interven- tion, and the representative transmits a copy of this letter to Vidal. Vidal makes contact with the representative again, no doubt in May, for the latter reminds the prefect of Vidal's merits and entitlements, and in a letter dated June 23, 1972 the prefect confirms his favorable intentions with regard to the candidate. Vidal writes to his representative on October 12 to thank him for his letter, tells him of his expectation of a favorable result, and concludes:

> I ceased my activity as a businessman fifty years after I established myself in the 2nd arrondissement, to which I remain and will always remain attached. For your refer- ence, I include two photocopied letters from my suppliers.

In January 1973, Vidal becomes impatient, and writes to the prefect to find out in which Ministry his file is waiting for attention:

> I am due to have an operation on my eyes, and will delay the surgery if I can find out when I will be able to know if I have been nominated. The operation that awaits me may have an uncertain outcome, since I will be 79 years old in a few weeks' time, and I would very much like to be alive and well if I am to have the joy of receiving this distinction.

However, Vidal is very disappointed not to see his name in the Merit Honors list at the end of January 1973. Vidal expresses this disappointment to Jacques Dominati, who declares himself to be "extremely and disagree- ably surprised." Since Vidal has asked him if he should delay his operation to wait for the next award list, Jacques Dominati admits that he cannot advise him to do so, given that the next roll of honor will not be published until July 14, and given also that he is not assured of success. So Vidal uses the cataract operation he is due to undergo to soften up Dominati, and at the same time he uses the wait for news as a pretext to put off the operation, which terrifies him. Dominati makes contact with the prefect again on February 6, 1973, and receives another, very positive reply, on the 22nd of the same month. After this, the representative writes to Vidal, on the 23rd, that he thinks victory is more or less assured. In the meantime, Jacques Dominati is re-elected, and on the very next day, Vidal leaves a short letter of congratulation on his "brilliant re-election" at the Boulevard de Sébastopol. He declares himself quite prepared to join a friendly meeting of the support committee. Dominati, spurred on by this letter, makes a further attempt to sway the prefect, who lets him know by his letter of March 30 that a favorable file has been transmitted to the Ministry of Commerce and Craftsmanship.

When he sees this letter, Vidal telephones the Ministry of Commerce, and learns that his name will not be included in the next honors list, nor in the one after that. He writes to Dominati on May 29 to inform him and to request

> your direct intervention to the Minister, which could make my file stand out from the rest. I am writing to appeal to your kindness towards me; I will soon be 80 years old, and as I am obliged to undergo some surgical operations, it would give me great pleasure to see my nomination succeed.

The representative replies that the change of government has resulted in the departure of the Minister who would have signed the nomination. However, he adds,

> I have the reputation, perhaps deservedly, of being tenacious. In your particular case, my dear Mr. Nahoum, I will do my best to deserve this reputation.

Jacques Dominati is elected president of the municipal council of Paris on June 14, 1973. This glory reflects on Vidal, who takes advantage of it to remind him of his request:

> I was very glad to learn of your brilliant re-election as Prime Minister of Paris, and expressed my joy to you by telegraphing my sincere congratulations to you this morning.
> We in the 2nd arrondissement were very proud to have had Mr. Paul Reynaud as our representative, and I am quite sure that we will be even prouder of you, my dear Mr. Dominati.
> Yours . . .
> P.S. Many thanks for you kind letter of June 6; I am hoping for a favorable response from you.

On July 7, Vidal sends another letter of congratulations after a dinner and debate which he attended with Corinne. Vidal encloses in his letter two posters for Paul Reynaud, which are forty years old, with the note: "On these posters, only the name needs changing."

Another letter on August 23 asks him again to intercede with the Minister:

> You wrote to me on June 6 that you have the reputation of being tenacious, and I am delighted to hear it and I am pleased about it for my own sake.

But the new intervention comes to nothing. We have no more letters between Dominati and Vidal on the subject after this letter of August 1973. However, Vidal does not give up. Jacques Dominati will become Secretary of State in the Ministry of War Veterans and Victims, and Vidal will remind him of his existence. The Minister will take advantage of an honors list intended for Algerian muslims and *pieds-noirs* to slip Vidal in amongst them. He is finally declared Knight of the national Order of Merit on December 19, 1979. It is very important to Vidal that the Minister should personally present him with the decoration. He encloses tracts and texts by Paul Reynaud from the thirties with his request. Jacques Dominati accepts by letter on January 23, 1980. The ceremony takes place in the reception rooms of the Ministry, in the Rue de Babylone, at the beginning of 1980. The family is invited, and the survivors from the older generations meet the new generations. Cousins are reunited. Edgar has invited those of his friends who know Vidal. The presence of people with famous names makes him happy. The Minister's speech presents an image of Vidal to which he listens with credulity and amazement:

"I would like first of all to speak of your youth, Mr. Nahoum, because it bears witness to your indissoluble attachment to France and to Freedom.

At your birth, you were, in reality, a subject of the Sublime Porte. But your father, Knight of the "Order of Léopold," attaché to the Belgian consulate in Salonica and representative of Bakou oil, gave you a solidly francophile education.

For that reason, when the allied army in the East landed in Salonica in 1915, you at once decided to sign up under the French flag.

You were afterwards posted to Marseilles in 1916, where you served until you were demobilized in 1919.

It was then that, as they say down there, you "came up" to Paris to open a business in the Rue d'Aboukir, already in the 2nd arrondissement.

In 1925, being aware of the need for responsible businessmen to participate in civic life, you became a member of the board of the treasury for the 2nd arrondissement's schools.

You were naturalized in 1931, and subsequently assisted the representatives of the 2nd arrondissement; I refer to Léopold Bellan, Paul Reynaud, Legaret, and finally myself and our friend Abel Thomas.

Your profound knowledge of people, problems and the Parisian social environment has made a useful contribution. Your remarks and suggestions, enriched by your long experience, are always welcome.

In the same way, the confidence that all those around you have in you, and particularly your friends and fellow businessmen, means that you are a friend to whom one listens and a model one wishes to imitate.

It is indeed your skill in the prudent management of a medium-sized firm, in spite of all the uncertainities and economic risks you have faced, that has earned you this unanimous acknowledgement of merit.

I would also like to salute your wife and your children, of whom, I know, you are very fond, and of whom you are justifiably proud.

It is for all these reasons that the President of the Republic has decided, at my behest, to award you the grade of Knight in the national Order of Merit."

Vidal listens, both stunned and convinced by what he has heard. As they are leaving, his son reminds him that the Minister has forgotten to mention his acts of heroism at Verdun and on the Marne. "Don't be nasty," replies his father.[79]

Nineteen Eighty-Six

Vidal was 76 in 1970. He ate well, drank well, and had no digestive problems, apart from occasional bouts of uninterrupted, spasmodic belching, which had begun after Luna's death, and which returned in periods of deep unhappiness and dissatisfaction. However, he felt the urge to urinate more and more frequently, and the pressure of this need would sometimes cause him to piss against a wall, in the street, which he would do without any feeling of shame, because it was a natural urge. Then he suffered a recurrence of his inability to urinate, which lasted twenty-four hours. He was terrified, but he took some medicine, and the normal flow resumed. The doctors advised him to have prostrate surgery, and Corinne encouraged him to have the operation, with Edgar's backing, but Vidal was fundamentally hostile to even the most minor surgical intervention on his body. He was victorious in resistance, and he did not have the prostrate operation! He had one or two subsequent urinary blockages, which were resolved with medicine. Vidal carried on living with his very frequent urges to urinate, which were a great nuisance to him if they arose when he was in the métro or on the bus.

Vidal had been wearing a hernia bandage since the sixties. Everybody had advised him to have an operation on his hernia, but he limited himself to changing the belt when the pressure was too great. In this case also, he was victorious in resistance.

As for his heart, Vidal occasionally had high blood pressure. Sometimes, he felt that his heart was beating strangely, and would go and see a cardiologist, who was a friend of his son's. Since he was always worried before the electrocardiogram, he would get Edgar to accompany him. The electros were fine, and Dr. Fortin recommended a special diet and a healthier lifestyle: he should eliminate salt, and take less fat and alcohol. Corinne took charge of this prescription: the diet allowed her simultaneously to care for, protect and bully Vidal. This explains why he was always impatient for his son to invite them to out to restaurants, where, in the festive atmosphere, Corinne would tolerate a few misdemeanours. He knew very well that Corinne always had a very small appetite and would not finish her dishes, which guaranteed him at least a meal and a half. Fortunately, he was not keen on cold meats, sauces or spicy food; that is, the food that was bad for him, and his excesses did him no harm. He also enjoyed the game with Corinne, and the pleasure of cheating, not only when he was not found out, but also when he was. It would amuse him to deny the evidence, saying: "Vicious slander!" And he would turn melodramatically to his son: "Go on, my son, go on, flesh of my flesh, avenge me!"

He still walked in a very sprightly manner; of course, he felt increasingly weary when climbing stairs, but he remained a good walker on the flat and did not hesitate, when there were public transport strikes, to walk to the Sentier to collect his mail.

In fact, it was his sight that would give him trouble at the beginning of the seventies. Both eyes were weaker, and one of them had become almost blind; a cataract operation was inevitable. Vidal mentions the forthcoming surgery in his letters to his representative in 1972, but in reality he resists the prospect fiercely. Corinne, for her part, fortified by her own operation, which has given her back her sight, and further fortified by the undisputed authority of Professor Offret, who is prepared to perform the operation on Vidal, nags him to do it incessantly. Edgar applies pressure on his side. Vidal mulishly resists. Nevertheless, his sight is weakening irremediably. Since Vidal refuses to resign himself to giving up roaming around Paris every morning as he goes about his business, he has taken to using a white stick, which allows him to part the crowd, get on the bus first, and cross the street authoritatively while casting disdainful glances at the cars, which he can only just make out. The pressure increases, and Corinne and Edgar finally get him to promise to have the operation at the beginning of 1974. Of course, he has managed to gain (or waste) a lot of time.

Vidal does not choose Professor Offret. He prefers a young woman, the daughter of a man his son knows. He imagines that a woman will be more gentle than a man, and that a young person will be more up to date than an old one, whose hand would probably be less steady. He is admitted to the Quinze-Vingts hospital in September 1974. Vidal does not want to be put to sleep, and they promise he will not be, but break their promise. When he awakes from the anaesthetic, he sees his son and his granddaughter Irène with his unbandaged eye. Realizing that he has been put to sleep against his will, he sits up and shakes an accusatory fist at Edgar: "Traitor, three times a traitor, you let your father be anaesthetized." He is forbidden to get up and urinate, and is given a bedpan fitted with a tube. He tries in vain. He can only piss standing up. His son tries to stop him, but Vidal feels an imperious, irresistible urge. His son panics: "You're not allowed to, I'll call the doctors."

Vidal gets up, snarling at his son with the insult of supreme exasperation: "Idiot!"

The operation has not been a complete success. Vidal only retrieves a few tenths of the vision in his eye, and it soon becomes urgent to operate on the other. Vidal has had the experience of the operation, but also that of the anaesthetic, which he does not want to go through again. He continues to resist for three more years, then finally gives in. He agrees to go to the Hôtel-Dieu hospital, changes his mind, and opts for a private clinic. His operation is performed at the Floréal clinic, in Lilas. This time, it is a complete success.

Therefore, in 1980, at the age of 86, Vidal is in bettter physical condition than he was in 1972. He can see clearly again, and can move around Paris freely once more. His hernia is more or less manageable with a belt. The state of his bladder has not worsened. He simply feels tired in the evenings, and wants to go to bed early. He avoids the métro because of the stairs, and takes the bus instead. But he is fit, with no lesions or disabilities. He still holds his back straight when walking, has kept all of his hair, his lively blue eyes, and prompt reflexes, and it is in the last years of his old age that he is most radiantly youthful.

XII

The Last Years

THE LOW PRESSURE-ZONE

The apartment in the Rue Laugier increasingly resembles a low-pressure zone in which cyclones form. Order, cleanliness and emptiness reign. Corinne no longer cooks more than the minimum for Vidal, hardly eats at all herself and is irritated when at every meal he urges her: "Eat, Poulette, it'll do you good." Vidal suffers her silences, and puts up with her reproaches. In spite of everything, eating and drinking put him in a good mood, as does his little daily swig of Benedictine. Corinne's afflictions continue in uninterrupted succession. Vidal is concerned for her, but at the same time he has become accustomed to it. He is fatalistic, and waits, hoping that the "Good Lord" will come and help him. He is very devoted to Corinne, but at the same time his main preoccupation is his daily meal, which he insists that she prepare for him whatever her condition. She urges him to eat lunch out, but he refuses obstinately. She wants him to leave, but she continues to protect him.

The explosive crises of rejection occur more and more frequently, leaving him completely at a loss. He bows his back beneath the storm, saying: "Yes, Poulette," or "I'm very sorry" in a tone of studied politeness, which exasperates her. He is increasingly dependent on her, and his dreams of emancipation have frayed and faded since Marguerite's death and Mrs. Ortona's refusal. His only dream, when he can take no more, is of an escape or return to Livorno or Salonica.

He feels increasingly tired. On September 17, 1981, he writes to his son, who is in San Francisco:

> I have been to see Dr. Milanolo about my tiredness, he can't find anything to worry about. He wants me to have blood and urine tests done. Yesterday, I saw Dr. Quercy, the cardiologist; Aunt Corinne came with me. Detailed examination, cardiograms, etc.; he left us 100 percent reassured and gave me some new pills for my tiredness and breathlessness, and advised me to have lung x-rays done in a few weeks' time.
> I was very pleased with both consultations, and now I'm not in the least worried. Both of them advised me not to travel or tire myself too much; I'm keeping an eye on myself and so is Aunt Corinne.

Two months later:

I feel increasingly weary, though I only go out once a day. I'm seeing the cardiologist next week.

His tiredness worries him; he finds it abnormal, and is afraid that his heart is getting weaker. The visit to the cardiologist temporarily alleviates his concern.

Before every journey, he envisages the possibility of his death, and wants his son to know the number of his bank account, the combination of his safe, and the address of the funeral directors.

It is not his death itself that preoccupies him, but his resting place. In Bagneux cemetery there are two family tombs, one of which is a double one, in the first row, where his father and mother are buried, and the other belonging to the "Hassid-Covo" family, where his sisters Henriette and Mathilde are buried alongside Élie Hassid and Liliane and Mony Covo. At Père-Lachaise, there is a Beressi tomb, where Salomon and Myriam Beressi are buried with their deceased children, Pepo and Luna.

Where should he go? He seems to have agreed with Corinne that they should both be buried at Père-Lachaise, in the Beressi tomb. However, as the situation at the Rue Laugier deteriorates, he no longer has the slightest desire to find himself in the same vault as his two sister-wives. He tells his granddaughter Irène in confidence about the torments the "Beressi sisters" have subjected him to, and of his desire not to be buried with them; he adds, transforming his last sigh into a sigh of relief: "Expiration . . . " then, filling his lungs and letting out the air again with an expression of infinite well-being: "Respiration!" However, he does not dare tell Corinne that he would prefer to be separated from her posthumously.

At one point, probably in 1977, after the death of Mathilde, whom he has buried next to her sister Henriette, he had envisaged having some work done on his parents' tomb in order to make room for one more. Was it for his brother Henri? For himself? The desire to join them was no doubt inhibited by the thought that it would be sacrilege to break open their coffins and move their ashes, and yet he did not imagine that he would be upsetting anyone else, or upsetting Corinne, by taking this decision. He had no desire to be placed in his sisters' tomb; his brother-in-law Élie, whom he had had to put up with out of family solidarity for decades, was in there too, as was Mony, his nephew by marriage, for whom he had never felt any great affection.

He finally found a solution that allowed him to avoid these posthumous difficulties. He decided to donate his body to the schools of medicine, and wrote a letter to this effect on January 19, 1982. In reply, a circular letter informed him that he must first become a member and benefactor of the René-Descartes University and its Center for the donation of bodies, by paying a minimal fee of 350 francs. Before making this payment, Vidal asked for two pieces of information:

Paris, January 29, 1982.
Parisian Center for the donation of bodies.

Dear Professor Hureau,
Thank you for your letter of the 26th of this month, and the enclosed form. In the first days of February, I will send you my contribution to become a member and benefactor.
On the form, I read: "If the body is accepted;" what are the conditions for acceptance?
Furthermore, as far as transport within eighteen hours is concerned, I have been thinking that if it should happen at home, at 7 o'clock in the evening, it would hardly be possible to make the declaration to the town hall until the following morning, after waiting for the report by the doctor from the Public Records Office, and waiting for the chief of police's authorization for the special ambulance. Would it be possible to get there within 18 hours?
I would be grateful if you would clarify this question, and I thank you in advance
. . .

He received a reply on February 2:

. . . Cases where donators' bodies are refused are very rare. In particular, this may happen in the case of people who have died of contagious diseases or whose bodies cannot be transported within the stipulated time limits..
If death occurs in the evening, the family should telephone 260-82-54, and an answerphone message will tell them what to do . . .

On February 17, Vidal received the card identifying him as a donator of his body to the schools of medicine. He prepared a little note, which his son found among his papers:

On the tomb in perpetuity in Bagneux, where my father David David Nahum, deceased in 1920, and my mother Hélène née Frances are resting,

engrave
Their fifth child Vidal
Knight of the Order of Merit
born March 14, 1894
died
has donated his body to science.

Vidal had often spoken to his son about his posthumous concerns, but he had not told him about the steps he had taken to donate his body. It was

Corinne, who did not like the idea, who told Edgar about it, and Edgar instinctively opposed the plan and asked his father to give it up. His father pretended to let himself be talked out of it, but he stuck to his decision.

Irène says: "One day when he wasn't well and I had arranged to visit him, my father entrusted me with the mission of persuading Papou to change his mind. I can see him now sitting in his armchair, smiling and slightly melancholy. I broached the subject with a bit of a lump in my throat: 'So what's all this about leaving your body to science?' Papou's reply is not philosophical, but precise, practical: 'It's easy . . . there's no fee . . . just a telephone call . . . the family doesn't have to bother about the body, or the funeral.' I interrupt him, appalled: 'but can't you see how upsetting that is for your Minou?' 'Oh, your father doesn't understand anything, he's just a child . . . ' Nona goes off to the kitchen to get him a home-made yogurt, like in Salonica. He leans forward and whispers: 'It's not just that, you see, I don't want to be buried with your grandmother Luna and your Nona in the Beressi tomb.' (It is then that Vidal says to her: "Expiration . . . . Respiration!")

By giving his body to be dissected in order to avoid posthumous cohabitations, Vidal revealed a remarkable conception of death. Although he believed that his parents' spirits remained present after their death, and continued to protect him, although he was disgusted by the thought of unsavory sepulchral proximity, although he went when necessary to funerary commemorations, and although he was a deist and talked about the Good Lord, Vidal considered his bodily obliteration with equanimity and was not in the least concerned about a "final resting place;" he felt no need for rites and ceremonies. Although all the religions take care, in their funerary rites, to ensure the proper liberation of the spirit and limit the corruption of the body, Vidal believed that the spirit departed for an invisible sphere whatever happened, naturally, and without any religious help, and that its only function or capacity was to protect its descendants. In this way, Vidal was at once completely materialist and completely spirtualist.

SUPER-PAPOU

Edgar had never ceased to discover Vidal's qualities, and had gradually begun to feel great admiration for his father, but this in no way prevented his mockery of him; on the contrary, the pleasure that his father took in inciting the mockery of those dear to him increased both his son's mockery and his admiration. In Paris, Vidal called his son every morning, and he still expected telegrams and phone calls whenever Edgar was away overseas. He also phoned the mother of Edwige, his son's wife, as well as the administrator at Edgar's center, or anyone else who might have news of him, beginning the conversation with: "Edgar's Dad here." His son was now a sixty-year old, but Vidal never ceased to be the Dad he had always been, both anxious and carefree. He pretended to insist on obedience and liked to remind his son of the scene from a film where the hundred-year-old hero, played by Noël-Noël, tells his eighty-year-old son: "Don't touch your beard." He probably dreamed of being respected by his son in the way that he had respected his own father, but since he was someone for whom teasing a person meant loving him, his son's disrespect pleased him because of its playful and teasing aspect.

Unfortunately, his son was still very often away from Paris, from France and even from Europe. Moreover, beginning in summer 1982, Edgar often spent time away from Paris with the parents of the woman he had recently married: her mother had suffered a heart attack in 1982, and Edwige wanted to be with her mother as often as possible, believing her to be constantly at death's door. Edgar accompanied her and worked on his manuscripts during these trips. Vidal never reproached him for it, but he must have thought that there was some injustice in his son's spending time away from him, with a family that was not his own. Edgar had the confused feeling that it was indeed unjust that he should be more often with these external relatives than with his own father, but he also felt, no less confusedly, that his father had become almost immortal, whereas his wife's mother seemed to be a condemned woman.

Vidal had always asked for his brothers' advice and opinions, and after they died only his son, and in a different way his granddaughters Irène and Véronique, could play the role of confidant for his problems, worries and concerns. So Vidal asked for their advice and opinions increasingly often, but he never followed them if they contradicted his own ideas. For Vidal, Edgar had come to represent a Gordian knot between the old and the new generations; while he remained Vidal's son and still a child in his eyes, he also found himself invested with the counselling role of Vidal's brothers, and even, as we have already mentioned, with a certain paternal function.

Of Vidal's generation, those born in Salonica, there was nobody left in his family, only a few old friends with whom he sometimes met up, like Marc Ezratti or Mordechai Benosillo. He had lost three of his nieces, Régine, Liliane and Aimée. But if the family had emptied from the top down, there had also been some demographic filling from below. Corinne and he were already Nona and Papou to Edgar's two daughters, Irène and Véronique, Fredy's son Michel, and Daisy's two daughters, Corinne and Marianne. Four great-grandchildren were born in their lifetime: Alice, Irène's daughter, Roland, Véronique's son, both born in 1982, followed by Inti, Corinne's son, and Gilles, Véronique's son, born in 1983 and 1984.

From time to time, the apartment in the Rue Laugier received visits from Irène, Véronique, Corinne and Marianne. Vidal and Corinne went to see their great-grandchildren. Moreover, Danielle and Nicolas Angel, young relatives on the Beressi side, loved Vidal and Corinne and visited them regularly. Nicole Angel writes:

Danielle met him one evening by what was then still called the Magasins Réunis. He was looking for a certain type of toilet paper. Corinne had phobias, special requirements: unpasteurized milk . . .

If it had not been for the depressive isolation and the crises, Vidal and Corinne would have been surrounded by people and fêted wherever they went. Corinne, during her periods of reprieve, was open, loving, confiding and curious, and he was always candid, warm and humorous with other people. There were a few happy dinners, when Corinne relaxed and Vidal thoroughly enjoyed himself. One of the last of these took place on New Year's Eve 1982, when Corinne and he were invited to the home of a friend of their son's, and Vidal ate, drank, joked, and sang to everyone's admiration.

WANDERINGS

However, they could no longer enjoy peace and gaiety at home, and they were condemned to seek it elsewhere, in unfamiliar surroundings. The formula was still working in the years between 1980 and 1982. In March 1982, they enjoyed their stay at the family guesthouse of Les Lavandes, Rémuzat, in the Drôme. At the beginning of June, they spent two weeks in a family house in Normandy, close to Caen. September saw them in a family center called La Porte ouverte [the Open Door], in Saint-Jorioz, Haute-Savoie. Vidal tries to choose different regions, gathers information, writes to tourist offices, and to the parents of Michel Grappe, Véronique's husband, who are from the Jura. He is delighted when he likes the food, disgusted when he doesn't. Corinne, on the other hand, is sensitive to noise, cleanliness and comfort. When they strike it lucky, they are happy and try to return to the same place, but often, at the time they want to go, everything is booked up and Vidal has to start looking again, and keep on looking . . .

The year 1983 begins with the same problems and the same difficulties. Vidal seems to have gone to Brussels with Corinne, at the time of his birthday (he is 89 on March 14), to spend some time with his nephew Edgard, his brother Léon's son. It is also a pilgrimage to the place from which the "Order of Léopold" had come to honor David Nahum, where Nahum Steel, which had been founded in Salonica, was established, and where his eldest brother, who had been head of the family after 1920, had lived, as well as his beloved brother Henri.

FIRST SEPARATION

A new crisis of rejection, in June or July 1983, results in the following compromise: Corinne will go alone to her daughter Daisy's home, in La Turbie, north of Monaco, and Vidal will go on vacation by himself. Daisy's husband, Sam, has booked a place for him in a seniors' residence, near Orange. However, in the meantime Corinne has forbidden Vidal to live in the apartment while she is not there. She doesn't want him "dirtying it." He gives his word, declaring that he will live with his granddaughter Irène, but as soon as Corinne leaves he secretly returns to the marital home. He gets used to being alone at night. He feels simultaneously upset and relieved at being on his own. He can go and have lunch at one of his granddaughter's homes, or with his son, who gets back from Buenos Aires on July 23. Edgar and Edwige (who is very fond of Vidal and is indignant at Corinne's attitude) leave at the end of July to stay with Edwige's parents in Villefranche-sur-Mer. Edgar vists Corinne at La Turbie; she is calm and rested. They have arranged that Vidal will come to Nice and that his son will drive him to the vacation home.

Accordingly, Edgar drops his father off at a beautiful residence, standing in extensive grounds. Vidal's room gives directly onto the garden. The next day, Vidal telephones Edgar and begs him to come and get him. As if enemies are spying on him, he refuses to give any explanation over the telephone, but insists that Edgar come as quickly as possible. Vidal has already announced to the administration that he is obliged to leave because of a serious family matter. When, in the car, his son asks him why he wanted to leave the residence, Vidal begins by saying that it's because there is no waiter service and everybody has to go and collect their own food, then because there are four tiring steps to get to his room. These reasons do not seem very convincing to his son. Finally, Vidal spits it out: "All the women are hideous and old, and all the men are civil servants, there's not a single businessman among them!"

Edwige's parents did not have a third bedroom in their apartment. Vidal looked for a hotel close by, in Beaulieu. Being the beginning of August, almost everything was full. By a stroke of luck, they found him a little room in a hotel facing the harbor. The heat was stifling, but Vidal could stand intense heat. Edgar persuaded him, with difficulty, not to telephone Corinne (who was due to join him two weeks later at the vacation home) and not to put pressure on her to come back before the agreed date. Every morning, Edgar would go and collect his father. After 10 o'clock, Vidal started looking at his watch to see if it was nearly time for lunch. When he had lunch alone, he would sit down at 11.30 on the terrace of the restaurant he had chosen and would wait impatiently for them to begin serving. He had some meals with Edwige's parents, who made a show of politeness, but in their hearts had little consideration for a man of Vidal's kind, who was far removed from their standards of honorability. For his part, Vidal was entirely unimpressed by their apartment at Villefranche-sur-Mer. Doubtless, by expressing with a grimace his dislike of the apartment, he wanted to express another kind of displeasure to his son. He made a show of being very relaxed and cordial during the meals in restaurants with Edwige's parents, and even confided, after a good meal, something he had never before revealed to his son: the reasons for his arrest in Salonica. Edgar felt ashamed and upset about staying with this external family instead of with his father. However, he could not think of leaving his wife; moreover, his papers and his typewriter were at Villefranche, where he was writing up a manuscript that he wanted to finish before the fall.

Vidal decided to return to Paris, and went back to his empty apartment in the deserted mid-August streets. His granddaughters were on vacation and his friends away. By chance, Violette, his son's first wife, picked up the phone, and asked him which restaurant he would like to have lunch in. Without hesitation, he chose the Brasserie de la Lorraine in the Place des Ternes. It was where the Nahums used to get together to celebrate whenever Léon, Jacques, Henri or Mathilde came to Paris. He was delighted with the enormous grilled sole he was served, drank a whole bottle of wine, and found an oasis in the desert of August. Then Corinne came back to Paris.

SECOND SEPARATION

Edgar and Edwige left for New York on September 8. They planned to stay until the end of October. Edgar was still frequently in touch with his father by telephone, and, indirectly, he received and sent messages through Marie-France Laval, who worked with him at his center, or via the telephone calls between Edwige and her mother. In mid-September, Vidal told his son that he was keeping to his bed and feeling very tired. During their next conversation, he was very anxious, and asked Edgar to come back to Paris. Edgar had to finish a seminar he was giving at the end of October. He took advantage of an invitation he had received at his meetings in Geneva to go to Paris on September 23. His father's health had improved, and most importantly, Vidal was reassured to know that, even if he was very far away, his son could answer his call. Corinne had been worried about him, but when she saw that he was out of danger, she began to rebuff him again whenever he complained: "But I'm the one who's ill, Vidal!"

Now that Vidal had recovered, Corinne's desperate melancholy became endemic that fall. She hardly slept at all at night, and would get up, go to the living room, and walk over to the window; when the urge to urinate woke him, he would murmur: "Come to bed, Poulette." She could no longer bear him. Vidal was distraught, and alerted Dr. Milanolo, Fredy, Henri and Edgar, but Edgar's intervention had become ineffectual, and Corinne would sometimes look at him distrustfully, as if he were conniving in Vidal's plot against her. Vidal would meet his son, either at Edgar's apartment in the Rue Vandrezanne or in the Sentier, and tell him of his unhappiness. But he was incapable of taking his distance, by going for lunch at a restaurant, for instance; more than ever, he wanted to leave, but was more than ever incapable of leaving. He often worried about his heart. Although he was now retired, Dr. Fortin probably came to examine him on November 24. His son took him to see Dr. Quercy on December 21. Each time they met, he would expect his son to give him his *semandica*, a small gift of food, especially *boutargue*, a Balkan dish that he loved of dried mullet eggs preserved in wax. In fall, he would ask for *marrons glacés*. He was delighted to receive these treats. More than ever, like his brother Henri in his days of misfortune, he put his hopes in a big win on the national lottery or the Crédit National. Each time they met, after sharing his somber thoughts, Vidal would say: "Don't worry, the Good Lord will help me and protect me."

There are no more breaks in the clouds. Corinne rejects Vidal with hatred and violence. Edgar is horrified, but he understands the causes of the tragedy that she is enduring and is making Vidal endure so well, and he knows that the only possible solution lies in them taking their distance from each other, so he does not want to prevent a separation which he believes to be absolutely necessary, at least for a time. A very violent scene takes place in January 1984; Dr. Milanolo and Edgar are both summoned to come at once. Corinne is shouting, screaming, weeping, imploring Vidal to leave. Vidal allows Milanolo and his son to persuade him, packs a little case and, before going to the door, asks timidly: "Do you want me to stay, Poulette?" "No!" she screams. Vidal allows his son to drag him away, and Edgar takes him to his apartment. There is a sofa bed in the sitting room, and Vidal spends the first night there. But he cannot bear to live and sleep on the twenty-sixth floor, and his son finds him a small hotel nearby, in the Rue du Sergeant-Bovillot. Then Vidal goes to spend a few days at his granddaughter Irène's home. Daisy decides to have her mother come and stay with her in Monte Carlo. Corinne does not want Vidal to occupy her apartment during her absence, and, before leaving, she pretends to have been locked out by a draught that blew the apartment door shut while she was standing on the doorstep without her key. She calls a locksmith, who changes the lock and then leaves, taking the keys with her. As soon as she has gone, Vidal fetches another locksmith, gets the lock changed again, checks out of the hotel, and secretly returns to his home. Vidal becomes accustomed to living alone. He goes for lunch to the little restaurant next door, where he becomes a regular: he likes the food and the welcome they give him: "They're charming people." He more or less controls his greed, but is no longer subjected to the restrictions that Corinne imposed on him for the sake of his health. When he gets home, he has his slug of Benedictine, then takes a little nap. He spends a lot of time calling people on the telephone during the day. In the evening, he has a yogurt, some honey, and perhaps some of the *boutargue* that his son has brought him. He goes to bed early, gets up early, and in the morning he goes to see his son, or one of his granddaughters, or else he goes to the Sentier. When on the bus, he is increasingly fond of going up to little old men and asking them their age, then comparing it with his own. Sometimes, they snub him. "That's none of your business, sir!" Other times, they answer him aimiably, and then he can say: "Guess mine." His interlocutor will hazard a guess in the range of 70 or 75, which allows him to announce triumphantly that he is 90, and arouse their astonished and admiring reply: "But you don't look it at all." Indeed, he still has all of his hair, much of which is still black. His face is almost unwrinkled, and his smiling expression is youthful. He is still slim, with an upright posture. He is animated when speaking, and still laughs like a child whenever embarrassed or amused by anything. But he walks slowly. Staircases exhaust him. In the evenings, he feels a profound and incomprehensible weariness.

Edgard in Brussels, who had been indifferent to the family in the past (like his cousin Edgar), now worries a good deal about his Uncle Vidal. On the telephone, he urges Edgar not to leave his father alone in the apartment, especially at night, and advises putting him in a retirement home. But Vidal refuses all of these suggestions. Edgard tells Edgar that at the very least his father should not leave the apartment, that he is in danger of falling down, and breaking his leg (as Edgard's father Léon had done) or being mugged, but Edgar refuses to consider shutting his father away. He would rather he took risks by going out, and lived a little, instead of surviving in confinement. Besides, he does not think that Vidal could survive if he were shut away.

Edgard is also very concerned about his Uncle Vidal's financial situation; by this time, he has scant resources. Edgard is afraid that he will be thrown out for good from the apartment which is also his own, but whose sole owner is Corinne, and he is afraid that Corinne's children will collaborate in this despoilment. Vidal's son knows that there is no danger from that quarter, and that they are ensuring that Vidal will not become destitute. Since his cousin continues to worry, he arranges a meeting in Paris between Sam and Edgard, and Sam explains to Vidal's nephew that he and his wife continue to provide for the needs not just of Corinne, but of the couple.

Vidal wants to stay at home, but he also considers other solutions. He thinks of renting a little studio near to Irène and Véronique; he starts his search, but does not get any further. He also thinks of going to spend a few days in Salonica, to see if he would be able move there. He is dreaming about Livorno again, too. At the same time, he still wants to reunite his family's dead at Bagneux, and he writes to one of Bouchi's nephews, whom the family had lost touch with, and who had emigrated to Argentina after the war. Here is the letter, which is returned to him marked "addressee unknown:"

Paris, 28 March, 1984
Dear Itzi, I have just found your address in a book of dear Mathilde's, and I hope that this letter will reach you. I hope that you and those around you are well.

Are you planning to come here for the vacation? I have just had my 90th birthday, and if God is willing and if the doctors let me, I very much want to go to Salonica for a few days. My son will come with me; his name is Edgar Morin, a well-known sociologist and writer.

If possible, I would also like to visit the grave of our dear Bouki. Do you have the address of the cemetery? If I can make this journey, I am going to find out if it is possible to bring dear Bouki's remains back to Paris, so that he can rest at the Paris-Bagneux cemetery, with Mathilde and all of my family.

I look forward to hearing from you,

With cordial regards, and love,

Vidal

In particular, it is the bachelor's life that this man "who loves being married" cannot bear. He has become accustomed to solitude, but only because he thinks it is temporary. On several occasions, his son prevents him from writing to Corinne, who is in the care of Professor Martin, a neurologist much liked by the Monte Carlo family, who has already admitted Émy, Corinne's sister, to his department at Nice hospital. Edgar has been to see Corinne during a short stay in the South of France, and encouraged her to continue writing her memoirs, which she had begun in a little notebook; he meets Martin (whom he already knows and is on friendly terms with) at his house, on March 10, and tries to give him some psychological information about Corinne. But Martin has more faith in chemistry than the psyche. Vidal has also written a letter, on February 24, to Professor Martin, which shows he perfectly understands that Corinne's illness is a result of the extreme violence of the shocks her soul has suffered, beginning with the death of her father:

39, Rue Laugier, Paris 17th arrondissement

Dear Professor Martin,

Please excuse me for taking the liberty of writing to you: as the husband of your patient Corinne Nahoum, I wonder if she has told you about her life. At 18, she lost her father, whom she adored, to a heart attack. She never got over her grief at his death. She then married, and in 1931, she lost her sister, who meant everything to her. Her sister was my wife, and left me with a 10-year-old son. She was on her way to Paris from the suburbs, and she died on the train. Corinne was inconsolable, despite all her husband's efforts. She wanted to look after my son, along with her own three children. The years between 1932 and 1934 were very hard with respect to her husband's financial situation, and she was very upset about that.

Then came 1939 and the war began, along with the Germans' racial persecution; she left Paris and in 1943 found herself in Nice with her husband, preparing to take the train to Lyon. Her husband, who had got down onto the platform, was arrested; she watched him leave and he made a sign to her to stay where she was. He was taken to Drancy and then Auschwitz.

I cannot describe what this misfortune meant to her. She pulled herself together, went to join her children, and my son, who was in the Resistance; she got through the Occupation, and then came the Liberation, bringing the very sad news of her husband's death.

In 1951 she, a widow, and I a widower, decided to get married, with the children's consent.

That gave me renewed energy, and I opened my business in Paris again. In 1964, having bought the apartment in which we now live, and having put all of her heart and all of her will into making it as she wanted, she suffered a depression that would not go away no matter how she wept. We left for Locarno, on the advice of our doctor, Dr. Milanolo (86, rue Cardinat, Paris 17th arrondissement), and since then he has been caring for her, with all the medication that she must have shown you. Every time deportees were mentioned, Corinne would change completely. Recently, she has been telling me that she regrets having remarried and not having kept her first husband's name!

Then comes the end of the year 1983; she is very tense, she sees me as the person who forced her to remarry! And you know the rest! Her children all remain very attached to me and are concerned about me, knowing that I am alone, for I am 90 years old.

Do you think I can come and see Corinne?

I ask you to forgive my intrusion, and I look forward to hearing from you.

Best regards,

Vidal Nahoum

Knight of the National Order of Merit

Nevertheless, Vidal had a few moments of joy during this sad period. His son had been told in 1983 that his name was on the honors list for the Legion of Honor, put forward by the Ministry for Scientific Research. His father was absolutely delighted at this news, and never stopped asking when the ceremony would take place and who would present the award. The son neglected to consider the question. If he had ever wanted a decoration, it had been after the war, and for his acts of resistance, but a hostile intervention had prevented his being honored at that time. In November 1983, Vidal told Edgar that he had seen President Mitterand on the television presenting the Legion of Honor, and he added that it would really make him happy if Mitterand could do the same for his son. So his son wrote to the President, whom he had known in the Resistance. For two months, Vidal asked Edgar incessantly: "Has the President replied to your letter? Have you had any news from the Elysée?" Finally, a letter from the chief of protocol informed Edgar that the ceremony would take place on February 13, 1984, at 6.30 in the evening, at the Elysée. Edgar invited the family and those of his friends who knew Vidal. Vidal put on his best suit, with of course the decoration which was sewn on to all of his jackets, and he admired the huge room in the Elysée where a hundred guests were present, to accompany the six people who were to be decorated. Everybody was standing, waiting for the President. Vidal asked for a chair, and sat down. Then, when the President commended his son, despite straining his ears, and making a hearing trumpet with his hand, he could not hear the President's praise. Nevertheless, he beamed with delight. Once the award had been made, Vidal rushed up to the President and, having introduced himself, handed him a letter that had been addressed to him in 1916 by the man who had protected him when he was 20, the socialist representative Jean Longuet. "We were already socialists back then," he said, convinced that his affirmation was true. He added with pride, expecting congratulations: "I think I am the oldest person at this gathering." "Not at all," replied the President, not realizing that he was hurting Vidal's feelings. "Professor Portman is here, and he is 92 . . . "

Then Vidal stormed the buffet, snatching up little sandwiches with the speed of an eight-armed octopus. His son, alarmed, went to drag him away, but whenever someone came up to speak to him, Vidal would dash over to the buffet again. After having been prised away a few more times, he wanted to go and speak again to the President, who was conversing with a circle of people standing around him. He was on the point of interrupting them all when his son dragged him back once more. Satisfied with his evening, he was one of the last to leave, and later he was very pleased to show the photographs of the President presenting the accolade to his son.

Two weeks later, Véronique gave birth to a boy, whom she named Gilles. Twice, Vidal, who now walked very slowly, made his way through the vast Pitié-Salpêtrière hospital to go and see his great-grandson.

During this period, Vidal experienced another moment of great joy when he was invited to lunch by Danielle and Nicole Angel: "He came at midday, very handsome, and impeccably dressed in a dark suit. He was happy to be back in our apartment, where he had been once or twice before with Corinne. To please me, he had brought some photos of Edgar being received, I think, by Mitterand. He was in some of the pictures too. Mitterand had complimented him on being the most senior member of the assembly, but I think he pointed out someone in the audience to him, who was almost as old as he was, and like him had stayed very young. He was happy that the ceremony had gone well, and that he had felt no tiredness or pain at that time."

"We sat down at the table. He asked after everybody in the family's health. He reassured me about my father: 'You can live for a very long time with angina.' He reassured me about himself. Yes, he was very well, he went to eat every day at a restaurant, the woman who ran it was charming, etc. In reality, he hated the restaurant, his precarious situation, and being deprived of Corinne, but as always he wanted to believe that tomorrow would be better, and never wanted to unburden himself on others. Our meal reminded him of Salonician cooking; in fact it was very simple: a selection of crudités (he carefully separated the red juice from the beetroots to stop it 'dirtying' the rest of the food on his plate); stewed courgettes, and coley.

He became animated, and seemed happy."

"Do you have any photos here?"

"Yes."

"See if there aren't any photos of Luna, my first wife [*Danielle's mother, Daisy Bourla, was a friend of Luna's at the Alliance in Salonica, and her grandmother, Ana Beressi, was a first cousin*].

"I'll have a look."

"I'm looking for photos of her." [*Had she remained alive to him? Was he thinking of her again?*]

"Naturally, I then asked him how he had met her. He began a long, very long description of the war in the Dardanelles, his journeys back and forth to France, and mentioned the address of cousins or intimate friends in Salonica, to whose house in France he went often. The story was precise, with a wealth of details, and finally, after half an hour, he ended with a single sentence mentioning the young girl, who was the family's daughter: 'Luna was there, Edgar's mother, we got on well together, and that was it.' And he waved his hand."

It was all there, the war in the Dardanelles, the hazardous journeys back and forth, but only "that was it" to describe the most important part, the one that doesn't get put into words, and especially not told to others.

There were meals at Irène's and Véronique's homes, with his great grandchildren, and in particular, there was a big party at Violette's for his 90th birthday, with his granddaughters and their husbands. Everyone praised him, joked about him, and teased him, just as he loved them to; he devoured an enormous quantity of food, emptied his wineglass as soon as it was filled, and suffered neither a headache nor indigestion. Then, as was his habit after meals on very special occasions, he lit a cigarette, which he held in the corner of his tightly clamped lips, where it protuded at an angle, not horizontally but sticking straight out, and he sucked in and blew out the smoke with a lordly air.

THE END

When spring comes, Vidal wants to return to the family guesthouses in Alsace which serve food he loves. He goes to the Maison-Rouge hotel, near to La Roseraie, in Saint-Pierre-par-Bach. By the end of May or beginning of June, Dr. Martin's treatment has improved Corinne's mental condition. Sam makes a few psychological soundings, which indicate that her allergy to Vidal seems to have attenuated. He therefore takes advantage of a meeting between Corinne, Professor Martin and himself to suggest to Corinne that she might get back together with Vidal. Corinne does not reject the idea, and Sam telephones Vidal and tells him to get ready to come to join them at La Turbie. At first, Vidal thinks he no longer wants Corinne back, then he becomes confused, and confides his confusion to his son, who is also confused. Finally, the desire to see Corinne again becomes pressing, and he reserves his seat on the train.

He asks his son to drive him to the station at 10 o'clock, as his train is at 11. Edgar is amazed that his father has not wanted to leave two hours in advance. They arrive at the station at 10.20, and Edgar discovers that the train is actually at noon. He is annoyed with Vidal, who has sat down on his suitcase in front of the departure board, which does not yet show his train's platform number. He scolds his father unkindly, but his father continues to sit there placidly on his suitcase, not saying a word. Did Edgar really have a meeting at noon, or was it out of irritation that he wanted to leave? He cannot recall, when he remembers this day, which is the last time he will see his father on his feet. In any case, he tells his father he has a meeting that he could have arranged for later if he had known the real departure time. "Go to your meeting, my darling, go on." The son does not accompany his father to the carriage, does not see him settled in his compartment, does not put his suitcase on the luggage rack for him, does not wave his handkerchief when the train leaves. He does not know that he is seeing his father as a fit and able man for the last time.

Vidal arrives at La Turbie and submissively throws himself at Corinne's feet. She makes him swear that he will stop causing her misery and grief, and that he will stop being mean with money. He swears to obey his queen in everything, and submits completely. Magnanimously, Corinne forgives him; a little later she says to Irène on the telephone: "Perhaps we can rekindle the fire from the ashes."

Daisy and Sam have given them their own room, which is on the ground floor, so that they do not have to go up any stairs. They decide to go to La Roseraie together, in Alsace, and Sam drives them there. Edgar is anxious, and telephones Vidal frequently; on some days, everything seems to be going very well, on others, badly, but the overall impression is positive. They return to La Turbie on July 15. On July 5 or 6, Edgar and Edwige move out of the high-rise that Edwige disliked, and return to the neighborhood Edgar had moved to in 1960. They set up their new apartment and plan to leave for Villefranche-sur-Mer, where they will be near to La Turbie, on around August 10.

On August 2, Vidal telephones Edgar and tells him that he is not happy at La Turbie, and he returns alone to Paris on Monday August 6. He asks his son to come and collect him at the station. Edgar tries to talk him out of it. He tells him that they will be nearby soon, in the South of France, and that he would be very sad to think of Vidal all alone in Paris in August. Vidal sticks to his decision. He leaves La Turbie on August 6, because beforehand he wants to attend two parties, one on the 4th, at Sam's sister's home, and the other on the 5th, for the birthdays of Sam and Daisy's two daughters.

Vidal has a good time at both parties; he eats a lot, drinks a lot, and as usual enjoys the festive atmosphere. During the night between Sunday and Monday of August 6, when he gets up as usual several times to urinate, he falls back on the bed and cannot get up again. In the morning, he does not feel very well, but he still wants to go back to Paris. A doctor is called; he advises against the journey and prescribes hospitalization. Vidal telephones his son to tell him he has had to delay his return, and that he does not want to go into hospital. The son insists that his father undergoes his tests at the hospital, and assures him that he will be arriving on the coast on Wednesday at the latest.

Irène: "On Monday August 6, at about 7 in the evening, I suddenly decide to call Papou at La Turbie. When he recognizes my voice, he makes his usual chuckle of delight, but he sounds rather surprised, which immediately worries me. "Oh, it's you Rirénou, I'm very happy to hear your voice, *mi alma*." He never says another word to me, because out of the blue he starts humming, for no reason; he drops the phone and I hear it fall; I shout his name several times, but he can't hear me any more, Papou has left me . . . "

On the telephone the next morning, Tuesday, Sam tells Edgar that Vidal has just been taken to hospital; he says that he is conscious, but that his condition is alarming: he seems to have had a brain haemorrhage. Edgar and Edwige hurry their preparations, but they are too tired to start driving that evening. They leave the next day, early in the morning. When they arrive that afternoon at the hospital in Monaco, they find Vidal unrecognizable. His nose is thinner, his open mouth no longer has the same lips, or any of its usual expressions, his eyes are lifeless, his face looks green. He is lying stretched out straight. He hears his son, feels his hand as it takes his own, squeezes it, and says, in a cavernous voice that his son has never heard before: "Yes, *mi alma*." He responds when his son strokes his hand. Then he asks him to help him get up and leave, and tries to lift his sheet. His son returns the sheet to its place, tells his father that he must stay in hospital so that they can look after him, and so on, but Vidal, with the obstination he has always shown whenever he wants something, keeps on asking to leave. From time to time, he seems to fall asleep, but then he starts asking to leave again. At one point, he imagines that Corinne is beside him, and says: "Corinne, you'll be the sweetest little Corinne in the world if you help me get up." Another time, he gets angry with his son when he prevents him from getting up. Finally, thinking it the best way to stop his father from trying to get up, the son leaves the hospital late that night to join his wife.

The next morning, Thursday August 9, he finds his father even more unrecognizable. His breathing sounds like a death rattle, is in fact a death rattle. His hand does not respond when his son's hand squeezes it. He seems out of everything; around him, in the other rooms or wards, the patients are watching television, which is broadcasting the rerun of some match; suddenly, in a cavernous voice, Vidal utters a single phrase: "When I'm back home, I'll watch television too."

The doctors reserve their judgment. New centers of the brain have been affected. So it is not the corporeal machine that is damaged: it could have carried on functioning perfectly for many more years. It is the computer, which, at a minimal but decisive point, has gone on the blink. Edgar sits there, stunned, next to this transformed creature who is more than ever his father. After lunch, Sam, feeling that the end is near, obeys Corinne's desire to see Vidal. He drives her from La Turbie to the hospital. She approaches the unrecognizable man, says "Oh," weeps, kisses him tenderly and caresses him. Perhaps he recognizes her. Then Sam comes to collect her, and takes her to the waiting room. Edgar comes to join her there, and Sam leaves to ask for some medical information. It must be 3.20 in the afternoon. Then he reappears and breathes to Edgar: "Go quickly, your father is dying." The son comes to a bed; some nurses are bent over it, bustling about. He takes his father's hand. Vidal's mouth is wide open, and he does not react to the hand. He stares into his father's face, then a nurse straightens her back and says: "He is dead." Edgar does not know who closes his eyes. A nurse takes off his wedding ring and gives it to him. He goes back to the waiting room, and hands the wedding ring to Corinne, who bursts into tears. It is 3.30. Vidal has died on August 9, as his own father had done.

He was in his 91st year. His son was 63, his granddaughters 37 and 38, his great-grandchildren 3, 2 and 1.

Vidal had repeatedly told Corinne, when they got back together again, that he wanted to donate his body to science. But now that his father had been thrown out of his home and rejected, his son could not bear the idea of his being tossed into the trashcan, so to speak, especially since his ninety-year-old body could be of no scientific interest. He asked for advice. Edwige thought Vidal should be buried, other people thought his wishes should be respected, and others that it was up to him, the son, to decide. Knowing that Vidal did not want to be buried at either Père-Lachaise or Bagneux, Edgar decided to have him laid to rest in a temporary plot of the very beautiful Monaco cemetery, which is arranged in tiers overlooking the Mediterranean. He also wanted there to be a group ceremony, to make up for the solitude of his father's last six months. And although his father had never wanted a religious ceremony, Edgar felt that he should be included within a community. Sam took him to see the rabbi of Monaco, who was of Morrocan origin, and therefore refused to countenance any laxity with respect to the ritual. All Edgar wanted was a religious presence at the burial; he did not want his father to be washed and wrapped in a shroud as the rites prescribed, nor did he want to perform the orphan's rites himself. But the rabbi refused to compromise: it was all or nothing. Edgar accepted. First the body was dressed so that it could be visited and displayed in a room of the cemetery's Athanée for a day. Then it was wrapped in a shroud. Vidal's granddaughters and their mother Violette came for the burial. There was a family party at La Turbie, with many children present.

Society column of *Le Monde* (deaths)

Mrs. Vidal Nahoum-Beressi
Mr. and Mrs. Edgar Nahoum
The Pennachioni, Grappe, Nahoum, Beressi, Pelosoff and Cohen families
Are sad to announce the death of
Mr. Vidal NAHOUM
Knight of the National Order of Merit
Bronze medal of the City of Paris,
in his ninety-first year.

The son only had his father's name inscribed on the tombstone he chose for him. From Vidal's terrace in the cemetery, you can see the sea that unites Spain, Italy, Salonica and France.

Corinne had a relapse of depression in September 1984; after suffering from a heart problem, she was admitted to the Princesse-Grace-de-Monaco hospital between February 11 and February 21, 1985. She believed that she was being persecuted there, and that she was in danger from a plot against her. In fact, ever since her marriage to Vidal and their move into the apartment in the Rue Laugier, she had been the victim of forces that persecuted her soul and gradually intensified their ferocity. The Rue Laugier was sold. Corinne had periods of remission and peace and calm in La Turbie, at her daughter's house, and later in a residential home where the apartments benefited from hotel services. She had to be admitted to hospital again, to Professor Martin's department at the Pasteur hospital in Nice, between September 9 and 21, 1985, and again in January 1986. She died on October 12, 1986, the day of her eighty-fifth birthday, and wanted to be buried, not in the tomb with her mother, her brothers and her sister Luna, but in the neighboring tomb with her grandmother Mathilde Beressi, who had died in January 1921, and whom she had loved more than her own mother. She had an inscription engraved there to the memory of her first husband, Joseph Pelosoff, who died in deportation.

Epilogue

Es claro que con la fin de mis dias a los de mi hermana no va a quedar el mas chico recuerdo de lo que estach hoyendo hoy.*
RAFFAELE NAHUM TO HIS CHILDREN

VIDALICO

Vidal: an appropriate name, lived up to by its bearer. It does not exist in French or English, and the adjective "vital" does not adequately translate the breath of life there is in Vidal.

Vidal had very great vitality. Energetic, multi-faceted, resourceful, not violent or violating, but endowed with strong desires and an obstinate will, fiercely attacking any obstacle in his path with the force of an the ocean wave, or on the contrary finding a way around it, smart, flexible, hard-working, laboring away ardently until he was 46, fit for service until the end of his life, running to Turin at 74 to get his sister out of hospital, at 85 going from the 17th arrondissement to the Sentier on foot to see an old friend, at 90 making his way through the vast hospital of la Pitié to see the face of his newly born great-grandson. As a friend of his son's wrote, on the day after his death: "It's wonderful, and fortunate, all the same, for him and for you, that he was able to live for so long while remaining fully alive" (C.L.). His vitality was expressed almost animalistically in the way he approached life, with both great spontaneity and intelligence; he was naïve and cunning, sincere and deceptive, very confiding and at the same time guarding his hideaways and his little mysteries, very open, candid, and at the same time very secretive.

His character remained constantly cheerful throughout all the misfortunes, trials, anxieties, blows of fate, suffering and mourning. Until the end, he was curious about everything, open to everything, events, the world at large, sociable with everybody, ready to enter a relationship in canine fashion with anyone he happened to meet.

He was unusual, without having either exceptional qualities or radical faults. Despite the apparent absence of mystery in this person who was receptive to everything, there was, as there is in everybody, a mystery, and Vidal's mystery was linked to his capacity to remain child-like.

His childishness remained the unchanging feature of his character. He remained youthful throughout his life, and his supremely and admirably child-like spirit became most apparent in his old age. He had remained a

285

happy child, the favorite whom his mother and his father had adored, and who was cherished by the great community of older brothers. The seriousness of maturity had all gone to his elder brothers Jacques and Léon; Henri remained a great adolescent, while Vidal remained both an adolescent and a child: unlike most adults, he needed milk and drank big glassfuls of it until the end of his life. He remained Vidalico for as long as he lived.

Since childhood, he had retained an immoderate taste for teasing and jokes. Until his death, he kept up the stamp collection he had begun in his youth, never classifying it, but continuing to amass it in boxes over the decades. He had increasingly childish hopes, like his brother Henri, of winning a jackpot on the Lottery. Lastly, he had retained an awe of decorations from the day in his childhood when he had seen his father decorated with the medal of the "Order of Léopold." His was not the typically French taste of a gentleman who needs to feel himself distinguished; it was a childish need, childishly conserved in adulthood.

He had been raised with tenderness, and had naturally aroused it in others throughout his life. He therefore felt an entirely understandable, but never imperious, need for it.

His incredible fixation on food was probably linked to his remaining childlike. As Irène says: "When we ate, he would commune with his childhood, with his Mom who had so gorged him with love that she had convinced him that eating and being loved are the same thing . . . Papou ate as if he were doing himself good, curing himself, praying, thanking somebody, and he did it seriously, religiously, methodically." It is because he believed that eating was salutary in every sense of the word that he constantly told Corinne, when, crushed with despair, she lost her appetite: "Eat, Poulette." It was his remedy for all ills, his panacea: eat! At the same time, his attitude to food expressed his uncouth, barely civilized animality: he concentrated on his plate, not just like a yogi on the syllable OM, which allows him to communicate with what is most sacred, but also like a voracious and vigilant predator, who devours his food hastily, instinctively lifting his eyes to sweep the horizon from time to time. And when he had eaten, he felt not only relaxation or satisfaction, but elation; it was a halleluia that he whistled or hummed, with a delighted expression on his face.

He was very glad to be alive and possessed "the most incredible quality of all: gaiety" (Irène). That was indeed the impression that the patriarch-child made upon those who only knew him in his eighties: "An enormous capacity for wonder" (Danielle and Nicole Angel). "His naïveté and possibly his candor often inspired my tenderness" (Evelyne Lannegrace, whose Oriental curves Vidal greatly appreciated). "I often felt old next to him. What enthusiasm!" (Angel). "The conversations we had when we saw each other, or on the telephone, used to cheer me up so much because of his enthusiasm" (Raphaël Benazeraf). "His enthusiasm at the end of meals . . . and his mischievousness . . . . his naughtiness" (Lannegrace).

Vidal spent his whole life singing. He sang and whistled like a bird every morning, at lunch, whenever he was relaxed and happy. In Salonica, his first attraction had been for Parisian *caf'conc'* songs; later, in France, he had made Marseillais, Neopolitan and Spanish songs his own. The sheet music he kept bears witness to his eclecticism as the century unfolded: *La Chanson du cabanon, Les Gars de la Marine, Guitare d'amour* (Tino Rossi), *Le Fanion de la Légion* and *Celui que mon cœur a choisi* (Piaf), *Le Chant des partisans, Plaine, ma plaine, Les Feuilles mortes, Si tu viens danser dans mon village* (Lucienne Delyle), *Ma Guépière et mes Longs Jupons* (Yvette Giraud), *Rose Blanche, le P'tit Quinquin, Che sera sera, L'Homme et l'Enfant* (Eddie Constantine), *Le Petit Bonheur* (Félix Leclerc), *La Complainte de la Butte* (Cora Vaucaire), *Bambino* (Dalida), *Colchique*, as well as a few Turkish songs which came back hauntingly at the end of his life.

Vidal approached life with inveterate optimism and inveterate fatalism. These two traits had always complemented one another, and helped him to bear trials and sorrows. His fatalism prevented him from taking a rebellious or angry stance against the blows of fate. His optimism, when faced with the same blows of fate, made him believe in the providential aid of the Good Lord, whom he saw as a magnification and a sublimation of his father. Moreover, although he was anxious about everything, including and especially the most insignificant things, (fear of missing trains, worry that his son was not using clean toilets), he felt no true anxiety, which is an inner emotion deeply linked to guilt. He never had the feeling that he had done wrong (nor did he ever boast of having done right), and had no experience of the feeling of guilt that was unconsciously gnawing away at Corinne, and consciously gnawed away at his son. Anxiety subjugated Corinne in body and soul, but Vidal remained serene in spite of being anxious.

Vidal was a faithful dog with a loving heart. His fidelity was directed first of all at his family, to whom he was naturally and totally devoted. He was capable of extending his devotion to friends, but his wonderful sense of fraternity was never addressed to people who were unknown, or distant; his devotion always went to concrete people, never to an idea. As for his loving heart, we can only imagine the loves of his youth, Wilhelmine and his secret lover in Marseilles, and we cannot mention the secret part of his life that he took with him to his grave, nor the one which his son will not divulge. However, we can marvel at his tenderness as a husband in his sixties, seventies and eighties, which was witnessed by young Danielle and Nicole Angel; they met Corinne and Vidal when he was over eighty, and say: "he loved her faithfully, graciously and without shame," which in no way prevented his libidinous dreams and his extramarital fantasies about other matrimonial arrangements.

He was entirely out of the ordinary as a father, which made him extraordinary. He was not a father like his own father, whose authority naturally inspired respect in his son, nor was he a carefree "modern" father. Or rather, he was naturally "modern," in the sense that his tenderness and his concern made him a maternal father. But his love had become an animal kind of love because his son was still-born, and condemned to remain an only child. Of course, parents' love always has an animal quality and origin. But Vidal's love was animalistic in its obsessive protectiveness. When his wife Luna died, he hypermaternalized himself for the ten-year old orphan. "He loved you insolently," Émy would tell Edgar.

Vidal's temperament did not make him either authoritarian or dominating. Being gentle and cheerful, he did not give punishments or sanctions, and he only ever slapped his son in very rare attacks of anger, leaving him absolutely stunned. However, until his son was 20, he got exactly what he wanted from him through blackmail and persistence. Out of concern to protect his life, he stopped him from living. By stopping him from living, he unwittingly encouraged him to risk his life. And ultimately it was because he wanted his son to live without risk that he gave him the chance to invent his own life by taking risks.

An immeasurable distance separated father and son between the son's tenth and twentieth year. Vidal's love imprisoned his son. His son, meanwhile, had shut himself off from his father; there was a very deep hostility in his filial love, which stemmed from the belief that his father had betrayed his mother. Is that why, as soon as he began to have a few ideas of his own, he saw commerce as deceit, family as a convention and society as a vice?

Vidal and his son could barely understand each other at all during the son's adolescent years. The father could not see any more sense in being a militant than in joining the miltary. The son who voluntarily took part in the Second World War saw his father as a sort of Salonician Schweik who had done everything he could to escape the draft. It was only with time that Edgar recognized Vidal's vital virtues: he recognized the virtues of his familial love, of his fraternity as part of a tribe, his openness to everything. He recognized the virtues of his scepticism, of his deeply irreligious and non–nationalistic secularity. He understood that the greatest gift Vidal had given him was the fact he had not transmitted to him any *culture*. Although he was an obsessive father, Vidal was a minimal father insofar as he had no ideas, no morality, no belief to teach to his son. He would have liked him to join his business, but only so that he could have his company in the store. ("But Vidal," Corinne would tell him emphatically, "you should be pleased and proud of what your son has become, he's not a nobody like you." "No," Vidal would say, "I'd still rather have had him in the store with me.")

Although neither of them knew it, the father was a Zen master to his son, educating him by letting him be; and so the son taught himself his own truths, and one of these truths was that the absence of education is an advantage. Finally, when Edgar recognized the beauty of Vidal's devotion, and that of his unchangeably youthful and childlike character, he was no longer suffocated, but cocooned by his father's love, and no longer embarrased by his failings and weaknesses, but admiring of his *vitality*. And thus his weak, feeble, uncertain, incomplete father became gigantic, immense, radiant, immortal!

However, neither respect nor veneration were associated with his admiration for his father: the son felt a need to tease and mock his teasing and mocking father. The reason was that a rotating relationship of paternity and filiality had gradually developed between them. Edgar had guided and protected his father during the Occupation; then, with the disappearance of his brothers, and his inner contradictions with regard to Corinne, Vidal had increasingly asked for the advice, and then the help of his son, but at the same time he had never ceased to be a father who gave his advice and assistance. And so, in spite of the father's blind spots, and the son's neglect and failings, a rotating loop had become established, where father and son changed roles incessantly, each becoming at once father-son and son-father to the other. The incredible bond which had begun in 1921 lasted sixty-three years, and the umbilical cord that tied one to the other had become an umbilical loop for both of them.

SECRET

Like everybody else, Vidal not only had a subterranean aspect to his life, but also a secret aspect (unknown to him) and a secretive aspect (unknown to other people). He had had an important secret love affair in Marseilles, and many romantic secrets afterwards. In the last years of his life, Vidal had eradicated all traces of love affairs in his past, and although he confided a great deal in his adult son, he avoided any confidence concerning his love life before his marriage (or concerning any extramarital affairs during his marriage with Luna), having made the belated discovery that his son had never forgotten his great childhood love for his mother. The only depositary of his secrets may have been his brother Henri, who died twenty years before him.

Vidal had once told his granddaughter Irène that he intended to give her a collection of love letters to keep for him, but he must have destroyed it instead. He liked to talk to her about Wilhelmine, and consulted her about cousin Marguerite. When he was about 80, he told his son to go after his death to see his friend Saltiel, a fellow Salonician, also in the hosiery business, whose store was in the Passage Saint-Denis, and pick up some personal documents. The son went to the address his father had given him, but did not find the store; he asked a neighboring store-holder, who did not recognize the name, and then he asked a prostitute who apparently occupied the entrance to the passage on a full-time basis, but she could not help him either. The depositary of the secret and the place where it was hidden had themselves disappeared.

WHAT WAS VIDAL'S PLACE?

What was Vidal's "place," meaning his social class, his cultural category, his necessary *habitus*? He was born into a respectable family in the Sephardic city, into its Livornese elite, in fact, and his sister Henriette and brother Léon were very conscious of belonging to the *gente alta* as opposed to the *gente bacha*.[81] Vidal had imitated the lifestyle of the Parisian middle classes, with their apartments, outings, restaurants and vacations. He had gone to live in the "good" neighborhood of the 17th arrondissement, which his sister Henriette and his brother Léon had chosen, but he had not incorporated their sense of honorability to any great extent. Like most small businessmen, he was not well-read (although he had retained his love for the verse of Corneille and Hugo, which he had learned by heart at the Franco-German school), and his musical tastes were for light-hearted songs, music-hall and *caf' conc'*. He was not overly concerned about looking elegant, except when he was going to an evening party or some solemn occasion.

He had not internalized bourgeois norms beyond a superficial degree, and because he was so sociable, he was naturally open to making friendships that ignored social categories, notably with his companions in the concentration camp or the regiment. He was something of an "interclassist," because he was both very sociable and not particularly socialized. He was relatively well at ease everywhere, including in prison and in the camp, and remained something of an outsider wherever he went. His arrest, incarceration, uprootings and rerootings, the good and ill fortune dealt to him by fate, and the precariousness of the Jewish destiny which he had suffered as a personal experience, had all in their way made him classless.

What did Judaism mean to him? It did not mean observing the Mosaic Law. He cheerfully broke the sacred fast of Yom Kippur. He did not believe in the rites. He had neglected his son's bar mitzvah. He had never been bothered by his son's marriages to gentile women. He felt a bond with a population (which to him meant a very big family); he was a "son of our people," *ben amenou*, although he did not include the Polacks (Ashkenazim); in his eyes, they only became part of the community when he began to feel, much later, a bond with and an interest in Israel. But, as we have seen, he did not see Israel as a homeland even then, for he could not really bring himself to think in terms of nation states. His Jewish identity was extended in a sense because of Israel, but his Sephardic identity was diminished because of Israel: the attachment he felt late in life to Israel made him shut himself off from Muslims, despite the fact that his family had always had good relationships with the Turks in Salonica, and although he himself had had friendly relationships for many years with Algerian stall-holders and small businessmen in the Sentier.

As for the *ben amenou* connection, he only experienced it (but he did so fully) during Seder, in the days leading up to Passover (Succoth and Purim, which the family had celebrated in Salonica, were abandoned in France). At Passover itself, his participation with the Jewish people was specifically Sephardic, with words and songs in Spanish to accompany the rites at table.

For the non-practicing Sephardim of Salonica, Passover remained the great celebration of their ancestral belonging to the people who were delivered from their slavery to the pharoahs. Although he was an atheist, Salomon Beressi celebrated Passover religiously. During the years between the wars, Vidal celebrated Passover with the family, either at his mother's house, or at Myriam Beressi's. After the war, he would spend Passover at a relative's house; later, after all the deaths, dispersion and dilution of identity in the next generation, Vidal and Corinne celebrated Passover at the Salonicians' Association (which they did not frequent on any other occasion). Once, invited by Edgar, who wanted to give them a treat, they celebrated Passover at the Rachi center. Towards the end of his life, when he and Corinne felt too tired, or were away from Paris, Vidal did not make much effort to take part in Seder. But those were the exceptions of the last years. The gaiety of the Passover holiday revived Vidal's Jewish identity along with his Salonician identity, and, every Passover, he said to himself, thinking of a pilgrimage rather than a definitive return, not "Next year in Jerusalem," but "Next year in Salonica."

His son does not remember whether Vidal kept a *mezuzah* at the door of his various homes, or whether the Nahums or Beressis did. However, when he was terrified before taking the plane for California, Vidal had spontaneously begun to recite prayers, putting his hat on his head. Nevertheless, he had never wanted a religious funeral for himself, and he had even excluded the ritual aspect of a non-religious burial by deciding to donate his body to science. But whenever he went to a cemetery, he would leave a pebble on the tombs he visited, and he would wash his hands before leaving, murmuring superstitiously: "*peche comeremos*" (we will eat fish). In his own way, he was a deist, asking for protection from the Good Lord, whom he thought of as a sort of supreme Father, but he was indifferent to all rites and temples. His true religion was that of the family, and included the worship of his dead.

He felt a sense of belonging, not to a "chosen people," but to a big family endowed with remarkable qualities, and he had a feeling of superiority, which was both slight and benevolent, not only with respect to gentiles, but Ashkenazim. He had never revealed this feeling to his son, but he had wanted to communicate it to his granddaughter Irène when she was a child, so she would know that, although she was the daughter of a gentile woman, she shared the virtues of the best people. She remembers:

"I was enthroned on the kitchen table (all primped and curled and dressed up by Nona) like a birthday cake, and Papou bent over me to tell me a big secret:

'Listen, Minou' (Papou called me Minou until I was a teenager, when I became Rirénou), 'I'm going to tell you a lovely story: there is a family on earth that is more beautiful, more intelligent and nicer than all the others; it is made up of Eskimos and Seraphim [*Irène had heard seraphim instead of Sephardim and Eskimo instead of Ashkenazi*]; and the Seraphim, which means us, your Papou, your Nona, your Dad, and therefore you, are even more beautiful and intelligent than the Eskimos.' Papou was interrupted by two objections, mine: 'What about Mommy?', and Nona's, in a scandalized tone: '*Atio*, Vidal, how can you say such stupid things to that little girl?' Papa stood back up, not in the least ashamed of himself, and reassured me: 'Your Mom is almost a Seraphim, because she married your Dad'; to Nona, he replied innocently: 'But I'm telling her the truth, Pouita.'"

How should Vidal be placed geographically? He was incontestably a man of the South, a Mediterranean. He was a Mediterranean in his love of the sun, the sea, harbor cities, and Turkish, Greek, Italian, Spanish and Provençal food cooked in olive oil. He was also Mediterranean in his belief in the evil eye, which is so profound in every part of the Mediterranean. For example, he was convinced that one should never boast, or congratulate oneself, for fear of attracting bad luck. When people admired his baby, he never concurred, and would reply: "Oh, he's not that cute." He would never have said that his son was handsome or intelligent (had he suspected that his son was intelligent, he would have called him *bovo* anyway as part of his permanent strategy against the evil eye). When Violette kept telling him how pretty her little baby Irène was, he would respond with a doubtful frown. "So you don't think she's pretty?" Violette would say, becoming indignant. "I do, I do . . . " "Well say so then!" At that point, Vidal would point at the ceiling and whisper: "Don't say it too loudly!" He never said that business was good, he always said: "Things aren't great," and avoided talking about his successes. He never said that things were going well for him or that he was in perfect health. He would answer: "Not too bad," or "Sometimes up, sometimes down."

Vidal could have adapted himself to life in Vienna, or another Germanic country, even Britain. He spoke German and English as well as French, Spanish and some Italian, but he would have fitted in better in Spain, and especially in Italy. The accidental nature of his coming to France, because of an arbitrary arrest, nevertheless corresponded to his childhood desire and his adolescent choice. He chose to become one of France's "inhabitants."

The East and West were strangely combined in him, and Salonica was the matrix of this combination. For fifteen centuries, the Sephardim had continued to practice their Eastern rites in Spain, but they had also been integrated into the Western world of the Middle Ages, which was both Christian and Muslim. Afterwards, they had taken with them and kept alive the Spanish language of the West in the Ottoman Empire of the East. In addition, Tuscanized families like the Nahums, Frances, Beressis and Mosseris had begun to absorb the first elements of the modern West's secular culture as early as the 17th century. In Salonica itself, these same families were profoundly marked by secular ideas during the 19th century, when they joined the "Progress" movement. French was now the language of ideas, and France the mythical country where life was sweet. "Poincaré, Poincaré, when will I be one of your inhabitants!" little Vidalico cried, when he became a teenager. Vidal said an inhabitant and not a citizen, for in Salonica he could not really grasp what was meant by the latter term. Although free and privileged, the Sephardim of Salonica remained subjects of the Sublime Port, and not citizens. Naturalized Italians like the Nahums were no longer subjects, but although they enjoyed privileges in the Turks' country, they did not live in Italy and so could not enjoy their rights as citizens.

In certain respects, Vidal is an Oriental-Western Sephardi of the medieval type, which existed before the Sephardim' inclusion within a nation-state. Under Nazism and the Vichy government, he continued to believe that modern anti-Semitic persecution was of a religious nature, as it was in the time of Isabella the Catholic. In other respects, Vidal was an Oriental Westerner of the modern type: although non-religious, and a naturalized French citizen, at heart he still retained a fearful and admiring respect for authority, congratulated his local representative and the President of the Republic after every election, and never dared take an active part in political struggles (he was never a militant and did not understand the weird compulsion that had taken hold of his son); when he became a citizen he felt that he had been given a title, not a right. In the same way, he held an Oriental-Western view of the law. He believed that the law was never totally impersonal and abstract. It was malleable and, by using one's skill and persistence when dealing with representatives of power, one could hope, not to get round it, but to make it bend. Lastly, he would introduce himself as Mr. Vidal to strangers or new acquaintances, partly through Oriental prudence, in order to conceal his true identity for a time, and partly because he wanted to be integrated into the French world. Thus East and West were combined in him and referred back to one another continually.

The distance covered from the imperial city of the East to the great capital of a Western State was at once very small (because Vidal was already Frenchified) and very great (because it took him a long time to grasp what is meant by a nation-state and a citizen, and in fact he never did completely grasp their meaning). His nostalgia for Salonica was mixed up with his regret for the Ottoman Empire, which had given the Sephardim a warm reception, protection, autonomy, prosperity and peace, and whose collapse had brought ruin, war, and ultimately the death of Sephardic Salonica. In fact, towards the end of his life a Turkish element, which had been introduced into his Sephardic culture, resurfaced in Vidal, in proverbs like: "Patience is the key to happiness," or: "The eye sees, the soul desires," and haunting songs, or curses.

In short, Vidal experienced an Oriental–Occidental poly-identity from which he derived great satisfaction: although he was first and foremost a Salonician, a child of Salonica, his small but true homeland turned paradise lost, essentially irreducible to any other place in the Sephardic world, he was also specifically Judeo–Spanish, more broadly a son of the Jewish people, and more broadly still Mediterranean, and he became a Frenchman both by chance and by predilection. He was Salonician, Sephardic, Mediterranean and French in a concentric and interwoven fashion. He was never from a single "place." He was neither nomadic nor sedentary, but sedentarized and nomadizable.

His sister Henriette and his brother Jacques spoke French without any trace of accent, and Mathilde, who was a polyglot, had a barely noticeable lilt; Léon's accent contained some intonations of mysterious origin, and his enunciation and manner of speaking seemed very British, devoid of gestures or exuberance, while Henri retained the Marseillais accent he had acquired in his twenties. But there was something guttural and indefinable in Vidal's voice, which was not the usual Salonician sing-song or the more Italian tonality that many of the Beressis and Mosseris possessed; instead, it was something harsh which gave French people the impression that it came from elsewhere, although they could not manage to place it.

Vidal's accent did not go away, but his transformation into a Frenchman was accentuated after his naturalization. Having become a French citizen, he experienced military camaraderie during the war, saw the introduction of gentiles into his family, with Edgar's successive wives and Fredy's wife, and himself became part of gentile families, the last of which included those of his granddaughters' husbands.

THE RELIGION OF THE FAMILY

In his ninety years, he lived through all the convulsions of the century, beginning with the eruptions in the Balkans that shook his city. As the scene of revolutions, and surrounded by would-be occupiers, Salonica went from Turkish into Greek hands, after having been threatened for a time by the Bulgarians. Vidal's life spanned the First World War, which arrived one day in Salonica, carried him away as a prisoner on a French warship and imprisoned him in the Frigolet camp, and the commercial failures of the post-war period, the 1929 crisis and the Second World War. Miraculously, Vidal survived these trials unscathed, and crucially, he was much less affected by imprisonment, persecution, danger, and external events than by the sorrows that befell him in his private life, his mourning, and the deaths of those close to him.

The reason was that his family was the substance of his life. It was a big family, with the *pater familias* presiding over his many children (six in Vidal's family), which expanded into a clan with the addition of uncles and cousins, and into a tribe with the addition of brothers and sisters-in-law. The family was an organic, legal, psychological, economic and indeed religious community. Until his generation, although marriages were no longer arranged by parents, they still required their consent, and when Vidal met Luna at Salomon Beressi's house, he asked her father's permission to marry the young girl. Later, it was the family that arranged his marriage to Sara Menahem.

The children's jobs, like their marriages, were subject to their father's approval. David Nahum had guided his sons' professional lives; he prevented Vidal from studying medicine, and, in spite of his disappointment, Vidal obeyed without protest or resentment.

After their father's death, authority was passed on to the eldest brother, Léon. Dispersal, far from slackening family ties, had made them stronger. The family's solidarity as a community became even more effective when its members were far from one another. The brothers continued to pay their mother an allowance; they did the same for their brother Jacques' widow as long as she lived, and when Henri ran out of customers, his brother Léon employed him in his business and, despite the fact that he was not very competent, kept him on with almost nothing to do. Léon and Vidal also helped Henri later when he was ill. Until Vidal's generation, the family had played the role of social security and health insurance. In his old age, Vidal even wanted to reunite his dead in the same Parisian cemetery.

Conflicts were resolved within the family by the father, and within the tribe by a relative endowed with authority. In Paris, it was his uncle by marriage, Hananel Beressi, whom Vidal invested with the role of judge and arbitrator.

The Nahum's post-Salonician diaspora corresponded to their father's plans, and benefited from bridgeheads of family and friends in France. The diaspora created a network of trust and mutual assistance that crossed over oceans and national boundaries. During the period between the wars, the Nahum family set up a communal network between Brussels, Paris, Belgrade and later Liverpool. When Vidal arrived in Paris, he began working in exports, like his new relatives Salomon and Samy Beressi, and later he continued to do some export business through the Benmayor family from Izmir, into which his niece Aimée had married. Family members, relatives and friends could trust one another's word, excluding the need for contracts or legal documents. There was never any abuse or conflict, nor even any squabbling, within this network of trust.

It was because the family was a concrete community in which he had invested both his interest and his disinterest that Vidal felt no compulsion to fight for an idea, nor any desire for revolution. However, immediately after his generation, the solidarity network would splinter under the pressure of centrifugal forces.

DIASPORA WITHIN THE DIASPORA

The Salonician diaspora extended into the world of relatives who had lost touch with one another. Many of the sons and daughters of David Nahum's brothers lived apart in different countries and lost all contact with their own sons and daughters. This had happened to the children of Salomon, David's brother, who had emigrated to Italy with their father, the representative for Fernet-Branca in Salonica. But Vidal had found and noted down the address of one of them, Raffaele, whom he never met, but whom his son got to know after he sent him the news of his father's death. (Raffaele could almost pass for Vidal's twin brother, in his face and expression as well as his vivacity and vitality.) Vidal also had the addresses of relatives he had never seen before, but whom he had been able to meet in Los Angeles and whom he almost met in New York.

The great breaks with the past occurred in the next generation. First of all, there was the break with Salonica, a city unknown to those who were born in the West, where the remaining members of Vidal's family, Azriel Frances and his children, were almost all wiped out.

The break was demographic, cultural and ethical, and it transformed the very structure of the family and the very notion of the individual. In David Nahum's generation, families had between four and eight children. In Vidal's generation, the nuclear couple with one or two children replaced the big family; in the next generation, the individualist ethos replaced family solidarity, and the national culture of the gentiles replaced Sephardic culture.

The diaspora of Vidal's generation had created an interfamilial network that was also international. The diaspora within the diaspora gradually broke this network up into separate micro-networks, which were themselves dissolved.

The descendants of the Nahums and Beressis have tended naturally, without any encouragement, to adopt a form of neo-Marranism, or double identity, one side belonging to the people of the Law, and the other to the Western "Franks."

The eldest child in the next generation, Liliane, Henriette's daughter, had married a Salonician, Mony Covo, in Paris, as tradition dictated. Liliane and Mony did not have children, but they practically adopted Véronique, the daughter born of Edgar's gentile marriage.

Aimée, Henriette's younger daughter, married a man from Smyrna (which would have been almost unthinkable in Salonica), and settled in Liverpool; her son Pierre, who was born English, made a gentile marriage to an Englishwoman, and his children are now definitively part of the British world.

Chary, Léon's daughter, married a man from Smyrna, whose family were of Livornese origin, and had married into an old Provençal family called

Naquet. They settled in Avignon, and had children who married gentiles and bore French names.

Régine did not marry; she had a passionate love affair with a gentile, an aviator from Toulouse, who was obliged to return to a base in North Africa and probably died during the war.

Hélène married an Austrian Jew, Paul Schrecker, and followed him to the United States, where she became an American citizen. She divorced her husband, moved to Ottawa, and broke off her relations with all of the Nahums, apart from her cousin Chary. She has recently married a gentile, of Canadian nationality, and has become a Canadian citizen.

Edgar and Edgard, the two cousins who were almost the same age, both experienced in their childhood, at school, what was for them the incomprehensible mystery of being Jewish, for they had never been initiated into the Mosaic Law. Edgar married three gentile women, while Edgard married one, and produced three children, who live in the gentile world.

Vidal's three cousins, Paul, Saül and Murat, married gentiles. Saül, who became religious after the war, nevertheless told his niece, who wanted to marry a gentile: "Go ahead, in the Bible it happens all the time" (Jews marrying non-Jews, that is).

In Genova, Italy, Raffaele Nahum married a Catholic; his three children also married gentiles.

On the Beressi side, Samy Beressi was the first to marry a gentile, before the 1914 war. He was from the same generation as Salomon Beressi, Luna and Corinne's father. His eldest daughter, Édith, married a gentile; his other daughter married a Veil, then separated from him and adopted a gentile daughter. His two sons, Alex and Roger, also entered the gentile world.

Élie Beressi married a gentile, while Hananel married a woman from Marseilles whose family came from Algeria.

Pepo, son of Salomon Beressi and Myriam Mosseri, married a Sephardi woman whose family had left Usküp for Salonica. Pepo's children, Jean-Marc and André, married Miss Tordjman, of Morroccan Jewish origin, and Miss Chazal, from the Auvergne, respectively.

Benjamin took a gentile for his wife and had a daughter by her, Odette, who was lost to her family after her father's deportation, and later found again by her aunt Émy and included in Maurice Cohen's tribe.

Émy married Maurice Cohen, who was born in Istanbul; her three children, Raymond, Marie-Claude and Maurice-Gérard were married, several times, to gentiles.

Among Corinne's children, Fredy married a gentile woman and had a son by her, called Michel. Henri remained a bachelor, in spite or because of Vidal and Corinne's efforts to marry him off. Daisy married Maurice's younger brother. Her daughter Corinne went to Bolivia. She had an affair with an Indian man there, and came back to give birth to a boy, to whom she gave the solar name of Inti. Her sister Marianne had a relationship with a Chilean who had taken refuge in France after General Pinochet's coup d'état, and she had a child by him whose Araucan name, Nahuel (which means "spring"), curiously begins with the same four letters as Nahum.

Edgar's daughters also married gentiles. Irène married the son of a Corsican general, and Véronique married the son of a Piedmontese proletarian and a Jurassian laborer, who, after having been in the maquis during the war, and a union leader and militant socialist after that, would study to become a certified architect.

Note that in this post–Salonician diaspora, not one of the Nahums or Beressis chose to live in Israel. Moreover, apart from the two Angel sisters, not one of them returned to the observance of Mosaic Law.

THE DEATH OF A CULTURE

The fire of 1917 had destroyed the Sephardic city. Hellenization, which began in 1912, continued in 1922 and became linguistic after 1930, had slowly begun to dissolve Sephardic culture before the Nazis exterminated almost all of its 56,000 representatives. History effaced what had been the only city in the world with a Spanish Jewish majority. In Salonica, two last vestiges remain: the Association of Survivors, whose existence is coming to an end, and the bookseller and publisher Molho.

Sephardic culture, which had been kept alive for four centuries nearly two thousand miles away from Spain, was diluted in France, as it was in the United States, in Argentina and in Israel.

It had its time of prosperity under Livornese influence, which necessarily led to its dissolution when the city and the empire were shattered by the upsurge of the new nation-states. Sephardic culture had once integrated secular culture; now secular culture integrated and disintegrated it in turn. The old Spanish *djidio* was spoken less and less among the 360,000 descendants of the line dispersed throughout the world.[82] It is because it is no longer spoken in kitchens that it is taught at the University in Paris today.

Thus, this culture died a double death: the atrocious one of Nazi extermination, and the gentle one of integration into the secular world of the gentiles.

Integration is also disintegration. It is both gain and loss. Should we accept and go along with the process? Try to delay it? The answer to both questions is yes. All cultures want to live. All cultures are mortal. As the wise man Hadj Garm' Orin said: "Like a human being, a culture should want to live and know how to die."

STATELESS AND POLY-STATELESS

Gentiles whose identities were formed by a nation-state see the "Levantine" Jews (a term which has long had an oily and treacherous connotation for anti-Semites) as stateless persons, and their dislike for them will only be increased by the tales of Vidal the Salonician's misadventures during the First World War.

However, when one examines the history of the Jews who settled in Spain, the most remarkable thing about them is their ability to put down roots in the Sepharad, and also, in spite of their expulsion, their fidelity to these roots, which they put down again unchanged in the East. They would probably have been very naturally integrated into the Iberian melting pot, if they had not been driven out by the Catholic Kings; and indeed the Spanish government belatedly recognized their right to reacquire Spanish nationality with the law of December 20,1924.

The Sephardim of Salonica put down roots there, and made it their homeland; it would take the great fire, Hellenization, and the Nazis to destroy this homeland. Sephardim will always put down roots if they are left alone for long enough. As a Salonician, Vidal had very strong roots, and he put down roots again in France. His was a sedentary nature, but history made a nomad out of him.

However, his ability to take root so easily also meant that the Sephardi was poly-rooted. Vidal was umbilically linked to a Mediterranean homeland with multiple Jewish, Hispanic and Italian roots. This Sephardi had known a motherland, made himself a fatherland, and put down roots; but he had no real experience of a nation-state, which was an invention of modern Europe, and represented another type of religion, as Toynbee saw very clearly, which brought its own hatred and intolerance with it. This religion, which has become that of the Nation of Israel today, was inconceivable to the Sephardim of the Ottoman Empire.

However, what was present in Salonica, which Paul of Tarsus once visited, and which was marked by Marranism, Shabbataism, and, we would add, Livornoism, all of which in their way broke with the constraints of the Mosaic Law, was a message, which was already latent in Paul's sermons and those of Shabbatai Zevi, in the experience of the Marranos, and later in that of the *Dönmes*. Once this message became non-religious, which it did as early as 1670 with Spinoza,[83] it agreed with the humanism of the gentiles: that beyond the divisions of populations and beliefs, there is the greater people of human beings, whose Homeland is the planet Earth.

"PASTELLICO"

Edgar, Vidal's son, experienced both the break between two generations, and the consequences of a deep inner rupture caused by the death of his mother. He felt estranged from his family, and especially from the Nahum family, loving only his Beressi grandmother without reserve. It was probably the unconscious search for a community, and the incredible void left by a mother who made him discover, lose and recover the infinite in love, which led him to join the Party of Revolution.

Having lost his culture early on, then retrieved it through his own studies, he became strongly aware of his neo–Marranism at the age of 40; he did not see neo–Marranism as incomplete in some way, but instead embraced its richness. At the time, he wrote: "I keep one foot, and get my kicks, in French society, but the other foot is in Italy, in Spain, in the East, wandering, always elsewhere . . . "

His life does not represent a break with Vidal's, but a continuation of it; his loss of culture is a logical consequence of the process of secularization that began in Livorno in the 18th century, and grew until it became almost complete in Salonica in the years between 1870 and 1900, followed by the emigration, itself logical, to France, and finally by the disintegration of the family in his generation. In the same way, by assuming a double identity, not a hidden one like that of the *Dönmes* or Jacob Frank, but half-open and half-closed, Edgar has taken Salonician Marranism and Shabbataism into the secular world. Even though he has lost his faith in earthly salvation, he has never ceased to be deeply moved by the "Messianism" that inspires those who break with the Jewish world without entering that of the gentiles, and who hope for a new world where – as Paul of Tarsus, another example of double identity, said – there would no longer be either Jews or gentiles.

Edgar has fully retained Vidal's Mediterranean tropism. He was delighted by his discovery of Spain and Italy; later, after some wavering and before knowing of his Livornese ancestry, it became clear to him that Tuscany was his true motherland.

This Parisian loves French cooking; he adores *andouillette* and *ris de veau*;[84] but he prefers Mediterranean cooking, with olive oil, and above all he loves Salonician-style eggplant gratin and *pastellico*. When Corinne still enjoyed cooking, she would always keep aside a portion for Edgar whenever she prepared gratins or *pastellico*. Edgar taught Edwige, a blue-eyed child of the North, how to make an eggplant gratin, and now when she wants to give him a treat when he returns from a journey, she makes him a *sfongattico*. Corinne taught Irène how to make *pastellico*. Liliane also taught Véronique how to make *pastellico*, and she makes a *pastellico* when she invites friends to dinner, and especially if her father is coming.

This family-sized *pastellico*, a large cheese tart roasted in the oven, and the *borekita*, a little single-portion pastry made with the same ingredients, has its origins in the depths of history. Spain has a kind of *borekita*, which emigrated to Argentina and Chile, where it became the *empanada*. *Boreks* spread throughout the Ottoman world, and there is a Greek version made with puff pastry, called *tiropitas*, which the Salonicians called "pastelles de *fojas*." In Tunisia, puff pastry *briks* are garnished with egg. In Morrocco, the equivalent of the *borek* is a sweet cake. Accordingly, the ancestors and cousins of the *pastellico* have scattered and flourished in their different varieties all over the Mediterranean, and are common to Moorish, Jewish and Christian Spain as well as to the Balkan peoples. It is probable that the Sephardim had been familiar with the *pastellico* for more than a thousand years in Spain, and that it accompanied them to Salonica, where, *hecho de las manos benditchas de la madre* (made by the mother's blessed hands), it was present at every family reunion and celebration. Then the *pastellico* crossed the Mediterranean again, and arrived in France with the Sephardim from the East. And when Sephardic culture became diluted among the Franks, its matricial kernel survived; as in every culture, this kernel is a gastronomic one, and the kernel of this kernel is the *pastellico*. Having become maternal food to its children, *pastellico* is now the only survivor, in Véronique's French and gentile world, of the engulfed world of Sephardic Salonica. It is not eaten eucharistically or mystically, but not in an exclusively material way either. It reminds those who knew and loved him of the look in Vidal's blue eyes.

Chronology

1391	Massacres of Jews in Spain. Massive conversions to Catholicism.
1430	Turks seize Salonica.
1453	Fall of Byzantium.
1480	Creation of the Inquisition in Spain.
1492	Fall of Grenada. Unification of Spain under the Catholic Kings. Departure of Christopher Columbus. Jews who do not convert to Catholicism are expelled from Spain and Aragon. Converts (*conversos*) become Marranos. The Ottoman Empire welcomes the Sephardim (Spanish Jews).
1498	Expulsion or conversion of Jews in Portugal and Navarre.
1500	Around 20,000 Sephardim settle in Salonica.
1515	First printing press in Salonica.
1523	Charter of liberation, according and guaranteeing autonomy to the Sephardim of Salonica.
1565–1566	Boycott of Ancona by Sephardic trade.
1568–1578	Salonica waits in vain for the Messiah.
1571	Turkish naval defeat at Lepanto (entrance to the gulf of Corinth).
1593	The grand duchy of Tuscany allows Jews to emigrate to Livorno.
1648	Dr. Fernando Cardoso, a Spanish Catholic, arrives in the Venice ghetto, where he becomes Isaac Cardoso. His younger brother Miguel also returns to Judaism, and becomes Abraham Cardoso.
1655	Shabbatai Zevi, born in Smyrna in 1626, proclaims himself Messiah. He preaches in Salonica. The Sephardic people begin waiting joyfully for imminent redemption. Abraham Cardoso, who has settled in Livorno, becomes one of his apostles.
1662	Manuel Boccaro Frances, a Marrano who has come to Livorno from Portugal via Amsterdam, and reconverted to Judaism, dies on the road to Florence. He may have been an ancestor of Vidal's maternal family.
1666	The Messiah Shabbatai Zevi converts to Islam.
1669	Seizure of Candie by the Turks. The decline of Venice, which will bring about that of Salonica, begins.

1676	Death of the messiah. His message lives on in secret sects, especially the Islamic sect of the *Dönmes*.
1699	Hungary and Transylvania achieve independence from the Ottomans.
1714	Catherine of Russia gains control of the Black Sea.
1718	Belgrade, Albania, Dalmatia and Herzegovina win independence from the Ottoman Empire.
1764	Beccaria publishes *Dei delitti e delle pene* in Livorno.
1765–1790	Pietro Leopoldo de Hapsburg, grand-duke of Tuscany, reigns as an "enlightened despot."
1770	Russian victory over the Turks.
1776	Birth of Lazare Allatini in Livorno.
	Last decades of the c.18th.
	Some of the Nahums, Franceses and Beressis leave Livorno for Salonica.
1796	Foundation of the Allatini and Modiano firms in Salonica.
1799–1814	Tuscany under French influence.
1803	*Birth of David S. Nahum in Salonica.*
1809	Birth of Moses Allatini in Salonica.
1817	Serbia obtains autonomy.
1826	Suppression of the Janissaries.
1830	Greek Independence. *Marriage of David S. Nahum to Miss de Botton. Birth of Joseph Beressi in Salonica.*
1831	Beginning of the era of reforms in the Ottoman Empire (Tanzimat).
1832	Cholera epidemic in Salonica.
1834	Death of Lazare Allatini. Moses Allatini, a doctor from Florence, comes to Salonica to take over his father's businesses.
1851	*Death of David S. Nahum. Posthumous birth of David D. Nahum.*
1852	Arrival of the first steam ship in the port of Salonica.
1856	Salomon Fernandez founds a modern Italian school in Salonica.
1858	Moses Allatini founds a modern French school in Salonica.
1858	Romania gains autonomy.
1861	*Birth of Salomon Beressi, son of Joseph Beressi.*
1862	*Birth of Dona Helena Frances.*
1866	Salem school opens.
1873	Universal Israelite Alliance school opens.
1874	The Matalon affair. Etz Haïm conservative society founded.
1875	Intimates Club created.
1876	Austria occupies Bosnia-Herzegovina. Beginning of Reign of Sultan Abdul-Hamid begins (1876–1909).

1877	Rabbi Gattegno attempts to impose a tax on the Franks. Non-religious Jews oppose him and he is defeated.
1877	Bulgarian Independence. *Birth of Myriam Mosseri.*
1877–1888	Rail link between Salonica and the West.
1878	*La Epoca*, first Spanish-language newspaper, founded. *David D. Nahum goes to the Universal Exposition in Paris. Joseph Beressi murdered.*
1878	Russo-Turkish war. Treaty of San Stefano. Congress of Berlin recognizes sovereignty of Danube and Balkan states.
1879	*Marriage of David D. Nahum and Dona Helena Frances.*
1880	Reform of the Talmud Tora, which begins teaching Italian and French.
1881	France seizes Tunisia (previously under Ottoman domination).
1881	*Birth of Henriette, eldest daughter of David D. Nahum.*
1882	*Death of Moses Allatini. David Nahum adds metallurgy to his import–export activities.*
1882	Great Britain seizes Egypt.
1883	*Birth of Léon Nahum.*
1885	*Birth of Jacques Nahum.*
1890	Individual taxation begins in the Ottoman Empire. City gas installed in Salonica.
1893	Tram system set up in Salonica.
1894	*Birth of Vidal.*
1896	Installation of drinking water supply to homes.
1897	Massacre of Armenians, Cretans and Macedonians by the Turks. *True birth date of Mathilde, last child of David D. Nahum. Birth of Luna Beressi, first child of Salomon Beressi.*
1898	*David D. Nahum becomes representative for the Mantachoff firm, importing petroleum from Baku to the Ottoman Empire.*
1898	*Birth of Pepo Beressi.*
1900	Salonica has more than 90,000 inhabitants; 56% are Sephardim (5% of whom are consular protégés), 20% Greeks, 11% Dönmes, 10% Turks, 4% Bulgarians and others. *Samy Beressi settles in France. Vidal begins to attend the Franco-German school.*
1901	*David Nahum mans the office of the Belgian consulate in Salonica.*
1902	Earthquake in Salonica.
1902	*David Nahum receives the civic medal, 1ˢᵗ class, from the King of the Belgians.*
1903	Bulgarian comitadjis blow up the Ottoman Bank in Salonica.
1904	*Henriette Nahum marries Élie Hassid.*
1906	*Birth of Liliane, daughter of Henriette and Élie Hassid.*
1906–1909	*Léon Nahum travels in Western Europe.*

1907	*Vidal and Cornelie Monday of Montreal exchange postcards.*
1908	*Death of David S. Nahum's widow, Vidal's grandmother. Hananel Beressi moves to Marseilles.*
1908	Young Turk revolution in Salonica. Ferdinand of Bulgaria proclaims himself Tsar of the Bulgarians. Austria annexes Bosnia–Herzegovina.
1909	*Birth in Paris of Roger Beressi, son of Samy Beressi and Gaby Lombard.*
1910	*La Solidaridad ovradera* reports on the first socialist conference in Salonica. *Vidal leaves the Franco-German school at 16, and works in his brother-in-law Élie Hassid's office. Léon marries Julie Menahem, whose father is a member of the Intimates Club.*
1911	Italy conquers Tripoli. *David Nahum, an Italian citizen, takes refuge in Vienna with his wife and his two youngest children, Vidal and Mathilde. Jacques and Henri take refuge Brussels with their elder brother Léon. Vidal gets a job in Vienna and falls in love with Wilhelmine.* Election in Salonica of Sephardic representative Emmanuel Carasso.
1912	Balkan States attack Turkey. Greece conquers Salonica and Macedonia.
1913	Balkan States go to war against Bulgaria.
1913	*Léon Nahum settles in Istanbul and oversees the construction of the Anatolian railroad. Birth of Émilie Beressi. Vidal makes a fruitless attempt to move to Paris.*
1914	First World War begins. Greece remains neutral. *Salomon Beressi leaves Salonica for Marseilles.*
1915	Anglo-French landing in the Dardanelles fails. The French set up camp in Salonica, and form the Eastern Army there (in October). Greece remains neutral, but Venizelos revolts against the king and forms a government in the enclave of Salonica. Bulgaria enters the war and crushes Serbia, whose army is forced back to Salonica. Italy joins the war on the side of the Allies. *Salomon Beressi's wife and children join him in Marseilles.*
1916	*Vidal and his brother Henri are arrested by the French military police on January 27, and then transferred by sea to Marseilles, where they are imprisoned. Then they are sent to the camp at Frigolet. David Nahum leaves Salonica to try and free his sons, and settles in Marseilles. Vidal and Henri have "Salonician" nationality recognized by the President of the French Council.*
1917	The Allies depose the King of Greece in July, and Venizelos brings Greece into the war. On August 5, a huge fire destroys the Sephardic city. *Vidal's secret love affair. Mathilde's engagement.*

1918	Armistice. *The Nahum family regroups in Marseilles. Mathilde gets married.*
1919	*Vidal travels to London to buy prefabricated houses. The collapse of the franc brings an end to the operation. Vidal goes to live in Paris, in the Rue Clauzel.*
1920	*Salomon Beressi meets Vidal in the Sentier in Paris, and invites him to spend Passover with his family. Vidal seeks permission to marry his daughter Luna. Vidal's marriage. David D. Nahum dies. Vidal tries his luck in Germany.*
1921	*Vidal moves to the Rue Mayran. Salomon Beressi dies. German Mark collapses. Corinne gets married. Edgar, Vidal's son, and Edgard, Léon's son, are born.*
1922	*Vidal opens a store in the Sentier, at number 52, Rue d'Aboukir, and becomes a hosiery wholesaler.*
1923	*Fredy born.*
1926	*Liliane gets married.*
1929	Wall Street Crash. *Death of Samy Beressi.*
1930	*Léon Nahum moves to Paris temporarily. Aimée gets married. Chary gets married. Vidal buys some land at Rueil.*
1931	*Vidal becomes a French citizen. Move to Rueil. Death of his wife Luna.* "Pogrom" in Salonica.
1932	*Vidal's son has foot-and-mouth disease. Émy gets married. Vidal has money problems.*
1933	Hitler takes power.
1934	Riot in Paris on February 6.
1935	*Vidal at his mother's house. Vidal at the Coq-Héron.*
1936	Popular Front. Spanish civil war begins. *Vidal's mother dies. Vidal remarries (in December).*
1937	*Vidal leaves his second wife (in June). He moves into the Rue des Plâtrières.*
1938	Munich.
1939	Second World War begins. Phoney war.
1940	*Vidal drafted to the Bourges munitions factory (in March).* German troops invade France (June). *Vidal retreats to Toulouse.* Marshall Pétain asks for an armistice. De Gaulle calls for Resistance (June 18). *Vidal returns to Paris (August). His store is put under temporary supervision (December).*
1941	*Mathilde in Italy (May).* German troops invade the U.S.S.R. (June). *Vidal leaves Paris for Toulouse (August).* German advance halted at the approach to Moscow (December).
1942	*Bouchi dies in Abbazia (February).* Jews obliged to wear yellow star in northern zone (May). Gemans invade southern zone. Italians control Nice (November). Stalingrad resists (November). *Vidal moves to Nice (November–December).*

1943	German surrender at Stalingrad (February). *Jacques and his family, Chary and her family take refuge in Italy (May).* Mussolini deposed and arrested (July). *Léon and his family take refuge in Italy (August).* German troops occupy Italy (September). Deportation and full-scale extermination of Salonica's Sephardic population. *Henriette and her family, unable to take refuge in Italy, go into hiding near Lyon (September-October). Joseph Pelosoff arrested at Nice station (October).* Massive Russian advance (Autumn). *Vidal moves to La Rochetaillée under the name of Louis Blanc.*
1944	Allies land in Normandy (June). Soviet troops enter German territory (June). Insurrection and liberation of Paris (August). *Jacques dies during the Florence insurrection. Vidal returns to Paris (September). He retrieves his store and apartment, and moves with Corinne and her children to the Rue Demours.*
1945	Germany surrenders (May).
1946	*Myriam Beressi dies.*
1947	*Henriette, Vidal's elder sister, dies.*
1947	*Mathilde gets married in Milan and immediately gets divorced. Vidal's first granddaughter born.*
1948	*Vidal's second granddaughter born.*
1949	*Vidal leaves his store in the Rue d'Aboukir and moves to the Rue Mulhouse where he tries his hand at the textile business.*
1951	*Vidal and Corinne get married.*
1952	*After his store in the Rue Mulhouse fails, Vidal opens another in the Rue d'Aboukir.*
1954	*Corinne and Vidal buy a piece of land in Vaux-sur-Seine.*
1955	*Vidal sells his apartment in the Rue Demours.*
1958	*Vidal opens a store in the Rue Beauregard. Pepo Beressi dies in the métro.*
1963	*Élie Hassid dies.*
1964	*Vidal receives the medal of the City of Paris.*
1965	*Henri dies.*
1966	*Vidal opens his last store in the Rue de la Lune.*
1967	*Maurice Cohen dies.*
1968	*Sophie, Jacques's widow, dies.*
1969	*Vidal saves Mathilde.*
1970	*Journey to California.*
1971	*Second journey to California. Léon dies.*
1972 (?)	*Pilgrimage to Spain.*
1973	*Pilgrimage to Salonica and Israel.*
1974	*Cataract operation.*
1975	*Pilgrimage to Livorno.*
1976	*Mathilde dies.*

1978	*Vidal records his oral autobiography.*
1979	*Liliane and Mony die. Vidal is decorated with the Order of Merit.*
1982	*Roland and Alice, Vidal's great-grandchildren, born.*
1983	*Gilles, Vidal's great-grandson, born.*
	First separation with Corinne.
1984	*Second separation with Corinne. Corinne comes back. Vidal dies on August 9 at the age of 91.*
1986	*Corinne dies.*

Edgar Morin
Diary of a Life

BY CRISTINA PASQUALINI

Edgar Morin was born in Paris in 1921. He has a multi-faceted personality and, coherently with the logics of complexity, he has always denied belonging exclusively to one disciplinary field, avoiding all kinds of labels and, in particular, the one of sociologist *tout-court*. Giovanni Reale – one of the greatest Italian philosophers of the 20th century – has called him one of the most prestigious personalities not only in French culture but in European culture in general. He has been called a sociologist but this expression becomes rather reductive in his case since he has the full stature of a philosopher. Actually, Morin likes to call himself simply Research Director for the French National Research Centre (CNRS) in Paris. Even though he does not shun being considered an intellectual, he does not presume to define himself as such. He does not feel that he is a master and when he is addressed as such he instinctively has the same reaction as the French writer, Georges Courteline, who, when any of his admirers called him master, would reply: you are treating me like an old fool. Morin is still in the sociology department of the CNRS, where he claims he would like to remain for the rest of his life even though he has often moved outside the field of sociology and some of his works are not sociological, strictly speaking, but historical, psychological, and political. They are, simply, multidisciplinary works.

Morin best identifies with the figure of the traditional intellectual precisely because, in trying to overcome the fragmentation of thinking and of knowledge, he tries to deal with human, moral, philosophical and political problems apparently in a non-specialist way, with the aim of reaching a general public, at times with a militant intent. Alain Touraine called him a planetary thinker, a planetary humanist, during the celebrations for his eightieth birthday at the UNESCO headquarters in Paris. As a matter of fact, Morin has a greater intellectual prestige than he likes to admit. We know, in fact, that he has had – and still has – prestigious roles in the international cultural and scientific panorama: besides being emeritus director of research at the CNRS in Paris for the department of human and social sciences, Morin is also president of the Agence Européenne pour la Culture for UNESCO in Paris, director of CETSAP (Centre d'Etudes Transdisciplinaires –

309

Sociologie, Antropologie, Politique) associated to the Ecole des Hautes Etudes en Sciences Sociales in Paris, President of the Association pour la Pensée Complexe, founding member of the Academie de la Latinité, co-director of the journal "Communications", and President of the Multiversidad Mundo Real Edgar Morin in Mexico. Over the past few years Morin has promoted and supported numerous events on an international level, including the setting up of Ce.R.Co. (Centre for Research on Anthropology and the Epistemology of Complexity) in Italy, at the University of Bergamo, and the Edgar Morin Study Centre for the Philosophy of Complexity, at the University of Messina (Italy). Moreover, he has collaborated with projects far and wide, which have met with great success not only in Europe but also in the rest of the world (Latin America, Mexico, Spain, China, etc.).

His scientific reflections have inevitably felt the effect of his formation, of his religious and cultural origins, of his background. Morin the man presents strong ties with Morin's man, in other words thinking and life blend, contaminate each other, are interwoven in the same Morinian scientific production (Morin and Pasqualini, 2007). If one goes over some of the significant events in Morin's life, his diaries and his writings shed light on the reasons for the centrality in his research of the issue of human identity and help us understand the distinctiveness of his approach. He has led a complex life, steeped in experiences linked to exceedingly different events – the perception of his birth as an extraordinary event, "a miracle" with regard to the death the doctors had forecast; his Jewish roots; his strong connections to the Mediterranean and to Latin America; the sudden, premature loss of his mother during childhood with the subsequent feelings of guilt and deep desperation which were kept hidden for years; the alternate political events during World War II, his involvement in the Resistance against Nazism and later against Stalinism; the Cold War and the fall of the Berlin Wall; the war in the Balkans; the tragic events of 11 September 2001 – all these facts have left their mark on his biography and have affected how he addresses the issue of complexity in approaching the study of socio-anthropological problems. A criterion based on the principle that an understanding of the human condition, marked by complexity, can only occur thanks to a "reticular" model and strategy of thought, moving in a "rhizome-like" manner by means of connections and not of reductions. Thus, if one's past experiences can direct one's intellectual reflections, it is interesting to identify the principal experiences which have generated Morin's obsession with the human condition and with the present, in other words the experiences which have caused him to become a planetary thinker/humanist, which are the root of the interesting as well as distinctive and rare fusion and synthesis between Morin the man and Morin's man.

THE STAGES AND THE INTERWEAVING OF
THOUGHT AND LIFE

We have a lot of information on Morin's family of origin, thanks to the biography *Vidal et les siens* (1989) and to the autobiography, *Io, Edgar Morin. Una Storia di vita* (2007). Edgar Morin's parents – Luna Beressi and Vidal Nahum – were Sephardic Jews; his real surname is Nahum, Morin is the surname he chose when he was in the Resistance movement during World War II. A nomadic family in Europe – both the maternal and the paternal branches of his family lived for a time in Italy, Spain, Turkey – Morin's family acquired Italian citizenship during the nineteenth century and, at the time of his birth, they were about to acquire French citizenship. In his family, his ancestors had been laymen for at least three generations; the word "Jew" was never uttered, it was replaced by the expression *los nuestros*, which, however, only referred to the Spanish Jews. He did not preserve any rite or belief of the Jewish culture; on the contrary, he was socialized initially with the French culture and later with the European one (Morin 1994). Morin himself said he was a "neo-Marrano", born of the cultural syncretism of different worlds, extraneous to yet at the same time participating in each of them. This explains his Mediterranean matrix and the decision to use a hybrid language when speaking in public in Latin American countries, a language he called "*fritagnol*", a mixture of French, Italian and Spanish. A language which made the audience love him since it returned him to and linked him to his origins.

The conflict between life and death characterizes Morin's life starting from childhood. In fact, in his books (Morin and Pasqualini 2007; Morin 1994) Morin states that the most important event which marked his life indelibly was his mother's death when he was only nine. It was important not only because of the shock and pain it caused him but also because of the effect this event had on his destiny. Morin developed two fundamental approaches to life from this tragic event: a generalized scepticism and the desire for a community. A permanent search for affection, which he did not direct to religion but which he initially and briefly, during the Resistance, believed he had found in the French Communist Party. The origin of his scepticism can also be traced back to his family, Jewish migrants originally from Salonika, who never transmitted to him a religious or political culture, and who practised a family and community ethics. Thus, we can conclude that his scepticism is the most evident result of the cultural void which Morin was living in during his formative years – the aspiring to a community is connected to his condition as the son of emigrants as well as to being an only child whose mother has died.

Although his mother died when he was still young, Morin recalls that the relationship between them was intense. We also know that this relationship was crossed and marked by death on two occasions. In fact, besides the death of his mother, Morin recalls another event which was significant for him, the "secret of his birth", which his father revealed to him much later. In *Vidal et les siens* (1989), Morin says he learnt later in life that he was not the son of a king, brought up by gypsies, but an embryo doomed not to be born because of his mother. It was necessary for him to die so that his mother could live, since his life was a threat to his mother's. Luna Beressi, Morin's mother, caught Spanish flu in the 1917 epidemic and risked dying; she subsequently suffered from a heart disorder but had not told her husband that doctors had forbidden her to bear children. When she fell pregnant, since abortion methods were ineffective, she had to resign herself to accepting the risks of her pregnancy. The doctors who were consulted said that if any complications arose during the delivery, they would choose to protect the life of the mother. Indeed, Morin was almost dead at birth as the umbilical cord had nearly strangled him, yet both mother and child managed to survive.

A few years after this first event, death appeared again in Morin's life, when his mother died, suddenly and tragically in 1931. The severance of the link with his mother caused him great suffering, which he tried to hide from his father, pretending to be happy and serene. As an adult, however, Morin reproached his father for not having had the courage to face the issue of his mother's death with him as a child, as well as for making him believe that his mother had left for a long journey when it was obvious that things were totally different (Morin 1994). Morin is deeply moved as he recalls the events occurring at the time of his mother's death: "I was at school. When I left school that day, my uncle Joseph, my aunt Corinne's aunt, was waiting for me. Strangely, I was very happy that day. It was a lovely spring day and I had written a short story called *The Bandit's Love*. My teacher had read it aloud in class. My uncle Joseph said: 'We'll go to my house because your mother and father have gone on a journey'. I clearly remember that we took a convertible taxi. I was standing up and looking at the landscape. I was calm and pleased. I went to Corinne's house and did not notice anything unusual. I believe the funeral took place two days later. My mother was buried at the Père-Lachaise Cemetery, a lovely cemetery built at the beginning of the nineteenth century. There's a small park near the cemetery where children go and play. Aunt Corinne's maid took me there, together with my cousin Fredy. I believe my father wanted to see me as he was leaving the cemetery. And I remember this very clearly. I was playing on the lawn in the park, breaking a rule that was in force in Paris, when I saw my father approaching, wearing a black jacket and shoes. He spoke strictly to me: 'Do not play here!'. I immediately understood everything, everything! But I pretended nothing was the matter. I had been deprived of an extremely important thing, a last farewell to my mother. The act of going to the cemetery is not only an act of compassion but it also means saying goodbye and seeing off someone who is dearly loved and who will never come back. But they took this away from me. There lies the root of my anguish, my dreams, my nightmares, my repulsion for lies" (Morin and Pasqualini 2007: 91).

Morin had to wait till the year 1962 in order to reach some kind of inner serenity, when he fell seriously ill and once again risked dying. In *Le Vif du sujet* (1969) – the diary-essay he wrote in 1962 when he fell seriously ill and was obliged to stay in a hospital in New York for a long time – Morin reflects on the meaning of life, on his mother's death and on his relationship with his father, accompanying himself in these reflections, walking towards himself, examining emotions/ideas that had lain untouched for too long, since adolescence. This interstitial "parenthesis", which presented itself unannounced, actually represented and produced a decisive, crucial turning-point: the many feelings of guilt which had linked him to his mother's death, and which had been his constant companions throughout his childhood and adolescence, gradually lessened. As a matter of fact, *Le Vif du sujet* was neither the first nor the only diary Edgar Morin wrote. He liked the diary-form as he found it interesting to investigate the workings of the mind, to see how his thinking as well as his reasoning evolved. In general, writing a diary helped him to avoid dissipating his ideas. Thus, a natural tendency gradually developed in him to take notes, to record his ideas and intuitions every day in a notebook, and then to transcribe his notes in the evening with the help of his Olivetti typewriter, an inseparable companion in the days before the PC became so popular.

A few years after his mother's death, the first signs of what would soon become World War II started to be worryingly present in Paris. The first struggles for workers' rights and wage demands were daily events which Morin witnessed with interest and preoccupation. In the years when he was still a student, Morin was luckily not excluded or rejected by his companions – even though a "violent" form of anti-Semitism was circulating in the Thirties. Indeed, this experience caused him to develop a heightened sensitivity and solidarity for all outcasts and people discriminated against by society, and made him approach Karl Marx's political and lay messianism.

Morin can boast of a distinctive formation, which was built on the field, the result of experiences which were often sought and often contingent, but heterogeneous as regards the sources they were drawn from. Ever since he was young, and thanks to his spirit which was open to the unexpected, Morin was fascinated by literary culture, by the cinema, by anthropology, sociology, philosophy, politics and religions. His family transmitted to him a love for Mediterranean traits, and his mother, in particular, passed on to him a passion for music and a sensitivity for classical and literary culture (Morin 1994). On the other hand, his father Vidal, a tradesman in Paris, would have liked his son to follow in his footsteps and become a trader rather than devote himself to classical studies. He dreamt he would one day call his shop *Vidal & Son*. However, Morin intended to follow his mother's suggestions and enrolled at the Lycée and later at University. Morin's first initiation into reading can be called "street culture", and it was thanks to this early socializing that even today he does not feel any of the cultural disdain which is typical of intellectuals coming from the "well-to-do" classes in society, the intellectuals who have always been dismissive of popular cultural forms such as songs or novels which at first sight may not present any literary claim, or films that are not "d'essai" (Morin, 1994). The films he loved include *Le Chemin de la vie*, 1931, a Russian film by Nicolaj Ekk; a German film, "*The Tragedy in the Mine*", and "*The Three-Penny Opera*", a film on emigration based on Bertolt Brecht's work. Morin, however, is not only the result of "street culture": ever since his early years at the Lycée he has had a passion for the great masters, like Montaigne, Pascal, Balzac, Zola, Tolstoj and Dostoevsky. He pursued these interests when he was studying at the Sorbonne in Paris and went to the lectures given by Georges Lefevbre on the French Revolution, or the private lectures given by Jankélévitch, and studied Marx and Engels's reflections on philosophy and economics in depth. His decision to enrol simultaneously at the Faculties of Humanities (History), of Law and of Political Science, was based on the fact that from a very early age Morin had always shown a multiplicity of interests in different fields of research, as well as a penchant for considering the complexity of the real. This led him to the study of history, economics, law, philosophy and sociology.

Towards the end of the Thirties, in the years in which the Spanish Civil War was being fought, Morin was studying at University and started his political commitment. At first, he collaborated with an anarchic organization called *Solidarité international antifasciste*, then became an active member of the Front Party. Morin recalls that this stage of his life was characterized by great worries and indecision because France showed a strong propensity to pacifism following the heavy cost in human lives and widespread destruction in the aftermath of World War I. In 1940, at the outbreak of World War II and as anti-Semitic laws were being passed, Morin was obliged to abandon his studies at university and decided to leave Paris, seeking refuge at first in Toulouse and then in Lyon. It was in Toulouse that Morin recovered his life and his freedom. As he is fond of recalling, at the very time when most people were being brutally deprived of their individual freedom, he had finally cut the umbilical cord that had tied him to his father, who had over the years exerted a strict control over his actions, most likely shaped by his excessive feelings of love and worry over his only child. In Toulouse, Morin discovered the warmth of the community, the warmth he had sought for years within the family domestic life and which he had, at least partially, learnt to do without. He soon became secretary general of a reception centre for refugees. In 1942, in Toulouse, Morin started becoming involved in clandestine actions, which led him to enrol in the French Communist Party and officially take an active role in the Resistance. However, this was not an easy decision for him to take, as it was fear which lay at the root of his greatest doubts. In those times of hesitation, before becoming committed to

314

Communism, Morin was actually considering leaving France clandestinely and going to Geneva, where Jean Piaget, among others, had settled. Retrospectively, Morin has always claimed that he made the right decision and that if he had not taken an active part in the Resistance this would have been a great existential loss to him.

The period of the Resistance which he spent between Lyon and Toulouse – as Morin recalls in *Autocritique* (1959) – was actually a time full of meetings, friendships, loves, important readings. Suffice it to note that once Morin had become clandestine, he was frequently obliged to change identity to avoid being identified and tracked down by the Gestapo. The origin of his name is both casual and odd. Morin had actually decided to use the surname Manin both because it was the name of the protagonist in a short story by Malraux, and because it was the name of a Venetian revolutionary. One day, while he was living in Toulouse, Morin introduced himself to a group of people as Manin, but they – for no evident reason – started calling him Morin. And that is the surname that has stayed with him to this day: Edgar Nahum Morin.

The period after the end of World War II was experienced by Morin quite differently to the period of the Resistance. On returning to Paris, he no longer had the community based on friendships, solidarity and strong ties, which he had been a part of in Toulouse and in Lyon. He was disoriented and, being strongly affected by the events he had experienced, he no longer felt the urge to finish his university studies or motivated to take up teaching as an occupation. Thus, he chose to work as a journalist for the PCF (Parti communiste français – the French Communist Party) – but this activity did not gratify him intellectually and actually made him perceive the excessive control exerted by the Party. At the time, he was still a militant, among other activities and on a more occasional and detached way, of the Party. He gave up being a journalist, decided to marry Violette Chapellaubeau – who had been his companion in the Resistance and who was to be the mother of his two daughters, Irène and Véronique – and went to work in Germany, in Lindau, on the Lake of Constance. In this novel milieu, Morin forged new, productive friendships and started writing his first book, *L'An zéro de l'Allemagne* (1946); in this book, which was greatly appreciated by the PCF, Morin distanced himself from the thesis of the collective guilt of the German nation.

After finishing *L'An zero de l'Allemagne*, Morin went back to Paris with an optimistic spirit of renewal. He and his wife, Violette, were sharing Marguerite Duras's flat, the elected headquarters of the *Group d'études marxistes*, a group of scholars and intellectuals, in whose debates Maurice Merleau-Ponty and Albert Camus also took part. Even though a good cultural milieu had been created, a new community of affection and thinking, an important need, not to be underestimated, was still present: finding a job. Although the Party had offered him a post as editor in the newspaper, *Humanité*, Morin no longer felt in harmony with the political-editorial orientation of the newspaper and decided not to accept. This meant that he was unemployed, but he did not have the courage to definitively leave the Party although he had not been actively engaged in it for over three years. This link was broken in 1951, when Morin was expelled from the PCF and became a researcher in Sociology at the CNRS in Paris; he published *L'Homme et la Mort* two years later, the result of two years' inter-disciplinary research.

Morin became a researcher at CNRS following the suggestion and encouragement of Georges Friedmann, a friend since the times of the Resistance, and presented a research project on industrial aesthetics, a topic which he was not really interested in. Thanks to the references provided by Georges Friedmann, Maurice Merleau-Ponty, Vladimir Jankélévich and Pierre Georges, Morin entered the CNRS and soon changed his research objective, turning to sociology of the cinema, instead an important opportunity which allowed him to travel and be present in many Film Festivals, including Venice and Cannes. There followed his publications *Le Cinéma ou l'Homme imaginaire* (1956) and *Les Stars* (1957). However, as he started to go more deeply into the sociology of the cinema, he realized that he could not isolate this medium from the overall horizon of mass culture. Hence, the volume *L'Esprit du temps* (1962). We can thus say that the Fifties and Sixties spent at the CNRS in Paris were marked by socio-anthropological studies on the cinema and on mass culture; this research which gave Morin visibility not only in France but also at an international level.[1]

At the end of the Sixties, Morin started travelling a lot – to Latin America, Peru, Bolivia, Mexico, the United States, and above all to California. The year he spent in California (1969) was recorded by Morin in his book, *Journal de Californie* (1970). As he was writing this diary, Morin was experiencing a rather unusual family situation: he had separated from his first wife, Violette, reached a balanced relationship with her, but was now feeling greatly attracted to Johanne Harelle, whom he would later marry, a charismatic woman who was connected to the world of the cinema.[2] Like Johanne, Morin decided to spend time in California to carry out his research. He found a country that was experiencing a cultural revolution, the 'hippy' movement was ending and its natural continuation was found in the Communes; there were frequent episodes of racial discrimination, especially in certain suburbs. Morin was greatly attracted to the American Communes, to their organization and culture, as they embodied and promoted a lifestyle and values he identified with and which allowed him to get closer to his truths, to himself, encouraging him to desist from techno-bureaucracy, from a bourgeois lifestyle and from unessential things. Morin probably found in the communes revitalizing traces of the communism he had experienced during the Resistance.

On a professional level, his stay at the Salk Institute for Biological Studies in La Jolla, California, invited by John Hunt and Jonas Salks, marked an important watershed in Morin's studies, opening a path which would lead to an epistemological turning point for him a few years later. At the Salk Institute, Morin became a student once more and investigated and felt enthusiastic about the research carried out by Norbert Wiener, Jacque Monod, Anthony Wilden, Gregory Bateson and other scientists. He approached the study of human biological fundamentals, in relation to the anthropological, historical and social aspects he had studied until then. However, the Californian experience fitted into a well-defined and coherent research path he had been following. We know, in fact, that before leaving for California Morin had become a member of a debate group promoted by Jacques Robin, which included scholars from various disciplines: they were known as the Group of Ten. Within this study group, Morin investigated several issues connected to anthropology, biology and cybernetics. Morin recalls, in particular, his meetings with the biologist Henri Laborit and with the cyberneticist Jacques Sauvan. Thus, the genesis of Morin's epistemological turning point is explained: on the one hand, his meetings with the Group of Ten, and on the other his stay in California. At the base of his epistemological turning point, which was concretized in 1971 on returning from California, there is Morin's conviction of the importance of connecting the sciences of the living, the most advanced biological research with the theory of information, with cybernetics, with the theory of the systems and, last but not least, with anthropology. Morin set up important relationships also with François Jacob, Henri Atlan and Heinz von Foerster. As a result, Morin founded a Centre for trans-disciplinary studies in 1971, CIEBAF (Centre international d'études bio-anthropologiques et d'anthropologie fondamentale). In 1971 and 1972, CIEBAF carried out important and impressive inter-disciplinary research, coordinated by Morin together with the Italian molecular biologist Massimo Piattelli-Palmarini; the results of this work were presented at an international conference and published in 1974 in three volumes. It was in this fervid cultural milieu that Morin conceived *Le paradigme perdu* (1973), which can well and truly be considered a programmatic manifesto announcing the epistemological turning point Morin had been working on for years. Moreover, *Le paradigme perdu* also contains in embryonic form all the elements which will subsequently give rise to his impressive, systematic work *La Méthode*. This work was, as Morin himself stated, a walk without a path, a walk where the pathway was traced and delineated whilst walking, and which will colonize his whole life; the products of this reflection – which form six volumes[3] – started appearing at the end of the Seventies and have continued to date.

Each book is the outcome of a research experience, a personal meditation, a journey made to a city, a country, a continent, but it is often Italy which has the privilege of being witness to the last revisions brought about to that book. Morin's escapes from Paris and from his commitments at the

CNRS are well-known: he seeks refuge in Tuscany, an oasis of peace and concentration, as he himself affectionately calls it. Italy, its colours and traditions, probably represent for Morin a synthesis of the Latin character and milieu, and the Mediterranean spirit where his family origins have their roots. Thus, in 1974 Morin left Paris in order to finish working on his first book of *La Méthode*; he set off in his Volkswagen, loaded with books, notebooks, documents, and hid out in the ruins of a castle on a hillside in the magic atmosphere of the Tuscan countryside (Morin 1999). The fact that he escaped from Paris to take refuge in Italy coincides, in Morin's life, with his need to find himself again, to find the strength that is required in order to complete the writing of his books. Over time, his relationship with his wife Johanne was consolidated as an important friendship, but it was only in 1981 that an extremely important change was to take place in his life. Once again, a series of extraordinary events caused a new beginning in his life, a new optimism. At Caldine, he was joined by Edwige L. Agnes, his wife today, whom he had met twenty years earlier, in 1961 at Santiago, in Chile. Moreover, a new community was being shaped, based on shared thinking and affection, as friendships were being formed with a group of Italian scholars: Mauro Ceruti, Gianluca Bocchi, Sergio Manghi and Oscar Nicolaus (Morin, 1994) – a group of scholars who are currently his closest disciples, even though Morin claims he has never truly had disciples. He recalls: "I have never had any teaching experiences in France. I have held classes in several foreign countries. I am not a professor who has disciples, who can cultivate his disciples and his disciplinary garden. Over the past years I have only disseminated by ideas in various parts of the world, working with various professional categories, with academics as well as non-academics. The person I feel closest to, nearest to, is Mauro Ceruti. That is obvious" (Morin and Pasqualini 2007: 122). Thus, the second half of the Seventies and the Eighties are characterized by anthropological and epistemological studies which cause Morin to elaborate the method of complexity, a methodological proposal for reading anthropological and socio-cultural phenomena from a connection rather than reductionist viewpoint. Starting from the Eighties, special attention should be drawn to the meetings at Ceresy, in which not only Morin but also many major exponents of the international scientific community were present. Indeed, the year 1987 was devoted to Edgar Morin, to his thinking, to debates on his ideas (Morin, 1990). Over the years, Morin succeeded in involving a surprising number of people, in connecting a group of people not only on the basis of intellectual affinities but also of esteem and friendship. In fact, in 1998 the First Inter-Latin American Congress on Complex Thinking was held in Rio de Janeiro, presided over by Morin and with the participation of many of those who formed that community of thinking and of affection which had built up over the years: Mauro Ceruti, Gianluca Bocchi, Oscar Nicolaus, Sergio Manghi, Alfonso Montuori, and many others.

As a matter of fact, although *La Méthode* can be considered to all intents and purposes Morin's central work of the past thirty years, we should point out that it is interconnected to three other important directions of his research: the political one, the one focusing on the reform of formative institutions, and the autobiographical one.

1. POLITICS

Morin's interest in politics and in the metamorphoses of the 20th century is not something new: suffice it to recall that after 1956, together with other intellectuals who were defectors of the PCF but had not yet abandoned the idea of communism, Edgar Morin founded the periodical *Arguments*, inspired by the periodical *Ragionamenti*, edited by Franco Fortini, which was to continue to be published until 1962, and dealt with the central political issues of the Fifties and Sixties: the suspension of the class struggles in the countries of "real Socialism", the new bureaucratic class, the war in Algeria, Gaullism. Subsequently, starting in the Eighties Morin analyzed the main contemporary geo-political transformations in his books, such as the Fall of the Berlin Wall, the conflicts in the Balkans, the Israeli–Palestinian conflict, the tragic events of 11 September 2001: *Introduction à une politique de l'homme* (1965); *De la nature de l'URSS* (1983); *Penser l'Europe* (1987); with Anne Brigitte Kern, *Terre-Patrie* (1993); *Les fratricides, Yugoslavie-Bosnie, 1991-1995* (1996); with Naïr Sami, *Politique de civilisation* (1997); with Jean Baudrillard, *La violence du monde* (2003); *Culture et barbarie européennes* (2005); and *Le monde moderne et la Question juive* (2006).

2. FORMATION

At the end of the Nineties, Morin took to heart the issue of school reform in France and the reform of education in general, and collaborated with numerous projects promoted by UNESCO. Some of the most significant results of his reflections appeared as a trilogy: *La tête bien faite* (1999), *Relier les connaissances* (1999), and *Les sept savoirs necessaries à l'éducation du futur* (2000). These three books became extremely successful in the international scientific community. In fact, Morin's reforming activities were not restricted to France alone, but progressively extended to other countries in Europe and, indeed, worldwide: Latin America, Spain, China, and, above all Mexico. It was here, in Hermosillo, that Morin took part in the opening of the *Multidiversidad Mundo Real Edgar Morin*[4] in 2004, the university which was inspired by his teachings in the books *La Méthode* and in *Science avec conscience* (1982). More specifically, *Multiversidad Mundo Real* originated from an event led by Ruben Reynaga Valdez and by a group of intellectuals of great sensitivity and culture. Ever since its foundation its objective has been to provide different educational offers thanks to a classical formation which is planned ad hoc and supervised by an International Scientific Council, made up of members belonging to the *Association pour la Pensée Complexe*, thereby in close agreement with Morin's ideas[5].

3. THE AUTO-BIOGRAPHICAL ELEMENTS

Within his vast intellectual production, Morin has devoted quite an important section to his autobiographical writing. Morin has always considered his diaries as belonging to a period in his life when he felt a strong need to meditate. Ever since his adolescence, Morin has liked to keep a diary but the first one to be published, *Le Vif du sujet* (1969), was written at the beginning of the Sixties; the second, *Journal de Californie* (1970), was written at the end of the Sixties and the third, *Journal d'un livre* (1981), at the beginning of the Eighties. Each diary is built up around a specific experience which is the starting point for general or detailed considerations. Apart from the diaries, Morin has also used autobiography: *Autocritique* (1959); *Mes démons* (1994); with Cristina Pasqualini, *Io Edgar Morin* (2007; as well as biography, *Vidal et les siens* (1989). Whilst *Autocritique* is an autobiographical work in which, as he tells the story of his life, Morin analyzes a specific experience in his life, i.e. joining the Communist party, his subsequent defection and the reasons underlying these decisions, in *Mes démons*, which is also an autobiographical work, he reviews his obsessions, his demons, certain significant events, people he has met, companions who are no longer with him and friendships he has found again. In the book *Io, Edgar Morin*, written in the form of a dialogue, Morin passionately and authoritatively recalls the principal stages in his thinking and in his life. Finally, the book *Vidal et les siens* is in certain aspects similar to a novel based on a true story, in which his father Vidal's life is accurately and minutely described by Morin as he narrates the most significant events that distinguished it.

HOW, WHEN AND HOW OFTEN?

Any attempt at summarizing Edgar Morin's life in this brief essay takes on the characteristics of a feat, precisely because Morin's life is not only dense with experiences, but above all because he opened up numerous courses of research, and has had an influence on different disciplinary fields and sectors. In fact, his lessons have been taken up by sociology, by philosophy, by the communication and formative sciences as well as by the natural sciences. We could spend a long time discussing how, when and how often Morin's thinking has become a part of the different fields of knowledge, within different countries[6]. Morin has made certain clear-cut decisions in the course of his professional career, never to fall into line with the prevailing system, trying to disrupt the sick, consolidated logic lying within the world of research and of academia, in particular. Morin has never held any official teaching post in Paris or in the rest of the world, even though he has taught everywhere, engaging in dialogue with the major contemporary exponents of different disciplines. The fact of being an eclectic free thinker, often breaking the mould, has caused him problems because he has not always been given the consideration that is his due. Morin accepted to work at the CNRS in Paris, elected as an ideal place, within which he has always made the most of his autonomy and freedom, of the availability of adequate times and milieus where he has carried out his research, which has often caused him to travel to other countries, and where he has learnt to deal with academia, even though he has never become a part of the latter. In spite of the fact that he is not an academic, Morin has given rise to a school of thinking and of research which has elected complexity as its paradigm to explain human nature, as well as social nature, the individual as well as society. We can say that after the Seventies it has become impossible for most scholars of the social sciences or of the natural sciences not to have an encounter with Morin in their own study courses, in their research. In fact, Morin has become an unavoidable reference point, an author whom one needs to interrogate. But, above all, what makes Morin such a well-known scholar, highly rated by the international scientific community, is the prehensility of his thinking, the multiplicity of issues, subjects and themes he has dealt with, always linking different disciplines. Researchers of disciplinary sectors which are (apparently) far-removed, read, study, communicate with Morin, each having different aims and interests. Morin's intellectual production is so huge and, in a certain sense, so heterogeneous that most scholars are only familiar with a section of his production, whichever is closest to that scholar's personal inclinations and disciplinary field. Thus, scholars focusing on the cinema and on communication studies are only acquainted with Morin's early works, while philosophers and scientists know *La Méthode*, and educators Morin's later works. What we need most today is not so much to promote, once more, the thinking of this major contemporary scholar, but to encourage the scientific community to bring together his thinking and acknowledge that Morin's apparently heterogeneous reflections – which have been produced in the course of over sixty years – are actually intimately linked in a complex project[7]. That is the manifest – and in a certain sense, ambitious – aim of this brief essay, in other words to return Morin in his complexity, in his relations, in his multidimensional nature, in his inter-disciplinary nature.

CRISTINA PASQUALINI
Researcher in Sociology
Catholic University of Milan (Italy)

NOTES TO EDGAR MORIN: DIARY OF A LIFE

1 As regards his studies and research on the cinema, on the star system, on young people and on mass culture, Morin can be considered a pioneer not only in France but also on an international level. In 1961, together with Roland Barthes and Georges Friedmann, Morin founded the journal *Communications*, which he still co-directs. Moreover, he collaborated with Jean Rouch – the film director and one of the founders of the nouvelle vague – in directing the film *Chronique d'une été* (1961).

2 The film produced by Claude Jutra in 1963, in which Johanne Harelle participated, was called *À tout prendre*.

3 For *La Méthode*, from the end of the Seventies Morin has written and published to date six volumes as follows: *La Méthode I. La Nature de la Nature* (1977); *La Méthode II. La Vie de la Vie* (1980); *La Méthode III. La connaissance de la connaissance* (1986); *La Méthode IV. Les idées. Leur habitat, leur vie, leurs moeurs, leur organisation* (1991); *La Méthode V. L'Humanité de l'humanité. L'identité humaine* (2001); *Éthique. La Méthode VI* (2004).

4 For further information consult the sites: www.multiversidadreal.org; www.edgarmorin.com.

5 The International Scientific Council is made up of scholars from various universities worldwide. They include: Mauro Ceruti, Giuseppe Gembillo, Mauro Maldonato, Sergio Manghi (Italy); Alfonso Montuori (USA); Edgar Assis Carvalho (Brazil); Gustavo Lòpez Ospina (Ecuador); Humberto Maturana (Chile); Raùl Domingo Motta (Argentina); Emilio Roger Ciurana (Spain).

6 Morin'a works have been translated in different countries but at very different epochs. For example in Latin countries Morin's translation began very early while in the USA it has begun only more recently. For further information please consult the site: www.ehess.fr/centres/cetsah/CV/morin.html

7 A complete acknowledgement of all Edgar Morin's works can be found in the book, Morin and Pasqualini (2007).

REFERENCES TO EDGAR MORIN: DIARY OF A LIFE

Anselmo, A. 2000. *Edgar Morin. Dal riduzionismo alla Complessità*. Messina: Armando Siciliano Editore.

Anselmo, A. 2005. *Edgar Morin e gli scienziati contemporanei*. Soveria Mannelli: Rubbettino.

Baudrillard, J., Morin, E. 2003. *La violence du monde*. Paris: Édition du Félin.

Bianchi, F. 2001. *Le fil des idées. Une éco-biographie intellectuelle d'Edgar Morin*. Paris: Seuil.

Bocchi, G., Ceruti, M. Eds. 1985. *La sfida della complessità*. Milano: Feltrinelli.

Bocchi, G., Ceruti, M. 2004. *Educazione e globalizzazione*. Milano: Raffaello Cortina Editore.

De Siena, S. 2002. *La sfida globale di Edgar Morin*. Lecce: Besa.

Gembillo, G., Giordano, G. 2004. *Epistemologi del Novecento*. Messina: Armando Siciliano Editore.

Giordano, G. 2006. *Da Einstein a Morin. Filosofia e scienza tra due paradigmi*. Soveria Mannelli: Rubbettino.

Manghi, S. 1987. Le sujet inachevé d'Edgar Morin: vers une théorie de l'acteur social. *Revue européenne des sciences sociales* XXV (75): 41–67.

Morin, E. 1946. *L'An zéro de l'Allemagne*. Paris: La cité universelle.

Morin, E. 1951. *L'Homme et la mort*. Paris: Seuil.

Morin, E. 1956. *Le Cinéma ou l'Homme imaginaire*. Paris: Minuit.

Morin, E. 1957. *Les Stars*. Paris: Seuil.

Morin, E. 1959. *Autocritique*. Paris: Seuil.

Morin, E. 1962. *L'esprit du temps*. Paris: Grasset.

Morin, E. 1965. *Introduction à une politique de l'homme*. Paris: Seuil.

Morin, E. 1969. *Le Vif du sujet*. Paris: Seuil.

Morin, E. 1970. *Journal de Californie*. Paris: Seuil.

Morin, E. 1973. *Le Paradigme perdu: la nature humaine*. Paris: Seuil.

Morin, E. 1977. *La Méthode I. La Nature de la Nature*. Paris: Seuil.

Morin, E. 1980. *La Méthode II. La Vie de la Vie*. Paris: Seuil.

Morin, E. 1981. *Journal d'un livre*. Paris: Inter-Editions.

Morin, E. 1982. *Science avec conscience*. Paris: Fayard.

Morin, E. 1983. *De la nature de l'URSS*. Paris: Fayard.

Morin, E. 1984. *Sociologie*. Paris: Fayard.

Morin, E. 1986. *La Méthode III. La connaissance de la connaissance*. Paris: Seuil.

Morin, E. 1987. *Penser l'Europe*. Paris: Gallimard.

Morin, E. 1989. *Vidal et les siens*. Paris: Seuil.

Morin, E. 1990a. *Arguments pour une Méthode. Autor d'Edgar Morin (Colloque de Ceresy)*. Paris: Seuil.

Morin, E. 1990b. *Introduction à la pensée complexe*. Paris: ESF.

Morin, E. 1991. *La Méthode IV. Les idées. Leur habitat, leur vie, leurs moeurs, leur organisation*. Paris: Seuil.

Morin, E. 1994. *Mes démons*. Paris: Stock.

Morin, E. 1996. *Les fratricides, Yugoslavie-Bosnie, 1991–1995*. Paris: Arléa.

Morin, E. 1999a. *Relier les connaissances*. Paris: Seuil.

Morin, E. 1999b. *Educare gli educatori. Una riforma del pensiero per la Democrazia cognitiva*. Roma: EdUP.

Morin, E. 1999c. *La tête bien faite*. Paris: Seuil.

Morin, E. 2000. *Les sept savoirs nécessaires à l'éducation du futur*. Paris: Seuil.

Morin, E. 2001. *La Méthode V. L'humanité de l'humanité. Livre 1: L'identité humaine*. Paris: Seuil.

Morin, E. 2004. *Éthique. La Méthode 6*. Paris: Seuil.

Morin, E. 2005. *Culture et barbarie européennes*. Paris: Bayard.

Morin, E. 2006a. *Itinérance*. Paris: Arléa.

Morin, E. 2006b. *Le monde moderne et la Question juive*. Paris: Seuil.

Morin, E., Piattelli-Palmarini, M. 1974. *L'Unité de l'homme*. 3 volumes. Paris: Seuil.

Morin, E., Kern, A.B. 1993. *Terre-Patrie*. Paris: Seuil.

Morin, E., Naïr, S. 1997. *Politique de civilisation*. Paris: Arléa.

Morin, E., Cotroneo, G. and Gembillo, G. 2003. *Un viandante della complessità. Morin filosofo a Messina*. Messina: Armando Siciliano Editore.

Morin, E., Motta, R. and Ciurana, È. R. 2003. *Eduquer pour l'ère planétaire. La pensée complexe comme Méthode d'apprentissage dans l'erreur et l'incertitude humaines*. Paris: Balland.

Morin, E., Pasqualini, C. 2007. *Io, Edgar Morin. Una Storia di vita*. Milano: FrancoAngeli.

Pasqualini, C. 2006. *Complessità, narrazione e agire quotidiano. Morin secondo Morin. In La vita che c'è. Teorie dell'agire quotidiano*, volume 1, Eds. De Simone, A. and D'Andrea, F., 211–246. Milano: FrancoAngeli.

Pasqualini, C. 2007. *Violenza del mondo e diritti umani. La proposta ri-formatrice di Edgar Morin. In Diritto, giustizia e logiche del dominio*, Ed. De Simone, A., 513–539. Perugia: Morlacchi.

Notes to Preface and Text

1   Translator's note (henceforth abbreviated to T.N.); cf. Albert Cohen's elegy to his mother, "Le livre de ma mère."

2   Paris, Éditions Entente, 1977.

3   Transcribed in italic script in this book.

4   Published in Salonica between 1935 and 1978 (Librairie Molho).

5   "We were thrown out of Spain, and in a bad way."

6   Joseph Perez, in *Isabelle et Ferdinand, Rois Catholiques d'Espagne* (Fayard, Paris, 1988), p. 317,

7   *Encyclopedia judaïca*, entry "Sevilla."

8   According to Joseph Perez (*op. cit.*), it is very difficult to estimate how many people left Castile.

9   Where, except in Northern Morocco, they eventually merged with the Berber and Arab Jewish populations.

10 T.N.: "Dialogic" is a key concept in Morin's work. According to the description he gives of it in vol. IV of *La méthode*, *Idées*, it is "the complete (complementary/concurrent/ antagonistic) association of logics that are collectively required for the existence, functioning and development of an organized phenomenon." (*op. cit.*, Seuil, Paris, 1991, p. 111)

11 On the history of Salonica, see P. Risal (pseudonym of Joseph Nehama), *La Ville convoitée: Salonique* (Perrin, Paris, 1913).

12 T.N.: A "macédoine" is a fruit or vegetable salad in which a variety of ingredients are cut into small pieces and mixed together; figuratively it means a mosaic or mish-mash.

13 Cf. Y.-H. Yerushalmi, *De la cour d'Espagne au ghetto italien, Isaac Cardoso et le marranisme* (Fayard, Paris, 1981) translated from English.

14 Cf. G. Scholem, *La Kabbale et sa Symbolique* (Payot, Paris 1966); Z'ev ben Shmon Halevi, *L'Arbre de vie* (Albin Michel, Paris, 1985).

15 G. Scholem, *Les Grands Courants de la mystique juive* (Payot, 1960 and 1968). *Le Messianisme juif*, Calmann-Lévy, 1974. *Sabbetaï Tsevi, Le Messie mystique* (Verdier, 1983).

16 D. Aubier, *Deux Secrets pour une Espagne* (Paris, Arthaud, 1964).

17 J. Nehama, *op. cit.*, vol. 6, p. 259. On the Livornese in Salonica, cf. p. 256 *et seq.*

18 That's enough, Mrs. Djamila,
    Stop arguing with the women next door
    About that wretched jug
    Of yours they broke.

19 The officers and intellectuals known as "Young Turks" formed a committee for Unity and Progress, whose goal was to impose a liberal empire. They

started the revolution of 1908, which forced the Sultan to reinstate the 1876 Constitution. However, the continual wars from then on led the Young Turk government to abandon their liberal approach in favor of pan-Turkish authoritarianism.

20 The bulk of the documentation for this prologue comes from Joseph Nehama's monumental and remarkably mulitdimensional work, the *Histoire des Israélites de Salonique*, in seven volumes. Nehama nevertheless wrote a "standard" history of Salonica, in both senses of the word. First, he considers Sabbetaïsm and its consequences to be a tissue of aberrations and delusions. In contrast, my intention is to show that Sabbetaïsm is integral to the original adventure of Sephardism in the East, and in Salonica in particular, and to recognize it as an original and valuable post-Marrano religious creation. Secondly, Nehama presents the Marranos, and the Livornese after them, as marginal elements in a whole which is seen as advancing or retreating frontally in the course of his history. I want to show that, through their very marginality, these groups played a decisive role in composing the culturally hybrid nature of Salonica's Sephardim. As far as the Livornese in particular are concerned, Nehama effectively indicates their role as the driving force behind the developments in Salonica in the 19th century, but such indications are scattered through the economy of his work. Naturally, it is because the author of these lines has wished to re-connect himself with his Livornese origins, and because he has always felt himself to be a neo-Marrano, that he has insisted on what (inevitably) seemed to him to be an underestimation in previously dominant notions about the Sephardim in the Ottoman world, and Salonica in particular. Being conscious of the retroaction of his personal identity upon the history under his consideration, he is able to accept and discuss criticisms, because he is capable of relativizing his own point of view. This ability to relativize is made possible precisely by his neo-Marrano consciousness. Is it this consciousness that has helped him to see what others did not see, or has it deformed his vision? Such a question cannot be decided by the asker.

21 Their descendants emigrated to France or Belgium at the beginning of the 20th century. Among them were a banker and philosopher, a journalist turned politician (Estier, born Ezratti), and the linguist who became the first holder of a chair in Hispanic Jewish studies, and who collaborated on this book.

22 Germany was increasingly present and economically active, but remained psychologically distant as a result of French cultural hegemony. Paradoxically, French cultural hegemony was completely out of proportion with its economic importance in Salonica. In 1900, it was Austria-Hungary, followed by Great Britain, Germany and Italy, which did most trade with the port; France only came in fifth place.

23 The Salonicians used to say "*Stambouli bovo*" (people from Stamboul are mooncalves); the Stamboulis retorted "*Selanikli fichugo*" (Salonicians are a pain in the neck).

24 Vidal explains Purim to his granddaughter Véronique in his oral biography: *I don't know if you have any inkling of the story. Amman was the king's favorite Minister, I can't remember which king it was, and he wanted to destroy all the Jews. But the king has just married Esther, hasn't he, that's in the Bible, when the Mardochée goes to see the queen, and says to her: "You can't let all your brothers be killed, speak to the king."*

So Esther picks her moment, speaks to the king, and he calls for his Minister, Amman was his name, and has him beheaded.

25   For instance, in Paris, at every family meal she will insist that Vidal's son who, being left-handed, holds his fork in his left hand, should eat with his right (although neither Vidal nor his wife make any attempt to force their son to conform in this way).

26   T.N.: A "joueur" is a gambler and a player, as well as a playful person.

27   The date is incorrect, not because Vidal has made a mistake, but because he wants to simplify matters.

28   P. Risal, *op. cit.,* pp. 307–308, 313 and 315.

29   P. Risal, *op. cit.,* p. 272.

30   Tripoli will be Italian!
Will be Italian to the rumble of the cannon.
Sail on, sail on, battleships!

31   The establishment of the first bridgeheads, at the end of the 19th century and the beginning of the 20th, encourages emigration, which increases considerably after the Balkan wars and the Hellenization of Salonica. These bridgeheads allowed families, almost in their entirety, to move from Salonica to France.

32   Where, ever since the 18th century, the Sephardim had enjoyed rights that the Ashkenazim did not obtain until 1868.

33   The *Sainte-Anne* stopped at Ajaccio on January 31.

34   Vidal seems to think that Christian practice is to eat fish on Saturday, and not on Friday.

35   T.N.: the French Chamber of Deputies corresponds more or less to the American House of Representatives.

36   T.N.: "Jerry", "Hun", etc. – an offensive term for "German."

37   His granddaughter Véronique asks him how he found his clients: *Well, for example, I sold DMC thread and embroidery cotton to Belgrade, so the boxes from the factory were all marked DMC. And just as they're delivering let's say twenty boxes to me, a gentleman comes in to the office: "Sir, are you the one who . . . And do you do the . . . ." He says: "Let me introduce myself, I am a trader in Bucharest, and I'm interested in this." Well, fine. And then there was another, I didn't know where he'd got my address from, he came from Czechoslovakia . . .* (oral autobiography).

38   The body underwent ritual purification, but we do not know whether it was wrapped in a shroud, or, whether, following the custom of the gentiles, it was dressed western-style in the handsome frockcoat.

39   T.N.: "Poche" means "pocket;" the play on words only works because of the proximity of "poste" and "poche," and hence is untranslatable from the French.

40   T.N.: The grimly ironic French expression literally means "maker of angels."

41   T.N.: The note is written in "Fragnol."

42   We may wonder why, on July 8, 1930, he has a general power of attorney drawn up in the names of Elie Hassid and his brother Léon, who has come to live in Paris for a year or two.

43   T.N.: The French school system begins with 11th grade and works its way up through the numbers to *Terminale* (final grade).

44   T.N. "ne suivra pas le sentier du Sentier." "Sentier" means path or trail.

45   T.N.: Morin's term is "matricielle," i.e. related to the matrix, meaning here both the maternal and the original.

46 T.N. "The year has barely finished its career . . . "
47 T.N. "O Time, suspend your flight!"
48 As if under the blissful influence of hashish.
49 Cf. Anne Benveniste's study, "Structure de la communauté judéo-espagnole du quartier de la Roquette entre les deux guerres," in *Traces*, special issue "Judaïsme, judaïcités," pp. 34–47.
50 In this capacity, he sends the following prescription to Vidal, who was worried about a wart he had (letter of May 27 1921):
    If your wart has continued to grow, even a very little, it must have got fairly voluminous since I received your last letter. Still, you should count yourself lucky that it has not had any babies. Lactic acid: 1g; salicylic acid: 2g; acetic acid: 0.50g; collodium q.s.p: 10g. Apply a very thin layer of this every evening, just covering the wart.
51 T.N.: Mortgage company.
52 Today it is the headquarters of the CFDT [T.N.: the Confédération française démocratique du travail, a trade union].
53 T.N.: "ce qui permettait de faire l'économie sur les vacances sans faire l'économie des vacances."
54 T.N.: In English in the text.
55 T.N.: A kind of soft white cheese made of curdled milk and whipped cream.
56 The divorce certificate indicates that Sara is of Czech nationality. Her family, who had been protected by Austria-Hungary at the time of the Ottomans, had acquired this nationality as a result of the dislocation of the Hapsburg empire, in an attempt to get the boys exempted from military service in the Greek army.
57 T.N. Slang name for Paris.
58 Edgar has been arguing about politics in the yard of the lycée since about 1934 or 1935. His friend Macé is a "red falcon" (socialist youth movement), and Salem calls himself an anarchist, while Edgar has begun to get himself a political education by reading the marginal leftist press, anarchist reviews, the journal of the SIA (*Solidarité internationale antifasciste*), the Piverto-Trotskyist students' magazine *Essais et Combats*, and *La Flèche*, produced by Bergery's frontist party, in which articles by dyed-in-the-wool pacifists like Georges Pioch, ex-communists like Rappoport, and reformers of socialism like Jean Maze and Bergery himself, appear side by side. He feels torn between the great surges of fraternalism and internationalism, which make him lean towards leftism, and realism, which makes him lean towards a moderate socialism within the national framework. He is a pacifist, not only because of his visceral fear of war (he is afraid of dying before he has begun to live), but also because he believes in the rights of populations (the Sudetenland is populated by Germans, Austria wanted the Anschluss), and he thinks it legitimate to criticize the treaty of Versailles, which was a victor's diktat. Although Soviet films have moved him deeply (*Le Chemin de la vie*) and inspired him with enthusiasm (*Eux, les marins de Cronstadt*), he has been immunized against Stalinian communism by all his reading, and by keeping up with current affairs. He joins the Frontist students in 1938, and among them he meets a student from Lycée Henri-IV, Georges Delboy, who will introduce him to Marxism. He has adopted as his own the hopes for freedom and fraternity which permeate the climate of the time, but he has not identified this hope with any particular face yet. He is reading a newspaper in Aunt Henriette's living room when

he hears the announcement that Barcelona has fallen over the radio, and raises the paper over his face to hide his tears.

59 Twenty-seven communist prisoners would be executed there in October 1941, after an attack committed in Nantes against a German officer.

60 Where the British fleet bombarded and destroyed the French fleet, on July 3 1940.

61 Cf. the article in *Nouveaux Temps* of January 12 1941, and the one in the *Petit Parisien* of July 9 1941.

62 Since Argentina is responsible for Greek interests in France during the Occupation, Mony and Liliane have managed to obtain this special protection.

63 Letter sent to his son in summer 1942, probably to Saint-Gervais, where Edgar and Victor Henri are mountain-climbing.

64 "I went to see Alida Valli, she was charming in *Invisible Chains*. On Saturday, we went to watch Liliane swimming with her friend Andrée" (July 19). "Liliane has just been for a swim in the sea; the weather is warm, but the constant breeze prevents us from feeling how strong the sun is, and it is always cool in the shade . . . Yesterday evening, we went with Léon's family and the children to the shore of the Big Blue and stayed until nearly 11 o'clock. The weather was beautiful, and everybody in Nice was there. This afternoon, we are invited to tea with one of our acquaintances from Paris, who came here a short time ago. She was one of the most elegant women at our darling Aimée's wedding" (July 16). "Tomorrow, I am going to the cinema to see the charming Alida Valli. I am spending the day with Liliane, who went to a bridge party in a beautiful garden. I sat under the trees watching the passers by, and some people playing tennis" (July 13). "Yesterday, I went to the cinema to see a lovely film with Emma Grammatica, it was quite wonderful. It's three o'clock, and at four o'clock cousin Elise is coming, and Edmée's mother has also announced that she will be coming. Every evening we get together on the terrace . . . " Liliane also writes to Mathilde: "We are having glorious weather, I have been swimming every morning. I have had a few lessons, which gives me the confidence to go further from the shore, and I am very pleased about it. Then I have bridge once or twice a week, which I love and which I find very interesting. Life goes on, you see, and we only want one thing, for it to keep going on this way until we can come home." (August 19 1943).

65 T.N.: A reference to the French national anthem, in which citizens are: "Les enfants de la patrie."

66 T.N.: "Avoir de la veine" is a colloquial expression meaning to be lucky.

67 T.N.: "Poulette" means "my little chicken."

68 T.N.: "Faire chabrol" is a custom in certain regions of France, including the Périgord: a small amount of wine is poured into the last drops of soup and drunk straight from the bowl.

69 T.N.: This letter in its entirety in "English" in the text.

70 T.N.: In English in the text.

71 T. N.: In English in the text.

72 T.N.: "Where are the scarves?"

73 He attempts in 1970 or 1971 to obtain an indemnity from the German Federal Republic: "For everything that I endured under the Occupation . . . I have made no request until now, but in my seventy-sixth year, everything that I

suffered then is taking its toll, and my business affairs, which were shattered by the occupation, have become increasingly difficult." But the deadline expired long ago and his attempt is in vain.

74 T.N.: A store selling clothing etc. for expectant mothers.

75 "One month later," Dr. Talamo writes to us, "I saw that I had received a case of liqueurs from Vidal Nahoum, along with an extra surprise: the Italian customs duty, which of course he knew nothing about. The most expensive liqueurs of my life, from that unforgettable and very dear friend Vidal Nahoum!"

76 T.N.: "Happy holiday and good health."

77 As a result, he had become capable of hostile feelings with regard to the Arabs, who were now the mortal enemies of Israel, and he was surprised that his son should take him to task whenever he made a remark against them. This hostility, we should note, was not directed at Muslims. He had spent his childhood and his youth in the shadow of minarets, and, in Salonica, he did not feel the anti-Islamic resentment of the Christians who were subjugated by the Muslims.

78 T.N.: The child's error in the last line is to add an m to *ignominieusement*, as a result of a confusion with *mignon*, meaning cute or pretty.

79 On June 12, 1988, nine years after Jacques Dominati had obtained the Order of Merit for his father, Vidal's son was examining the letters and the information concerning this decoration. Fate decreed that he should be living in the 3rd arrondissement, to which Jacques Dominati had since moved, and where he had become deputy Mayor, that the second round of the legislative elections should be on June 12, and that Jacques Dominati should have as his opponent the socialist Jacques Benassayag. Edgar thought of voting for Benassayag, but wanted his wife, who agreed, to vote Dominati in memory of his father. However, Edwige had an accident which rendered her immobile on voting day. Edgar went off to the polling station, feeling very torn, thinking at one moment that he would vote Benassayag, out of loyalty to the Left, and the next that he would vote Dominati, out of loyalty to his father. He found civic reasons for voting Dominati (an excellent mayor, who promoted parks, helped the destitute and the underprivileged, was supported by the ecologist candidate who had withdrawn in his favor, etc.). But he also found opposing arguments ("I have never voted for the Right, I ought to be voting for an idea, and not because of the past," etc.). He debated a bizarre and novel problem: "Should one vote in memory of one's father?" But, as he made his way to the Rue de Turenne, he came to a decision: he *ought to* make this gesture which, if not Oriental, was at least Mediterranean, in any case not at all western, of voting, not so much as his father would have done, but, via Dominati, *for* his father. The idea that Vidal would be present in his voting slip did him good.

80 It is clear that at the end of my days, or those of my sister, not the least little memory will remain of what you have heard today.

81 T.N.: "upper" as opposed to "lower" classes.

82 Sixty thousand Spanish Jews emigrated to France and 3,000 to Belgium in the first three decades of the 20th century.

83 "In this time, there is absolutely nothing that the Jews can attribute to themselves which would place them above the other peoples."

84 T.N.: *andouillete* is a sausage made from pig's intestines; *ris de veau* is calf sweetbreads.